FOR THE
PUBLIC RECORD

Recent Titles in
Contributions in American Studies

FOR THE PUBLIC RECORD

A Documentary History of the League of Women Voters

Barbara Stuhler

Contributions in American Studies, Number 108
Robert H. Walker, Series Editor

GREENWOOD PRESS
Westport, Connecticut • London

Library of Congress Cataloging-in-Publication Data

Stuhler, Barbara.
    For the public record : a documentary history of the League of
Women Voters / Barbara Stuhler.
        p.   cm.—(Contributions in American studies, ISSN 0084–9227
; no.   108)
    Includes bibliographical references and index.
    ISBN 0–313–25316–1 (alk. paper)
        1. League of Women Voters (U.S.)—History.   2. Feminism—United
States—History.   I. Title.   II. Series.
    JK1881.S78   2000
    324.6′23′0973—dc21   99–22094

British Library Cataloguing in Publication Data is available.

Library of Congress Catalog Card Number: 99–22094
ISBN: 0–313–25316–1
ISSN: 0084–9227

First published in 2000

Greenwood Press, 88 Post Road West, Westport, CT 06881
An imprint of Greenwood Publishing Group, Inc.
www.greenwood.com

Printed in the United States of America

The paper used in this book complies with the
Permanent Paper Standard issued by the National
Information Standards Organization (Z39.48–1984).

10 9 8 7 6 5 4 3 2 1

Copyright Acknowledgment

Contents

Photo essay follows page 152.

Preface

In the third decade of the life of the League of Women Voters of the United States (LWVUS), Anna Lord Strauss, who was then president, made this telling observation: "the League has an enviable record for pricking the conscience of our public life."[1] That enviable record, told in the words of several generations of League leaders, is what this book is all about. With fifty years of selected documents, *For the Public Record* is intended to serve as a useful complement to *In the Public Interest: The League of Women Voters, 1920-1970,* Louise M. Young's narrative history of the League's first half century of achievement.

The documents chosen *For the Public Record* serve to illuminate Young's history by providing the reader with the original sources that prompted her insights and interpretations. They also reflect my own judgment of what is important and of lasting interest. I found the speeches made by League presidents at national conventions or council meetings most helpful because they summarized the activities, accomplishments, problems, and shortcomings of the League in a given period. These speeches also articulated the philosophy and the values of the League over the years, and both have remained constant.

In addition, I chose materials representing the broad range of issues that have been of enduring concern to League members over the years. Although the specifics have varied from time to time, certain themes persist:

international cooperation, education, human welfare and development, effective and accountable government, the protection and enhancement of the natural environment, individual liberties, and civil rights. My selections also represent an attempt to put a human face on the League and its leaders, especially in its first decades. Many of us looking at the pictures of early leaders see only serious miens that belie their grace and good humor. Although there were substantial differences of opinion that arose from time to time, sparking personal criticisms and conflict (witness the confrontation between Carrie Chapman Catt and Maud Wood Park in Chapter 5), the women of the League liked each other. They laughed, and they had fun together. Lasting friendships emerged from their association in the mission of active citizenship on behalf of the public good.

In her first chapter of *In the Public Interest*, Louise Young established in five pages the framework for this valuable history of the LWVUS. It spans the League's first fifty years, beginning with its conception by suffrage leaders and maintained by their successors as a significant first step in the political liberation of women. Young asserts—with considerable justification—that "because changes on the anticipated scale had not occurred, it was possible to assume that nothing had altered."[2] Measured by voter turnout or election to office in the aftermath of women winning the vote, it is true that not many women went to the polls in the 1920s. Their failure to participate can be attributed to their uncertainties as novice voters, to their reserve about crossing from the domestic realm to the public sphere, and to their lack of knowledge about candidates and issues. All reasons foreseen by the League's founders who knew that winning the vote was the beginning of women's participation in the political arena. They foresaw that the process was not a matter of a single election but of years of effort (a fact that became clearer as voter turnout by both men and women declined throughout the 1920s). Postsuffrage women were wooed by the political parties but those who entered that arena, for the most part, did not rise to any positions of influence until the 1930s. Few women sought public office and fewer succeeded, except by death of a father or a spouse (at the national level, in local—and less visible—races, women did experience more success). Yet those measures of voting and election to public office represented only two yardsticks of women's political interests and activities.

Their most significant contribution took the form of political action through voluntary associations. In her impressive study, *The Grounding of Modern Feminism*, Nancy Cott states that "it is highly probable that the greatest extent of associational activity in the whole history of American women took place in the era between the two world wars, after women became voters and before a great proportion of them entered the labor force." Nor were these organizations apolitical. Cott and other scholars as well have argued, with evidence to back their assertions, that women's organizations created and shaped the modern methods of pressure group politics. The League of Women Voters played a highly visible role in that evolution.[3]

Neither *In the Public Interest* or *For the Public Record* should be regarded as comprehensive. While each volume highlights the frustrations, disagreements, innovations, and achievements of the League's first fifty years. *For the Public Record* extends its documentation in the epilogue, albeit briefly, beyond 1970 to the present time. The raw materials of this unique organization of political women yield many tales worth telling of civic education and activism. Scholars and students should continue to explore the LWVUS Papers for stories of individuals and their collective efforts on behalf of good government. Despite the old-fashioned phrasing, good government remains a consummation devoutly to be wished and in democratic societies still depends on the participation of a well-informed citizenry. That was the founding principle of the League of Women Voters and one that has guided its actions for more than seventy-five years.

The League attracted as members women who were well educated, middle-class, and progressive in their political thought. There were, of course, variations on the theme: some members were rich, some poor; some, despite their station in life, became active in the League because of their frustrations with the way things were; a few became members as a means of expressing their new U.S. citizenship. The League was not—to use a contemporary term—multicultural. It is interesting to note that the League established a 1925-26 fellowship for a woman graduate to study "the American Indian problem." The decision was prompted by a League study, revealing the "dearth of authentic material on the general Indian problem." The League was interested not in recruiting Indian women as members but to determine how best to improve the administration of Indian affairs.[4]

In the same vein, the League formed a Committee on Negro Problems, later changed at the request of black members to the Committee on Interracial Problems. Although the committee was headed by prominent League leaders: Julia Lathrop (1921), Minnie Fisher Cunningham (1921–25), and Adele Clark (after 1925), nothing really came of their efforts. The League appeared to be less interested in recruiting African-Americans as members than with addressing issues that might improve their social and economic circumstances. Evelyn Brooks Higginbotham notes sadly, "By the end of [the 1920s] the League of Women Voters had lost, largely by its own choice, the potential for being an important mobilizing force among black women."[5]

In recent years even though the League has embarked on a course of action that has succeeded in diversifying its membership in terms of age (especially now that eighteen-year-olds can vote), its gender, and its ethnic and racial composition, the membership has remained in large part white, middle-class, middle-aged, and female. One significant sign of that success was the election in June 1998 of Carolyn Jefferson-Jenkins of Colorado, the first African American to serve as president of the LWVUS.

For many potential members with limited discretionary time, the League may not be the primary organizational choice. The nation has witnessed a veritable explosion of organizations addressing very specific issues, and the interests and needs of women (and men) wanting to improve housing in their community, for example, may support a neighborhood group working on that issue rather than the League even though it, too, is engaged in the same enterprise but perhaps with a more detached and impersonal approach. However, there is still a role for the League as a multi-issue organization that couples education with advocacy, a group where like-minded women and men can come together on issues important to them and who desire to participate in the democratic process in a very direct and effective way.

In the exuberance of energy associated with what is often referred to as the second wave of the women's movement in the 1970s, a variety of other women's organizations came upon the scene, notably the National Organization for Women (NOW) and the Women's Political Caucus, as well as a host of new women's political groups interested in pursuing reforms and highlighting particular issues. While they were all engaged in advancing the cause of women, each went about the task with a different style. On occasions, such as the fight for the failed Equal Rights Amendment (ERA) and the continuing struggle to insure the right to privacy, the League actively aligned itself with these groups. The League, from its inception, has never turned its back on coalition building or, for that matter, on feminism.

Not everyone agrees on the meaning of feminism, a term imported from France in the early part of the twentieth century. In essence it conveys the simple concept that men and women share a common humanity, and it follows from that premise that the rights of women should be equal to those of men. It is common to hear women say, "I'm not a feminist, but I believe in equal pay for equal work." That rejection of the term *feminism* came about because some women viewed those espousing the idea as uncompromising and strident in their advocacy. Some of those advocates, it is true, articulated a kind of feminist fundamentalism as if equality did not imply choice, as if there existed some kind of creed that required obeisance. The opportunity for women to choose is part of what feminism is all about—the right to choose whether or not to be a scientist, an athlete, a homemaker, a politician, a child caregiver, or a carpenter. This does not necessarily imply that men and women are identical in every respect but simply that men should not dominate women, that women should have equal opportunities to choose what they want to be, and to receive equal compensation and equal representation.

In that sense, the League has always been a feminist organization, from the part its predecessor played in the great suffrage campaign to its own struggle to enable women to be citizens in the fullest sense. It has also played an important leadership role. The evolution of the League's philosophy from protecting women workers to the idea of equal pay and equal opportunities for advancement has been in the mainstream of women's thought and action as these have evolved in the second half of the twentieth century. No organization has worked harder to secure equality for women from serving on juries to retaining their American citizenship (as men did) when they married foreign nationals. The Cable Act of 1923, which addressed that latter issue, was one of the League's first victories and one of its finest. The League came into being because leaders of the suffrage association recognized that women would have to be schooled in citizenship. The League accomplished this by mounting and maintaining a comprehensive educational program in government and politics. The League also trained its members to be citizen advocates. As they observed governmental bodies in action, many of the Leaguers said, "I can do that." And they did—the women office holders who have been League members credit the League for sparking their interest and for building their confidence and competence.

Generations of suffrage women struggled to win their cause for seventy-two long years before a national League of Women Voters was born. The LWVUS has now been in existence for nearly eighty years. For 152 years all told, suffrage women and League women have recognized that political know-how—including both the substance of issues and the skills of the process—has been the key to political power and influence. In acquiring this knowledge and these skills, League members have been mindful of their long heritage of constituent government in the public interest as well as their commitment to the politics of openness and integrity. The documents in these pages tell that story.

NOTES

1. *Report of Anna Lord Strauss to National Convention.* Grand Rapids, MI: League of Women Voters of the United States, August 26, 1948, 3.

2. Louise M. Young, *In the Public Interest: The League of Women Voters 1920–1970.* Westport, CT: Greenwood Press, 1989, 1.

3. Anne Firor Scott, *Natural Allies: Women's Associations in American History.* Urbana and Chicago: University of Illinois Press, 1991. Nancy F. Cott, *The Grounding of Modern Feminism.* New Haven, CT: Yale University Press, 1987, 97. See, for example, Suzanne Lebock, "Women and American Politics, 1880–1920," in Louise

A. Tilly and Patricia Gurin, Eds., *Women, Politics and Change*. New York: Russell Sage Foundation, 1990, 279.

4. Leagues have continued to reach out to Indian women in a variety of ways. Efforts to establish Leagues on reservation communities were made (for example, with the Ogala Sioux in Pine Ridge, South Dakota in 1952) to interest individual Native American women, wherever their residence, in participating in League programs and to provide information to all citizens about their concerns, interests, and achievements. The University of Minnesota Press will release the *fifth* edition of the Minnesota League's study by Elizabeth Ebbott titled *Indians in Minnesota* in 1999.

5. News Release, February 16, 1925. LWV Papers on film, Part II, Series A. Reel 6, Frame 0706. Evelyn Brooks Higginbotham, "In Politics to Stay: Black Women Leaders and Party Politics in the 1920s," in Tilly and Gurin, *Women, Politics and Change*, 215.

Acknowledgments

In 1989 Greenwood Press published a history of the first fifty years of the League of Women Voters of the United States (LWVUS). Years before, in the late 1940s, Louise M. Young had been instrumental in persuading the Library of Congress, which had not as a rule accepted organizational archives, to acquire the League's papers—more than two tons of them! A prominent and experienced scholar, Young then took on the task of cataloging those papers. In the process she became intimately familiar with the League's history, and her accounts of the League past to the League present at national conventions and other meetings excited members, who learned that theirs was a distinguished history of education and advocacy. The League, Louise Young assured them, had made an indelible mark on the progress of American democracy, and they, as members, were part of a great tradition of which they could be rightly proud.

As Young explained in her foreword to *In the Public Interest: The League of Women Voters, 1920–1970*, Julia Stuart, LWVUS president (1964–1968), had asked her to write a history that would be part of the League's fiftieth anniversary celebration in 1970. But this book, as books often do, took longer to complete than anticipated, and a variety of other circumstances delayed its publication until 1989.

Robert H. Walker, Series Editor of Greenwood's Contributions in American Studies, represented the press in offering contracts to Louise Young and Mary Ann Guyol for companion volumes: a narrative and documentary history of the League's first fifty years. The two works were to be mutually supportive, reflecting parallel organization and published simultaneously. The two volumes were considered equally important and their total value as substantially greater than the sum of the parts. The basic outline was the product of long discussions between the two authors, with the senior editor sometimes a passive participant. Subsequently Guyol received valuable advice from the recently retired deputy director of the LWVUS, Martha T. Mills, and, in spite of a succession of incapacitating strokes, Guyol managed to select a significant number of the documents before her death in 1994. Susan Ware's introduction to the guide for the League Papers on microfilm brought to life Guyol and her enthusiasm for the League.

The real vitality of the League lay at the local level, but once again, the experience varied widely, based on the temperaments and needs of individual members. For some women, especially those in small communities, the League was the most exciting thing that ever happened. Mary Ann Page Guyol, who joined the Red Wing, Minnesota chapter during the Depression, recalled: "It filled a tremendous void in my life . . . . I was right in the middle of the action, and I simply adored it." Guyol seconded the observation of Belle Sherwin that the League was "a university without walls" when she observed: "You see, women rarely thought about going back to college or graduate school when the kids were gone. They couldn't afford it for one thing—and for another, it just wasn't done. So the League became our university, our graduate school—it was, well, just everything." [1]

I was approached in 1996 to complete the work, and agreed to do so, starting in 1997. I was privileged to have Professor Walker continue serving as editor and adviser for the project and to be able to call on my long friendship with Martha Mills for her memory and knowledge to supplement my own League recollections and research. Meetings with Martha during the League's Forty-third National Convention in San Diego in June 1998 proved to be indispensable to the book's completion.

Robert Walker urged me to send my draft to Ralph Young who, during his mother's extended illness, had done the final editing of *In the Public Interest.* For several years Professor Young has been teaching at the University of Manchester in England, and I sent him one of the initial drafts together with the collection of documents. His suggestions and very careful editing have contributed enormously to the final product.

The documents selected for inclusion in *For The Public Record* come primarily from the rich collection of LWVUS Papers in the Library of Congress, which I reviewed in two separate visits. Most of the documents in that collection were available to me on microfilm at the Wilson Library of the University of Minnesota. These included transcripts and records of national conventions and council meetings, program files, publications, and correspondence.

I want to express my appreciation especially to Karon Schmitt, neighbor and computer guru who did the hard work of preparing *For the Public Record* for publication. I am also grateful to the Elmer L. and Eleanor J. Andersen Foundation for financial support, to Caroline Reis who helped with copy editing, to Jane Hilken who did the index, and to Jean M. West, who helped me proof the manuscript in its early stages. I am indebted to the Greenwood Press, especially to editor Meg Fergusson who was unfailingly helpful in overseeing the project. Staff members at the University of Minnesota's Wilson Library, the Library of Congress, and the League's national office were helpful as always. Thanks also go to my friends who once more put up with the idiosyncrasies of a writer at work.

A word to readers: In the interest of avoiding peppering the book with "[sic]" to indicate misspelling or other minor errors of punctuation, I have taken the liberty of correcting such small mistakes as well as errors found most frequently in the transcriptions of national conventions and council meetings, an audio tradition of record-keeping inherited from the history-minded National American Woman Suffrage Association. It would be understandably difficult to discern the difference between the spoken "affect" and "effect," for example, or to transcribe with total accuracy the great variety of voices recorded in those debates and speeches.

It should be noted that the National LWV became the League of Women Voters of the United States with a change in the organization's bylaws in 1946. While both terms are used interchangeably—in reference, for example, to the national board of directors, the national convention, etc., citations of publications will reflect that 1946 change of name. I have also shortened LWVUS throughout to LWV in part to reflect the interactive relationship among the national, state, and local leagues. (References to specific state and local leagues are appropriately identified.) Most of the speeches and convention debates reprinted in these pages, although excerpted, contain the essence of the content. Finally, as a member of the League of Women Voters for fifty years, I confess to a certain partisanship on behalf of the organization and its mission of political education and advocacy.

NOTE

1. *Papers of the League of Women Voters, 1918-1974.* A microfilm project of University Publications of America, Research Collection in Women's Studies. General Editors: Dr. Anne Firor Scott and Dr. William H. Chafe, Advisory Editor: Dr. Susan Ware. League of Women Voters of the United States, 1986, Part II, xii.

FOR THE
PUBLIC RECORD

Chapter 1

Women and Politics

Women won the vote with the enactment of the Nineteenth Amendment in 1919 and its subsequent ratification by thirty-six states in 1920. Susan B. Anthony and Elizabeth Cady Stanton, national leaders of the woman suffrage movement, anticipated that the Fifteenth Amendment enfranchising black men would also include "sex" in the language stipulating that "the right of citizens of the United States to vote shall not be denied or abridged by the United States or by any State on account of race, color, or previous condition of servitude." The exclusion of women angered Anthony and Stanton and prompted them to sever the close alliance previously enjoyed by abolitionists and suffragists. As they prepared to work on behalf of a sixteenth amendment enfranchising women in 1869, the two intrepid women organized the National Woman Suffrage Association. In that same year Lucy Stone and her husband, Henry Blackwell, formed the American Woman Suffrage Association. While the two associations shared a common goal, they differed in their tactics—a condition that would also characterize the suffrage movement in the early twentieth century as well as the women's movement from 1970 on.

Three other amendments (the income tax, the direct election of senators, and prohibition) would be adopted in the subsequent forty-three years, prompting suffragists to refrain from reference to a numerical identification. They chose instead to speak of a "federal" amendment (to distinguish it from state suffrage amendments). In the later years of the campaign, the

Congressional Union for Woman Suffrage (an offshoot of the National American Woman Suffrage Association, representing the 1890 merger of the National and American suffrage associations) called it the Susan B. Anthony Amendment. By whatever name, the amendment was first introduced into Congress on January 10, 1878, by Anthony's close friend, Senator Aaron A. Sargent of California. Forty-seven years later Congress acted favorably, prompted by support from President Woodrow Wilson, whose opposition had been overcome in large part by the extraordinary roles played by women in World War I. Congress, equally impressed with women's wartime contributions, was also influenced by the fact that delegations from the fifteen states that had already adopted full women suffrage via state amendments were more inclined to be supportive, mindful of the fact that they represented women as well as men.

Within the first four months following congressional approval, seventeen states had ratified the Nineteenth Amendment, but other states—even suffrage states—failed to act. Carrie Chapman Catt, president of the National American Woman Suffrage Association, led a delegation on a "Wake Up America" campaign. Their efforts paid off, and the final battle for suffrage took place in the border state of Tennessee where, after weeks of intrigue and intensive lobbying by supporters and opponents, the Nineteenth Amendment was finally ratified. Tennessee's certificate of ratification was duly signed and made official with the signature of the U.S. Secretary of State on August 26, 1920.

When Carrie Chapman Catt called to inquire about the outcome, Secretary Bainbridge Colby invited her to come to the Department of State to see for herself. Maud Wood Park, chief congressional lobbyist for the national association and the recently named president of the newly organized League of Women Voters, was one of those in the party. Later, she wrote of that moment: "We almost had to stick pins in ourselves to realize that the simple document at which we were looking was, in reality, the long sought charter of liberty for the women of this country."

The amendment process is described in the following Article of the U.S. Constitution.

DOCUMENT 1: ARTICLE V OF THE U.S. CONSTITUTION

The Congress, whenever two-thirds of both Houses shall deem it necessary, shall propose Amendments to this Constitution . . . which . . . shall be valid to all Intents and Purposes, as part of this Constitution, when ratified by the Legislatures of three-fourths of the several States. . . .

The phrasing of the "long sought charter of liberty for women" is short and sweet.

DOCUMENT 2: ARTICLE XIX OF THE U.S. CONSTITUTION

[Proposed June 4, 1919; declared ratified August 26, 1920]

The right of citizens of the United States to vote shall not be denied or abridged by the United States or by any State on account of sex.

Source: Jacqueline Van Voris, *Carrie Chapman Catt: A Public Life.* New York: The Feminist Press, 1987, 155–62, 246 n. 2. Maud Wood Park, *Front Door Lobby.* Edited by Edna L. Stantial, Boston: Beacon Press, 1960, 276. Constitution of the United States.

Chapter 2

The Politics of Woman Suffrage

The materials presented here trace the origins of the suffrage movement, identify some of its leaders and the influences that shaped its ideology and operations, describe the political milieu and the schisms that divided the movement, and conclude with the birth of the movement's most visible and enduring legacy—the LWV.

William Blackstone, the leading writer on English common law, stated in 1769 that "by marriage, the husband and the wife are one person in the law . . . the very being or legal existence of the woman is suspended during the marriage, or at least is incorporated and consolidated into that of her husband under whose wing, protection, and cover she performs everything . . . her condition during her marriage is called her *coverture*." That prevailing attitude of female dependence and servitude, which found its way to American shores, was initially protested by only a few brash and bold women. By the nineteenth century, however, women began to do an end run around "coverture" by creating a politics based on altruism. This took a variety of different forms, including missionary support, temperance groups; organizations devoted to the salvation of fallen women, and anti-slavery societies. The most important of these activities proved to be the abolition campaign, for as they learned about the discriminations against black Americans, women became increasingly sensitive to their own deprivations. That sensitivity was enhanced by male abolitionists who welcomed their participation but only in separate "female" societies. Nevertheless as Eleanor Flexner, a pioneering historian of the suffrage movement, noted: "It was in the abolition movement that women first learned to organize, to hold public meetings, and to conduct petition campaigns. As abolitionists they first won the right to speak in public, and began to evolve a philosophy of their place in society and of their basic rights. For a quarter of a century the two movements, to free the slave and liberate the woman, nourished and strengthened one another."

Source: William Blackstone, *Commentaries on the Law of England*. New York: William E. Dean, 1853, 375–76. Eleanor Flexner, *Century of Struggle: The Woman's Rights Movement in the United States*. Cambridge, MA: Belknap Press of Harvard University Press, 1959, 41.

At the first world antislavery convention in London, England in 1840, there was a historic meeting of two minds. Lucretia Mott, president of the Philadelphia Female Anti-Slavery Society, had been elected a delegate. Elizabeth Cady and her new husband, Henry Stanton (also a delegate), had made their journey to London a honeymoon voyage. When Lucretia Mott along with other American women delegates were banished from the floor because the convention authorities would not recognize their credentials, Mott and Stanton began to spend time together. The more they were together, the more concerns they shared, particularly those relating to the status of women. They resolved to do something about women's rights on their return to the United States.

That resolve dissolved as Mott found her time taken up with internal Quaker arguments and Stanton began having babies. In 1848 Mott came to Waterloo, New York, a twin town to Seneca Falls where the Stanton family was living. They and three other women met over tea, and Stanton's rhetoric about her life inspired them to write a call to a convention for the purpose of discussing the social, civil, and religious condition of women. Eight days later, three hundred women and men crowded into the Weslyan Chapel. In that short interval Stanton had composed a "Declaration of Sentiments" detailing the repeated "injuries and usurpations" suffered by women and several resolutions to redress those injustices.

All the resolutions were approved, though one seemed likely to fail: "That it is the duty of the women of this country to secure to themselves their sacred right to the elective franchise." It was not until Frederick Douglass, the former slave and then publisher of the North Star newspaper in nearby Rochester, New York, provided an eloquent seconding speech that delegates were persuaded to approve the controversial resolution.

*Why was there such opposition to women voting? Because it so
challenged the prevailing view of women's roles. It was seen as an
attempt to replace male authority with female autonomy, to change the
role of women from subordinate to equal within the family structure;
and to enable women to cross the threshold from the domestic sphere
to the public realm. Such assumptions were still largely entrenched in
popular culture, and Americans—men and women—were not ready to
abandon old ways. Despite these reservations, and the ridicule and
mockery to come, the convention delegates at Seneca Falls initiated
their seventy-two-year-long struggle by American women to win the
right to vote.*

DOCUMENT 1: THE DECLARATION OF SENTIMENTS

When in the course of human events, it becomes necessary for one portion
of the family of man to assume among the people of the earth a position
different from that which they have hitherto occupied, but one to which the laws
of nature and of nature's God entitle them a decent respect to the opinions of
mankind requires that they should declare the causes that impel them to such a
course.

We hold these truths to be self-evident: that all men and women are created
equal; that they are endowed by their Creator with certain inalienable rights; that
among these are life, liberty, and the pursuit of happiness; that to secure these
rights governments are instituted, deriving their just powers from the consent of
the governed. . . .

The history of mankind is a history of repeated injuries and usurpations on
the part of man toward woman, having in direct object the establishment of an
absolute tyranny over her. To prove this, let facts be submitted to a candid
world.

He has never permitted her to exercise her inalienable right to the elective
franchise.

He has compelled her to submit to laws, in the formation of which she had
no voice.

He has withheld from her rights which are given to the most ignorant and
degraded men—both natives and foreigners.

Having deprived her of this first right of a citizen, the elective franchise,
thereby leaving her without representation in the halls of legislation, he has
oppressed her on all sides.

He has made her, if married, in the eye of the law, civilly dead.

He has taken from her all right in property, even to the wages she earns.

He has made her, morally, an irresponsible being, as she can commit many
crimes with impunity, provided they be done in the presence of her husband. In
the covenant of marriage, she is compelled to promise obedience to her
husband, he becoming, to all intents and purposes, her master—the law giving
him power to deprive her of her liberty, and to administer chastisement.

He has so framed the laws of divorce, as to what shall be the proper causes,
and in case of separation, to whom the guardianship of the children shall be
given, as to be wholly regardless of the happiness of women, in all cases, going
upon the false supposition of the supremacy of man, and giving all power into
his hands.

After depriving her of all rights as a married woman, if single, and the owner of property, he has taxed her to support a government which recognizes her only when her property can be made profitable to it. He has monopolized nearly all the profitable employments, and from those she is permitted to follow, she receives but a scanty remuneration. He closes against her all the avenues to wealth and distinction which he considers most honorable to himself. As teacher of theology, medicine, or law, she is not known.

He has denied her the facilities for obtaining a thorough education, all colleges being closed against her.

He allows her in Church, as well as State, but a subordinate position, claiming Apostolic authority for her exclusion from the ministry, and, with some exceptions, from any public participation in the affairs of the Church.

He has created a false public sentiment by giving to the world a different code of morals for men and women, by which moral delinquencies which exclude women from society, are not only tolerated, but deemed of little account in man.

He has usurped the prerogative of Jehovah himself claiming it as his right to assign for her a sphere of action, when that belongs to her conscience and to her God.

He has endeavored, in every way that he could, to destroy her confidence in her own powers, to lessen her self-respect, and to make her willing to lead a dependent and abject life.

Now, in view of this entire disfranchisement of one-half the people of this country, their social and religious degradation—in view of the unjust laws above mentioned, and because women do feel themselves aggrieved, oppressed, and fraudulently deprived of their most sacred rights, we insist that they have immediate admission to all the rights and privileges which belong to them as citizens of the United States.

In entering upon the great work before us, we anticipate no small amount of misconception, misrepresentation, and ridicule; but we shall use every instrumentality within our power to effect our object. We shall employ agents, circulate tracts, petition the State and National legislatures, and endeavor to enlist the pulpit and the press in our behalf. We hope this Convention will be followed by a series of Conventions embracing every part of the country.

Resolutions: Whereas, The great precept of nature is conceded to be, that "man shall pursue his own true and substantial happiness." Blackstone in his Commentaries remarks, that this law of Nature being coeval with mankind, and dictated by God himself, is of course superior in obligation to any other. It is binding over all the globe, in all countries and at all times; no human laws are of any validity if contrary to this, and such of them as are valid, derive all their force, and all their validity, and all their authority, mediately and immediately, from this original; therefore,

Resolved, That such laws as conflict, in any way, with the true and substantial happiness of woman, are contrary to the great precept of nature and of no validity; for this is "superior in obligation to any other."

Resolved, That all laws which prevent woman from occupying such a station in society as her conscience shall dictate, or which place her in a position inferior to that of man, are contrary to the great precept of nature, and therefore of no force or authority.

Resolved, That woman is man's equal—was intended to be so by the Creator, and the highest good of the race demands that she should be recognized as such.

Resolved, That the women of this country ought to be enlightened in regard to the laws under which they live, that they may no longer publish their degradation by declaring themselves satisfied with their present position, nor their ignorance, by asserting that they have all the rights they want.

Resolved, That inasmuch as man, while claiming for himself intellectual superiority, does accord to woman moral superiority, it is pre-eminently his duty to encourage her to speak and teach, as she has an opportunity, in all religious assemblies.

Resolved, That the same amount of virtue, delicacy, and refinement of behavior that is required of woman in the social state, should also be required of man, and the same transgressions should be visited with equal severity on both man and woman.

Resolved, That the objection of indelicacy and impropriety, which is so often brought against woman when she addresses a public audience, comes with a very ill-grace from those who encourage, by their attendance, her appearance on the stage, in the concert, or in feats of the circus.

Resolved, That woman has too long rested satisfied in the circumscribed limits which corrupt customs and a perverted application of the Scriptures have marked out for her, and that it is time she should move in the enlarged sphere which her great Creator has assigned her.

Resolved, That it is the duty of the women of this country to secure to themselves their sacred right to the elective franchise.

Resolved, That the equality of human rights results necessarily from the fact of the identity of the race in capabilities and responsibilities.

Resolved Therefore, That, being invested by the Creator with the some capabilities, and the same consciousness of responsibility for their exercise, it is demonstrably the right and duty of woman, equally with man, to promote every righteous cause by every righteous means; and especially in regard to the great subjects of morals and religion, it is self-evidently her right to participate with her brother in teaching them, both in private and in public, by writing and by speaking, by any instrumentalities proper to be used, and in any assemblies proper to be held; and this being a self-evident truth growing out of the divinely implanted principles of human nature, any custom or authority adverse to it, whether modern or wearing the hoary sanction of antiquity, is to be regarded as a self-evident falsehood, and at war with mankind.

Resolved, That the speedy success of our cause depends upon the zealous and untiring efforts of both men and women, for the overthrow of the monopoly of the pulpit, and for the securing to woman an equal participation with men in the various trades, professions, and commerce.

Source: Elisabeth Griffith, *In Her Own Right: The Life of Elizabeth Cady Stanton*. New York: Oxford University Press, 1984, 37–39, 42–52. Excerpts from the "Declaration of Sentiments" in Anne Firor Scott and Andrew Mackay Scott, *One Half the People: The Fight for Woman Suffrage*. Chicago and Urbana: University of Illinois Press, 1982, 56–59.

From the outset of the new woman's movement, suffragists depended on existing antislavery societies to be their publicists and collaborators in seeking freedoms and rights denied to both African Americans and women. That unity of purpose disintegrated in the aftermath of the Civil War with the enactment of the Fourteenth and Fifteenth Amendments to the U.S. Constitution. Section 2 of the Fourteenth Amendment introduced the word male into the Constitution for the first time. The Fifteenth Amendment omitted the word sex but did include "race, color, or previous condition of servitude" as reasons not to deny voting rights.

Elizabeth Cady Stanton and her friend and colleague, Susan B. Anthony, were mad as wet hens over the exclusion of women from the two amendments and did not accept the proposition that this was the "Negro's hour." Consequently, in 1869 they organized the National Woman Suffrage Association, and, in the same year, Lucy Stone and her husband, Henry Blackwell, formed the American Woman Suffrage Association. It was the first time that American women had organized on behalf of their own interests.

DOCUMENT 2: ARTICLE XIV OF THE U.S. CONSTITUTION

[Proposed June 13, 1866; declared ratified July 28, 1868]

Section 2. Representatives shall be apportioned among the several States according to their respective numbers, counting the whole number of persons in each State, excluding Indians not taxed. But when the right to vote at any election for the choice of electors for President and Vice President of the United States, Representatives in Congress, the Executive and Judicial Officers of a State, or the members of the Legislature thereof, is denied to any of the male inhabitants of such State, being twenty-one years of age, and citizens of the United States, or in any way abridged, except for participation in rebellion, or other crime, the basis of representation therein shall be reduced in the proportion which the number of such male citizens shall bear to the whole number of male citizens twenty-one years of age in such State.

DOCUMENT 3: ARTICLE XV OF THE U.S. CONSTITUTION

[Proposed February 26, 1869; declared ratified March 30, 1870]

Section 1. The right of citizens of the United States to vote shall not be denied or abridged by the United States or by any State on account of race, color, or previous condition of servitude.

Section 2. The Congress shall have power to enforce this article by appropriate legislation.

Source: Ellen Carol Dubois, *Feminism and Suffrage: The Emergence of an Independent Women's Movement in America, 1848–1869.* Ithaca, NY: Cornell University Press, 1978, 51, 59, 164, 174–75. Constitution of the United States.

There were many talented leaders who emerged in the seventy-two year struggle to achieve woman suffrage. They included the founders—Mott and Stanton—described by one contemporary as the soul and mind of the movement; Susan B. Anthony, who was the energetic extension agent, carrying the message to the far reaches of a young nation; and Carrie Chapman Catt, who would twice serve as national president of the suffrage association.

Despite the enthusiasm and efforts of suffrage supporters, their successes were few and far between. In 1869 the territory of Wyoming became the first political entity in the United States to have woman suffrage and carried that suffrage into statehood in 1890. Other western states followed suit: Colorado in 1893, Utah in 1895, Idaho in 1896. As Carrie Chapman Catt made clear at the 1895 national suffrage convention, suffragists were strong on rhetoric, less effective organizationally. Among the tasks Catt identified were surveying each district, contacting and persuading voters and recording those contacts, arranging district meetings, forming committees to enhance organizational and public relations efforts, and educating poll watchers about election laws and what constituted violations of those laws. Susan B. Anthony's comments on Catt's remarks contained a grain of truth when she noted that "there never was a young woman who did not feel that if she had the management of the work from the beginning, the cause would have been carried long ago. I felt just so when I was young." Even though the delegates responded with empathetic laughter, Anthony knew, too, that a more effective organization was an imperative confronting the movement. Four years later, Anthony chose Catt to succeed her in 1900 as president of the National American Woman Suffrage Association. The final victory was due in no small measure to Catt's organizational genius. Catt understood the ways of politics, and her knowledge helped win suffrage in Idaho and—nearly twenty-five years later—in the United States.

Source: Report of the Plan of Work Committee and Comments by Susan B. Anthony, National American Woman Suffrage Association Convention, Atlanta, GA, January 31–February 5, 1895. Robert Booth Fowler, *Carrie Catt: Feminist Politician.* Boston: Northeastern University Press, 1986, 119.

The suffrage movement was strengthened by its association with other women leaders and other organizations and movements. When Frances Willard became president of the Woman's Christian Temperance Union (WCTU) in 1879, she brought with her a strong commitment not only to temperance but also to suffrage. Although a member of the less flamboyant American Woman Suffrage Association, she dared to ask Susan B. Anthony to speak at the WCTU convention of 1881, prompting a walkout by a number of conservative members. Willard, however, stuck to her suffrage guns—"arguing for the ballot as a defense of the home"—and established a Department of

Enfranchisement in 1882, which in time became the organization's leading department. As a result, and despite the reservations of some members, the WCTU took the place of the anti-slavery movement as the greatest ally of suffrage. Although the strength and size of the WCTU undoubtedly helped (by gaining the support of the largest women's organization then in existence) more than it hindered (by generating the fierce opposition of the liquor interests), Anthony remained apprehensive about men confusing the two organizations and their primary missions.

In the later years of the suffrage campaign, the settlement house movement, or what Arthur Schlesinger Jr. has described as "this middle-class mission to the poor," became an important adjunct primarily for the leadership it brought to the campaign and for the issue orientation it inspired the League of Women Voters to adopt. He also credited middle-class reformers for initiating the demand for a child labor amendment, for maximum hour and minimum wage standards, and for social insurance. These social innovations came not from the unions but from organizations like the Women's Trade Union League (formed in 1902 by a coalition of working class and elite women to strengthen the influence of wage-earning women in labor unions). Jane Addams of Hull House, Florence Kelley of the National Consumers' League, and Julia Lathrop, who became director of the Children's Bureau, were among the pioneering women of social reform whose work and activities reinforced the notion that women deserved full citizenship.

Jane Addams was a leader both by virtue of the high offices she held in the National American Woman Suffrage Association (NAWSA) and by her intellectual creativity. Hull House, which Addams established in Chicago in 1889, served as a model for the settlement house movement whose leaders pioneered the new profession of social work, important in providing career opportunities for women as well as remedies for the social ills they addressed. Addams gave voice to a new strain in the suffrage movement. While not rejecting the concept of "sameness," that is, women's shared humanity with men that entitled them to equal justice under the law, she also articulated the concept of "difference" in the particular contributions women could make as efficient managers of civic affairs.

Jane Addams's contention that women as experienced housekeepers could solve a variety of municipal problems struck a responsive chord. Women had helped to build the infrastructure of communities—the hospitals, libraries, parks and playgrounds, charitable organizations, and cultural institutions. Lacking the vote, *they were beginning to be appreciated as reformers and doers with a high regard for integrity, accountability, and morality. The concerns of women like Addams, Kelley, and Lathrop meshed with the new progressive movement. It was no wonder that Theodore Roosevelt gave full credit to the social workers "who are doing . . . invaluable work" or that Jane Addams returned the compliment by seconding Roosevelt's nomination as the presidential hopeful of the Progressive Party in 1912.*

Source: A. F. Scott and A.M. Scott, *One Half the People,* 21. Arthur M. Schlesinger Jr., *The Age of Roosevelt: The Crisis of the Old Order, 1919–1933.* Boston: Houghton Mifflin Co., 1957, 24–25.

DOCUMENT 4: JANE ADDAMS ON CITY HOUSEKEEPING

It has been well said that the modern city is a stronghold of industrialism quite as the feudal city was a stronghold of militarism, but the modern cities fear no enemies and rivals from without and their problems of government are solely internal. Affairs for the most part are going badly in these great new centres, in which the quickly congregated–population has not yet learned to arrange its affairs satisfactorily. Unsanitary housing, poisonous sewage, contaminated water, infant mortality, the spread of contagion, adulterated food, impure milk, smoke-laden air, ill-vented factories, dangerous occupations, juvenile crime, unwholesome crowding, prostitution and drunkenness are the enemies which the modern cities must face to overcome, would they survive. Logically their electorate should be made up of those who can bear a valiant part in this arduous contest, those who in the past have at least attempted to care for children, to clean houses, to prepare foods, to isolate the family from moral dangers; those who have traditionally taken care of that side of life which inevitably becomes the subject of municipal consideration and control as soon as the population is congested. To test the elector's fitness to deal with this situation by his ability to bear arms is absurd. These problems must be solved, if they are solved at all, not from the military point of view, not even from the industrial point of view, but from a third, which is rapidly developing in all the great cities of the world—the human-welfare point of view . . .

City housekeeping then failed partly because women, the traditional housekeepers, have not been consulted as to its multiform activities. The men have been carelessly indifferent to much of this civic housekeeping, as they have always been indifferent to the details of the household . . . The very multifariousness and complexity of a city government demand the help of minds accustomed to detail and variety of work, to a sense of obligation for the health and welfare of young children and to a responsibility for a cleanliness and comfort of other people. Because all these things have traditionally been in the hands of women, if they take no part in them now they are not only missing the education which the natural participation in civic life would bring to them, but they are losing what they have always had.

Source: Jane Addams, "The Modern City and the Municipal Franchise for Women," NAWSA Convention, Baltimore, MD, February 7–13, 1906, in Vol. 3: 178–79. Elizabeth Cady Stanton, et al. *History of Woman Suffrage*, 6 Vols. Rochester, NY: Susan B. Anthony; New York: National American Woman Suffrage Association, 1881–1922, Vol. 5: 178–79.

In the early 1900s higher education for women became increasingly popular, and colleges like Vassar, Mount Holyoke, Smith, Wellesley, and Bryn Mawr were respected institutions of single-sex education. These colleges, as well as certain coeducational institutions, attracted increasing numbers of women and proved to be a fertile ground for suffrage support. M. Carey Thomas, president of Bryn Mawr, also served as president of the National College Equal Suffrage League from 1906 until 1917 when it disbanded (the first College League had been founded in 1900 in Boston by Radcliffe student Maud Wood Park and her friend Inez Haynes Gilmore who was later prominent in the National Woman's Party). As her biographer makes clear, Thomas, frequently controversial and often contentious, nevertheless made the most of her presidency as a vehicle to demonstrate her support for suffrage. The National College League gave the movement an important intellectual dimension with the presidency of Thomas and with its establishment of a traveling library that circulated among member colleges; it contained some two dozens works ranging from Mary Wollstonecraft's *Vindication of the Rights of Women* to *The Doll's House* by Henrik Ibsen. Eleanor Flexner, the distinguished biographer of the suffrage movement, characterized Thomas as a vital and compelling personality who aroused antagonism by her impatience and self-assurance. Carrie Chapman Catt called Thomas "Her Holy Smokes."

Source: Helen Lefkowitz Horowitz, *The Power and Passion of M. Carey Thomas.* New York: Alfred A. Knopf, 1994, 400–01. Flexner, *Century of Struggle*, 371, n. 18.

Like the division of the suffrage house in 1869, a similar schism emerged in the 20th century. An impatient coterie of young women who had revived NAWSA's dormant Congressional Committee had more ambitious plans to achieve suffrage. In March 1913 the committee organized a big parade in Washington, DC and upstaged Woodrow Wilson's arrival on the eve of his inauguration. Invigorated by their success, Alice Paul, Lucy Burns, and others formed the Congressional Union. In time, tensions mounted between the two suffrage groups, and Paul and Carrie Chapman Catt agreed to disagree. The final break came when the Congressional Union introduced partisanship into the movement by campaigning in suffrage states against all Democratic officeholders in the 1914 elections (Paul *and Burns had been graduate students in England and had been drawn to the practice of British suffragettes to hold the party in power responsible for inaction on the suffrage issue). In 1917 the Congressional Union was transformed into the National Women's Party, and members began picketing the White House. After an uneasy truce with the authorities, the pickets began to be arrested for obstructing traffic and imprisoned. When they protested with hunger strikes, the women who had been "jailed for freedom"[1] were forcibly fed. While these tactics prompted public sympathies, Carrie Chapman Catt and her associates, who were trying to win President Wilson's support, found them counterproductive.*

DOCUMENT 5: RECONCILIATION FAILS

Another problem came before this convention—the policy of the recently formed Congressional Union to adopt the method of the "militant" branch of the English suffragists and hold the party in power responsible for the failure to submit the Federal Suffrage Amendment. They had gone into the equal suffrage States during the congressional campaign of 1914 and fought the re-election of some of the staunchest friends of this amendment, Senator Thomas of Colorado, for instance, chairman of the Senate Committee, which had reported it favorably, and a lifelong suffragist. The press and public not knowing the difference between the two organizations were holding the National American Association responsible, and protests were coming from all over the country. Some of the younger members, who did not know the history and traditions of the old association, thought that there should be cooperation between the two bodies. Both had lobbyists actively working at the Capitol, members of Congress were confused and there was a considerable feeling that some plan for united action should be found. Miss Zona Gale, the writer, offered the following motion, which was carried without objection: "Realizing that all suffragists have a common cause at heart and that difference of methods is inevitable, it is moved that an efficiency commission consisting of five members be appointed by the Chair to confer with representatives of the Congressional Union in order to bring about cooperation with the maximum of efficiency for the successful passage of the Susan B. Anthony Amendment at this session of Congress...."

At the conference Mrs. Catt explained to Miss Paul that the association could not accept as an affiliated society one which was likely to defy its policy held since its foundation in 1869, which was neither to support nor oppose any political party, nor to work for or against any candidate except as to his attitude toward woman suffrage. Miss Paul would give no guarantee that the Congressional Union would observe this policy. It was thought that some way of dividing the lobby work might be found but in a short time the Union announced its program of fighting the candidates of the Democratic Party without any reference to their position on the Federal Amendment or their record on woman suffrage. They offered as a reason that as the Democratic Party was in control of the Government it should have the Federal Amendment submitted. There never was a time when the Democrats had the necessary two-thirds of the members of each house of Congress, but enough of them favored it so that it could have been carried if enough of the Republicans had voted for it. It was plainly evident that it would require the support of both parties. The policy of the Congressional Union, put into action throughout the presidential campaign of 1916, made any cooperation impossible.

Source: Excerpts from the *Proceedings of the NAWSA Convention*, Washington, DC, December 14–19, 1915, *History of Woman Suffrage*. New York: Fowler and Wells, Vol. 5, 453–55.

In Woodrow Wilson's speech at the 1916 suffrage convention, he stated that he had now put behind him any quarrel as to the method of achieving suffrage. His was a personal journey from early opposition to siding with the advocates of state suffrage amendments to endorsement of the federal amendment, a journey influenced by the important contributions of women in World War I, the presence at his front gate of the pickets of the National Woman's Party, and pressures from his three daughters. The President, accompanied by Mrs. Wilson, had a customary retinue of distinguished men and, of course, the secret service. He had asked to speak last and listened as the president of the National Women's Trade Union League, head of the Women's Bureau and others addressed issues of concern to women. When it was his turn, Woodrow Wilson spoke of the "gathering force" for suffrage. He then set aside the quarrel about means and addressed the women, saying that suffrage will "prevail," and that he was there to affirm and welcome that fact and to congratulate them. Carrie Catt kept reminding Wilson of the critical wartime contributions by women, arguing that if the world was to be made safe for democracy, saving it at home should be the starting point. On September 30, 1918, he addressed the Senate of the United States.

DOCUMENT 6: THE WINNING PLAN

At the close of the convention, Mrs. Catt called a session of the Executive Council, made up of the national officers of the Association and the presidents of its state branches. During the unusual heat of the preceding week she had conducted three meetings a day. She had borne, with no outward sign of disturbance, the responsibility of having the President as speaker at a time when fears for his safety were especially acute. She had found opportunity to confer with women from every part of the country, whose help was needed for the execution of her plans. That afternoon she intended to get a binding pledge of their cooperation.

The scene in the crowded stuffy room in the basement of the hotel where the Council met is something I shall always remember: the tired faces of most of the women there; the huge map of the United States, hung on one of the walls; and, most vividly of all, Mrs. Catt herself, when, after the routine business of the Council was over, she took up the typed pages in which she had outlined the work of the coming year.

To her preamble, which was a brief restatement of reasons for undertaking a more energetic drive for the amendment, I listened with a good deal of inward protest. I could not forget that the only woman suffrage planks in both the major party platforms called for action by the separate states, not by the Congress. I believed that, hard as the advance, state by state, was bound to be, we had to have a good many more states in which women could vote before the drive for a federal amendment would be successful. Even after Mrs. Catt stated that the Association's Congressional Committee in Washington was to be enlarged and much more spacious headquarters were to be taken there, I was still skeptical.

Then she started to explain that no amount of work in Washington was likely to bring about the submission of the amendment unless new victories were won in the states. At that point I began to listen more carefully, for it was clear that Mrs. Catt had no intention of letting her federal program lessen efforts to secure state action. On the contrary, as I soon learned, her plan was essentially a demand for legislative activity in every part of the country during the coming sessions of the state legislatures.

Pointer in hand, she stepped to the map and traced four divisions of states, to each of which she assigned a particular form of legislative work. First, she called on our organizations in the equal suffrage states and in Illinois to secure from their legislatures resolution requesting the Congress to submit the woman suffrage amendment. In the case of the income tax amendment, she explained, resolutions from the state legislatures had proved extremely helpful.

Next she pointed out several states—New York among them—in which there was a chance of carrying a state constitutional amendment to enfranchise women. In all those states she urged our workers to prepare at once for a campaign to get their legislatures to submit such an amendment and the voters to support it.

For most of the remaining states she advised trying for presidential suffrage, i.e., the right to vote for presidential electors, which could be given by the legislatures without referring the question to the voters. For a few of the southern one-party states, where success in the primary is equivalent to an election, she told the delegates that they ought to make an attempt to get suffrage in the primaries, a form that could also be granted outright by the state legislatures.

In brief, confronted with the choice between work in state campaigns and work for a federal amendment, Mrs. Catt declared, "We must do both and do them together."

When the fourfold plan had been made clear, she described the procedure necessary to put it into effect. An immediate start upon the work was imperative, she explained, in order to have everything ready at the beginning of the legislative sessions, most of which opened in January. If our campaigns were simultaneous, the opposition, taken by surprise and unprepared for a fight on so many fronts at once, would be forced to concentrate on a few states or else to spread itself too thin to be effective. Then, warning her listeners that the plan would fail if its scope leaked out, she requested from them a definite pledge that they would disclose no details except such as were required in each state for its own project.

Last of all, she presented a compact to be signed by the representatives of suffrage associations in at least thirty-six states. She reminded us that, since thirty-six was the minimum number of states necessary for the ratification of a federal amendment, a failure on the part of a single state would mean ultimate defeat for all.

When the full number of signatures had been affixed to the compact and we filed out of the room, I felt like Moses on the mountain top after the Promised

Land had been shown to him and he knew the long years of wandering in the Wilderness were soon to end. For the first time I saw our goal as possible of attainment in the near future. But we had to have swift and concerted action from every part of the country. Could we get it? Could we get it?

Often since then, remembering how hard it was at best to win our vote in the Congress and the subsequent ratification by 36 states, I have speculated as to what would have happened if Mrs. Catt's plan had not been presented on that sultry afternoon in 1916. Undoubtedly a woman suffrage amendment would have been adopted at some time, even if Mrs. Catt had never been born; but, if success had not come when it did, the cause might easily have been caught in a period of postwar reaction, and victory postponed for another half-century. That women all over the United States were able to vote in 1920 is due, I believe, to the carrying out of the plan prepared and presented by an incomparable leader.

Source: Maud Wood Park, *Front Door Lobby*. Boston: Beacon Press, 1960, 15–18. Carrie Chapman Catt, "Report: Campaign and Survey Committee," Papers of the National American Woman Suffrage Association, Library of Congress.

Carrie Chapman Catt's strategy of supporting American preparedness for subsequent participation in World War I and continuing the suffrage campaign turned out to be both wise and effective. She was able to maintain her commitment to both despite her deep ambivalence regarding the first. On principle, Catt opposed war as a means of settling conflict, but she also believed that the failure of suffrage organizations to support the war effort would place the issue of suffrage in jeopardy. At the 1917 NAWSA convention she succeeded in persuading delegates to prepare for war. Two months later when the United States Congress approved the declaration of war, Catt kept the organization on course. But she was not without her critics on both sides of the issue. The Women's Peace Party ejected her from membership and other pacifists denounced her. Throughout the war, NAWSA members worked with the Red Cross, served soldiers in canteens, and stood in for farmers in the production of food, thereby deflecting critics who falsely accused suffragists of being disloyal and pro-German. The antisuffragists, eager to pounce on Catt and stretching the truth about her motives, even went so far as to urge her deportation. Nevertheless, most Americans applauded the contributions of suffragists during World War I and began to respond affirmatively to their proposition that they had, by virtue of their patriotism, earned the vote. Given Catt's aversion to war, her tactics might have seemed cynical, but, as Robert Fowler, one of her biographers, observed: "She never had any interest in a politics of purity in the impure world. To her the fact was that she could not stop the war, but the NAWSA's opposition to war could seriously delay women's enfranchisement. . . . Her devotion in subsequent decades of her public life to the cause of world peace was not an act of expiation. It was rather a resumption of the peace mission, which she had never lost sight of. But it was a long-range goal and she had no intention of losing momentum for women's enfranchisement because of it."

Source: Robert Booth Fowler, "Carrie Chapman Catt, Strategist," in Marjorie Spruil Wheeler, *One Woman, One Vote: Reconstructing the Woman Suffrage Movement.* Troutdale, OR: New Sage Press, 1995, 299–302.

Carrie Catt had put the hard work of persuading members of Congress into the capable hands of Maud Wood Park. Her rules for suffrage lobbyists were direct and clear. While their business was serious, it was also leavened by laughter, one example of the good humor that permeated the movement.

DOCUMENT 7: DIRECTIONS FOR LOBBYISTS

During January 1917, our lobby, in addition to members of the Congressional Committee, consisted of twenty-nine women in sixteen different states, who stayed in Washington at their own expense for periods ranging from six days to four weeks. For their use we had our lobby rules drawn up in the following form:

Directions for Lobbyists

I. Preparation

1. Read our records of each member before calling on him. Also read biographical sketch in Congressional Directory. *Records must not be taken from the office.*
2. Provide yourself with small directory. Your own representative is the best source of supply.

II. Interviewing

1. If the member appears busy ask whether he would prefer to see you at some other time.
2. Be courteous no matter what provocation you may seem to have to be otherwise.
3. If possible learn the secretary's name and have a little talk with him or her. The secretary, if inclined to be interested, should be invited to headquarters.
4. If the member is known to be in favor *show that you realize that fact* and ask him for advice and help with the rest of the delegation. This point is *very important.*
5. Be sure to keep his *party* constantly in mind while talking with him.
6. Be a good listener. Don't interrupt.
7. Try to avoid prolonged or controversial argument. It is likely to confirm men in their own opinion.
8. Do not stay so long that the member has to give the signal for departure.
9. Take every possible means to prevent a member from *committing* himself definitely *against* the Federal Amendment. This is *most important.*
10. Leave the way open for another interview if you have failed to convince him.

11. If the member is inclined to be favorable invite him and his family to headquarters.

12. Remember to hold each interview confidential. Never quote what one member has said to you to another member. It is not safe to talk of your lobby experiences before outsiders or before servants. We can never know by what route our stories may get back to the member and injure our cause with him. We cannot be too cautious in this matter.

III. Reports

1. Do not make notes in offices or halls.
2. Do find opportunity to make notes on one interview before starting another. If necessary, step into the "Ladies" dressing room to do this.
3. Write full report of your interview on the same day giving—
   a. Name and State of member.
   b. *Date* and hour of interview.
   c. Names of lobbyists and name of person making report.
   d. Member's argument in detail, especially with view to follow-up work.
   e. Any information you may glean about his family or friends that may be useful to the Washington Committee.
   f. Hand-written report to *Miss Bain*, not later than the day following the interview.
   g. Promptness in turning in reports is most important in order that lists and polls may be kept up to date.

When I was sufficiently familiar with the work to have a little sense of humor about it, I condensed those rules into a series of "don'ts":

Don't nag.

Don't boast.

Don't threaten.

Don't lose your temper.

Don't stay too long.

Don't talk about your work where you can be overheard.

Don't give the member interviewed an opportunity to declare himself against the amendment.

Don't do anything to close the door to the next advocate of suffrage.

The last "don't" was the one I dwelt on most in my talks with our workers, partly because it was the most difficult to follow. Knowing that the effect of our work in the case of doubtful members was cumulative, I used to say over and over again, "If we can't do any good, at least we must be sure that we don't do any harm."

Many of our lobby meetings were as entertaining as a good comedy. One of the women had the gift of ironic wit. Another was a capital mimic and gave us side–splitting imitations of some of the men whom she had interviewed. She was wise, too, for she cautioned us never to tell outside that any of our number had ventured to "take off" members of the Congress. I sometimes found it hard to stop my own laughter long enough to give out the next assignments.

Source: Park, *Front Door Lobby*, 38–40.

Miriam Leslie, who officially changed her name to Frank Leslie after her husband's death, took charge of his declining publishing empire and restored it to its former glory, was interested in the suffrage movement and usually contributed $100 a year to the cause. Catt's courtesy and competence must have prompted Leslie to stipulate in her will that nearly one million dollars go to Catt for "the furtherance of the cause of suffrage." Three years later, in 1917, following a legal contest with Leslie's family, which consumed nearly half of the legacy, Catt finally won the first round. (The lawsuits lasted until 1921.) With that initial payment of $500,000, Catt formed the Leslie Woman Suffrage Commission establishing a Bureau of Suffrage Education and purchased *The Woman's Journal* from Alice Stone Blackwell, merging it with two other suffrage publications. *The Woman Citizen* became the official journal of the National American Woman Suffrage Association and later of the League of Women Voters. That bequest from Miriam Leslie made a big difference in the ability of NAWSA to intensify the campaign through expanded outreach efforts of education and publication.

Source: Madeline B. Stern, Leslie, Miriam Florence Folline, *Notable American Women*, Vol. II, 393–94. Flexner, *Century of Struggle*, 272–73. Mary Gray Peck, *Carrie Chapman Catt: A Biography*. New York: The W. W. Wilson Company, 1944, 222, 265.

As victory drew nigh in Congress, Carrie Chapman Catt's engaging letter to Maud Wood Park in February 1919 reflected her good-natured willingness to accept either victory or defeat. She was accepting of one more defeat because she was so confident of the final outcome. At this stage, NAWSA was hopeful that the congressional Democrats, who had lost to the Republicans in the 1918 elections but who still controlled the lame duck session, would decide to bring the suffrage amendment to a vote and take credit for its passage. They did so on February 10, 1919, but the Senate again defeated the suffrage amendment, this time by a margin of only one vote.

DOCUMENT 8: CARRIE CHAPMAN CATT TO MAUD WOOD PARK

Apparently our chances have not been changed except by the additional earnestness of our friends and bitterness of our foes . . . Well, if fate perches on our bedraggled and outworn banner, we shall all be glad and perhaps we shall even feel jubilant. We shall shed no tears at any rate. But if our familiar experience is repeated, I want you to know that I am quite resigned and I think to the point that I shall not suffer. Editorials are written and ready for *The Citizen*. Mrs. Shuler is bringing the telegrams to send out if we go through, and bulletins if we do and if we don't, are ready too. In any event the delay cannot be long. Those who will eventually triumph can afford to be patient and forgiving.

I wish I might put you in a very tender embrace and steady your nerve and courage for these next days. If it is a go, you will steady yourself with joy, but if it isn't it will be a temporary shock and disturber of poise, which if I could I would ease for you.

If through we go, dance a jig and go to bed for a week of sweet sleep. If through we don't go, swear a few swears and go to bed and sleep a week just the same. If through we go, it was you who did it; if through we don't go, no other human being could have put it through. Nothing has been left undone, except the Lord's creation of certain creatures who pass for statesmen. HE MIGHT have done a better job!

So many of our officers are curious to see those queer Senators, inspired by much the same curiosity as the public by the ads of the Wild Man, that someone must stay home with finger on the trigger while they look through the bars of the senatorial cage. At the same time I am mending my physical incapacities so as to be in better trim for the next battle and I therefore will not be down for the Victory Dinner.

With the most loving and complete confidence one human being can feel for another, I am

Yours for victory
Yours for defeat
Yours anyway

Source: *Congressional Record*, 65th Cong., 3rd sess., 1919, 57, part 3:3062. Carrie Chapman Catt to Maud Wood Park, February 9, 1919. Women's Rights Collection, Schlesinger Library, Radcliffe College, Cambridge, MA.

NOTE

1. The expression, "jailed for freedom" is taken from the title of a book by Doris Stevens (New York: Liveright, 1920).

Chapter 3

From Jubilee to Victory

One and a half years before victory was achieved, Carrie Chapman Catt proposed the organization of a League of Women Voters "to finish the fight." Catt and others realized that the winning of suffrage would not be not an ending but a beginning—the beginning of full citizenship for American women. They would have to be trained in the rudiments of voting: how and where to register; how to assess candidates and ballot issues; and what to do at polling places. If the votes of these newly enfranchised citizens were to be effective, the citizens had to be informed about a wide range of issues. Among those already of interest were education, social services, child labor, governments that were open and accountable, women's rights, and world peace. These and other concerns constituted issues of the day affecting all citizens but representing a special bonding of the sentiments of women. An instrument for the political education and involvement of women was what Catt meant by "finish the fight." An organization, however, does not spring full-blown from the mind of one person, even one as erudite as Carrie Chapman Catt. There were many matters to attend to, not the least of which would be the relationship of the new organization to the political parties and the selection of League leaders.

Catt made her proposal a few months before congressional passage of the Nineteenth Amendment to delegates of the National American Woman Suffrage Association assembled for the fiftieth anniversary convention in St. Louis. In the call to convention, Carrie Chapman Catt first mentioned the idea of a League of Women Voters and elaborated on that idea in her opening convention address. The principal theme of her speech, which must have taken two hours to deliver, called for a national crusade against illiteracy and ignorance so that the American electorate would be "intelligent and clean."

DOCUMENT 1: CALL TO CONVENTION

To the Fiftieth Annual Convention and double anniversary of the National American Woman Suffrage Association, 1869–1919.

The National American Woman Suffrage Association calls its State Auxiliaries through their elected delegates to meet in annual Convention at St. Louis, Statler Hotel, March 24th to March 29th, 1919, inclusive.

In 1869, Wyoming led all the world by the grant of full suffrage to its women. The Convention will celebrate the fiftieth anniversary of this event.

In 1869, the National and the American Woman Suffrage Associations were organized—to be combined twenty years later into the National American Woman Suffrage Association. The Convention will celebrate the fiftieth anniversary of the founding of the organization, which without a pause has carried forward during half a century, the effort to secure the enfranchisement of women.

As a fitting memorial to a half century of progress, the National American Woman Suffrage Association invites the women voters of the fifteen full suffrage States to attend this anniversary Convention, and there to join their forces into a League of Women Voters, one of whose objects shall be to speed the suffrage campaign in our own and other countries.

The Convention will express its pleasure with suitable ceremonials that since last we met the women of England, Scotland, Ireland, Wales, Canada and Germany have received the vote; but it will make searching inquiry into the mysterious causes which deny patriotic, qualified women of our Republic "a voice in their own government," while those of monarchies and erstwhile monarchies are honored with political equality.

Suffrage Delegates, Women Voters, there is need of more serious counsel than in any previous year. It is not you, but the Nation that has been dishonored by the failure of the sixty-fifth Congress to pass the Federal Suffrage Amendment. Let us inquire together. Let us act together.

Source: "Call to Convention," The Woman Citizen, February 15, 1919.

DOCUMENT 2: CARRIE CHAPMAN CATT'S SPEECH TO THE CONVENTION

Every suffragist will hope for a fitting commemoration of this 50th Anniversary of our national organization and the Golden Jubilee of the first grant of full suffrage to women. She will hope for a memorial dedicated to the memory of our brave departed leaders, to the sacrifices they made for our cause, to the scores of victories won.

She will not be content with resolutions of self-congratulation; with speeches of tribute; nor will any suffragist propose a monument built of marble which only a few would see and fewer comprehend. What then shall it be? I venture to propose a memorial whose benefits will bless our entire nation and bring happiness to the humblest of our citizens.

What vainglorious proposal is this, do you ask? I propose no marvel; merely the most natural, the most appropriate and the most patriotic memorial that could be suggested—a League of Women Voters to "Finish the Fight" and to aid in the reconstruction of the Nation.

What could be more natural than that women having attained their political independence should desire to give service in token of their gratitude? What could be more appropriate than that such women should do for the coming generation, what those of a preceding period did for them? What could be more patriotic than that these women should use their new freedom to make their nation safer for their children and their children's children? I put the question to you, fellow suffragists; would not such a League express the spirit of our movement and our common feelings of gratitude upon this occasion more clearly than any other form of Memorial?

Let us then raise up a League of Women Voters—the name and form of organization to be determined by the voters themselves; a League that shall be non-partisan and non-sectarian in character and that shall be consecrated to three chief aims.

1. To use its utmost influence to secure the final enfranchisement of the women of every state in our own Republic and to reach out across the seas in aid of the woman's struggle for her own in every land.

2. To remove the remaining legal discriminations against women in the codes and constitutions of the several states in order that the feet of coming women may find these stumbling blocks removed.

3. To make our democracy so safe for the Nation and so safe for the world, that every citizen may feel secure and great men will acknowledge the worthiness of the American Republic to lead.

Source: Excerpts from *"The Nation Calls,"* Proceedings of the NAWSA National Convention, St. Louis, MO, March 24, 1919. LWV Papers on film, Part II, Series A, Reel 1, Frames 0021–32. (Future citations will be abbreviated, as for example, II. A.1. 0021–32.)

Meanwhile, the business of winning the vote had to be attended to. As the deadline for still another congressional vote on the suffrage amendment approached, Maud Wood Park, NAWSA's congressional chairman, sent out an urgent appeal to congressional chairmen in all the states. A week later, on May 21, 1919, the House passed the Nineteenth Amendment by a vote of 304 to 89. On June 4, the Senate followed suit with a vote of fifty-six to twenty-five.

DOCUMENT 3: MAUD WOOD PARK TO CONGRESSIONAL CHAIRMEN

This is a RUSH request to fill an imperative NEED. The newspaper reports that the federal amendment is sure of passage have turned tremendous anti-pressure upon the members of both houses. This is the crisis. The passage of the amendment depends upon YOUR work in holding the men already pledged and turning the doubtful ones to our side. Will you do the following things?

DOUBTFUL MEMBERS. Here is your most important task. Please organize to get all possible pressure and many letters and telegrams to these men, beginning the first day of the session, May 19th and continuing until the vote is taken.

NEW MEMBERS, FRIENDS. Next in importance is sending all possible letters and telegrams to these men telling them that their aid is counted upon.

OLD MEMBERS, FRIENDS. If you have not already made clear to these men that you are counting on their votes and therefore have asked their constituents not to bother them with letters [make sure a letter to that effect is sent before the end of next week].

NEW MEMBERS, OPPONENTS. As much pressure and as many letters and telegrams as possible should be brought to bear upon these men, since there is always more hope of those not recorded as having previously voted against us.

OLD MEMBERS, OPPONENTS. Do as much work on these men as your patience and energy permit. We are trying to secure a vote within the first ten days of the session. Whether we can get our friends among the absentees in Europe and elsewhere back within this time is still a question.

The situation requires prompt attention. YOUR work may assure the victory. Please take none but those committed in writing for granted as pledged to vote for us. Please take none but those most bitterly opposed for granted as being hopelessly against us. Success to you.

Source: Maud Wood Park to Dear Chairman, May 14, 1919, Women's Congressional Rights Collection, Radcliffe College, Cambridge, MA. Congressional Record, 66th Congress, 1st sess. 1919, part 1: 93–94 and 635.

Even before congressional enactment in 1919 and ratification by three-fourths of the states in 1920, Leagues had sprouted in states where women were already voters or "near voters." At NAWSA's last convention in Chicago in February 1920, the League of Women Voters was formed with Maud Wood Park at its first president. Meantime, the hard work of enactment by Congress and ratification by three-fourths of the states remained at the top of the new national organization's agenda. On August 26, the deed was done. After the last celebratory suffrage parade in New York City, Carrie Chapman Catt made the following remarks at the Astor Hotel.

DOCUMENT 4: SUFFRAGE SACRIFICES AND VOTING RESPONSIBILITIES

The vote is the emblem of your equality, women of America, the guaranty of your liberty. That vote of yours has cost millions of dollars and the lives of thousands of women. Money to carry on this work has been given usually as a sacrifice, and thousands of women have gone without things they wanted and could have had in order that they might help get the vote for you. Women have suffered agony of soul which you never can comprehend, that you and your daughters might inherit political freedom. *That vote has been costly. Prize it!*

The vote is a power, a weapon of offense and defense, and a prayer. Understand what it means and what it can do for your country. Use it intelligently, conscientiously, prayerfully. No soldier in the great suffrage army has labored and suffered to get a "place" for you. Their motive has been the hope women would aim higher than their own selfish ambitions, that they would serve the common good.

The vote is won. Seventy-two years the battle for this privilege has been waged, but human affairs with their eternal change move on without pause. Progress is calling to you to make no pause. Act!

Source: The Woman Citizen, September 4, 1920.

Five months earlier, at the founding congress of the League of Women Voters (held in conjunction with NAWSA's last convention in Chicago), Carrie Chapman Catt urged her listeners not just to be voters but to become active in the party of their choice in order to enhance their effectiveness as citizens. At the same time she foresaw the difficulties and misunderstandings that might confront members of an organization, ostensibly nonpartisan, who also participated in the political parties and supported or opposed legislation. Yet she believed that League members should and could play leadership roles inside the parties through knowledge of issues and support of enlightened legislation.

DOCUMENT 5: POLITICAL PARTIES AND THE LEAGUE OF WOMEN VOTERS

What I am going to say is not necessarily your interpretation of what the League of Women Voters is, or ought to do, because it is only my own personal view. We have certain opposition to the League of Women Voters and that opposition is largely political. The people who are interested in enrolling large numbers in political parties have expressed here and there rather cutting criticisms of the League of Women Voters. They have represented it according to their own viewpoint, which is a different view from that which we hold.

These critics seem to think that it is going to keep women out of the political parties. Fellow suffragists, we have come to a turn of the road. For about sixty years we have been appealing to political parties to give us the vote, for there was no possible way of ever getting that vote until the political parties were willing that we should have it. I don't think we have ever won the vote in a single state, even by a state referendum, where one or both of the political parties have not tacitly given their consent that it should go through. Certainly ratification would not have been possible without their aid.

Well then, is it our intention to continue on the outside of those political parties where we have been for sixty years and to go on appealing for their favor as we have always been doing? Are we going to petition them as we have always done? Well, if so, what was the use of getting the vote? (Applause)

It certainly was never any idea of the proposed League of Women Voters that we should remain out of the parties and appeal to them for the things that we wanted to do. The only way to get things in this country is to find them on the inside of the political party. (Applause) More and more the political parties become the power through which things are accomplished. One cannot get congressional action or legislative action unless the political parties represented there are willing, so powerful are they.

It is not a question of whether they ought to be powerful or ought not to be powerful: they are. It is the trend of the present political development and instead of appealing to them for the things you want, it is better to get on the inside and help yourself to the things you want (Applause) . . . .

Be a partisan, but be an honest and an independent one. Important and compelling as is the power of the party, the power of principle is even greater. Those who have struggled in a sixty years' old battle for political freedom should not voluntarily surrender to political slavery—and one kind of partisanship is little more than that. It is possible, even though unusual to be a partisan and an independent.

More, there may be another danger. You know we suffragists have had a very ingrowing time these last five or six years. The controversy was virtually over long ago. There was a thrill in our campaign when we could go out and challenge the real doubts of the people. But of late our opponents have merely been calling us names. That environment may have made us too timid and too conservative. If we are going to trail behind the democratic and republican parties about five years, and our program is going to be about that much behind that of the dominant political parties, we might as well quit before we begin. (Applause)

If the League of Women Voters hasn't the vision to see what is coming and what ought to come, and be five years ahead of the political parties. I doubt if it is worth the trouble to go on. (Applause)

Traveling in the rear of the procession is too dusty and germ laden for the comfort of the self respecting; traveling in the midst of the procession is too crowded. The place where the spaces are broad and the air clear and bracing is ahead of the procession, in the lead. Let us travel there.

To sail between the Scylla of narrow-minded partisanship on the left and the Charybdis of ultra conservation on the right, is the appointed task of the League of Women Voters; through that narrow and uncomfortable passage it must sail to wreck upon the rocks or to glorious victory.

I have confidence that the conscientious purpose and the high noble outlook of this body will furnish an unconquerable morale, and that its new and splendid Board of Directors will prove clear–eyed pilots who will guide us all to the glorious promise which our hopes and aims inspire. Yet let no one of us lose sight of the fact that power to build a higher welfare for all lies within the parties and not without.

Whether our Nation attains that welfare depends upon the conduct of the voters who compose the parties. Independent, intelligent, lofty principled voters make great parties and great parties make great nations. (Great Applause)

Source: Carrie Chapman Catt, Excerpts from "Political Parties and Women Voters," Congress of the League of Women Voters, Chicago, February 14, 1920. LWV Papers on film, II. A.1. 0153–57.

In the aftermath of victory, some of the bitterness and division that had characterized the suffrage campaign faded away. Typical was the assessment by Carrie Chapman Catt and Mary Peck, one of Catt's close colleagues in the struggle, as they came to recognize that the National Woman's Party had made important contributions to the success of the suffrage campaign. It provided a needed militancy, and the Party's radicalism supplied a useful counterpoint to NAWSA's middle-of-the-road respectability. Neither organization, they concluded, needed to apologize for their efforts, nor did either deserve full credit for the outcome.

While Carrie Chapman Catt had clearly laid down the framework for the operations of the League of Women Voters, she declined to play a role in its administration. A board of directors and a president must be selected. Catt had already divided the League into seven regions, and the board of directors would consist of those seven regional directors, together with the officers. A ballot listing ten names was presented to the delegates, and they were instructed to vote for four. (It is not clear who made up the list.) In any event Maud Wood Park, Edna Fischel Gellhorn of St. Louis, Missouri, Marie Stuart Edwards of Peru, Indiana, and Pattie Ruffner Jacobs of Montgomery, Alabama were the top four vote getters. They were told to select the officers from among themselves. Park, who earned her living on the lecture circuit, was the most mobile and, given her invaluable experience and outstanding performance as NAWSA's Congressional Chairman, she seemed an obvious choice for president. Gellhorn became vice-chairman, Edwards treasurer, and Jacobs secretary; and they—like Park—proved to be exceptional leaders. Associated with them in the League's beginning years were other unusually talented women such as Julia C. Lathrop, Katharine Ludington, Mary Foulke Morrisson, and Harriet Taylor Upton.

On the shoulders of these women fell the responsibility of getting the organization under way. Washington, DC, the nation's capital, easily won over Chicago, the central location, as the headquarters site. The program content derived from reform measures cited in Catt's speech to the Jubilee Convention in St. Louis plus some additions in the form of more than sixty resolutions approved by the League Congress in 1920, including one to oppose Republican Senator and longtime suffrage opponent James Wadsworth of New York in the forthcoming elections. The resolution not only passed but was loudly cheered—a momentary slip in nonpartisanship! Almost immediately, two actions—although it was not recognized at the time—would become League traditions. The first came about when the newspapers printed Mabel

Costigan's passionate rhetoric about the need to curb the "meat trust." The criticism did not go unnoticed in a city that was "Hog Butcher for the World," and a representative from the Swift Company asked to be heard. He was, and the League's habit of hearing both (or all) sides of an issue had its initiation. Soon thereafter, the same Mabel Costigan became the first representative of the new League to testify before a congressional committee. In the aftermath of that testimony on May 21, 1920, she sent telegrams to state League presidents urging "immediate expression from consumers so that the public demand action on the Kenyon-Kendrick Bill to regulate the meatpacking industry." It proved to be the first of what now must number in the thousands of requests for member action in support of or opposition to proposed legislation.

The new officers faced an overwhelming task of organization. The implications of the magnitude of the program had to be dealt with. At a post-convention meeting of the officers and directors, the standing committee chairmen (who had been reappointed), and several state presidents agreed that the national board should have authority over the disposition of the adopted program—a major policy decision. Subsequently the board, attempting to bring order out of what Maud Wood Park described as a "kettle of eels," proposed a revision of the bylaws that would be submitted to the next convention in 1921. Questions relating to the content and the size of the program, and its organizational form have persisted throughout the League's long life. Then, too, there was the question of financial support—from dues, contributions, pledges assigned to states or some combination thereof. Over the years, the League has continued to struggle to achieve an equitable and responsible assignment of shared responsibility for its funding. There was also the matter of staff. A suggestion that the women's colleges might act as "research laboratories" was not implemented, but in time the national headquarters served as a way-station in training college women as staff resources, and it still does. As Louise Young noted:

> In no area did the League develop sophisticated techniques more rapidly than in the preparation of materials in support of its program. It became a veritable training ground in the social sciences in the formative years under such academically minded executives as Maud Wood Park and Belle Sherwin.

In fairly short order, the League located a Washington office that was occupied by Maud Wood Park, one assistant, and one secretary. Edna Gellhorn took on the monumental job of organizing citizenship schools all over the country from her home in St. Louis, while Marie Edwards managed financial affairs from her home in Peru, Indiana. Together these women and other leaders—many from the ranks of both experienced and younger suffrage workers—laid the groundwork for an organization destined to be respected for its contributions to governance in the public interest.

Source: Unidentified, undated manuscript (probably an early chapter draft by Louise Young). LWV Papers on film, II. A.1. 0040–42, 0046, 0049–51, 0057, 0059–60. Fowler, Feminist Politician, 153.

Chapter 4

The Decisive Year

Enthusiasm, energy, and explanations marked the first year of the League of Women Voters. Almost immediately the new League leaders prepared platform planks to submit to the political parties assembled in national conventions in the summer of 1920. A variety of materials also were created to clarify the League's purpose and nonpartisanship, and to entice women to join.

In 1920 the Nineteenth Amendment enfranchised women, and the National Suffrage Association launched the League of Women Voters. It was indeed a decisive year! The 546 delegates assembled in Chicago for NAWSA's Victory Convention knew that they needed ratification by only three more states to make votes for women the law of the land. The announcement that went out set the tone.

DOCUMENT 1: CALL TO THE 1920 SUFFRAGE CONVENTION

Suffragists, hear this last call to a suffrage convention!

The officers of the National American Woman Suffrage Association hereby call the state auxiliaries, through their elected delegates, to meet in Annual Convention at Chicago, Congress Hotel, February 12th to 18th, inclusive.

In other days our members and friends have been summoned to annual conventions to disseminate the propaganda for their common cause, to cheer and encourage each other, to strengthen their organized influence, to council as to ways and means of insuring further progress.

This time they are called to rejoice that the struggle is over, the aim achieved, and the women of the nation about to enter into the enjoyment of their hard-earned political liberty.

Of all the conventions held within the past fifty-one years, this will prove the most momentous. Few people live to see the actual and final realization of hopes to which they have devoted their lives. That privilege is ours.

Turning to the past, let us review the incidents of our long struggle together before they are laid away with other buried memories. Let us honor our pioneers. Let us tell the world of the ever-buoyant hope, born of the assurance of the justice and inevitability of our cause, which has given our army of workers the unswerving courage and determination which has at last overcome every obstacle and attained its aim.

Come, and let us together express the joy which only those can feel who have suffered for a cause.

Turning to the future, let us inquire together how best we can now serve our beloved nation.

Let us ask what political parties want of us, and we of them.

Come one and all, and unitedly make this last suffrage convention a glad memory to you, a heritage for your children and your children's children and a benefaction to our nation.

Source: "Call to the Victory Convention of the National American Woman Suffrage Association, 1869-1920." LWV papers on film, II. A.1 0005.

The happy delegates were joined by uncounted numbers of alternates and visitors. Carrie Chapman Catt called them all to "disorder" and concluded her remarks with "You've won! . . . rejoice, applaud, and be glad!" For nearly one hour, two thousand women expressed their joy with songs and shouts; they paraded and waved banners and flags. The Republican elephant and the Democratic donkey walked to the platform arm in arm to be greeted by the smiling Carrie Catt. It was a memorable occasion.

Once they settled down, delegates went about the business of dissolving the National American Woman Suffrage Association and forming the League as a new and independent national society. Following the Jubilee Convention in 1919, some state and local Leagues had already been organized.) The League experienced the customary growing pains of a newborn organization. Suffragists knew what they wanted the League to do, but they did not have a clear sense of how to achieve their objectives, partly because they differed as to the most effective means. Nor did they anticipate some of the issues with which they would have to contend. At the same time that they had to work out their relationships with the political parties and with other women's organizations, suffrage leaders had to engage in the final battle for ratification in Tennessee. But before that final effort, attention turned to the transition from suffrage to the League of Women Voters. The infant organization intended to mobilize suffrage women in a new commitment of time, energy, and money. Not all suffrage women joined the League.

Some simply drifted away and some younger suffragists found the new behavioral freedoms of the 1920s an enticing distraction. Other women followed their reform-minded inclinations into organizations focused on education, world peace, and other interests or participated in like-minded groups based on religion (Jewish and Catholic women), on professions and business, and on auxiliaries of veterans' organizations. If there was one development that characterized the postsuffrage era, it proved to be the myriad opportunities for participation of women volunteers in a host of associations reflecting a wide range of programs and projects. The age of the woman as volunteer was about to come into full flower.

Maud Wood Park responded to common questions being asked about the new instrument for civic education and action.

DOCUMENT 2: MISPERCEPTIONS ABOUT THE LEAGUE OF WOMEN VOTERS

A sequence of questions is likely to follow on mention of the League. These questions occur again and again in much the same form and can be stated briefly as follows:

1. Does the League of Women Voters intend to become a separate party of women?

Emphatically not! We urge our members to enroll in the political parties of their choice and expect to have their assistance inside party lines in securing party support for our measures.

2. Will not the League duplicate the work already being done by other organizations of women?

In pieces, yes, but as whole no. At various points we overlap slightly and with relation to these branches of the work we arrange for cooperation with already existing organizations, but no other organization is devoting its energies exclusively to education in citizenship and the interests of women as voting citizens. Other organizations are eagerly welcoming our assistance along the lines where their interests touch ours, and this movement presents the coordination on a large scale of women's energies and women's interests.

3. Does it not interfere with the work of women for their political parties?

No, the work for the parties and the work for the League are not in any sense antagonistic but rather supplementary. Well-rounded human life needs a period for consideration and reflection, and then a time for action. Too hasty action brings results which must be reconsidered. The League of Women Voters gives women time to learn all sides of public questions as a basis for their choice of party affiliation. In the same way, it gives women an opportunity to come together as women and consider the measures women want and to see the advantages of these measures not from the point of party bias and party advantage but of public welfare.

4. Isn't it a mistake to segregate women as voters in a request for special legislation for women and children?

We hope it will not be necessary to do this long, but it is necessary until we catch up with the present inequalities of legislation which has been enacted from the masculine point of view.

5.   Are we merely the suffrage organization under another name?

No, because our organization numbers in its membership many women who were indifferent or opposed to the granting of the ballot to women and who in this new field for women's work are manifesting a splendid spirit and a desire to make their vote effective.

As a valuable by-product of the League of Women Voters, I list the power to call attention to what is going on in legislative bodies. Every legislative body is beset by persons who want personal favors or local or business benefits. We cannot over-estimate the importance of arousing the average good citizen who never takes the trouble to let his representative know what he wants. The majority of legislators hear only from their constituents who want personal or local favors.

A great organization in working for personal or sectional advantage by following legislation on questions of benefit to all citizens is actually helping because there are members of all legislative bodies who wish to act for the interests of all the people but who are often discouraged in their efforts because they get no support nor assistance from their constituency. The League can furnish directly at the seat of legislation encouragement and support for such right-minded legislators and can also through its local branches and through its material sent to the home districts of those legislators rouse the better class of citizens to intelligent interest and support of what the man himself is trying to do. I regard this as one of our most valuable contributions to the development of citizenship.

Source: Condensed minutes of the Victory Convention, 9:416, Minnesota Woman Suffrage Association Records, Minnesota Historical Society, St. Paul.   Maud Wood Park, "Five Questions," *The Woman Citizen*, November 20, 1920.

One of the high priorities for the new LWV in the presidential election year of 1920 was to gain the support of both political parties for the legislation members deeply desired to be enacted. President Park composed the thirteen planks and headed delegations to both conventions. The Republican convention endorsed five of the thirteen; the Democrats endorsed twelve (declining to support the proposed federal department of education). The apparent enthusiasm of the Democrats was misleading, however, because they were now the minority party, and the dominant elements in each party reflected the public mood, turning its back on the progressive movement that had been receptive to concerns of social justice. In the aftermath of the Republican convention's rejection of most of the League's proposed platform planks, pressure was brought by Republican women in the League to arrange a meeting with candidate Warren G. Harding. On what was designated as "Social Justice Day," a delegation of women, including the national board and Carrie Catt, made the pilgrimage to Harding's home in Marion, Ohio. Having been briefed in advance by LWV board member (and Republican) Marie Edwards, the candidate endorsed the Sheppard-

Towner bill, the women's and children's bureaus, supported the idea of elevating education and welfare to cabinet status, and promised to name a woman to his cabinet (he did not). On the League of Nations— a subject of great interest to women—he was notably silent. His silence prompted Catt to cast her personal nonpartisanship to the winds and endorse the Democratic candidate, James M. Cox, also of Ohio. The press called her action a "bombshell."

DOCUMENT 3: SUGGESTED PLATFORM PLANKS BY THE LEAGUE OF WOMEN VOTERS

I.   Child Welfare. Realizing that the hope of the nation lies in the children of today, the citizens of tomorrow we pledge ourselves to support:
   Adequate appropriation for the Children's Bureau;
   The prohibition of child labor throughout the United States;
   The protection of infant life through a Federal program for maternity and infancy care.
II.   Education.   We recognize that the appalling percentage of illiteracy among both native and foreign born in the United States is a blot upon our civilization; the lack of understanding of the essentials of good government, a menace to our future. We therefore advocate:
   A Federal Department of Education;
   Federal aid where necessary for the removal of illiteracy and for the increase of teachers' salaries;
   Instruction in the duties and ideals of citizenship for the youth of our land and the newcomer to our shores.
III.   The Home and High Prices. As a means of increasing the efficiency of the home and reducing the cost of living, we favor:
   Increased Federal support for vocational training in home economics;
   Such Federal-regulation and supervision of the marketing and distribution of food as will tend to equalize and lower prices, and the enactment and enforcement of such other measures as will freely open the channels of trade, prevent excess profits, and eliminate unfair competition and the control of the necessities of life.
IV.   Women in Gainful Occupations. In order to promote the welfare of millions of women engaged in gainful occupations, we advocate:
   The appointment of women in the Mediation and Conciliation Service of the United States Department of Labor and on any industrial commissions and tribunals which may hereafter be created;
   The establishment of a joint Federal and State employment service with women's departments under the direction of technically qualified women;
   A reclassification of the Federal Civil Service with the merit system of appointment and promotion, free from discrimination on the ground of sex, and with a wage or salary scale determined by the skill demanded for the work and in no way below the cost of living as established by official investigation.
V.   Public Health and Morals. We commend the effort for moral protection of the fighting forces of the nation made, during the World War, and we urge a continuance of appropriations to carry on an active campaign for the prevention of venereal disease and for public education in sex hygiene.

VI.   Independent Citizenship for Married Women.   Believing that American-born women resident in the United States should not forfeit their citizenship by marriage with aliens, and that alien women should not acquire citizenship by marriage with Americans, but rather by meeting the same requirements as those provided for the naturalization of alien men, we urge Federal legislation insuring to the women of the United States the same independent status for citizenship as that which now obtains for men.

Source: Planks to be Presented by the National League of Women Voters to the Platform Committees of the Political Parties, 1920 LWV Papers on film, II. A.1. 0166. Louise Young (unidentified, undated document). LWV Papers on film, II. A.1. 0060 and 00067.

In a letter to a fellow board member who was a prominent Republican, Maud Wood Park told of an encounter with the Republican Advisory Committee on policies and platform. No wonder the Republican Convention was so unreceptive to the League's proposals!

DOCUMENT 4: MAUD WOOD PARK ON MEETING WITH REPUBLICAN ADVISORY COMMITTEE ON POLICIES AND PLATFORM

To begin with, our hearing before the Republican Advisory Committee on policies and platform was exactly what Mrs. Catt called it, "a farce." . . . Mr. Mills did most of the talking, as I understand he has done on similar occasions when other bodies have appeared before it, and in the main his talk was the most violent and unreasonable and ill-mannered denunciation of us for advocating anything that could by any possibility be construed to mean the extension of Federal power in state matters. . . . I have never heard anyone attack a witness with rare savage violence than to fell upon Mrs. Catt in the beginning, and the rest of us, i.e., also Ludington, Mrs. Pinchot and myself, when it came our turn to speak. He seems to be a Monomaniac and curiously his mania is the historical Democratic doctrine of state rights. I have not yet got over the "Alice in Wonderland" feeling which it gave me to have the chairman of a Republican committee make a Republican war cry out of that old Democratic shibboleth which has given us so much trouble on the lips of the South. Well, this is more than enough of that.

Source: Excerpt from Maud Wood Park to Mrs. Harriet Taylor Upton, May 20, 1920. LWV Papers on film, II.A.3. 0054.

All that was left for the Nineteenth Amendment to become the law of the land was ratification by three-fourths of the states. The suffragists wanted to be able to vote in the 1920 presidential elections, and, when all was said and done, they did. But it was not an easy self-imposed deadline to meet. Within a month after the U.S. Senate vote in June 1919, eleven states had ratified the amendment; by the end of September, seventeen. Then came an inexplicable pause, prompting Carrie Chapman Catt to embark on a personal "Wake Up America" tour. By year's end, five more states had been added to the ratification roster. In 1920, thirty-five states had approved the amendment, but eight had defeated it. Other remaining states were either expected to oppose ratification or their governors were not expected to call special sessions of their legislatures. There was one last hope—Tennessee. All the proponents and opponents converged on the border state for the final showdown. After three months of intense political maneuvering in the hot summer months, Tennessee became the thirty-sixth state to ratify the Nineteenth Amendment. Even after the victory in the Tennessee legislature, a victory dramatized by the affirmative vote of twenty-four-year-old Representative Harry Burn who had been admonished by his mother to "be a good boy" and vote for ratification, the matter of woman suffrage was still not resolved. Reconsideration by the House and an injunction to prohibit the governor of Tennessee from certifying ratification were tactics employed by unyielding opponents to defeat suffrage. When these efforts came to naught, efforts were made to persuade U.S. Secretary of State Bainbridge Colby—whose signature on the Tennessee certificate of ratification would make the Nineteenth Amendment official—that the action by Tennessee was unconstitutional. This too, failed. Votes for women became the law of the land on August 26, 1920.

Source: Anastasia Sims, "Armageddon in Tennessee. *The Final Battle Over the Nineteenth Amendment,*" Marjorie Spruil Wheeler, ed. *One Woman, One Vote: Rediscovering the Woman Suffrage Movement.* 345–48.

A 1921 brochure stating some reasons to join the League of Women Voters provides ample evidence of the commitment and purpose guiding the new organization.

DOCUMENT 5: WHY JOIN THE LEAGUE OF WOMEN VOTERS?

BECAUSE it is the only organization in existence for the political education of women.

BECAUSE it develops the intelligence of the individual voter through forums, discussions and the spread of information on public affairs.

BECAUSE it gives disinterested unpartisan information on parties, candidates and measures.

BECAUSE it offers programs for practical civic work in your state, your city, your town.

BECAUSE it works for better law enforcement.

BECAUSE it works for better legislation on matters for which women should be primarily responsible.

BECAUSE it provides a meeting ground for women of all parties and all groups, where they may exchange ideas, make plans and work together for things in which they have a common interest.

BECAUSE it urges women to enroll in the political parties and work through them to improve the machinery of government.

BECAUSE it is organized in every state and you can accomplish more through a great National organization than by working alone.

BECAUSE it unites the country's woman power into a new force for the humanizing of government.

"If ever the world sees a time when women shall come together purely and simply for the benefit and good of mankind, it will be a power such as the world has never known."—Matthew Arnold.

Source: "Why Join the League of Women Voters?" 1921 brochure, LWV Papers, Library of Congress.

The relationship of the League to political parties was fraught with misunderstanding, particularly on the part of partisans, again and again in the early years. The great influx of women voters—or so it was supposed—made nervous nellies out of the professional politicians, who feared that the League's effort to reach women with information about registering to vote would benefit their opponents. Over time both Democrats and Republicans have articulated similar sentiments, probably a good measure of the League's even-handedness.

DOCUMENT 6: PARTISANSHIP OR VOTERS SERVICE?

The League of Women Voters is bound to be non-partisan. Some ardent Republicans, and some equally ardent Democrats, each charge it with really holding the scale pretty even.

A curious instance happened of this undue nervousness. The League of Women Voters in a certain state had been trying to carry out the program of the National, and to secure as large a registration of women as possible. It had urged them to register and vote, but of course had not given them any advice as to how.

A formal request was sent to the State Headquarters of the League by a local party organization of women belonging to the dominant political party of the state. The League of Women Voters was asked to cease its effort to get women to register, on the ground that this was outside its purpose (to foster good citizenship and secure uniform legislation), and also that such action belonged properly to the party organizations. Of course, the request could not be granted.

But let no one set this down as an example of the odd things that women may be led to do through their inexperience in politics. At about the same time, the League of Women Voters in the capital city of the same state induced the movies to put on the screen a notice of the time and place where women should register to vote. There was nothing partisan about it. No hint or suggestion was given that they should vote one way or the other. Yet the men's State Headquarters of the dominant party in that state protested to the League of Women Voters against their telling the women when and where they could register!

Source: "Was it Partisan?" Alice Stone Blackwell editorial, *The Woman Citizen*, November 20, 1920.

After the election that brought Warren G. Harding to the White House, Governor Nathan L. Miller of New York vented his ire about the League of Women Voters before the state League convention. "He said that they had no reason to exist, they were a menace to the institutions of the republic (because they were not a political party), they were evil, and he was opposed to the social welfare legislation the League advocated." There was no applause when he finished, but Carrie Chapman Catt responded in her usual spirited fashion. She later dismissed the furor that followed, commenting that "when the governor charged the League with being a 'menace' as he did four times, he was so far over-reaching facts as to be amusingly ridiculous."

DOCUMENT 7: THE VALUE OF NONPARTISANSHIP

A few days ago a group of Republican women meeting in Albany devoted a considerable period to a discussion of the League of Women Voters. If the press reports are correct, they showed an enormous amount of misinformation and so shocking a spirit of intolerance as to be wholly un-American. If there is any one thing to which our Republic is more sacredly pledged than to another, it is to free thought, free speech, freedom of organization and freedom of political action. These are and ever have been the four corner stones of our boasted American liberty. Yet these women were quoted as saying that members of the League of Women Voters are not wanted in the Republican Part. That was apparently said by more than one delegate. Even the Governor is reported as warning the women to beware of groups.

In view of the fact that many thousands of members of the League of Women Voters are Republican by tradition, this challenge takes on peculiar significance. Can it be that the Republican Party of the State of New York means to demand of women that they choose between the Party and the League of Women Voters? That women cannot belong to both? Does it issue this demand as an ultimatum?

Since when has the Republican party renounced this principle of free organization and free political action? What is it that Republicans find objectionable about the League of Women Voters. Its national constitution defines its objects:

"The object of the national League of Women Voters shall be to foster education in citizenship and to support improved legislation. The national League of Women Voters urges every woman to become an enrolled voter but as an organization it shall not be allied with and support not party." Do Republicans find "education in citizenship" or "improved legislation" dangerous aims? As matters stand it is not the League of Women Voters which needs to rise to defend its platform, but Republican women within the League of Women Voters do merit an explanation.

It is true enough that this is a government of parties and that every voter should therefore join one, but while that is the truth, it is not the whole truth. Parties administer government but progress is compelled by groups. I can recall no really important change in our institutions which has been brought about by party initiative and I can think of no policy more certainly destructive of normal progress than the dissolution of those organizations which are promoting measures of reform. As a matter of historical fact every great act of any political party has been brought about by group action.

The very part these political ladies serve was for years a group before it was a party. It pommelled Whigs and Tories with its unanswerable appeals, and as parties do, they shirked and dodged the issue, until the nation arose in revolt and blew both old parties into oblivion and made a young fighting party of what had been a fighting group.

Prohibition has never been noticed in the national platform of either political party, yet by group agitation it's a law. The examples are plentiful. The facts are that no party adopts an idea until that idea is supported by sufficient senti-ment to indicate that the party will lose votes unless it takes it up; or because the idea promises additional votes. In so doing, parties merely obey the law of self-preservation. Whoever fails to recognize that behind the parties are the people; and that among them independent groups are at all times educating, agitating, arguing, contending, urging, appealing for their various causes, has missed the determining factor in governments by the people. Those ideas swell and grow and press for recognition and parties give heed when they can evade action no longer. Ours is a government by majorities but the compact, consecrated earnest minorities compel the majorities to think and to act. The League of Women Voters aspires to be a part of the big majorities which administer our govern-ment, and at the same time, it wishes to be a minority which "agitates and edu-cates" and shapes ideas today which the majority will adopt tomorrow. Its members in the main will wish to be partisans if by so doing their individual freedom to think and act according to the mandates of their own consciences, is not curtailed; collectively the organization will remain non-partisan. Women to whom party loyalty is a superstition and a fetish will not be able to hold to both aims; they will be partisans only. Women who fail to see good in parties be-cause they know much they cannot admire, will be Leaguers only, but the ma-jority will possess the vision and the fundamental knowledge of how changes are wrought in such a nation as ours, and will follow the lead of majority and minority without confusion of thought or act. The League has a work to do and it invites cooperation and friendly relations with all parties. If it receives them, its work will be soon done.

Source: Van Voris, *Carrie Chapman Catt*, 164–65. Excerpts from speech of Carrie Chapman Catt at banquet, State [New York] League of Women Voters, Hotel Ten Eyek, Albany, NY, January 27, 1921. *The Woman Citizen*, February 9, 1921, 949–51.

Even though Carrie Chapman Catt named the new organization the League of Women Voters, all the to-do about women and the parties prompted her suggestion to change the name to the League of Voters, an idea that still surfaces at League conventions, although men have been members since 1974.

DOCUMENT 8: CARRIE CHAPMAN CATT CALLS FOR MEN AS MEMBERS

I wish also to make a suggestion, which I intended to forward to Atlanta, but didn't. I would like to have somebody serve notice to amend the Constitution by taking out the word "women" from the title, leaving it *League of Voters*, and that a strong and urgent invitation should be extended to independent-minded men to become members and unite in an independent political policy for the Nation. You have perhaps observed that the political women are throwing innuendoes at the League of Women Voters as a sex-segregated institution. The Republicans have moved to found a National Republican Women's Club, and the will be just as much a segregation when they get going again. Why not step boldly to the front and do away with sex segregation and beat the political women in a race of progress. Do you realize that the country is full of independent-minded men who are "all dressed up" with independent ambitions and "have no place to go"? If it is not too late to introduce to give such a notice and nobody else will, I will give it provided you do not find it objectionable. You who are to lead the League of Women Voters should be the judge of what it ought to be.

Source: Letter from Carrie Chapman Catt to Edna Gellhorn, Marie Edwards, Elizabeth Hauser, February 17, 1921. LWV Papers on film, III. A.3. 0456.

A little more than a year after the League was founded, a meeting took place between League officials and representatives of NAWSA (although officially dissolved in 1920, the dissolution, due to technical and legal reasons, did not occur until 1925). The discussion centered on the program load, a concern that became a perennial issue within the League. The League, said Carrie Chapman Catt, was trying to do too much. Her suggestions, however, were not agreed to, and the League continued to address a variety of public policies deemed by the organization to be in the public interest.

DOCUMENT 9: CARRIE CHAPMAN CATT ON THE NEED FOR PROGRAM FOCUS

Mrs. Catt stated that the future of the League was one of deep concern to her and that she had certain opinions concerning it which she wished to present with no feeling of criticism, realizing that the League must work out its own destiny. Among other charges which she has heard as being brought against the League are the usual ones: that nobody knows just what the League stands for; there is no outstanding objective; that it has a program stolen from other organizations. . . .

Let the Sheppard-Towner Bill end the work of the Child Welfare Committee. Dismiss it and turn it back to the Federation. Ask Industrial Groups to take over the work of the Women in Industry; the work of Social Hygiene Committee should be taken over by groups already organized for that purpose. In short dismiss Committees on Social Legislation, and retain our political groups or Committees, working primarily for the education of women in citizenship and for the removal of illiteracy.

Our primary interest should be to work for the political development of this country largely through the removal of illiteracy, the education of the voter, improvement in political methods, the conduct of campaigns, the management of municipalities, etc. We should drop the Committee on Election Laws and Methods, and the first thing we should stand for is EFFICIENCY IN

GOVERNMENT, which should be all its name implies and not a committee, but should be the big work of the Board.

Source: Minutes of Conference between the Board of the National American Woman Suffrage Association and the Board of the League of Women Voters, April 10, 1921. LWV Papers, Library of Congress.

Maud Wood Park had already made her mark in the suffrage movement as a highly effective lobbyist during the last years of the suffrage campaign. When Carrie Chapman Catt chose not to put herself forward as a nominee for president of the League of Women Voters, Park was a logical second choice. Younger than Catt by twelve years, Park possessed impressive suffrage work credentials. In 1900, much to her surprise, she found herself at age twenty-nine the youngest delegate present at NAWSA's national convention, prompting her to organize the first College Equal Suffrage League. Following her work organizing other college Leagues, serving as president of the Massachusetts Woman Suffrage Association, and then as vice president of the national college league organization, she was free to travel, not just in the United States but around the world. Her first husband died in 1904, and in 1908 Park had secretly married again. She and Robert Hunter, a theatrical agent, did not have a house but met in hotels during her lecture tours and spent time together at her vacation home in Maine. In 1917 Catt recruited Park to manage the Nineteenth Amendment campaign in the U.S. Congress, and it was in this arena that Park made her most notable contributions to the ultimate success of the suffrage movement.

Source: Sharon Hartman Strom, "Park, Maud May Wood," in Barbara Sicherman and Carol Hurd Green, Eds., *Notable American Women: The Modern Period.* Cambridge, MA: The Belknap Press of Harvard University Press, 1980, 519–22.

Chapter 5

Possibilities, Hopes, Dreams

As the League of Women Voters struggled to establish its presence and to persuade citizens of the need for a nonpartisan political organization, differences emerged as evidenced by debates in national League conventions. Although Carrie Chapman Catt had demurred from assuming a position of League leadership (she did accept the designation of Honorary President), she did not hesitate to make her views known, especially when they varied from those of President Maud Wood Park. Those differences sometimes escalated into open disagreements. Catt's propensity for giving the limelight to the League ran counter to Park's more modest demeanor, and that difference sparked a civil and amusing debate between the two.

Great debates and new beginnings marked the 1921 League convention in Cleveland, Ohio. Nearly one thousand delegates from forty-six states responded to the announcement from Maud Wood Park.

DOCUMENT 1: CALL TO THE SECOND ANNUAL CONVENTION OF THE NATIONAL LEAGUE OF WOMEN VOTERS

A dream has come true. Equality of suffrage is a fact. It is the result of a crusade, an exalting and holy crusade. The world has seen none more wonderful. We shall have need again and again to draw on this example of tireless effort and high courage bequeathed to us.

We have not wasted our year. The League now stands organized in every State in the Union. The woman voter has already proved herself an earnest and selfless worker.

By faith we have won the fight for suffrage. By belief in the efficacy of the ballot and the value of good citizenship, we have come thus far. Let us know no pause. From the whole stock of our several experiences and combined wisdom, let us lay our plans more effectively for the future.

Heed the call! The League is established. The League has power. How best shall we use this power to become a vital and helpful force in our country? How best continue in the work of educating a conscientious, well–informed electorate?

Answer the call! Send a delegate from every congressional district in the United States of America.

Source: Call to the Second Annual Convention of the National League of Women Voters, 1921. LWV Papers on film, II. A.2. 0398.

While the national organization could report no legislative accomplishments and little in the way of governmental improvements or reforms that had occurred in the aftermath of woman suffrage, delegates from state and local Leagues painted a mixed picture of successes and failures. The Minnesota League, for example, in 1921 had won legislative passage of seven of nine measures, including: a $5 increase in the monthly pension maximum for mothers of dependent children, a street trades bill forbidding children under age twelve from selling newspapers, and three bills making women eligible to serve on juries.

One of the great debates that took place during the six days of the convention related to the nature and length of the program. It was the beginning of a protracted quarrel between the Pennsylvania League, which advocated civic education as the League's primary focus, and the national organization, which supported both education and the advocacy of legislation (reflecting what turned out to be the majority League opinion). Although it is reasonable to conclude that one is not possible without the other, Lucy Miller of Pennsylvania and Marie Edwards, a national officer from Indiana, articulated their disagreements on the convention floor.

DOCUMENT 2: THE BEGINNING OF THE DEBATE ON LEAGUE PROGRAM

MRS. JOHN O. MILLER (Pennsylvania):

We are facing in this National League of Women Voters and in our State Leagues, the fact of whether or not (we fought this out on the last Convention floor) the State Leagues and the National League are going to limit their scope of membership by taking up in their very infancy not only controversial bills but so many bills that it is impossible for us to do honest work if we are honest with ourselves.

This last clause robs us of making this decision. You can come to no decision. You can't say whether you want to put education first or go to the Legislature and get these long lists of laws and put them first.

Pennsylvania started out—we may be wrong, but we started out—with a definite policy. That policy was we were going for a certain goal. We thought that if we didn't have a definite goal, we couldn't live, because we are over-organized now.

We thought we had something nobody else had to offer in teaching citizenship. There are three Committees we have never appointed Chairmen for because we never could handle them with our budget, office force, or the meager intelligence we have on our Board. We thought they should come, not paralleling, but to a point in the Board, and as a Board we were going to push them because we had to send our members from the various Districts and we pushed them with the idea that we would grow in membership and grow more intelligent in membership.

I think we have to make that decision. We are one year old. Are we going out for legislative programs that are exceedingly long and sometimes exceedingly controversial that our membership doesn't understand or are we going to begin by building up a membership and make them think about something?

If this League in going to do anything, it has to keep the woman voter on the job 11 months of the year, and if it doesn't do that, my League may get the best possible legislation through the Legislature, but as long as my county sends a certain gentleman down from Pittsburgh whom I might name, we have failed because he will have five bills through the House against our one. At present he has more power than all the women do in the State, apparently.

Are we going to make the men back of him know that we have a constituency that is going to be out months before the primaries and that we are going to have something to say as to the kind of candidate that will be elected?

That is the choice we have to make. Can we do it with the long programs we have? Remember, Pennsylvania is not saying whether or not those programs are good. We are perfectly willing to say we don't know anything about them.

Are we going to build up membership or build legislative programs? If you put that amendment, you haven't made any decision at all and you will go home through the same door you entered at this Convention. (Prolonged applause)

MRS. RICHARD EDWARDS (Indiana): I do believe Mrs. Miller has confused the issue here. I am as much in sympathy with one point she is making as any member of the Convention could be, but I do believe the essential thing is being lost sight of. It is not to insist on a broad legislative program but a broad educational program that is being brought up. (Prolonged applause)

We have no right to insist on any State conducting any legislative program.

That is for the State to decide. But, I think we have a right to insist it should be open to the members of any State League to obtain information of the widest kind on the general projects whose principles are endorsed at the National Convention.

Our whole plan of building up a self-accounting and self-determining electorate, formed on these questions, our whole idea rests on the very theory that this information, which is at the hands of our specialists in Committee work, should be at the disposal of our individual members in every League in the country. (Applause)

I think our educational program must be as wide as the demand for it from the individual Leagues. I think our legislative program must be as narrow as the State Board at the State Convention decides. (Applause)

And, if we are going to be better able to decide the questions than the men, (and we must be better informed than the men) and if great sources of information are shut away from our members by failure to provide the channels from the National to the State, then we are not getting that information to our State members.

I am heartily in sympathy with the State that is stripping its legislative program to meet its own needs and efficiency. I am not in favor for a minute of restricting our avenues of approach for the bettering of the education of our members.

Source: Barbara Stuhler, *Gentle Warriors: Clara Ueland and the Minnesota Struggle for Woman Suffrage.* St. Paul: Minnesota Historical Society Press, 1995, 192. Proceedings of the Second Annual Convention of the National League of Women Voters, Cleveland, OH, April 11–16, 1921. (hereinafter referred to as the Second Convention), LWV Papers on film, II. A.1. 0812–15.

Carrie Chapman Catt, weighing in with a variation on the issue of education versus legislation, proposed that a department of efficiency in government be the prime focus for League attention. By this means, the League could work for improvements in governmental organization and operations, leaving social reform efforts to other women's organizations: "I repeat that if the successor of the Suffrage Association does not take up politics as its chief work, no other group of women will, and there is a tendency to do the things which are most normal and natural for women to do, and that is to protect the children and the home, and so on." While such a department was approved by the Convention, so too was an ambitious legislative program. Delegates left Cleveland with the existing ambivalence between action and education still unresolved.

DOCUMENT 3: THE LEAGUE'S LEGISLATIVE PROGRAM

At the Convention in Cleveland the National League of Women Voters endorsed the Sheppard-Towner bill and adopted the following principal planks, endorsing the principle but no special bills. The plan adopted at Cleveland being "that the Executive Committee appointed by the National Board decides the order in which legislature measures shall be stressed." When any of the measures endorsed by name or in principle comes up for hearing, an official representative of the League is present to state the stand the League has taken.

Principal planks as adopted in Resolutions and Recommendations of Standing Committees:

Opposing any weakening of the National Prohibition Law.

Endorsing the Sheppard-Towner bill for the protection of maternity and infancy care.

Endorsing the principle of physical education in schools, through state action with federal aid.

Asking for generous appropriations for the Federal Children's Bureau.

Urging the enforcement of all child labor and school attendance laws.

Urging Congress to make adequate appropriation for the Interdepartmental Social Hygiene Board.

Urging equal punishment for men and women offenders against the moral law.

Endorsing the 8-hour day, and the prohibition of night work for women in industry, and the establishment of living-wage conditions.

Urging the appointment of qualified women in all boards having to do with women's work.

Asking for a reclassification of the Civil Service on a merit basis, without discrimination against women.

Recommending an equal interest by husband and wife in each other's property acquired after marriage.

Asking for direct citizenship for married women.

Supporting increased appropriations for vocational training in home economics.

Endorsing jury service by women, with exemption for mothers of young children.

Endorsing the principle of the Towner school bill, but leaving action in support of it to the discretion of the Board of Directors.

Endorsing the principle of protection of National Parks and Monuments and keeping them inviolate for the use and enjoyment of the people.

Endorsing the creation of a federal department of Public Welfare and urging the appointment as head of the department of a woman who is an expert on social problems.

Recommending the regulation by Congress of the meat-packing industry.

Encouraging the organization of legitimate co-operative associations within the states.

Asking Congress to appropriate money to complete the Alabama nitrate plants for the benefit of agriculture and to furnish needed electric power to a large territory in the South.

Urging the National Government to do everything possible for the women held in harems in the Near East.

Asking Congress to make August 26th, the date of ratification of the Federal Suffrage Amendment, a national holiday.

Opposing any attempt to repeal State Direct Primary laws, and in favor of making nominations more representative of the voters.

Source: "Recommendations Committee on Election Laws and Methods by Mrs. Carrie Chapman Catt, Chairman." LWV Papers on film, II. A.1. 0531–52. "Principal Planks as adopted in Resolutions and Recommendations of Standing Committees." LWV Papers on film, II. A.1. 0430–41.

Some measure of hyperbole can be found in this letter from Senator Albert J. Beveridge (R., IN) to Carrie Chapman Catt, who had written him after his speech to the Cleveland convention in support of the primary as a political reform. Nevertheless, it reveals the general esteem (probably coupled with a good measure of apprehension) with which elected officials regarded the League.

DOCUMENT 4: ALBERT J. BEVERIDGE TO CARRIE CHAPMAN CATT

Thank you very much for your generous words concerning my visit to Cleveland and my talk on the Primary. . . .

I have said to everybody wherever I have gone since the Cleveland convention, that no public assemblage, whether of men or women, ever appealed to me more powerfully than did that historic meeting of women. In sagacity, in dignity, in accuracy of procedure, you women approached perfection as nearly as human beings ever are allowed to do. Moreover, the impression that Convention made upon me at the time, has grown upon me steadily ever since I have said publicly on a good many occasions, that I consider your Convention to have deserved the important word "historic"; for I look upon it as the distinct beginning of a great epoch. I feel quite sure that it was the most determinative assemblage that was held anywhere in America at the same time.

Source: Albert J. Beveridge to Carrie Chapman Catt (undated but probably written in 1921). LWV Papers on film, III. A.3. 0454.

The most dramatic happening of the Cleveland Convention occurred when Carrie Chapman Catt tore up her prepared remarks and made a rousing speech against war. At an evening meeting, Judge Florence Allen spoke about the need for "righteous" international law. Her conclusion was a rigorous call for high moral standards in government:

> We shall be tested most of all by our purpose that right shall be done in government. We must demand of our public officials the same energetic, devoted, incorruptible services that we demand in our most important private matters. We must solemnly determine that our influence shall be thrown behind morality in all public business and most of all in international matters. We must never tolerate aggression by this nation and we must support the upbuilding of systems by which law shall be substituted for rapine among nations. We shall be false to our trust if we admit that decency and honor are not necessary between the nations of the world and that the law of the land is that might makes right.

> Only by demanding that this standard be maintained by America, and advanced in the world at large, shall we be found worthy in our moral testing—only then shall we prove ourselves fit descendants of the great women who won for us our freedom.

This moving statement was followed by an impassioned speech by Will Irwin, a well-known and respected foreign correspondent and author of a new book, The Next War. Realizing that Irwin had gone beyond his time limit, Maud Wood Park rose to ask him to finish. She was held back by Carrie Catt who had reached out and grabbed her skirt and pulled her back into her chair. Very soon thereafter, Irwin did finish and, he later wrote, "Mrs. Catt passed me. She was taking the floor without introduction and, as she walked, she was tearing up her manuscript. As soon as she could get a hearing—for the house had risen with her—she swept into such a fiery, eloquent denunciation of war and all its works as I had ever heard." Joseph Lash, writing of that moment, said, "Mrs. Catt may have been 'clear cold reason' (quoting Eleanor Roosevelt) on the subject of direct primaries and other measures to weaken the control of political bosses, "but she was all flame and passion when she ripped into President Harding, who in his first address to Congress a day earlier, had declared 'This Republic will have no part in the League of Nations.' " That speech set the stage for Catt's later crusade on the Cause and Cure of War.

DOCUMENT 5: CARRIE CHAPMAN CATT ON WAR AND PEACE

There isn't an audience in this country nor in any other one in all the world where that sort of appeal doesn't stir the hearts of the people. There isn't an audience to which a speaker may allude to international peace that doesn't win a response from that audience. There isn't anybody in all the world who is willing to say that he wants another war. There isn't anybody who doesn't want peace, but the question is, how are we going get it? That is the practical question, and it is not only a question for us to decide in our country, in our own states and cities before we can act collectively with other nations, but it is for ourselves individually to think our way through.

We don't settle that question when we have a million different points of view, and we don't settle it when we don't have any point of view at all and wait for somebody else to act.

Mr. Irwin was very careful to tell you that he hadn't any specific way of getting a solution of this question; everybody in this time is extremely careful about being non-partisan. I don't care a rap about it. I am for disarmament. (Applause)

I was for a democratic League of Nations. I am for a Republican one, or any other kind. (Applause) I believe in taking action upon questions of this kind and not waiting too long and now that the Republicans are in, I believe it is the duty of everybody who wants disarmament, of everybody who wants the prevention of that future war, to compel action at Washington, (applause) and it does not matter what party is in or who is President, our country is not judged by its parties, it is judged as a nation. (Applause)

Today there isn't anybody in the world that knows what we are going to do, nobody in any other nation and nobody in this nation knows what we are going to do. (Applause) But I ask you if there is anybody anywhere at this moment with an earnest crusading spirit who is campaigning to arouse America to lead in this matter. Oh, no! We are as stolid and as indifferent apparently, and as inactive as though there was not before us the greatest question that was ever presented to the nations of the world.

It is a curious kind of psychology that is upon our nation. We have always been a nation in favor of arbitration. It was this country, I believe, that signed the first treaty of that character. We were leaders in it. We don't believe in wars as a nation. We are a peaceful people, and we are the believers in the ideal of the voice of the people settling questions and not force.

Well then, we are the appointed ones to lead in this question. It is difficult, as Mr. Irwin has said, for anyone here to believe what has been the result of the war on the other side. It is not possible to quite comprehend it without seeing the effects for oneself. Over there, where they are war-torn still, where they are still trying to call themselves together, trying to build up their old life on their bad money and bad economic conditions and bad feelings of every kind—while we live in paradise over here, we are disgustingly fat and altogether too well clad.

All of this we have. Then it becomes us to lead. How are we going to lead, to do it? Not by standing back and waiting for somebody else to speak. Not by waiting, waiting. We will get another war while we are waiting. It is only by action. There isn't anything that can't be done in this country as a result of popular opinion. (Applause) It is the government. There never was a President and there never was a whole Congress, and I am not so sure about a Senate (laughter) that would not yield to popular opinion. It can do anything.

The people in this room tonight, were there no others interested in all the world, could put an end to war if they would put themselves to it. (Applause) One vote is of no value. Two votes are of no value. A thousand votes standing for a common cause can be a wedge which will set the pace for political parties in the direction of those thousand people. (Applause)

If we but stand together and know what we want, we can get it. We want peace. We all want peace. We want to abolish that antiquated, barbarous, ridiculous method of quarreling and killing each other. We all want it and we all stand back for somebody else to act.

Well, let us make a resolution tonight, each and every one of us, and let us consecrate ourselves individually and collectively to the business of putting war out of the world. (Applause)

It isn't necessary for a Republican to become a Democrat, nor a Democrat to become a Republican, but it is necessary to rise above the partisanship of either and both of those parties and say, "Here is a national issue, greater than any party or any man." (Applause)

Let us work then; let Mr. Harding know; let the Senate know; (hardly anybody else counts) (laughter) let them know that we as a constituency of Congress expect action.

You know, it is a terribly grinding thing to any one of us who has ever so little international interest, to know what they say of us. I don't like to have people say that we are a provincial nation, and I don't like it because I know we are. (Laughter)

The other day a letter came from the President of the Suffrage Association in France. She said in telling something of the new spirit that has come in France as a result of the difficulties over the reparations that they have withdrawn the invitation for the next Suffrage Congress to be held in Paris because the feeling is such that if German delegates were to come, they might not be treated well. She said, "Oh, if we could only know what the United States is going to do."

That I have heard from one, two, three, four nations, the complaint that nobody knows what we are going to do.

Our aloofness, our isolation, our silence upon the question. Oh, Americans, let us be silent no more; let us send a message across the sea and join hands with the men and women of every land who want to put this terrible thing out of the world. (Applause) We can do it. But, if we will, there must be no timidity among us; there must be no cowardice.

You know the most popular thing that anybody can say upon a public platform today is to say, "Let us stand for international peace." The most unpopular thing that anybody can say is, "Let us stand for it in this particular way." (Laughter) He who wants to stand for this question and really wants to get behind this question and boost, must do it with the understanding that he can afford to be unpopular; that he can afford to stand against the world, and I tell you, good friends, it doesn't matter if there are only four or five together who are in the right, they may stand and stand fast and all the world will come to them, and all the world will surrender to them. (Applause)

Then, let us get this vision: here we are called. How infinitely greater and higher is that call than anything of all the wonderful things that have been discussed here. I say to you women, you know war is in the blood of men; they can't help it. They have been fighting ever since the days of the cave men. They can't help it. There is a sort of an honor about it. But, it seems to me, that God is giving a call to the women of the world to come forward and stay the hands of men and say, "No, you shall no longer kill your fellowman."

The audience arose and applauded long and enthusiastically.

Source: Excerpts from the Proceedings of the Second Convention. LWV Papers on film, II. A.1. 0357–58. Van Voris, *Carrie Chapman Catt,* 187. Joseph P. Lash, *Eleanor and Franklin.* New York: W. W. Norton and Co., 1971, 263. Excerpts from the Proceedings of the Second Convention. LWV Papers on film, II. A.1. 0938–44.

In her presidential address Maud Wood Park put a bright face on the League's growing pains before the convention delegates. While she analyzed in considerable detail and with total candor both the League's achievements and its frustrations, she concluded with an optimistic outlook for the League's future.

DOCUMENT 6: MAUD WOOD PARK ON THE LEAGUE'S PURPOSE AND ADVERSITY

The Purposes of the League as defined in the By-laws are two:
   a)   To foster the study of citizenship, and
   b)   To promote improved legislation.

There is a third result to which we did not pledge ourselves directly but which I sometimes think may prove to be of even greater service than our specified aims. This is what might be called the by-product of our efforts.

In the days when some of us sacrificed all other possibilities of social service in order to give our whole time and strength to the suffrage movement, we were sustained in this course by our belief that in working for political equality we were working for the fundamental principle upon which this nation was built and thus, in the broadest sense, we were helping to make its ideals a reality. We believed, too, that the ballot in the hands of women would be the most potent means of accomplishing the special ends of the various forms of social service in which we were interested.

Faith In Democracy: In much the same way the faith in the possibilities for good of democratic government which is the foundation stone of the League of Women Voters is a necessary answer to the disillusionment and skepticism of many men who have grown weary in well–doing because it has seemed to avail nothing in the face of self-seeking and trickery in the conduct of public affairs. Let us be thankful that we are hopeful, for abiding belief in what the whole people can and will do was never more sorely needed.

Solidarity of Women: Among women themselves the all-partisan attitude of the League can go far to maintain understanding and sympathy and a common purpose when these bonds are threatened by party alignments. However they may differ as to methods, the great majority of women earnestly desire such things as proper care and well rounded education for all children, the safeguarding of girls in industry, the promotion of social hygiene, the removal of civil and legal discriminations on the ground of sex. It is therefore well for them and well for the community that women of all parties have an opportunity to come together in an organization devoted solely to the interests of women as voters and there take counsel together for the accomplishment of their common aims, which are far more likely to be attained if a program is outlined by an inclusive group of women than they would be if left solely to the initiative of political parties.

Help to Men In Public Office: Another kind of service can be rendered to the man in public office, beset by seekers for personal favors, business concessions, or local or sectional benefits, who sooner or later tends to forget that the average citizen wants none of those things because the average citizen neglects to make it clear that his desire is for the common weal. . . .

Service to the Political Parties: To the political parties, whether they realize it or not, we are a source of benefit because we put them upon their mettle to defend principles with facts which bear the test of intelligent examination. No right-thinking party man or woman wants a party success won by misstatement or misinformation; but when only one side is heard or considered there is a wide opportunity for the unscrupulous to make points and votes by misrepresentation. An all-partisan organization presenting all sides of public questions tends to check this danger and thus to help the party in its legitimate purpose, the promotion of definite principles of government.

Moreover, the League can scarcely fail to develop in its members a saving sense that the saints are not all in one party and the sinners in another and a steadfast determination to see that their own party, whatever it may be, follows its real statesmen rather than its unscrupulous wire-pullers. Every political party needs members who refuse to be blindfolded and then herded to a goal. Every political party needs members who adopt its principles because they understand these principles and who follow its leaders because those leaders have proved themselves worthy to be followed. Therefore an organization that teaches voters to examine and reflect before choosing a party and then to insist upon that party's living up to its purpose is helping the party.

Conclusion: Our aims are still largely possibilities, hopes, ideals. They will not become realities without dust and tears, hardships and disappointments. Our task will not be completed in an election or a year. Let us have no illusions about that.

We are met to find out how we can best carry out our purposes by methods that are practical as well as far-reaching. We shall not find these methods always sharply defined, but we must avoid the mistake of those who "did not know the road but only saw the goal."

In Governor Bradford's history of the Plymouth Colony there is a chapter which tells of the hardships and dangers that the Pilgrims knew they would have to face in coming to the new world, the length of the voyage, the perils of the sea, the danger of savage tribes, the possibility of disease and starvation. Bradford enumerates all these and then he goes on to say: "But it was answered that all great and honorable actions are accompanied by great difficulties and must be both enterprised and overcome with answerable courages."

The work to which the League of Women Voters has dedicated itself—the work of helping women to become self-directing, conscientious and effective voters—is "a great and honorable action." Let no one doubt that the difficulties by which it is accompanied will be "enterprised and overcome with answerable courages."

Source: Excerpts from the Proceedings of the Second Convention. LWV Papers on film, II. A.1. 0270–96.

Carrie Chapman Catt, who had been named Honorary President of the League at the Jubilee Convention in 1919, had second thoughts. She wanted to maintain a free voice, and because she did not believe in such honorific designations, she had tried to resign in December 1920. "I have trimmed and repressed and kept silent for thirty years, and now in my few declining days I long for the opportunity to speak my mind, but when I do speak my mind, I jar the League of Women Voters. . . . I do not think that I shall develop into a very menacing sort of radical, but I would like to have a little soul freedom, and it would be grand to be able to speak out through the Citizen." (Both the Suffrage Association and the League used The Woman Citizen as a publication outlet.)

DOCUMENT 7: CARRIE CHAPMAN CATT ON RESIGNING AS HONORARY PRESIDENT

In discussing the future of *The Citizen*, I suggested that in order to cut loose in every respect from the old connections, it might be well for me to resign as Honorary Chairman of the League of Women Voters, and it is upon that particular point that I wish to ask your judgment. As a matter of fact, I was not elected in the normal and parliamentary way.

The question was raised, put and carried in a moment of impulse and it is not in the Constitution. Whatever influence I may have had has been given freely to the League of Women Voters, and I think I might now be dismissed from that

post; or if the act would be misunderstood by any, I might continue until the Convention in April and then express my very sincere disbelief in honorary presidents for such organizations. I have trimmed and repressed and kept silent for thirty years, and now in my few declining days I long for the opportunity to speak my mind, but when I do speak my mind I jar the League of Women Voters. I understand that I nearly demolished it at the dinner in New York. Of course I do not think that any organization can amount to much if its members are unable to speak their honest convictions. On the other hand, I know that we were stronger as a suffrage association, when we did repress our views upon other subjects. I do not think that I shall develop into a very menacing sort of radical, but I would like to have a little soul freedom; and it would be grand to be able to speak out through *The Citizen* for a few months.

Will you please give me your judgment on this problem at the earliest moment that you can? Please be perfectly frank and honest with me. I imagine that you will be glad to be rid of me—at least I hope so.

Here is a Merry Christmas and a Happy New Year for you, and my love and admiration now and always.

Source: Carrie Chapman Catt to Maud Wood Park, December 22, 1920. LWV Papers on film, II. A.2. 0828.

Although she was persuaded not to step down, Catt was correct in anticipating that she and the League would not always be of one mind. She continued, however, to respect and support the organization. Presiding at a session at the Cleveland convention in 1921, she held forth on a number of matters in her customary candid manner.

DOCUMENT 8: CARRIE CHAPMAN CATT'S VIEW OF THE LEAGUE IN 1921

CHAIRMAN CATT: Mr. Bryce said five years ago that the obvious difficulty of government by public opinion was the difficulty of ascertaining it. Well, it is difficult from two ends of the problem. One is the machinery of finding out what the people want, but the other difficulty is with the people themselves to discover what they want, and this is one of the questions that is likely to be a deluded one in the next two years. . . .

After all, it is a very long process—this finding out how to govern by popular opinion. It has been about a thousand years since the present processes have been in daily and yearly evolution, and we have a long way to go before we find the perfect system. . . .

I want to say just a word about the League of Women Voters. It became an independent group a year ago, with its plans all yet to be made. It was organized upon a new scheme. Whether the women who had fought for the vote would like to continue in an organization to make that vote effective remains to be seen. There have been a good many criticisms upon the whole idea of woman suffragists continuing working together. We have learned a great deal in the last year, and some things are clear now that were not clear a few months ago. One of the things that we have to do, and I think perhaps it is the greatest task before us, we men and women have to learn to work together. We never have. It is a very difficult process. There are men who have been so long accustomed to telling women what they ought to think, that it is going to be very difficult for them to let women do their own thinking, and there are so many women who have been accustomed to think that men are infallible that it is a good deal of a joke to them to discover that some are not, and in that process of working together, it seemed a few months ago as though it were going to be a very simple thing and come to us very quickly because just before the election, the political parties were quite hectic in their desires and efforts to gather in the women voters, and great were the promises made of equality and all that sort of thing. . . .

I want to say that having observed this convention, I am satisfied, absolutely satisfied, that whatever the criticisms may be upon the League of Women Voters, whether they come from political leaders as has been the case sometimes, or from women's organizations who thought we were overlapping, whatever the criticisms may be, and from whatever source, I am convinced that the League of Women Voters is strong enough to withstand any criticism which may come. (Enthusiastic applause) The League of Women Voters was an experiment. It was a wholly new thing, and no one could tell a year ago in which direction its evolution would go, but I am satisfied now that every woman here, as a delegate, is convinced that there is a work and a big, tremendous work for the League of Women Voters to do, that there is the old comradeship, that there is a new inspiration, that there is a broader field for work which opens before you and that the League of Women Voters is going to give the greatest service in all the world to womanhood. I can't express to you the confidence I feel in the spirit that has been manifested here. . . . So I look to the League of Women Voters to really lead us out of this stage of discontent, which is common to our own country and to all the others in the world. I am proud of you, and I am so glad to see so many young women here who have their lives before them, for there is a long service for you to perform.

Let me repeat, there is nothing that is good, nothing that is right, and nothing that is progressive that you cannot accomplish—if you want to. The only thing is to stand together. Make the big things look big and do make the little things look small. (Enthusiastic applause)

Mrs. Park, you really should now take the convention or may I have the pleasure of introducing you? If there was anybody who had any doubt a year ago—I don't think there really was—as to the wisdom of the choice for President, I am sure that doubt has long ago faded away. We have the right woman in the right place. (Enthusiastic applause) She has given you a wonderful year of sacrifice and effort and constructive service. She is going to go on as a great leader of a great organization. She will never disappoint you; she will *never* be unfair; she will never be hasty; she will never be impulsive; she will always be the same calm, loving, fair-minded, judicious person that she has been every minute of the last three hundred sixty-five days.

The women all arose and applauded enthusiastically.

Source: Excerpts from Proceedings of the Second Convention. LWV Papers on film, II. A.2. 0226–33.

Maud Wood Park responded graciously to Carrie Chapman Catt and reminded the delegates of their impressive heritage.

DOCUMENT 9: MAUD WOOD PARK'S RESPONSE TO CARRIE CHAPMAN CATT

MRS. PARK: I think you will all allow that there is nobody in the world whose praise I would rather have, (applause) or rather deserve.

This is almost the end of our week of convention. The Vice-Chairman of the League, who was Chairman of the Program Committee, spoke truly when she called it a "Working Convention." I thought that was a good slogan. I didn't realize that it was going to be so completely a reality. We have had session after session after session on which we have been working to find our service and ourselves. Mrs. Catt has said that in the beginning we weren't quite sure, we didn't know what we wanted to do altogether ourselves. Some of the women who had had the inspiration of working in the old suffrage association were a little afraid that we were going to lose our single-minded idea in undertaking to do the great number of things that the League of Women Voters seems to be undertaking to do. . . .

And so the thing I particularly want to say to the members of this Convention is that we haven't any less an ideal than we ever had. On the contrary, we have more. Three generations of women have toiled and suffered and sacrificed in order that we might have the opportunity that is ours today. If we don't make good on that opportunity, their sacrifices have been largely in vain. Now, then, it is ours to make good for the splendid, wonderful leadership that we have had. (Enthusiastic applause)

Source: Excerpts from Proceedings of the Second Convention. LWV Papers on film, II. A.2. 0237.

Jessie Hooper, president of the Wisconsin League, had been one of the many delegates electrified by Carrie Chapman Catt's speech against war, and she took this moment to suggest means whereby they might implement Catt's call for an alternative to war.

DOCUMENT 10: JESSIE HOOPER'S CALL FOR ACTION ON BEHALF OF WORLD PEACE

MRS. HOOPER: Women of the Convention, I am not going to keep you but one moment. Ever since we have been at this Convention, we have applauded when the name of Mrs. Catt has been mentioned. We have applauded when we saw her pictures. We have cheered. Did you mean it?

"Yes" from the audience.

Yesterday we passed a resolution unanimously calling upon the President of the United States and our Congress to take the first initiative in trying to get disarmament in the world. Did you mean it?

"Yes" from the audience.

Well, prove it. I call upon this Convention to go home and not only find out whether there is a sentiment for it, but if there isn't, make it. (Applause)

Dr. Shaw passed away before she had an opportunity to see whether we meant what we said when we told of the people who were working so hard for us that we would make good when we got the vote, Mrs. Catt is with us. I beg of you to do something now, rather than wait to put up a monument to her when she is dead. (Applause)

We have the power in our hands tonight, and it is for us to decide whether we will make that opinion so strong in these United States, that not even one Senator stands against it, but stands for disarmament of the world, and we will offer our services to the women of Europe to see that it is done on the other side.

I ask every woman here to go home and make a campaign in every club, men's or women's clubs, to see that that pressure is brought on Congress to get the quick action that this world may be at peace forever. I want every woman in the Convention who is willing to go home and work for world peace to rise.

The women all arose and applauded.

Source: Excerpts from the Second Convention, 1921. LWV Papers on film, II. A.2. 0237-38.

Another momentous happening earlier in 1921 marked a resurgence of differences between the suffragists now organized in the League of Women Voters and the National Woman's Party (NWP). The militant NWP regarded the achievement of suffrage as but a way station along the road toward complete equality and began a state-by-state campaign in support of equal rights legislation. While their perception of other existing inequalities experienced by women was valid, it ran up against the campaign being waged by a number of women's groups on behalf of social reform—including the League, the General Federation of Women's Clubs, Business and Professional Women's Clubs, the YWCA, the National Consumers' League, and the Woman's Trade Union League. Theirs was a more gradualist approach involving a variety of reforms to better the conditions of working women, to curb child labor, and to provide needed services for the urban poor. But Alice Paul equated protective legislation as an implicit "recognition of the inferiority of women." And thus the issue would be joined until the early 1970s when many women's organizations, such as the LWV, which had earlier opposed the Equal Rights Amendment, came out in support of the amendment.

A second conflict between the National Woman's Party and the League arose with the NWP's initiative to place in the U.S. Capitol a statue of three of the leading suffrage pioneers: Susan B. Anthony, Lucretia Mott, and Elizabeth Cady Stanton. The statue was unveiled in the Rotunda in a ceremony on February 15, 1921, the anniversary of Susan B. Anthony's birthday. The League, however, was not present, an absence explained to the National Board and to the State Leagues, in a communication from Carrie Chapman Catt.

DOCUMENT 11: CARRIE CHAPMAN CATT ON THE STATUE OF SUFFRAGE PIONEERS IN THE U.S. CAPITOL

A prominent and reliable suffragist reports that Alice Paul told her that the National American Woman Suffrage Association had never returned a reply to the invitation of the Woman's Party. As these rumors seem to have been spread, broadcast and presumably with intention, I lay the facts before you. . . .

The Board of the National Association and the Board of the National League of Women Voters have declined to join in the ceremonies.

It had been our hope that this fact need not be publicly mentioned since the fewer disagreements between women that are advertised, the better. However, the inevitable misrepresentation has followed. The Board held that since for seven years the two associations had worked upon different policies, and that the National had made repeated statements to the effect that there was no connection between the two associations and no private understanding, as always charged by the antis, that it should not now give evidence that our claims may not have been true. At every step the National Association met misrepresentation and has abundant proof of much absolute untruthfulness emanating from that society. It has been very careful not to mention these facts in a public way. It has never attacked the Woman's Party and has never mentioned that body except when necessary to correct some misrepresentation on account of which the cause would suffer.

The busts also revived an old difficulty of the National Association. In the year of the World's Fair (1893) Miss Johnson made three busts. Because the National Suffrage Association was incorporated for the sole purpose of gaining suffrage, it could not legally undertake to finance the busts. Therefore three members of the National Association, one its Treasurer, formed a private committee and made a very incomplete contract with Miss Johnson. Altogether $3000 was to be paid her and the busts were then to be placed in the Capitol. Something over $2000 was paid to her (I believe $2300) and the remainder collected. That money was not paid because it developed that the Capitol would not receive busts of suffrage pioneers at that time and that Miss Johnson would not give up the busts even when paid for unless they could be placed in the Capitol. A controversy, therefore, arose which aroused a good deal of bitterness of feeling.

All this occurred before I was a member of the National Board but the ripples of disagreement trickled through the after years.

Miss Johnson held that she should have been paid all the money and that she should have been permitted to keep the busts. The National suffragists held that since the busts were not satisfactory, she should have been satisfied to give them up if paid for. There was at the time a great deal of criticism by the Stanton family concerning the bust of Elizabeth Cady Stanton and Miss Shaw and Lucy Anthony were equally critical of the bust made of Susan B. Anthony.

Later, these same three busts were reproduced by Miss Johnson and are said to have been improved. The busts now to be presented are a third reproduction of the same busts. This is a bare statement of the facts.

The National Board does not wish to reflect in any way upon Miss Johnson's talent as a sculptress nor upon her character as a businesswoman, and therefore desires to make no public statement concerning the causes which led to the vote it took upon the matter.

Source: Sara M. Evans, *Born for Liberty: A History of Women in America.* New York: The Free Press, 1989, 187–88. Clarke A. Chambers, *Seedtime of Reform: American Social Service and Social Action, 1918–1933.* Minneapolis: University of Minnesota Press, 1963, 171–73. Carrie Chapman Catt to the Board of Directors, Presidents of former Suffrage Auxiliaries, and Chairmen of State Leagues of Women Voters, undated, LWV Papers on film, III. A.3. 0756–58.

Two days later, the statue was removed to the Crypt, a room on the ground floor (but often called the basement) that was originally built to house George Washington's remains and later used as a store room. There the three suffrage leaders languished until 1997 when the statue was elevated temporarily to a more prestigious and public location. Contributions of individual women, beginning in 1995 on the occasion of the seventy-fifth anniversary of the Nineteenth Amendment, paid for the move. Possibly not all, but certainly many, contemporary feminists would agree with Catt that "the busts are not satisfactory."

Source: New York Times, September 22, 1996.

The relationship between the National League of Women Voters and the General Federation of Women's Clubs, had its roots in the years of suffrage. The federation had been suspicious of what members perceived to be the radical ideas of suffrage and did not encourage suffrage club affiliation, elect suffragists as club officers, or, for that matter, endorse suffrage until 1914. With the organization of the League in 1920, the older Federation felt that the new upstart organization was treading on its toes. A women's collaborative effort in the legislative arena was advanced to placate the Federation's president, Alice Ames Winter, who had been upset at the possibility of the League (according to Carrie Catt) "stealing the Federation's thunder." Fortunately, Winter, a graduate of Wellesley College (where she also obtained a master's degree), had also been a suffrage supporter. She joined with Maud Wood Park, a graduate of nearby Radcliffe, trying to put petty turf jealousies aside with a joint communication to the state presidents of both organizations.

DOCUMENT 12: MAUD WOOD PARK AND ALICE AMES WINTER ON LWV/GENERAL FEDERATION OF WOMEN'S CLUBS' RELATIONSHIPS

A notable joint letter has been signed by the presidents of the two great women's organizations, the General Federation of Women's Clubs and the National League of Women Voters. To further the work in which women are interested, Mrs. Thomas G. Winter and Mrs. Maud Wood Park have addressed to the Club and League State Presidents a call for the utmost measure of coopera-tion. The letter reads:

"There are before us at this time so many important issues that it is even more than usually wasteful of strength for women agreeing upon great issues not to get the full force to be derived from cooperation. The General Federation of Women's Clubs and the National League of Women Voters are both organi-zations of progressive women interested in the right development and the right conservation of our country's resources; they are both organized in each one of the 48 states; they are both supporting certain state and federal legislation, in many instances the same bills.

" . . . Obviously, since the work of the General Federation is primarily so-ciological and educational, and the work of the League concerns itself with women as voting citizens, there is a good and sufficient reason for cooperation. These differences are in emphasis only and not in sharp distinction. The Fed-eration has always done legislative work, and the League is doing educational work; but the 'overlapping' should be used to promote mutual strength and un-derstanding, never rivalry or antagonism.

"It is with great pleasure, therefore, that we, the National Presidents of these two organizations, announce to our auxiliary members our mutual understand-ing of the value of both organizations and our earnest desire that the most cor-dial relations of cooperation shall exist between all state and local branches and the members in general of the Federation of Women's Clubs and the League of Women Voters to the end that the work in which we are all interested may be forwarded with the least possible waste of effort."

Source: Van Voris, *Carrie Chapman Catt*, 121. Barbara Stuhler, *Gentle Warriors*, 71–72. Maud Wood Park and Alice Ames Winter, "Joint Letter to Local Branches of National League of Women Voters and General Federation of Women's Clubs," *The Woman Citizen*, October 22, 1921. LWV Papers on film, III. A.1. 0620.

The League's first major legislative success came with the enact-ment of the Sheppard-Towner Act for the protection of the welfare and health of mothers and children in late 1921. A year earlier, Maud Wood Park — following up on a promise of a collaborative legislative ef-fort—had assembled the heads of major women's organizations and proposed that they form a coalition to magnify their effectiveness in achieving common legislative goals. Thus the Women's Joint Congres-sional Committee was formed with Maud Wood Park, a highly experi-enced lobbyist, as chair. While the legislation for maternal and infant health education established a modest program with an annual appro-priation of slightly over $1 million (no more than $50,000 was to be spent each year in administration by the Children's Bureau), it did rep-resent the first time that Congress appropriated funds for the states to use for a social purpose. In this respect—and even though it was not renewed in 1929—Sheppard-Towner was the prologue to the body of legislation enacted in the 1930s that laid the foundation for the mod-ern welfare state.

DOCUMENT 13: MAUD WOOD PARK ON THE SHEPPARD-TOWNER ACT

The Sheppard-Towner Bill for the protection of maternity and infancy has become a Federal law. Ten million voters, representing the most influential women's national organizations that have been supporting this measure, are rejoicing in this notable Thanksgiving gift to the women and children of America. It is not alone a great victory for forward-looking legislation, it is recognition of the wishes, not the women as women, but of the great new electorate who have sprung full-fledged, into the responsibilities of citizenship.

The National League of Women Voters is delighted over the large majority by which the Congress passed this bill. Selecting this as the one measure to which they would devote their energy, the League has steadily worked to this end, cooperating with other women's organizations in every way possible. On July 22 the bill passed the Senate by a vote of 63 to 7; on November 19 it passed the House by a vote of 279 to 39; on November 23—Thanksgiving Eve—with the President's signature, it became an act.

Meantime, six states which held legislative sessions last spring, anticipating the passage of the Sheppard-Towner bill by Congress, passed legislation to enable them to begin state welfare work under Federal control as soon as the bill became an act. Minnesota, New Hampshire, New Mexico, Pennsylvania, South Dakota, Delaware, whose Congressmen so bitterly fought the bill—all these states are ready to begin. Pennsylvania, whose annual appropriation for its Child Welfare Department totals about $6,000,000, telegraphed immediate readiness to begin cooperation with the Children's Bureau.

Women—millions of them—wanted the preventable deaths of mothers and babies stopped. And they "made their wants felt." So, as Judge Towner said of the men of Congress, women may also say: "We have done something at least to make this country a little better and safer place in which to live."

Source: Maud Wood Park, "A Triumph for Women," *The Woman Citizen*, December 3, 1921, 16.

In another context, Catt had felt moved to voice her irritation with the Republican Party for being critical of the League and angry that prominent partisans were urging Republican women to leave the League. (The Oklahoma Congresswoman referred to by Catt was Alice Mary Robertson, a former vice president of the Oklahoma Association Opposed to Woman Suffrage. In perhaps the ultimate irony, she was the first woman to be elected to Congress in 1920 at age sixty-two. She ran for Congress as a Republican from Oklahoma's second district, campaigning on the principles of "Christianity, Americanism, and Standpattism." Robertson was defeated in 1922, having offended Republicans, Democrats, women, and veterans.) Nor did the Democrats escape her ire. No matter that she had earlier advocated leaving social reform to other women's groups, Carrie Chapman Catt wanted to make it very clear that the League should be credited for passage of the Sheppard–Towner legislation.   Thus began a dispute over who should get credit for the act's passage.

DOCUMENT 14: CARRIE CHAPMAN CATT, "WHO'S SCARED?"

The Woman's National Republican Club has just given a semi-public luncheon in New York City in honor of Mrs. Harding, who pled indisposition and did not come.

What happened there makes the occasion notable among the tens of thousands of such events which take place every day.   One scans the press report in vain for a program to be served by Republican women, a proposed aim to support a principle to rally around—but none is mentioned.   There was, however, a curious and seemingly well-disciplined unanimity of advice.

Said Congresswoman Robertson: "If there are any Republican women in the League of Women Voters, get out."   Said Mrs. Medill McCormick: "The time has passed for a separate women's organization whether you call it the League of Women Voters or the Woman's Party."   Said Mr. Adams, chairman of the National Republican Committee: "About the poorest thing a woman can do politically is to be a non-partisan. There is just as much logic in forming a party of women as there would be in green-eyed, red-haired or bald-headed men forming a party."

Mrs. Harding sent a letter and even she added her mite to what appeared to be the main object of the meeting: "If I did not feel that the nation could, and in the long run must, be served best through parties, I should not be a partisan Republican. But I do feel this, and therefore, am convinced that the maintenance of effective party organization and unremitting work is a duty second to none."

With wide-eyed astonishment those who read the account have ejaculated with one voice: "What is the matter with the G.O.P.? Is it scared?"

But the women have manifested new symptoms, heretofore wholly unknown to political experience.   They neither hurled anathema at their one-time party rival nor spent time or breath praising their own party record and leaders—the only problem in the entire world which troubled the speakers, male and female, was the existence of the League of Women Voters!   Why? The Federation of Clubs, W.C.T.U., the Y.W.C.A., The University Women and countless other women's organizations which "carry on" do not disturb the Republican peace of mind—it's only the League of Women Voters which has aroused their ire.

Why?   Because it has already more to boast of in the way of political achievement than Republican and Democratic women put together.

"If you want to do something, do it within the party" said they.   Well, well, the members of the League of Women Voters are usually members of the parties, but when the maternity bill [Sheppard-Towner] went through, neither the Republican or Democratic women as such were the power behind it. . . . The Oklahoma Congresswoman who decries the League, spoke against the bill in committee and on the floor and hysterically spoke against it.   Has she and have other Republican women (and Democratic women) made the removal of legal discriminations against women, naturalization of married women, and the correction of illiteracy which are the next aims of the league, a party program? How can Leaguers trust a party to do these things when it has made no pledge to that effect?

Source: Angie Debo, "Robertson, Alice Mary," in Edward T. James, Janet Wilson James, and Paul S. Boyer, Eds., *Notable American Women: A Biographical Dictionary.*

Cambridge, MA: The Belknap Press of Harvard University Press, 1971, Vol. III, 177–78. Excerpts from Carrie Chapman Catt, "Who's Scared?" *The Woman Citizen*, January 28, 1922.

Needless to say, such plain talk caused something of a brouhaha, and Maud Wood Park wrote Catt, saying, "I hate like mischief to bother you about trifles like hurt feelings, but, alas, Mrs. Yost has stirred up a regular hornet's nest, on the one hand with the Republicans and on the other with the Joint Congressional Committee, apropos your article in The Citizen of January 28." Park also noted a call from "a friendly representative" of the joint committee who feared that there "might be real trouble" with some of the committee's other organizations unless some statement from Park appeared in a future issue of The Woman Citizen. *Park enclosed a copy of the statement she had drafted.*

DOCUMENT 15: LETTER FROM MAUD WOOD PARK TO *THE WOMAN CITIZEN*

May I ask you to make clear in your columns the great service rendered in the passage of the Sheppard-Towner Bill by the organizations represented on the Woman's Committee on the Sheppard-Towner Bill, which is a sub-committee of the Women's Joint Congressional Committee?

When this sub-committee was organized, Mrs. Florence Kelley, representing the National Consumers' League, was made chairman. On the Committee were representatives from the following organizations:

American Association of University Women
American Home Economics Association
General Federation of Women's Clubs
Girls' Friendly Society of America
National Board of the YWCA
National Congress of Mothers and Parent-Teacher Associations
National Consumers' League
National Council of Jewish Women
National Federation of Business and Professional Women
National League of Women Voters
National Society, Daughters of the American Revolution
National Woman's Christian Temperance Union
National Women's Trade Union League

Through the membership of these organizations and their united efforts, there was recorded in the Congress such an overwhelming demand for the bill that Honorable Samuel Winslow in reporting it to the House of Representatives said: "The proposed legislation has undoubtedly stirred up more sentiment, wisely or unwisely created, than any bill which has been before the Congress in ten years, or maybe 100 years."

In my judgment it was this demand, together with the interest of the President, the help of Mrs. Harriet Taylor Upton, and the efforts of friends of both parties in the Senate and House, which made possible the passage of this bill.

Source: Maud Wood Park to Carrie Chapman Catt, February 13, 1922. LWV Papers on film, III. A.3. 0485. Maud Wood Park, letter to *The Woman Citizen*, February 14, 1922, LWV Papers on film, III. A.3. 0493.

Carrie Chapman Catt sent a long dissenting letter, filled with affection for Park but bemoaning her lack of ego and unwillingness to take credit for what essentially had been the League's doing, namely the passage of the Sheppard-Towner Act. She sent letters the same day, making similar terse observations, to national board members Marie Edwards and Belle Sherwin.

DOCUMENT 16: RESPONSE OF CARRIE CHAPMAN CATT TO MAUD WOOD PARK

I was rather sorry that there were others present yesterday so that I could not have quite as frank a talk with you as was resting upon my soul. I saw that you were very busy and further that you looked awfully tired. I did not want to distress you, but I did think that we ought to have this difficulty fought out to the end, so that we shall quite understand each other and that we here in the office of *The Citizen* shall understand just what relations you wish us to assume toward the League.

I am awfully sorry that I have been guilty of doing anything which has made your work the slightest bit more difficult. At the same time I know, and I think you do, that all the trouble that arises in Washington is stirred up by a very small handful of Republicans—women who are after your scalp and Mrs. Upton's scalp and Miss Hay's scalp and my scalp. There are different reasons for their attacking us, and we are not put in the same class by any means, each of us having in an especial way challenged their enmity. These women were all in our suffrage association. They were all good and loyal workers then. I have never been able to understand the reason for their animus except that the moment the high appeal of principle was removed, they descended into the pit of the darkest kind of narrow partisanship.

There was a time when the Democrats were after us too, but because the Democrats are now out and disorganized we don't hear anything from them whatever and the battle is between the Republicans and the rest of us. This enmity is subterranean, secret, maligning, lying and thoroughly dishonorable in every respect. I have no patience with the policy that caters to it, placates it, apologizes to it, in order to make temporary peace. This is the forced policy that politicians have assumed in times past, and which has eventually led to war.

Now if the League of Women Voters does not know that there is trouble ahead for it in this underhanded campaigning, they are less well informed on the general subject of human nature than I supposed they were. In your letter (in order to make peace in Washington) you have sent to *The Citizen* you have politely called me a liar! Of course you didn't mean to do that, but you couldn't do what you did do in any other way. What I did was to give the League of Women Voters credit for having put through the Maternity Bill. You politely say in your letter that they had almost nothing to do with it except to allow their name to stand on the committee. In your effort to let everybody else have full credit, you have renounced absolutely all credit for the League.

Now I do not believe this is true, but if it is, the question arises in my mind—what has the League been doing in Washington for two years? Why have we contributed in solid cash in two years, $30,000 for the maintenance of the League, if the only thing that shows in the way of legislation is a bill that it had nothing to do with?

Your greatest fault, my dear girl, is a cavity where your bump of conceit ought to be, and this time you have positively done your organization a decided wrong by belittling its work and influence.

Since you are going off on a long journey where I cannot consult you and do not want to put any more burdens on you, you put me in the position of having to do one of two things. Either publish your letter without any comment whatever which announces that the President of the League of Women Voters has called me a fabricator, and put into the hands of this little group of Republican women a billy with which to beat me over the head; or I must make comment and in some way announce that I am right and you are wrong. In any case you have put the League and me and you all in a very bad kind of hole to get out of.

Undoubtedly it seems to you that it is of the utmost importance to keep the Joint Congressional Committee, and therefore you want to make peace with them. That committee was set up at the suggestion of the Federation as I remember it. The Republicans continually stirred up against the League by these few women make it impossible for the League to get anything through, I suppose, without the aid of these women whom you are obliged to put forward.

Then the truth of the matter is this. That this group of Republicans stirred up such a mess down there that the League in order to accomplish what it wanted to accomplish was obliged to put forward the women representing kindergarten organizations against which the men had no prejudices, and you merely kept in the background and pulled the strings. Now you virtually say that you didn't even pull the strings.

Very well, are you ever going to be able to do anything in Washington if that Republican group continues to hound the League? Already the Federation says that it is much more popular than the League, and the Republicans of course condemn the League whenever any woman of some other organization goes to see them, and these women are naturally gradually turning against the League and think that they could do the whole thing.

In order to pull the League out of this undignified and worrisome attitude something must be done, but the thing to do is not to crawl before those who are criticizing.

Just at this moment I am in doubt as to which of two attitudes I ought to assume. Either to fight for you who don't want to be fought for and smoke out into the open these people who are trying to get Mrs. Upton out of her position and kill the League if they can; or whether I should wash my hands of the whole business and never again say anything about the League.

Your letter arrived too late for this issue of *The Citizen*, and I think that was very fortunate. I had meanwhile prepared an answer to the come–backs from the Republicans, etc. And there is another one coming next week in response to the come–backs of the Democrats, and in that combination your letter will have to go in. But I want to warn you now that I shall make comment about it although at this moment I do not know what.

I am writing this letter not to trouble your peace of mind, but to apologize to you for having spilled your beans, and to apologize to me for your having spilled my beans.

My dear Maud, my affection for you is as deep as the ocean, and as broad as the horizon.   My confidence and faith in you is unlimited, but I have one "senatorial reservation" and that reservation is that you can't be trusted an inch when it comes to beating your own tom-toms. If I had been present at your creation I should have had put into your make-up a nice fat ego in which case you would have been absolutely perfect.

Since you told me that Miss Sherwin and Mrs. Edwards thought your letter should be even stronger than it was in repudiating the League's responsibility for the bill, I am going to send a copy of this letter to both of them, for perhaps I shall get some come-back from them which I do not expect from you.

I beg you, do not try to answer this letter but just read it in order that you may know how I feel about it.

Source: Carrie Chapman Catt to Maud Wood Park, February 18, 1922. LWV Papers on film, III. A.3. 0485–88.

Marie Edwards responded to Carrie Catt, explaining the need for great diplomacy in dealing with the members of the Women's Joint Congressional Committee, and the value of Maud Park's tact, skill, and intelligence in managing that organization. Belle Sherwin added her two cents worth, and Catt replied to both; but to Edwards she provided interesting information about the origin of the WJCC although the League did take the lead role in its organization and operations.

DOCUMENT 17: CARRIE CHAPMAN CATT TO MARIE EDWARDS

It was quite unnecessary for you to send me that long letter of explanation since you, Miss Sherwin and Mrs. Park want the statement printed as she sent it. I am quite satisfied that that is the way it ought to be done. It has gone into *The Citizen* this week.

You need not worry about any further "spilling of the beans" for I have taken a very iron-clad resolution, and that is that when there seems to be a necessity of the League being defended, someone else will do it. I shall in that way keep off everybody's toes and there will be no pain or embarrassment.

You remember "that Mrs. Shuler insisted that the Convention should order the Board to form a Joint Committee." No my dear, you are away off. Mrs. Winter was our guest. She was disturbed all the time because we were stealing the Federation's thunder. Mrs. Winter, Miss Sherwin and Mrs. Pennybacker came to me with this complaint and I asked if they couldn't devise some way of working together. I told them that none of us had any time then to give a thought to anything. They went away and spent a half day together, and then came back with the proposal of the Joint Congressional Committee which they sent up to me when I was presiding. I handed it to Mrs. Shuler and asked her to introduce it. It was not her motion at all, and she knew nothing about it. The initiative came from the Federation.

Perhaps you will remember that at the last Congress in Cleveland I went before your committee and suggested that despite the Joint Congressional Committee, there were innumerable complaints and much friction and suggested that the League should drop everything on its program which was already being done by any other large or several large organizations and devote itself to the things which it alone could do. The entire Board arose as one man and sat down on that proposition. I am sorry that so much energy has to be spent in keeping them all in line.

I still do not think it is profitable, but since all the rest of you do think so and you are the officers, I have no complaint to make.

I beg of you do not come down to New York to tell me about the League of Women Voters. I haven't time to hear about it. I am clear "up to my eyes" and haven't a minute to spare, but there are others down here who would like to hear about it and would be very glad to see you at any time you choose to call around this way. Don't include me in the party, because I am writing a book and I don't know anything but that book, and I don't care anything about anything else but that book until it is through.

Source: Carrie Chapman Catt to Marie Edwards, March 3, 1922. LWV Papers on film, III. A.3. 0501.

In the aftermath of the argument about the League and the Women's Joint Congressional Committee, and on the eve of the League's third national convention in Baltimore, Park offered to give up the presidency for someone who would chart a course for the League more to Catt's liking.

DOCUMENT 18: MAUD WOOD PARK TO CARRIE CHAPMAN CATT

I have been hoping ever since I came back that I should be able to get to New York this week to have a talk with you, but the enormous amount of extra work brought on by the loss of my clothes and papers in the fire—particularly my report for the convention which was nearly done—makes it evident now that I cannot steal even a few hours before I have to go to Baltimore.

You know how hard it is for me to write, so please pardon the shortcomings in what I am sure I could have put much more clearly if I had had an opportunity to talk with you.

This is it—I feel very strongly that you do not approve of the general course that the League has been taking or the special things that it has tried to do. I cannot honestly agree with your view in most of these matters, but I have for so many years recognized your extraordinary qualities of leadership, and I feel so much appreciation of all your personal kindness to me that I would rather have it go your way even though I cannot agree that it is necessarily the better way.

The League was your idea. It is your child. You shaped its first policies, and until that meeting just before the last convention I had thought that we were carrying them out. I have an indescribable feeling that we are somehow astray from the fold when we are not wholly in accord with you.

My term expires this year. No nominating committee has asked me to stand again, but I suppose they are going to. However—and I say this with the most complete sincerity—I do not want to be at the head of an organization that is in any sense at odds with you. I wish you would think this over and try to suggest a candidate for the presidency who does seem to you to have the right conception of the League's work. I have thought of Miss Wells and Miss Sherwin and Miss Ludington as possibilities for the future, if not for the present. Mrs. Edwards would, to my mind, be the best fitted if she had no family. But I think that any of the others would be admirable, and they are all more or less familiar with the work of the League. I should honestly be glad to support any of these, or probably anybody else whom you wanted to suggest, and myself to take a vice-presidency in order to help through the period of a changing administration.

I do mean this with all my heart, and I do want you to consider it seriously. We shall have five days before our own convention begins in which to look round after we reach Baltimore, so it is not necessary for you to reply to this letter until we have a chance to talk.

Always with deepest admiration and love. . .

Source: Maud Wood Park to Carrie Chapman Catt, April 14, 1922. LWV Papers on film, III. A.3. 0902–03.

> But while Carrie Chapman Catt confessed her unhappiness with "the way the League is drifting" programmatically, she maintained her confidence in the ability of Maud Wood Park to lead the organization.

DOCUMENT 19: CARRIE CHAPMAN CATT TO MAUD WOOD PARK ON THE LEAGUE

I have just received your letter and make haste to reply.

There is no one in this big wide world who *could* be president of the League and compare at all favorably with your own masterly, tactful, all–wise management of things. There is no one who doesn't want you there and every member does want you there. So let's say nothing else about it. Don't think for a minute of wasting energy on a successor. When you see the time coming, as some day you will, that you can go on no longer, then you must cast about for some one to take your place, but that I hope will be a long way ahead.

No, dear Maud, I do not like the way the League is drifting, but that doesn't matter in the least. The convention elects officers and composes a program. The officers in turn carry out the policy and really create it. That is big machinery and I have no intention of bucking against its combined judgment. I have the utmost pride and admiration and confidence in the entire board, individually and collectively, and a supreme confidence in the president.

The League is going in the direction it had to go doubtless, and if the rest of you see no breakers ahead on the route it is taking then the fact that I think I see them is of no concern, and your combined judgment must be right. At any rate I shall utter no criticism and no one will rejoice so heartily over every achievement as I, even when I think it out of place. Don't worry about me, dear girl. I'd throw out Child Welfare and let the Federation have it. I'd throw out Social Hygiene and let the W.C.T.U. have it, and I'd throw out Food and let the Packers have it, and then stand on a clear-cut Better Government plan. It is easier to explain. When I've made a speech here and claimed it as an agency for political education, I've been utterly routed by a question on that maternity bill which has no more to do with good citizenship than diamond tiaras. My mind isn't big enough to see the goal ahead through such a cloud of other things—that's all. You think otherwise and so does Miss Sherwin for I talked with her. That is enough for me. I surrender. Dear Maud, forget it, you have trouble enough. . . .

Poor little Maud what a lot of woe has come to her. Big masterly brave Maud, how she does conquer all things! She's my heroine, my hope and my abiding faith!

Source: Carrie Chapman Catt to Maud Wood Park, Easter Sunday, 1922. LWV Papers, Library of Congress.

At the Baltimore convention, President Park took a few minutes to explain the organization and workings of the Women's Joint Congressional Committee and, contrary to Carrie Catt's opinion, felt that credit should be shared where credit was due.

DOCUMENT 20: MAUD WOOD PARK ON THE WOMEN'S JOINT CONGRESSIONAL COMMITTEE

Mrs. Edwards has asked me to speak about the method of work of the Women's joint Congressional Committee in Washington. That was formed a year ago last November, and now there are 14 organizations represented on the Women's Joint Congressional Committee. . . .

When we came to the day of the first meeting some of us realized we were going to have to face a rather difficult problem of organization in this work; that no two organizations had endorsed exactly the same measures, and that of course, no organization could be held to the support of any measure it had not endorsed. So we adopted the plan of making the Joint Congressional Committee only a clearinghouse. The Committee itself does not support any measure before Congress, nor does it inaugurate legislation.

This does not mean that the organizations represented on the Joint Congressional or on its sub-committees may not inaugurate legislation, but the Committee itself does not inaugurate legislation; it merely acts as a clearinghouse.

According to the by–laws recently adopted, whenever any bill has been endorsed by three of the organizations represented on the Joint Congressional Committee, a sub–committee on that particular measure may be formed, and the work for the measure is done through the sub–committee.

The work for the Sheppard–Towner Bill was never done in the name of the Women's Joint Congressional Committee; it was done by the Women's Committee on the Sheppard–Towner Bill, which is a sub–committee of the Joint Congressional Committee.

We have eight of these sub–committees; each sub–committee elects its own officers, and the Joint Congressional Committee elects its officers; the Joint Congressional Committee has its own stationery, and when the subcommittees get active enough to need stationery they print their own letterhead printing there the names of the organizations which have endorsed any particular measure.

When a representative appears before the Congress representing the whole Committee, if that seems the best thing to do, that representative does not appear as a representative of the Joint Congressional Committee, because there might be on the Joint Congressional Committee some organization that has not endorsed the bill. You may ask, "Of what use is the Joint Congressional Committee?" It has a great deal of use, as a clearinghouse, because at every one of the meetings there is a report from the sub–committees, and these organizations that may not have endorsed a particular measure get the benefit of knowing what the measure is, and then they get the habit of looking ahead.

We had this year what I think has proved extremely useful, a Lookout Committee. This is a committee, which keeps its eye on legislation of interest to women, but legislation that has no sub–committee in the Joint Congressional Committee.   There are several measures in which a good many of us are interested where we have not had endorsements enough to appoint any sub-committee; the Lookout Committee tells us about those measures, and we are really getting a considerable amount of information in that way.

I have been asked to explain who is eligible and how membership in the Congressional Committee is determined.

Originally the League of Women Voters sent out invitations to the national organizations that we knew were doing legislative work. We invited representatives of what were at that time ten of the great national organizations of women to meet in our office and talk over the possibility of forming a clearinghouse for measures before Congress in which women's organizations are interested.   We had very cordial responses from these organizations.   Then other organizations applied for admission.   Also we now have a Committee on Admissions that studies methods of work of an organization and decides whether it is eligible; if it is not doing congressional work, it is not eligible.

I think that this plan is the best possible plan for everybody, if everybody will play fair with regard to it, to warn the League of Women Voters always to remember that the thing we are after is to get the thing done and not necessarily to get the credit for it."

Source: Excerpts from proceedings of the Third National Convention (hereinafter referred to as the Third Convention), Baltimore, MD, April 24–29, 1922. LWV Papers on film. II. A.3. 1537–39.

The significance of the Third National Convention, however, lay not with such intramural disagreements but rather with the prelude to that convention, a conference with women of Latin America. It represented the League's first venture in what would prove to be a continuing commitment to work with women of other nations. Although the League had inherited an association with the International Woman Suffrage Alliance, that relationship proved to be more off than on in the postsuffrage years and did not represent the centerpiece of the League's international activities. The Pan-American Conference, held in Baltimore from April 20 to 23, set the stage for future activities abroad, activities that gained momentum in the years after World War II. At the request of the U.S. government, the League, under the aegis of the Carrie Chapman Catt Memorial Fund, exported its skills of civic participation in visits and meetings to women in Germany, Italy, and Japan, helping them develop institutions that would give them a political voice.

Chapter 6

The Pan–American Convention

In its third year the League of Women Voters took a global initiative, inviting representatives of Latin American nations to participate in a Pan–American conference of women and to attend the League's national convention. Carrie Chapman Catt used the conference as a forum to challenge the women of Latin America to exert their influence and gain the vote. As usual, she also advanced the proposition to the assembled League members that social issues, while important, were hardly the stuff of training for citizens in the political process. In her presidential address, Maud Wood Park, in her gentle way, took issue with Catt's assertion, suggesting that social issues were in fact appropriate venues and that no concern of policy should be exempt from civic attention and action. She also took the opportunity to advise members that they should not deplore but rather applaud the diversity of opinion that existed within the organization.

In 1922 the League, in a bold, innovative step, combined its Third National Convention with a Pan–American Conference in Baltimore representing the League's first venture into the circles of high diplomacy. Officials of the city of Baltimore, the director of the Pan–American Union, and Secretary of State Charles Evans Hughes were persuaded to support the idea of inviting women from member states of the Pan–American Union.

DOCUMENT 1: CALL TO THE CONVENTION AND THE
PAN–AMERICAN CONFERENCE OF WOMEN

The National League of Women Voters calls its Affiliated and Associate Members to send delegates to the Third Annual Convention of the League at Hotel Belvedere, Baltimore, Maryland, from April 24th to 29th, 1922.

The League calls Women from All the Americas to meet in Conference from April 20th to 23rd, 1922, on subjects of special concern to women—Education, Child Welfare, Women in Industry, Prevention of Traffic in Women, Civil and Political Status of Women and International Friendliness.

PEACE among nations is essential to the work that women have most at heart. A definite step towards the maintenance of peace has been taken by the Conference on Limitation of Armament. The League has borne its full share of responsibility for making known to the Conference the profound hope of the people of this land that war may cease.

But this hope can never be wholly realized until friendly cooperation for common ends takes the place of international rivalry. The League believes that friendliness with our neighbor countries will be stimulated and strengthened when women from all parts of the Western Hemisphere come together for sympathetic study of their common problems.

In the Third Annual Convention of the League its members, rejoicing over the successes of the past months and earnestly mindful of the things that are yet to be done, will have opportunity to review the work of officers and committees, to hear the experiences of state leagues and to determine upon plans for the coming year.

The League needs the counsel of all its workers. Its usefulness has been made clear. Its field for service is wide. It has faith in the ideals of government by the people and zeal for their fulfillment. Its goal of intelligent, conscientious, effective citizenship will be won only by wisdom and consecration.

The League calls YOU to come and give of your best.

Source: LWV Papers on film, II. A.2. 0308.

Delegates from twenty-two countries of the Western Hemisphere and scores of others—representatives of women's organizations and students attending U.S. colleges and universities—were present for all or part of the five–day Pan–American conference convened in Baltimore and the four-day League convention that followed. In her welcoming address League president Maud Wood Park said:

> The women who are turning their thoughts on this conference today realize with us that we women have problems in common that are not defined by national or international boundaries—problems that belong to women all over the wide world, and we believe that in the combined wisdom of the women who are here we shall all receive help in our common problems. . . .

The National League of Women Voters is eager to learn from the experience of these women who have honored us with their wisdom here today. We realize that we have much to be taught, and we are deeply grateful to you who have taken this long journey to bring us the benefit of what you know about the subjects in which we also are interested. . . . If you could look into our heart today you would no doubt see the warmth of our welcome and the depth of our appreciation.

It turned out to be a successful venture and constituted the League's first step toward a wider international engagement.

Source: Excerpts from the Proceedings of the Pan–American Conference (hereinafter referred to as the Pan- American Conference), Baltimore, MD, April 20–23, 1922. LWV Papers on film, II. A.2. 0364.

A highlight of the conference was a visit by Lady Nancy Astor, born in Virginia and married to a British citizen. In 1920 she became the first woman in the history of Great Britain to be elected to the House of Commons. Some of her wit, charm, and candor come through in these remarks to the delegates at the Pan–American conference.

DOCUMENT 2: LADY ASTOR ON VOTES FOR WOMEN

Mrs. Catt . . . said all the reporters here were not interested in women's votes, but in me. I should like the reporters to know why I am here: It is because women have votes. (Applause)

Think what a disaster for the world it would be if my peculiarities had been hidden in a two-room cottage instead of the House of Commons. (Laughter)

But it is all very well for people to look at me and say "Lady Astor has got whatever she has," but it is on account of the wonderful work that the women did that I am here at all today. (Applause) . . .

I should also like to say one thing more. There has been a slight misunderstanding about what I think of the Washington Conference [on disarmament]. Some of the reporters said that Lady Astor did not think much of the Washington Conference. I do not think much of the Washington Conference! Why, I think it was the beginning of civilization! (Prolonged applause) They did not know what they were talking about. (Applause) You cannot think what the results of the Washington Conference meant to Europe, how they were received in England and in Europe. I was in England, but I saw the European papers. The people of England, I know, were looking to Washington, and they are going to keep looking to Washington until they keep on conferring more and more. (Applause) I want that to be right. Everybody in the world ought to be grateful to the Washington Conference. (Applause)

I have felt, and always feel, that I should apologize that I should be the first representative women have in the House of Commons, because I want none of you to forget what splendid work the women who were the pioneers in the movement had already done. (Applause) I read an editorial that Lady Astor did not smash windows and things like that. (Laughter) Lady Astor did not have to do it—that was done by others before her, and I do feel very deeply that none of us should ever forget what the women have done in the very beginning, and I know what it is to be a pioneer. So I look back and I apologize to all these people for having gotten a few of the glories which they worked for and which they should have had. But it is always that way: The people who do the real work never get the credit for it but people like me come on and reap all the fruits of it. I really mean it. People like me should remember that it was these pioneers who made it possible for us to be where we are and it does not matter whether we get the glories or not. Never forget that. (Applause) All during the great suffrage movement, I really did nothing for the cause—I was too busy populating the world, but I was with them in spirit and a great many of my friends went to prison.

What was it all about? What were we doing it for? It was not for notoriety. I do not believe any right-minded woman liked notoriety, and I have had plenty of it. I truly do not like it. I have never seen a right-minded woman in my life who liked notoriety, but we are willing to have it and suffer it, even if it hurts. (Laughter) There has been a great deal of misunderstanding about the woman's movement, but some day the world will see. All great movements are misunderstood about the woman's movement, but some day the world will see. All great movements are misunderstood when they begin.

I am told that some of the Pan–American ladies are not suffragists. If that is true, I do not know what they are here for, but I am sure that they will be. (Applause)

I know how difficult it is, particularly for the Catholic women. They have a difficult time of it. I cannot for the life of me see what having the vote has to do with religion. (Applause) I thought the most beautiful thing about religion was that all men and women are equal. (Applause) That to me is the saving grace of religion. (Laughter) I like to think there is a God that looks into our hearts and not our sex. . . .

Now, I am not going to say anything else. I would beg the reporters who are here today to remember me—if they came here to see me—that there is no greater believer in woman suffrage than I am, and I agree with the lady from Nicaragua that if we had had the vote the world might have been very different. But the world won't be different by our having the vote; the world might be different by our using the vote. (Applause) You see, having the vote without using it is like having religion without using it, and it is not much use. I am not telling you how to use your votes. I have not come over for that, but because you have asked me, and I bring you greetings from all the women in England. (Applause)

Source: Excerpts from the Proceedings of the Pan–American Conference. LWV Papers on film, II. A.3. 0966–71.

In the closing minutes of the Pan–American Conference, the elder stateswoman of U.S. suffrage spoke to the delegates. Her remarks inspired the delegates from North and South America to form the Pan–American Association for the Advancement of Women. The friendly feeling so manifest at the opening of the conference came into full flower as a firm bond of friendship at its close.

DOCUMENT 3: CARRIE CHAPMAN CATT'S CHARGE TO THE WOMEN OF LATIN AMERICA

I want you to take this message home. It does not matter whether you are interested in this question or not. I want you particularly to remember this: There are six continents in the world and there is only 1 continent where no woman has the vote and that is South America. Will you be content to be the only women in the world without the vote? No! Because there is as much spirit, as much aspiration, as much ambition in the Spanish and the Portuguese women as in any other women in the world. (Prolonged applause) I do not forget that some 300 years ago there was a women's movement, a great movement, and it was led by the women of Spain and Portugal. I do not know what happened afterwards, but it was forbidden by the law and it disappeared and these women come forward rather tardily now, nevertheless they will come. It is unthinkable that women shall be sitting in legislatures, and Parliament, and in Congress, making the laws for nations, when the women of another continent have not so much as the privilege of a vote.

I am sorry indeed to tell you that there will be a long fight ahead. I have become somewhat acquainted with women of many nations and I have never known the women of any nation where they did not have the vote, where the women did not profoundly believe that their men would not long deny them the vote. I have never talked with such women who did not feel that the procuring of the vote would be a very easy matter. . . .

Now, dear friends from South America and Central America, if you think that you do not want to be a suffragist, and do not want to start a movement in your own country, well, don't do it; but if you don't somebody else will. (Applause)

You cannot escape destiny and the destiny of this time is to lead the women of the world. (Applause)

And, if you are afraid of us, why just get over it. (Laughter)

One of the delegates told me when the invitation to this conference came to her country, it created a great deal of talk, that every newspaper printed it and the men and women said it was a bad thing for any woman from that country to come to this conference because they would only be entangled in politics. Now, I am going to promise to you that I am sure the women of the National League of Women Voters will treat you with great tolerance as a respect to you; but I confess, so far as I am personally concerned, I am going to entangle you if I can. (Applause and laughter)

You are going to need education. You are going to need laws, you are going to need greater freedom, as your countries have greater population and pass from the agricultural to the industrial stages, and you can do a great deal more with the vote than you can without it, and you will find that men and women give you a great deal more respect when you have the vote than when you have not got it. (Applause and laughter)

Source: Excerpts from the Proceedings of the Pan–American Conference. LWV Papers on film, II. A.3. 0949–57.

As the nearly weeklong Pan–American Conference of Women came to an end, delegates turned their attention to the business of the convention. The debate over program and focus continued. Lucy Miller of

Pennsylvania took up the cudgel on behalf of a shorter program of political education, leaving the cause of social reform to others. Carrie Catt took still a slightly different view, again arguing that the League not equate the achievement of social work objectives with political work.

DOCUMENT 4: CARRIE CHAPMAN CATT ON THE LEAGUE MISSION

When the League of Women Voters was brought into existence, I had one thought in my mind. I did not say it to you. That was that if the League was to go on and function with value that it ought to have its own initiative and it ought to develop and move in its own direction, and I was particularly anxious that it should be entirely divorced from the old suffrage association so that no one could say that it was being run by the old suffrage board or the old suffrage leaders.

The Convention was very kind and courteous and, without consulting me, made me an honorary president. I protested, but it was again given to me at the second convention, with a vote.

Now, you can bear me out when I say that I have never voted. I have not done so because I did not by so much as a single vote on the Board wish to affect the policy of the League of Women Voters.

I have determined not to use what little influence I might have to balance any question one way or another.

I do not know whether any of you have noticed it, but I have been very quiet and well–behaved notwithstanding. . . .

The average person who knows about the League of Women Voters knows it is an organization that helped in the maternity bill; they know that it has stood for social hygiene and for social questions a great deal more than political activities. That is the point that I make as my sole objection. . . .

I do not agree with those who say that social hygiene and social welfare are training for citizenship. I don't believe that getting rid of venereal disease is any more of a quality of good citizenship than getting rid of tuberculosis or a hundred other things that we can get.   But that is for the convention to decide. . . .

Now, to my mind, there is this that no one in the League of Women Voters should ever forget. I heard someone say that if any committee of the League should be dropped someone else would come along to do the work, but there is no other political party or organization to do the political work, and I for one regret that even in this convention where the time has of necessity been so shortened because of the many foreign delegates and other things that have entered into it, I regret that so much time has had to be given to reports adopted in other conventions, and we have had no time to discuss whether there is any way in which we as a whole can elect more women to the courts and to the legislatures. I regret that there has been no opportunity for free and frank and resolute discussion as to how the women may more effectually influence political parties for good and I can name many other questions which, it seems to me, belong to this amendment and have not been discussed here because there have been so many other things that have taken their place. . . .

Now, dear girls (laughter), we have a difference of opinion, not a very wide one, but somebody asked me something about a faction. I was entirely unaware of any faction in the National League of Women Voters. I say we have a little difference of opinion, that some of us think we ought to do a little more political work, and some of us think we ought to do a little more social work. Don't any of you who want political work go home disgruntled and say you won't work for the League any more. Don't any of you who want social work go home and quit working. . . .

Now, the Convention has adopted this program. Let us be loyal to the League of Women Voters, each and every one of us, and then let us work and work very very hard. I am going to, but don't go and try to change the policy of the League if it doesn't suit you. It is not a good idea to bring a motion just at the last minute and expect it to go through without proper consideration. But it is proper for you to go home and prove in your own state that you are ready to carry out the policy of the League and that your idea as to its policy, whether it be the political policy or the social policy, is right and the only way you can prove it is right is by doing better work in your state than any other state is doing. (Applause)

THE PRESIDENT: The Chair has known that there was unanimous consent for the breaking of all rules of time limits when the Honorary President was speaking. She did not have to ask that, she knew it. (Applause)

The Chair wants to say one word more and that is if this organization does not try to live up to its founders it is a mighty shame to every one of us.

Source: Excerpts from the Proceedings of the Third Convention. LWV Papers on film. II. A.3. 0340–48.

Maud Wood Park's presidential address took issue with Carrie Catt's preference to concentrate on the machinery of government and rejected her proposal to join with men in a progressive bloc of American voters.

DOCUMENT 5: MAUD WOOD PARK'S PRESIDENTIAL ADDRESS

Today we turn to the problems of our own organization and ask ourselves what we have been doing and what we ought to do hereafter to be worthy of our place in the world's sisterhood of earnest, thoughtful women. (Applause) The idea that I should like to put before you as a guide for our own deliberations is stated in the motto printed on the Convention program: "The education of citizens is the safeguard of a republic." . . . Because this government by the people was founded to bring about the safety and happiness of the citizens through a political system clean, efficient and just, and because the women of the United States have at this time a peculiar opportunity given by their recent enfranchisement to help in the full realization of this great ideal, we are banded together to do our part. That faith I take to be the cornerstone of the League of Women Voters.

This faith must rest upon three convictions. The first of these is the belief that whenever a majority of the voters are intelligently and actively interested in public affairs, good government is assured for the reason that good government is plainly to the advantage of the vast majority of men and women. Therefore, anything and everything that tends to arouse and sustain public interest in public affairs, to bring about intelligent consideration of public questions, and to stimulate activity in our common concerns is so much to the good.

Our second conviction is that women are particularly able to help at this time, not because they have a monopoly of wisdom or virtue—we know better than that—but because owing to the enfranchisement of approximately twenty millions of them as potential new voters, there is the greatest opportunity that this country or any other has ever known to train to the activities of good citizenship on enormous number of persons who, on the whole, are well meaning and realize that they have much to learn. . . .

Women as voters are in the first flush of youth. Youth is ordinarily the period of enthusiasm, and enthusiasm can sometimes leap over obstacles that laborious care has been unable to remove. Perhaps that is why we are so hopeful about what we can do. At any rate, our belief in our possibilities, whether wholly justified or not, is a tremendous advantage now.

The third conviction upon which our faith rests is that women have a contribution all their own to make to public affairs. They are not going to help much if they merely learn the political wisdom of men and repeat it parrot–like. If that is all they can do, they only double votes without affecting the equation of results.

Men have done and are doing their part to solve public problems chiefly on the basis of their distinctive experience in the economic world. The conduct of large business affairs is almost wholly in the hands of men and men make up the greater number of wage earners outside the household. Naturally, therefore, and properly, men have the viewpoint of business interest. And that is an important and necessary viewpoint—but it isn't the only one.

Women by virtue of their distinctive experience in life have a tendency to see affairs of government in such terms as education, public health, public morals—the human development made possible by a peace-loving and a forward-looking civilization. This is the point of view of social welfare, and it should be reckoned with quite as fully as should the point of view of business interest.

I do not mean that the business viewpoint should no longer be considered now that women have votes. Proper respect for business experience is essential if we are to be a prosperous nation; but we shall be a better and happier nation when equal respect is given to that half of the people who know best how to care for human life. The needed adjustment between the two tendencies is far more likely to be brought about if women voters are mindful of their own experience and firm in seeing that it has due weight in public affairs.

Heretofore women have had to make the best of things governmental: now they have a chance to make those things better and they should not permit themselves to be set aside as contributors to the common weal either by the authority of men's experience or by undue humility on their part. . . .

If we believe that women have a special service to perform in bringing their distinctive viewpoint to bear upon the problems of democracy, it is evidently not enough for the League to devote itself wholly to proposed improvements in governmental machinery, as we are sometimes urged to do. Efficient governmental machinery can do much to bring about results, but efficient machinery alone may be a profound menace. The purposes for which the machinery is to be used are more important than the machine itself. Obviously, efficiency in government is one thing for despotism and something quite different for a democracy. This generation has seen what was probably the most efficient governmental machinery the world has ever known grinding out incalculable disaster to itself and to civilization because it was used to further the ambitions of a small group of leaders. In the last analysis, that efficient machine turned out as its product the supreme inefficiency of world–wide war. Let us remember that fact and be careful to distinguish between seeming and actual efficiency in government.

The latter demands not only good machinery but the material of a developed social consciousness if we are to have the right sort of output. That is why we set before our members social standards by which that output may be tested, and why our committees on social welfare are a necessary part of our program. No voter is properly trained for citizenship who lacks comprehension of measures in behalf of child welfare, education, the protection of girls in industry, social hygiene, a reasonable solution of the problems involved in the cost of living, and the simple justice of the removal of unfair discriminations against women. No citizen is trained in citizenship who is not eager to promote every honorable means whereby abiding peace may be secured.

Moreover, there is no better way of learning about the existing practices of government than by working in a legislative body for an urgently needed measure or by following processes by which that measure is enforced. . . .

It is true that the very extent of our work sometimes makes it seem to the casual observer to lack unity. "You are doing so many things that I find it hard to tell what you really are doing," says one kindly critic. "You need to devote yourselves to a single splendid undertaking," says another, who adds that our extremely well–organized organization is "All dressed up with no place to go."

Her comment would have been more apt is she had said all dressed up with too many places to go; for our real danger is not in lack of outlets for the enthusiasm of our members but rather in the multiplicity of opportunities for their efforts. Only by a wisely chosen and carefully followed program, with provision for concentration on one piece of work at a time, can we avoid that danger. If we do choose with wisdom the most important next step, we shall find that the other needs group themselves in proper order as we go on.

We shall find, too, that the variety in our work is a strength rather than a weakness to the organization provided we do not forget the goal to which all our efforts are tending—the goal of workable and working democracy. With that end always in mind, we shall not lack unity of purpose which is the only unity that really counts.

Moreover, the differences in methods will go far to save us from that most dangerous of all pitfalls to the enthusiast, faith in a universal panacea, a royal road to good government, a system that can be trusted to work itself. From the beginning the League of Women Voters has been spared much bitterness of spirit by its tacit admission that no one change or reform can bring about the complete realization of the democratic ideal. . . .

If we may assume that our chief work is not primarily the promotion of a special measure or measures but rather the awakening of the average citizen to active interest in the duties of citizenship, is there any way in which we can estimate our task?

Sometimes I like to compute it arithmetically, by reckoning that of the estimated twenty-five millions of potential women voters, surely fifteen millions can be made alert to the dignity and importance of the opportunity that enfranchisement has brought. If that is really done and fifteen million women set to work, I have no doubt of their making sure enough to enlist the interest and help of at least ten millions of men voters. . . . Let no one suppose that I am advising the formation of a new party or the support of any particular set of political opinion. What we want and need is a majority of citizens who are willing and able to form their own opinions and to support them with acts.

Is it an impossible task to secure this majority? It is doubtless hard, but it should not be impossible, particularly when we remember that we are not alone in the effort. . . . All these together make up a good force already enlisted in the cause of good citizenship.

Of course we have and shall continue to have opponents. The group most in evidence likes to voice itself in loud denunciation of the League and its members. To tell the truth, I do not give much weight to that sort of opposition. When it is due to honest misunderstanding of our purposes, it is bound to be temporary. . . .

But there is a kind of opposition that will never be done away with, that will grow as our strength increases; that is the covert but extremely bitter opposition of those who have personal ends to serve such as our doctrine of good citizenship. . . .

Wherever the self-seeker is looking for an opportunity to advance his own interests at the expense of others, whether they be interests of politics, of commerce or vice, he or she will know that we are standing in the way of such illegitimate advancement; and that fact will be resented. We shall be fought secretly with all manner of false statements; attempts will be made to create misunderstanding and dissension in our ranks; articles belittling our work will be bought and paid for in the press; a systematic campaign will be carried on to prejudice against us—persons in high places who are not familiar with what we are doing.

We should not deceive ourselves about these hostile forces. They will be powerful and persistent and we may not, if we would, fight them with weapons like their own. We have only our sincerity of purpose and our loyalty to one another with which to ward off our attacks. But if we do have sincerity and loyalty, we need not fear. . . .

By far the most serious of our opponents is the colossal inertia of large numbers of persons. If this nation ever faces final disaster, it will be because what "is everybody's business is nobody's business except the self-seekers." We need to rewrite the old adage and to supplant the age long experience that gives it authority in order that what is everybody's business may indeed be everybody's business, because when that happens everybody's needs will be seen to. In this respect ours is a stupendous undertaking, for inertia is a thoroughly uninteresting opponent. Thrills do not come easily in a struggle against sheer dead weight, but that weight must be moved if we are to succeed.

Have we the courage to try and to keep on trying? Our entire history as an organization will be forecast by our answer to that question. If we have the courage to try, we do not need genius or even extraordinary qualities in order to succeed. All that we shall require is steadfast faith in democracy, common sense and persistence. No two of these requisites without the third are enough. But if we have all three—and keep them together—we are invincible. (Long sustained applause)

Source: Excerpts from the Proceedings of the Third Convention. LWV Papers on film, II. A.3. 0450–63.

In an effort to clarify the process and the respective roles of the Leagues, the delegates, and the national board, Park made these illuminating comments.

DOCUMENT 6: MAUD WOOD PARK ON THE CONVENTION PROCESS

Now, in general, about the business of this convention let me say this: You are the absolute authority in matters coming before the National League of Women Voters. Between conventions the Board of Directors has power to act upon the methods of carrying out recommendations of the convention. The Board of Directors is not entitled ever to formulate your policy; you have that authority, you are the authority; you are the government of the National League of Women Voters. Your vote determines what our plans and policies shall be for the coming year; the Board of Directors suggests programs of work; the standing committees suggest programs of work, but this convention is the final authority; you are the supreme court and the whole law–making body in one; there is no appeal from your decisions. The Board of Directors has no authority to act contrary to your decisions upon any matter; it has authority to carry out your decisions to the best of its ability. That means that you must carefully consider what decisions you give in this convention and then you must be willing to abide by the majority vote of the convention or by the two-thirds vote, if it is a matter that a two–thirds majority is required on; that is, you cannot take action in this convention and then wonder why the Board of Directors tries to carry out that action. You have given a mandate to the Board of Directors and the Board of Directors has no authority—that is if it is an honorable body—except to do its utmost to carry out that mandate. Is that clear?

It is pretty hard for the majority of human beings to learn esprit de corps. I think this body of the National League of Women Voters has developed a very remarkable esprit de corps, but frequently I find some misunderstanding person who has not read her copy of the minutes of the convention. I have no doubt that the incoming board will endeavor to do as much to carry out the mandates of this convention as the outgoing board has tried to do with respect to the policies and mandates of the last convention; you can call the board to account if they do not carry out your wishes, but you cannot hold anybody except yourselves responsible for the policy of this association. (Applause)

Source: Excerpts from the Proceedings of the Third Convention. LWV Papers on film, II. A.2. 0669–74.

A special committee had been convened to address the vexing issues relating to the League's programmatic philosophy and focus and to a number of operational measures as well. National board member, Belle Sherwin, served as chair, and Lucy Miller's membership on that committee gave her an opportunity to express her opinions in support of a narrower definition of political education.   In the process, Miller's view did not prevail, and her fellow Pennsylvanians continued to dissent from the commitment to the broader concept held by the majority of League members. As the convention debate continued, President Park felt obliged to comment.

DOCUMENT 7: MAUD WOOD PARK ON DIFFERENCES OF OPINION

The Chair wishes to take a few moments to say a few words. I find there are a few members of the convention who are distressed because we have differences of opinion. I should feel distressed if we did not have now and then these highly proper differences of opinion. Everybody here should have definite views as to what the organization ought to do and if these views are carried out in the votes of the organization, if these views are your views truly and honestly, then you should work by every fair means to make your opinions prevail. You are good League of Women Voters when you do that whether your opinion is the opinion of anyone else or not. What we ought to do, not only as good citizens but also as good members of the League is to be willing to abide by the decision of the majority, whatever that may be. Let us take our case and cheerfully accept the decision of the convention and then if that decision is not mine, I will try to work and have my opinion prevail next year, but in the interval I will try to abide by yours. That is the only way to train for citizenship in a country which is living under such a constitution as we live under.... Some one approached me in the elevator on the way up this afternoon and ... they asked me if I did not think that we women wasted a good deal more time than the men did in talking about what we were going to do. I replied that after having sat for a good many years in the gallery of the United States Congress I felt we were remarkably expeditious.

Source: Excerpts from the Proceedings of the Third Convention. LWV Papers on film, III. A.3. 0303–4. See Chapter 5 for the essence of the Miller argument.

Chapter 7

"An Every Woman's Organization"

The League scored impressive legislative victories in its first four years, among them the Sheppard-Towner Act, legislation providing safe food and milk supplies, civil service classification reform, and the establishment of the Women's Bureau. With the passage of the Cable Act in 1922, the League advanced citizenship rights for women. In 1907 Congress had passed legislation depriving American women—but not men—of their citizenship if they married foreign nationals. At its first convention in 1920, the LWV submitted to the platform committees of the Republican and Democratic parties (as well as the Prohibitionist and Farmer-Labor parties) a plank to rectify this inequity, and it was adopted by all four parties. In her subsequent testimony before a congressional committee, Maud Wood Park said, "A woman is as much an individual as a man is, and her citizenship should no more be gained or lost by marriage than should a man's." The Congress concurred and when the bill passed the House in 1922, Representative John Cable (R., OH) gave full credit to the League for securing its passage by a large majority, stating, "It was because of your ability and wisdom that the independent citizenship bill was reported out of committee, and because of your active interest and support and that of the National League of Women Voters that the vote stood 206 in favor of the bill and but nine against. You have my sincere appreciation and also respect for your ability in undertaking and carrying out the work you are now doing as President of the National League of Women Voters, as well as in securing the passage of the bill yesterday."

The Cable Act became law with the signature of Warren G. Harding in September 1922. In a speech to delegates at the Des Moines convention in 1923, Minnie Fisher Cunningham described the League's role and that of Maud Wood Park in the Cable Bill victory.

DOCUMENT 1: MINNIE FISHER CUNNINGHAM ON THE CABLE BILL

I will try to give you a history of that Cable Bill which was the most dramatic and wonderful piece of legislation from two standpoints. One of these was the gratifying, glorious fact that it was over—the removal of the greatest discrimination of women after the suffrage bill was passed. The other one was that when it got underway, the Cable Bill became the winner of the blue ribbon for speed in passage over any piece of women's legislation I have ever known anything about. . . .

So she [Maud Wood Park] came to Washington, in the heat of August, looked over Congress, saw various people about the Cable Bill and they all said, "We can do nothing about the Cable Bill until the Bonus Bill is passed."

Then, she continued to go to see important and influential people and I was privileged to go with her. She would go to see a member of a committee and the gentleman in charge of the work would tell us to sit down, and then he would say, "We are interested in that legislation; you have really converted me to it and as soon as we get around to it we are going to pass the Cable Bill, but—but I have a few words I wish to say on the Bonus Legislation. My mind is on that."

Then he made that speech, which he was going to make on the floor of the Senate, to Mrs. Park. She listened to every word of it, with the utmost interest, and a smile, and then she said, "Yes, Senator, but"—and then I knew it was going through. When she had finished, he said, "Well, I do not think we can get a quorum of the Committee because it takes 6 and I believe only 6 are in town and I am not sure they will all be favorable, and even if they are I do not believe in this hot weather you can get men together for Committee meetings—I do not believe it can be done, Mrs. Park." And Mrs. Park said, "Well, would you like us to help you get the Committee together, Senator?"

He looked a little surprised and then he said, "Yes, anything you can do for us will be appreciated! We will have our Committee meeting on Tuesday (or Wednesday morning, or whatever it was), and you can see if you can get the gentlemen to come." So Mrs. Park called up a few of her assistants and she said. "You are responsible for so and so, and you are responsible for so and so," and she said, "It is hot weather but they must come to that committee meeting," and they came.

There were six of them and they all came to the Committee and voted favorably. That is to say, in the end they voted favorably. Mrs. Park sat on a bench outside of the door and checked them off as they came in, and if your man did not come in, woe unto you, for you had better have had him in the first place, because you had to have him there in the last place. Mine was a gentleman who was so busy that no one dared to ask anything of him, but I went meekly to his office and asked would he please come and go to the committee meeting.

Then it came up in the Senate. There was an adjournment meeting. The Bill had to lay over to another day, and all had to be done over again. Finally, however, it did go through the Senate and it was passed without any amendments, which were bad for it, to keep it from passing in the House. Then it went from the Senate. We thought it went straight to the President, but you learn things all the time about legislation in Washington.

It did not go straight to the President at all. We had to find out where it did go. Finally we learned that it was proper to refer it to the departments which were affected by it. We found it had to be referred to two departments: the Department of Labor because the Immigration Laws were affected by it; the Department of State was affected by it because of the passports and international relations.

It went to one and was forgotten, and was rapidly approaching the day when Congress would adjourn. Mr. Cable was as anxious about it as we were. He is running for office in his state and he wanted to find the Bill and get it decided before he went back home to his constituents.

Mrs. Park was called away and charged us with seeing that the Bill was signed before Congress adjourned, and we were more than anxious that it should be, so we began chasing around, looking for the Bill. We had everybody else chasing around, too, and trying to find out why it was tarrying.

I will never forget Mr. Cable's anxiety about his Bill. He would call up the League's headquarters 6 times a day, asking what progress we were making or reporting something. And one time he said, "The Parliamentarian for the Senate says, 'All right, not to be signed before Congress adjourns,' but, Gee Christmas, I don't believe him. I think it should be signed, now—because, Gee Christmas, it has to be signed before I go home to Ohio."

It was signed one morning when Miss Sherwin was having a meeting. Mr. Cable had his picture taken with the Bill. We were all so happy about it and then he took his pen in hand and wrote a letter to Mrs. Park, telling her of the wonderful achievement—and it was one of the most wonderful achievements; and to express to Mrs. Park his great appreciation for helping to pass the Cable Bill, he presented the pen to Mrs. Park.

I had the privilege of presenting it to her in Boston. We had our pictures taken while I was holding the pen in my hand, presenting it to Mrs. Park. Miss Sherwin was there and she said, "Mercy Mrs. Park, please smile, you look like Edward Everett Hale at the Boston Tea Party."

Source: Betty Goetz Lall, The Foreign Policy of the League of Women Voters of the United States: Methods of influencing Government Action, Effects on Public Opinion and Evaluation of Results. Ph.D. dissertation, University of Minnesota, 1964, 212, 220–21. Statement of Mrs. Maud Wood Park, Hearings before the Committee on Immigration and Naturalization, House of Representatives, 67th Cong, 2nd Sess., June 8, 1922, 570. Rep. John Cable to Maud Wood Park, June 21, 1922, LWV Papers on film, I. A.1. 0350. Minnie Fisher Cunningham, Excerpts from remarks, Fourth National Convention, Des Moines, IA, 1923. LWV Papers on film, 11. A.5. 0119–26.

It was ironic that at the League's Fourth National Convention in Des Moines, Iowa, the state's most famous native daughter, Carrie Chapman Catt, was not there, her absence, as a press release made clear, being due to an extended lecture tour in South America. Her tour resulted from Catt's promise in the previous year at the Pan- American Conference of Women to help the women of that continent.

DOCUMENT 2: PRESS RELEASE ON 1923 LEAGUE CONVENTION

The 4th annual convention of the National League of Women Voters will bring women from all parts of the country to Des Moines on April 9th, and it is expected that women from the West will play a larger part in the deliberations than ever before. League leaders are delighted that Iowa is to play host for 1923 for Iowa bulks large in the history of the woman movement. Mrs. Carrie Chapman Catt came out of Iowa to lead the suffrage cause to victory. . . .

By common consent the veteran suffrage leader is ranked as the greatest American woman, and the National League of Women Voters is largely her idea. She felt the need of women for political education and for higher ideals of citizenship and the League was organized to work for these ends. Since its organization in Chicago in 1920 it has enrolled 2 million women in 45 states, has secured the passage of innumerable laws for the betterment of the condition of women and children and for the general good.

It is the conviction of Mrs. Maud Wood Park, president, that for many years women will be interested chiefly in such legislation. The League does not credit women with superhuman wisdom. It seeks only to put to public use the special knowledge age-old experience has given them. Just now Mrs. Park says there are few women who can be of assistance in solving great National problems— the tariff, the labor question, for examples—but there are millions of clear thinking women who can help secure better schools, better working conditions for women and children, better care for defectives and delinquents for these are matters in which they have special experience.

Mrs. Park will preside at the convention and it is thought that Mrs. Catt, honorary president, will not end her lecture tour of South America early enough to be present. The convention will be chiefly a "work" convention. The League is an efficient and practical organization which carries out its plans after due deliberation and is not be lead astray by sentiment. Its organization is efficiency itself. The 48 states are divided into seven regions with a regional director to consult with state leaders and coordinate the work so that there shall be concerted action for the same end everywhere. The seven divisions of League work, child welfare, social hygiene, women in industry, uniform laws, living costs, education and international cooperation to prevent war, are in charge of National Standing Committee Chairmen, and their departments for such work as efficiency in government and training in citizenship, with a publication department and a wonderful managed speakers' bureau.

The League is not out to put women in office and it is not a woman's party. It will work for the election of qualified women for office and it wishes to see qualified women on school boards and commissions but its numbers will not support any woman merely because she is a woman.

"Women in Office," says Mrs. Park, "will for some years be judged by a standard of perfection. Men are judged merely by the average their predecessors have maintained. For this reason we must have the best women for office, not merely the woman who 'will do.' Good government is our aim, not the advantage of women merely because they are women."

The League urges every woman to enroll in a political party and to be active in it.

The League Program, in short, is a thing all thinking women can heartily approve whether they were formerly suffragists or not.

Source: LWV Papers on film, II. A.4. 0470–71.

In her presidential speech Maud Wood Park chose not to read the prepared text of her address. Consequently, her remarks were far less formal and far more amusing but still informative. Because her printed text included more references to the League's substantive program, emphasizing international cooperation, the control of child labor, and the need for "a campaign for effective citizenship," establishing ambitious goals for an increased voter turnout in the 1924 presidential election, excerpts from the prepared text are also included. In her conclusion to both speeches, Park expressed her concern that the League not be an organization for "experts who do remarkable things brilliantly" but should be representative of "men and women in every walk of life." Quoting one of our "wisest members," Park asserted that the League should be "an every woman's organization."

DOCUMENT 3: MAUD WOOD PARK'S 1923 SPOKEN PRESIDENTIAL ADDRESS

PRESIDENT PARK: Madam Chairman, gentlemen and ladies. (Laughter)

I don't know that the delegates to this Convention have yet been informed of everything that is expected of them. I was not aware myself of quite all the contract we were under, until our Press clippings a few days ago brought in a syndicated press article, which has evidently gone all across the country, and which predicts what is going to happen at this Convention. It carries the pictures of the Nominating Committee, and the article is headed, "Women arrange a fine, fancy Feminism fight." Just think of all that alliteration. Then the article goes on to tell us, and since it gave me a great deal of information, I will repeat that information to you. It goes on to tell us what we are expected to fight about.

First, whether to maintain aggressively the line of cleavage that has separated the suffrage activities of the League from those of the National Women's Party. (Laughter)

Second, whether to give official organization standing to the League of Nations.

Third, what part the organization shall play in the movement for international cooperation to prevent war.

Fourth, whether the organization shall hereafter specifically endorse candidates for public office. In addition to those issues, concerning which there already is much palpitation in League circles, there seems certain to develop a fine factional fight over the election of the seven Regional Directors. However, there are also to be elected two Vice-Presidents and a Treasurer."

Then the article adds a little despondently, "Mrs. Maud Wood Park holds office for one year more." (Laughter) . . .

Now, I never have claimed any particular gift of prophecy, but I want to make one prediction, and at the end of the Convention, I want you to decide whether the writer of that article, or the present speaker is the better prophet. What I predict for this Convention is that we shall have frank, fair, friendly freedom of speech and of action. (Applause)

Now, there has been another press clipping that I have seen of late that has attempted to make a partial prophecy with regard to the League of Women Voters, and that statement I should like to analyze a little more seriously with you. In a Sunday full-page article, printed in one of the New York papers recently, there was a record of the history of the New York State and City League of Women Voters during the three years of its existence, and that history reported the struggles that the League had had, and the obstacles that it had overcome, and then it ended with this query: "The League of Women Voters has weathered adversity. How will it bear prosperity?" . . .

There was a time when always in Republican States we were held to be a Democratic organization, and always in Democratic States we were held to be a Republican organization. I said two years ago, in my first annual talk to the League that I believed. . . that kind of an argument against us was the best possible proof that we were steering an even, unpartisan course—we, who are composed of the women of all political parties. . . .

I suspect that as time goes by the average citizen will find out about us what we firmly know about ourselves, that we are neither reactionary nor radical that we are advancing firmly, steadily, straight–forward, along that middle road of which we believe means sane and orderly progress towards the realization of the great ideal of our nation. (Applause)

Source: Excerpts from the Proceedings of the Fourth Annual Convention of the National League of Women Voters (hereinafter referred to as the Fourth Convention), Des Moines, IA, April 9–14, 1923. LWV Papers on film, II. A.5. 0857–64.

DOCUMENT 4: MAUD WOOD PARK'S 1923 WRITTEN PRESIDENTIAL ADDRESS

"The most powerful factors in the world today are clear ideas in the minds of energetic men and women of good will."

The Convention as a Mirror

I believe the chief use of the president's address is to hold up a mirror in which the larger aspects of the work are sharply outlined. What have we been doing this past year? How far have we gone toward carrying out our purpose to aid women in making intelligent and helpful use of their votes? What do we need to do more or differently? These are the questions that the Convention must answer.

Essentials of Useful Citizenship

As a standard of measurement, I propose to take the words on the cover of your programs, "The most powerful factors in the world today are clear ideas in the minds of energetic men and women of good will." This quotation is really a summary of the essentials of useful citizenship, which are good will, clear ideas, and energy; and it is quite worth our while with these ends in view to take reckoning once more of ourselves and our activities as an organization.

To begin with, I believe that we may take the element of good will for granted. Otherwise it would be hard to explain why the organization has members at all, since the only inducement it offers is the opportunity for hard work, not for personal ends, but for public service. In respect to good will I doubt that we differ much from the great majority of our fellow citizens. Men and women everywhere and in great numbers mean well. The trouble is that most of us never get beyond that point in our relation to government, or to any other set of duties that life thrusts upon us. Good will is an excellent starting point but no more.

What we chiefly need to concern ourselves with is, first, the clearness of our ideas and, second, the energy with which we carry them out.

Three Definite Ideas

I think that if we analyze our work we shall find it grouped around three perfectly definite ideas. The first, briefly stated, is this: if government by the people is to mean efficient government, the average citizen must be interested enough to vote at all elections in accordance with the best information that he or she can get. The second recognizes that women, in addition to their general duties as voters, have special responsibilities in regard to public provision for the welfare of children and the home and for adequate protection for women in industry, together with fair opportunity for all women under the law. The third affirms that since peace is essential to the orderly progress of civilization, the establishment of some international means of preventing war is a fundamental concern of the United States and all other nations.

When I wrote that sentence, not so long ago, I thought that was a very moderate statement. Within the last few days I have come to believe that it is almost a revolutionary remark, because of the curious propaganda that has been going across this country from one end to the other, tending to confuse the mind and seeming to prove, in its extraordinary manifestations, that anybody who believes in sane and reasonable methods of preventing war is trying to leave our country defenseless against force, and thus to undermine the Republic.

We want no revolutionary government. We have no desire to proceed along the path of progress by any except evolutionary methods, but we do claim the right that every American citizen has—we should claim it for ourselves and for other organizations—we claim the right to spread our opinions under the American guarantee of free speech.

We do not expect to be called traitors when we say that we believe if civilization has any sense at all, it will use its best resources against another breakdown of civilization such as the World War was.

All the other ideas in the League's plans and programs are but corollaries of the three just mentioned, or expansions of them. Take, for example, the thousands of citizenship schools which the League has arranged, some of them in great universities, others at crossroads—the courses of study in the principles and practices of government, national, state or city, the institutes on efficiency in government arranged for the discussion of admitted defects in governmental machinery and proposed remedies, the digests of state election laws, the handbooks and manuals of state and city affairs, the questionnaires to candidates for public office which the state and local Leagues have sent out, the all partisan pre-election meetings which they have carried on, together with the efforts made to give practical details about time and place and qualifications for registration and voting and the proper legal marking and folding of a ballot—all these are but details to meet the requirements of that idea of ours about the primary duties of citizenship.

Our belief in regard to the special responsibility of women is illustrated in every one of the programs of our standing committees which were established as far back as the St. Louis convention before the League was an independent body. The idea is illustrated, too, in the bulk of our legislative work in state and nation, and in all the efforts that our members make to have a reasonable number of properly qualified women in party and public positions of trust.

In a similar way the efforts of the League to strengthen and make articulate public opinion in support of the Conference for the Reduction of Armaments, our study courses, the Pan–American Conference of Women at Baltimore, the round table discussions and the public meetings which the League has arranged in order to bring about a general understanding of international problems and through that better understanding to help in developing effective means of international cooperation to prevent war—these are all corollaries of our idea about the importance of international friendliness.

No one should suppose that we think our fundamental ideas are in any way novel or the exclusive possession of the League. The only novelty is that the League tries to carry them out. That is the reason why I consider energy the most important of the three essentials named in our convention motto and why I want to speak in detail of ways in which we may further develop that energy in well doing, directed by common sense which is one of the rarest and most valuable qualifications of human beings.

Special Work at Special Times

If energy is to be wisely used it must be directed to special work at special times. During the coming year, for example, the work should be planned with reference to the facts that legislatures will be meeting in only a few states, that the Congress will not convene until December unless an extraordinary session is called, that the presidential election is ahead, and that many local elections are to be held. For these reasons it is a year in which local affairs should be particularly stressed.

Law Enforcement

I therefore urge that special attention be given to intelligent preparation for local elections and that study should be made of the local enforcement of laws for which the League has worked. These include six federal measures and many state laws. Together they make an impressive number of legislative achievements, but if they prove to be like many other laws, forgotten almost as soon as they are entered in the statute books, the list might better be called a list of failures. Unless the League is willing to make sure that the laws which it has mothered are carried out, we shall have done harm rather than good in our legislative work because every neglected statute is one more contribution to a widespread menace in the United States today—the lawlessness of individuals and of mobs. Whether this lawlessness be the result of self indulgence on the part of average citizens, or of inefficiency or venality on the part of officials, whether it be flippant or deliberately ferocious, it means the breakdown of orderly government. That any citizen of the United States should tolerate in this day the rule of masked mobs, much less join in their iniquitous proceedings, seems incredible. Yet the facts show that considerable numbers of citizens in various parts of the country are upholding this grim menace. If, therefore, the most terrifying manifestations of American tendency to lawlessness are to be stopped, we shall need to foster much more responsibility for law as law than we now have. Efficient citizenship demands the average citizen's obedience to the law whether he likes it or not, and I might add that the obligation to obey is not lessened even in the case of laws which he is doing his best to have repealed.

There is no better way in which the League of Women Voters can help to establish respect for law than by taking thought of the way ill which laws that the League has worked for are being carried out. I therefore hope most earnestly that the program of every state League will emphasize this duty and I suggest that three measures be chosen for special watchfulness in the community: first, the local administration of the Sheppard-Towner Act; second, a state law, educational, industrial, or sanitary, which the state league has sponsored; and, third, a city or town ordinance of importance to the well being of the community.

The advantages of such a plan will be two–fold. It will establish the connection between legislation and law enforcement and it will turn the attention of the League members to local conditions, in regard to which I believe that women have special aptitude for effective service. Furthermore, it will unify our activities throughout the country and thus give the added strength that comes from combined effort.

International Cooperation to Prevent War

The coming year is also one in which important decisions in regard to our relations with other countries are likely to be made. The close of the 67th Congress left without action the proposal for the entrance of the United States into the Permanent Court of International Justice, and also resolutions for an economic conference, and for the complete outlawry of war. The kind of international cooperation needed to prevent war is a fundamental concern of the United States and all other countries, and the members of the League of Women Voters should take great pains to inform themselves upon these important issues in order intelligently to support the methods that seem wisest. I shall not go into the plans that are proposed for this purpose. They have special emphasis in the program of the Convention, but I cannot express too earnestly my own conviction that the coming year is the time for extraordinary effort toward the establishment of abiding peace.

Child Labor

Another proposal, which will come up in the next Congress, is the constitutional amendment to permit the Congress to make laws in regard to child labor. This subject also is a timely one for present study as a basis for future action.

Campaign for Efficient Citizenship

For our further work, a work which will require all the energy we can muster, all the clear ideas we can bring to bear upon it and all the good will we can feel and foster, I urge a campaign for efficient citizenship in its primary phase, the performance of the duty of voting in all elections in accordance with the best information which can be obtained. . . .

Suppose that we were to seek the irreducible minimum of the successful working out of democracy. It would certainly be the requirement that at least a majority of persons eligible should care enough about the government to vote when they have an opportunity. Judged by that standard the United States today is still unsuccessful as a government by the people, for in the last presidential election less than one–half the citizens of voting age took the trouble to vote.

That fact alone is a serious one, but when it is remembered that the presidential election brings out a considerably larger percentage of the potential vote than state or local elections, the situation is notably worse. . . .

If we are to be really a democracy, it is high time that we were about it, and the League of Women Voters can do no more important piece of work between now and the next national election than to set a goal of reasonable increase in the percentage of votes cast, make a definite and carefully thought-out plan for attaining that goal, and enlist the help of public-spirited men and women from one end of the United States to the other in carrying out the plan.

Suppose we set 75 per cent of the vote that could have been cast in 1920 as our goal in the presidential election of 1924. That means a gain of about 25 per cent. What must we do to reach that goal?

First of all, we must begin in time. That is why I am bringing up the subject a year and a half in advance of the election. If plans were left until the League's next convention, there would be no chance to get them under way in many states before the presidential primaries, and in states in which early payment of the poll tax is a prerequisite for voting, all efforts to increase the vote would be futile.

Second, we must make it plain that our campaign is not in the interest of any person or party, but is a straightforward effort to have all opinions counted.

Third, we must be ready with accurate figures, precinct by precinct, election district by election district, to show what the vote was in 1920 and what it should be in 1924 if at least 25 per cent is to be gained.

Fourth, we must enlist the help of the press, the churches, and as many other groups of public–spirited citizens as possible.

Fifth, we must urge them as well as ourselves to compare membership lists with lists of registered voters, and point out to members who have not registered the importance of doing so. I suspect that we shall have a good many surprises even in our own circles if we do the work thoroughly.

Sixth, we must continue to collect and give out in brief and simple form information about the qualifications of voters and the places and dates for registering and voting.

Seventh, we must gather and disseminate, as many of the Leagues have done in the past, unpartisan information about candidates themselves and their stand upon important issues, including candidates for the national party conventions.

Eighth, we must hold pre-election meetings, at which candidates of all parties can address voters of all parties and of no party.

Ninth, we must call attention, through press and pulpit, to the importance of election day and the need of kindly urging of neighbors and friends not to overlook the privilege which it offers.

Tenth, we must organize our forces precinct by precinct, street by street, and in crowded districts, block by block.

In other words, we must organize a campaign for active citizenship such as this country has never before known. We must "sell" the idea of voting to every possible voter. We must get out the vote. . . .

Don't be skeptical because what we are asking of the average citizen appears to be a small thing. If everybody did that much—or that little—we should have no occasion for worry over our national future. The success of democracy doesn't depend on a few persons who do great things, but upon many persons who do small things faithfully.

And don't be discouraged, because this campaign for efficient citizenship is really a very large undertaking. Nothing that I know of seems to bewilder men in public life more than the hard work that women are willing to do without any personal ends in mind. Again and again I am asked in Washington how it happens that so many women's organizations are interested in this, that, or the other public measure. Those men in whom public spirit is completely lacking, are always certain that the organization has a secret sinister motive, or that the individual women are paid huge salaries to enlist the support of other women, or else that they are in pursuit of public office. The newest explanation that I have heard is that of a senator who, having been obliged reluctantly to admit that no one of these previous statements was true, burst forth with the charge, "Well, they must all be neurotic. That is the only way you can account for them." The simple fact that he overlooked is the inspiration of working together for something that is bigger and more important than our personal interests.

The Vote and Human Relationships

The most thrilling thing about the League of Women Voters is that it helps its members to be useful in the largest series of human relationships to which women have been admitted, their relationship with their fellow citizens. Heretofore, women have known the intimate affection of family and friends, the pleasant intercourse of social groups, the comradeship of fellow workers in trade and profession, the fervor of religious faith shared with the members of their church, but important as all these are, no one of them reaches so wide or so far as the relationship to our fellow citizens which the vote brings and which extends through our fellow citizens in this nation to other lands and other peoples. That is why this League of ours is worth making big sacrifices for so long as it kindles in the hearts and minds of women the warmth and light and good cheer of conscious kinship in the common weal. . . .

An Every Woman's Organization

In that belief, I hope, for the future of the League of Women Voters—not that it will become a body of expert persons who do remarkable things brilliantly—but that it will continue to be in fact what one of our wisest members once called it, "an every woman's organization." There can never be any organization of citizens in this great country of ours worthy to continue unless that organization combines the experience and the wisdom and the practical common sense of women and men in every walk of life. For this reason we are now "an every woman's organization," and our future is assured so long as we hold to that fundamental purpose.

Source: Excerpts from the Proceedings of the Fourth Convention, April 1923. LWV Papers on film, II. A.5. 0524–32.

At the close of the convention, the League got into high gear to launch the 1924 Get Out the Vote campaign.

DOCUMENT 5: A CALL TO A CRUSADE

I call the League of Women Voters to a crusade, to set to work to restore democracy and to rouse the public to an understanding of the simple duty of every qualified voter to the community, the state, and the nation. I urge a campaign for efficient citizenship in its primary phase: the performance of the duty of voting in all elections in accordance with the best information which can be obtained.

Fewer than half—49%—of the eligible voters voted in the presidential election in 1920. In 1922, 33 states elected governors and only a little more than one-third of the possible voters cast their ballots. In primary and local elections, the percentage is often much lower.

We are ruled by a minority. This is not due to the less responsible citizens alone. It is a common failing of thousands of well-intentioned and well-informed men and women who excuse themselves on slight pretext from registering their good intentions and their knowledge in the only place in which they will count toward good government—the ballot box.

Every member of the League of Women Voters is called to a crusade to remedy this dangerous condition. If we are to be really a democracy, it is high time we were about it! Let us set a goal of reasonable increase in the percentage of votes cast, make a definite plan for attaining that goal, and enlist the help of public-spirited men and women from one end of the United States to the other in carrying out the plan.

Let us fix as our goal for 1924, 75% of the vote that could have been cast in 1920. That means a gain of about 25%. Then let us find what that actually means in the number of votes in our state, our county, our city or town, our ward, and our precinct. In other words, we must organize a campaign for active citizenship such as this country has never before known. We must "sell" the idea of voting to every possible voter.

It will be worth all the work that must be put into it and if successfully carried through, it will do more to make government by the people real than anything else which has been attempted, or can be attempted.

It can be done and it is up to us to do it.

Source: Excerpts from Maud Wood Park in the Proceedings of the Fourth Convention. LWV Papers on film, II. A.5. 0533.

DOCUMENT 6: SEVEN STEPS TO EFFICIENT CITIZENSHIP

*Get Out
the Vote*

7   Organize forces,
precinct by pre-
cinct, street by street—

6 Collect and give out
unpartisan information
on candidates and issues.

5   Hold pre-election
meetings and invite
all candidates to speak.

4   Collect and give out in—
formation on who may
vote and when and where.

3   Enlist help of press,
churches, individ—
uals, and organizations.

2   Use figures of last
election as basis for

1   work for 25% increase. Begin in time, by
work in local and primary elections

THERE ARE SEVEN STEEP STEPS
to the First Stage of Efficient Citizenship.
From 49 per cent of the possible voters in 1920
to 75 per cent of the possible voters in 1924

Source: LWV Papers on film, II. A.5. 0534.

As in 1920, the League again submitted planks to the Republican and Democratic parties in 1924. Interestingly, Eleanor Roosevelt chaired the committee for the Democrats "to consider planks of special interest to women."

DOCUMENT 7: LEAGUE PLATFORM PLANKS OF 1924

International Cooperation to Prevent War

Entry of the United States into the Permanent Court of International Justice; as the means of taking part in an established Court to which 47 Nations belong; as an important step in substituting law for force.

Participation in international conferences; to continue the policy initiated by the United States in the Conference on the Limitation of Armament.

Cooperation with international agencies; informal cooperation has already proved successful, as in the case of the Reparations Commission of 1924, therefore it should be made official.

Public Welfare in Government

Federal laws for the protection of children in industry following the passage and ratification of the Child Labor Amendment; as the means of securing to all children in their formative years freedom from labor and corresponding education.

Appropriations

For Vocational Education in Home Economics; as a means of increasing the efficiency in the home and reducing the high cost of living.

For the Women's Bureau in the Department of Labor; as the Government bureau organized to secure facts about the conditions under which women in industry work, and to show the relation of those facts tot he welfare of the nation; annual appropriation since 1920.

For the Children's Bureau in the Department of Labor; as the Government bureau created to make scientific studies of all that concerns the welfare of the children of the country; annual appropriations since 1912.

For the administration of the Maternity and Infancy Act: in order to continue the stimulation of appropriations in the states, to establish a program for the promotion of the welfare and hygiene of maternity and infancy; appropriations authorized 1922 to 1927.

Equalization of educational opportunity; for the purpose of reducing illiteracy and fitting children in every school district to meet the responsibilities of life; by the principle of Federal aid, an established and successful method in the field of education since 1862.

Removal of legal discrimination against women: by special measures not prejudicial to women's labor laws or to social welfare legislation. Any legislation for equal rights between men and women should be drawn with most careful consideration of each specific type of law involved, instead of attempting to deal with the subject by blanket legislation such as the so-called Equal Rights amendment.

Efficiency in Government

Merit system in the Federal civil service: as the means of appointing public officials because of proved ability and fitness rather than for personal or partisan reasons, by Act of Congress, 1883; should be extended to all the units of the service, as they are created by law, in order to secure efficient administration and enforcement of law; should be strengthened by legislation providing for new methods of personal administration as they are proved to be sound and constructive; should receive appropriations adequate to set up those methods.

Source: LWV Papers on film, II. A.7. 0315–16.

In an address to convention delegates the following year (but some months before the November 1924 elections), Minnie Fisher Cunningham, who had served as the League's Executive Secretary from 1921 to 1923 and was then Second Vice President in charge of organization, described some of the League's early experiences with candidates and the beginning of the League's well-known service to voters at election time.

DOCUMENT 8: MINNIE FISHER CUNNINGHAM ON VOTER EDUCATION

Now, another political aspect of our work is the work among candidates. That work has not been uniform throughout the United States. Different leagues have used different methods in doing their work with the candidates as they saw it in their field. There have been different phases in that work and some of those phases are endorsement of candidates and some are questionnaires. This is the most widely used method: Some meetings for all candidates, impartial non-partisan and meetings to which all candidates are invited, and a perfectly splendid method which was used in the 1922 election, particularly, was the impartial, non-partisan presentation of, first, the office itself, telling in a printed publication just exactly what the office to be filled was, what its salary was, what the duty of the office would be, how many appointive people were under that office and what its obligations in general were, and then on the opposite page giving the names of the men candidates to that office and as much of their background as the league cared to present on that subject in a completely, impartial manner as between candidate and candidate, but in an educational manner as regard to the office itself.

That, it seems to me, was one of the most magnificent pieces of work with candidates that I have ever seen wherever it was carried on, because it was to be placed in the hands of every voter and it was for them to take home and study at their leisure. Those other methods of working with candidates, I am not going to discuss because you are all more or less familiar with them, but just for a moment I am going to contrast the method of political parties with candidates. The business of a political party is to elect the candidate that they have nominated, and so, naturally, they are going to present that candidate in the most favorable light possible. And, I, for one have been, well in my earlier days I will say, much shocked in going to political conventions to see and hear men going around the convention halls saying perfectly terrible things about the candidates they were not supporting while they were saying glorifying things about the candidate they were supporting. When the candidate was nominated, to find that same individual standing in a chair and waving his hat and cheering his head off for that particular man, that is not the League of Women Voters' method with candidates.

Another one of the political phases of our work is elections. The work that we do with elections is tremendously interesting I do think. We do lots of things with elections. We study about them. We study about elections for the purpose of having election laws, for the purpose of having those who are on the statute books executed. Honestly, we study about them for the purpose of finding out what their defects are, and I think all of us admit that these election laws fall a shade below absolute perfection, too. Then we study about them to find ways of improving those election laws that are already on the statute books.

Then, we teach the mechanics of voting. We have demonstration classes to teach the mechanics of voting. When we get out the vote, we try to arrange way stations on the way, some time before the election, wherever one of these voters can come and find out how to mark the ballot, not who to mark it for, but how to vote it.

I remember teaching in a Citizenship School in one of the Northwestern states just before the 1920 election, and we invited a distinguished gentleman to come to us and talk about city government. That distinguished gentleman came with a large roll of papers, which we thought was about the city and the city government. I was presiding over the meeting, and I introduced him, and there were copies of the official ballot that they were going to vote on the next election day, and he was to tell them, not only how to vote, but how to vote for "A." He began on his list of preferred candidates, and I mentioned mildly that we wanted him to talk on city government. He said if he had known we wanted him to talk on city government, he would have come prepared to talk on that subject, but he wanted to tell these women how to vote, they were all there together and he could do it.

That is not the League of Women Voters' way of teaching voting. We teach how to vote, but not how to vote for "A," and that is a trifle different from the way the party organization has to do it, because, why a party organization? Why, for the purpose of putting the party over!

Source: Excerpts from the Proceedings of the Fifth Annual Convention of the National League of Women Voters (hereinafter referred to as the Fifth Convention), Buffalo, NY, April 24–29, 1924. LWV Papers on film, II. A.6. 0122–25.

One of the most intense moments in the life of the young League organization came as a consequence of accusations leveled against all fifteen members of the Women's Joint Congressional Committee and the National Council for the Prevention of War as part of the "Socialist-Pacifist Movement, for being an integral part of International Communism," The "Spider Web Chart," prepared by a woman librarian in the U.S. Army's Chemical War Service in the Department of War, documented their so-called interlocking directorates and impugned the motives and reputations of their leaders as well as individual women like Carrie Chapman Catt, Jane Addams, Helen Gardener, Florence Kelley, Belle Case LaFollette, and Rose Schneiderman. Helen Gardener wore many hats: author, suffragist, and the first woman (1920) appointed to the U.S. Civil Service Commission (by Woodrow Wilson when she was sixty-seven). Florence Kelley was a suffragist, social reformer, and long-time head of the National Consumers' League. Belle Case LaFollette, the first woman to graduate from the University of Wisconsin Law School, was the spouse of Robert M. LaFollette, who served as governor of Wisconsin, as U.S. Senator, and as the Progressive Party candidate for the presidency in 1924. When he died in 1925, Belle turned aside the pleas of enthusiastic supporters to be his successor, and her son, Robert Jr., took his father's place in the U.S. Senate. Unlike the other women in this group, Rose Schneiderman was an immigrant from Eastern Europe, widowed at a very young age and poor. Although initially suspicious of the coalition of workers and well-to-do reformers represented by the Woman's Trade Union League, Scheiderman later came to regard the organization as "the most important influence in my life." It was through the League that she learned the art of trade union work, and she played a key role in the successful organizing drives of the International Ladies Garment Workers Union from 1909 through 1914. Schneiderman served as president of the New York WTUL from 1919 to 1949 and as national president from 1926 to 1950 when it disbanded.

Source: Adelaide Washburn, "Gardener, Helen Hamilton," Vol. II, 11–13; Louise C. Wade, "Kelley, Florence," Vol. II, 316–19; Louise M. Young, "LaFollette, Belle Case." Vol. II, 356–58, *Notable American Women.* Nancy Schrom Dye, "Schneiderman, Rose," *Notable American Women: The Modern Period,* 631–63.

The Spider Web Chart was used by General Amos A. Fries, head of the Chemical Warfare Service, to allege (among other charges) that the Sheppard-Towner Act had been drafted in Moscow. These allegations were intended by the military to discredit peace-minded women and their organizations. Behind the rhetoric of the accusers lay the fear that military budgets would be reduced. In an unscheduled speech at the 1924 Buffalo convention, Maud Wood Park described the process by which she learned about the Spider Web Chart.

DOCUMENT 9: MAUD WOOD PARK ON THE SPIDER WEB CHART

Perhaps some of you have realized almost as vividly out in the country what we have realized in Washington for some months past, that there has been going on a subtle undercurrent of attack on women's organizations in this country, on the ground that they are disloyal. When those statements first began to be made, they sounded so ridiculous that I just laughed at them. I could not believe for one moment that anybody would think that the great women's organizations of this country were guilty of the things of which they were being accused. But, more and more, I came to realize that there was some background for those accusations that it was necessary to find out about.

After I went out to the national convention, Biennial Convention of the National Council of Women, last autumn,   in Decatur, I discovered that there was a printed so-called "photostat". . . which impugned the loyalty of every organization in the Women's Joint Congressional Committee.

I was asked to speak that evening, I was there on the activities of the Joint Congressional Committee, and I was told that while I was speaking, there was passed through the audience copies of this photostat, one copy handed about, and the person who handed that copy about was a woman who had apparently come out there to get through that convention an armed-to-the-teeth resolution. The woman who handed that about stated that she had access to the private records in the Department of War, which proved the charges made upon this chart.

I do not know whether it is large enough for you to see, but down the center column there is an assumed list of the organizations in the Women's Joint Congressional Committee. At the top, there is a heading that I will later read to you, from the correspondence; at the bottom, there are some very scurrilous verses, and along the side there is a list of supposed terrible creatures with a summary of their wrong doings.

Now, it does so happen that only three or four of those women who are fringed around the edges belong to the organizations represented in the Joint Congressional Committee, but if the charges against all the others, whom I do not know at all, are as absurd as they are against those three or four women, whom I do know, there is no truth to any of the charges.

When we got that chart—and let me say that it was through the activities of one of the State Presidents of the League that I was able to get a copy of the chart—the Women's Joint Congressional Committee, to whom I presented it appointed a special committee to investigate the source of circulation of the chart, and take such measures as were necessary to have its misstatements corrected.

Source: Excerpts from the Proceedings of the Fifth Convention. LWV Papers on film, II. A.5. 0738–42.

The denouncement of this episode is revealed in an exchange of letters from a special committee of the Women's Joint Congressional Committee chaired by Park with two other representatives—one from the American Association of University Women and the other from the Service Star Legion— with Secretary of War John W. Weeks (his tenure as senator from Massachusetts had been terminated by the organized opposition of suffragists who vowed to defeat him for his stand against women voting) and his reply of capitulation. Secretary Weeks's first effort to placate the Women's Joint Congressional Committee failed, prompting a second letter from the special committee. This time, Weeks acquiesced in their demands, but by then the damage had been done. Because of the circulation of the charts, the League and other groups continued to be suspect in the eyes of those who saw the red menace behind every effort to advance cooperation among nations, and that perception was to reach new heights in the Senator Joseph R. McCarthy (R., WI) era during the early 1950s.

DOCUMENT 10: LETTER PROTESTING THE SPIDER WEB CHART

An attack has been made upon the Women's Joint Congressional Committee by means of a chart compiled and circulated by a subordinate in a bureau of the War Department which is exceedingly irritating to the organizations comprising the Women's Joint Congressional Committee and to the 12 million women voters composing these organizations. They cannot understand why an employee of a government bureau should be permitted, with the knowledge of the head of that bureau, to attack the women's organizations of the country and the women voters in these organizations. They wonder where the funds come from whereby these attacks are made. The following is a statement of the objections, which the organizations make to the chart above-mentioned:

A. The Purpose and Method of Organization of the Women's Joint Congressional Committee

The Women's Joint Congressional Committee, which is attacked in the chart, was organized in 1920. It is a clearinghouse for 17 national women's organizations, which have representatives in Washington for the purpose of keeping in touch with Federal legislation of interest to women. The committee as such, initiates no policy and supports no legislation and no organization joining it is committed to any policy except that of cooperation, whenever possible. The members bring to it the endorsements of their organizations. After a measure has been endorsed by 5 or more member organizations of the committee, a sub-committee of representatives of endorsing organizations is organized, elects its officers and carries out a campaign of action for the enactment of the measure by the Congress.

An accurate list of the member organizations of the Women's Joint Committee in 1922-23, the year to which the chart refers, and of the sub-committees is appended.

B. The Chart

This chart has for its caption the heading "THE SOCIALIST PACIFIST MOVEMENT IN AMERICA IS AN ABSOLUTELY FUNDAMENTAL AND INTEGRAL PART OF INTERNATIONAL SOCIALISM."

1. This heading is scurrilous, libelous and criminal as applied to the Women's Joint Congressional Committee and we protest strongly against its use in this chart circulated with the knowledge of a branch of the government.
2. At the bottom of the chart appears the following verses:

> "Miss Bolsheviki has come to town,
> With a Russian cap and a German gown,
> In a women's clubs she's sure to be found,
> For she's come to disarm America.

> She sits in judgment on Capitol Hill
> And watches *appropriation bills*
> And without her O.K. it passes Nil
> For she's there to *disarm* America.

> She uses the movie and lyceum too,
> And alters text-books to suit her view,
> She prates propaganda from pulpit and pew,
> For she's bound to disarm America.

The make of the species has a different plan
He uses the bomb and firebrand,
And incites class hatred wherever he can
While she's busy *disarming* America.

His special stunt is arousing the mob,
To expropriate and hate and kill and rob,
While she's working on her political job
AWAKE! AROUSE!! AMERICA!!!

These verses are scurrilous and libelous and insulting to every woman voter in these women's organizations. We again protest in the strongest terms against the use of them in this connection.

3. In the third place the chart is false and inaccurate in listing the organizations which belong to the Women's Joint Congressional Committee. An accurate list appended here. Of those listed on the chart, the Women's International League for Peace and Freedom does not belong to the Women's Joint Committee. The Women's Council for World Disarmament does not belong and has never belonged to the Women's Joint Congressional Committee. Yet these two organizations are connected by lines with one of the Women's Joint Congressional Committee and both are included in the list in the middle column of the chart of organizations belonging to the Women's Joint Congressional Committee. The intention to vilify is perfectly clear.

Again only seven, not all, of the member organizations of the Women's Joint Congressional Committee are participating organizations in the National Council for the Prevention of War. The General Federation of Women's Clubs is not a member of the National Council for the Prevention of War, the National Congress of Mothers and Parent–Teacher Association is not a member, the American Home Economics Association is not a member, the National Consumer's League is not a member, and the Girl's Friendly Society is not a member.

In addition to the heading and the verses, the second offense is in the list of women forming the border of the chart. Here is a list of names of women about whom scurrilous remarks criticizing their patriotism and citizenship are made. As to the truth of these remarks we have no evidence. If not true they are libelous. The point of interest before us is that three names are linked by lines with the Women's Joint Congressional Committee through the Women's International League for Peace and Freedom and the Women's Council for World Disarmament, when neither of these is a member of the Women's Joint Congressional Committee. The intention to vilify the Women's Joint Congressional Committee is perfectly clear and we protest against it.

C. Author of Chart and Connection with General Fries

Investigation has revealed the fact that the author of the chart is known as librarian of the Chemical Warfare Service of the War Department. When a request for the chart was made of her, the author stated that it must be referred to General Fries. When General Fries has been approached with requests for the chart, these have been referred to the author in several instances. Such a request is known to have been answered by letter from General Fries. The chart is said by the author to have been distributed to various official and private agencies. In other words, the Chemical Warfare Service of the War Department, a branch of the government, is engaged in this contemptible attack on the women's organizations in the country.

D. What We Request

1. We request a statement from General Fries to the effect that the chart is misleading in general and untrue in particulars and that the War Department has no information with which to support it.

2. We ask, further, that the files of the Chemical Warfare Service be examined and that copies of the above statement be sent to every person or agency or organization to whom the chart has been sent from the address of the Chemical Warfare Service.

We are sure that although this attack has been perpetrated by a subordinate in a bureau of the War Department immediate redress will be made to us. We should like to say, however, that if such redress is not made immediately by the War Department we intend to secure it in some other way. Twelve million women voters in these organizations do not propose to bear this scurrilous and contemptible attack by a subordinate in a government department without redress.

DOCUMENT 11: SECRETARY WEEKS'S LETTER OF APOLOGY

With reference to the letter from your Committee, dated April 2, 1924, complaining of the injustice done your organization by the circulation of a chart by a subordinate in the War Department you are informed that all the charts complained of in the possession of the Chemical Warfare Service, have been ordered destroyed. General Fries has been directed to inform all persons to whom these charts have been distributed from his office that there are errors in the chart and to request their destruction.

I regret that charts containing the errors pointed out by your committee were circulated by any branch of the War Department.

DOCUMENT 12: MAUD WOOD PARK ACKNOWLEDGES THE APOLOGY

Permit us to thank you on behalf of the Women's Joint Congressional Committee for your letter of April 16th, stating that all of the charts to which we objected in the possession of the Chemical Warfare Service have been ordered destroyed and that General Fries has been directed to inform all persons to whom the charts were distributed of the inaccuracies and to request their destruction.

We presume that in informing these persons to whom the charts were distributed of the inaccuracies in them, General Fries will point out the particular inaccuracies to which we objected, that is, that the Women's Joint Congressional Committee is in no way connected with most of the persons to whose activities the Chemical Warfare Service has found objection, and that the caption and poem and other remarks have no bearing whatever on the Women's Joint Congressional Committee. It will be apparent to you that the mere statement that there are inaccuracies in the chart would not have the effect of disabusing the minds of the persons who have seen them of the erroneous impressions of the Women's Joint Congressional Committee which they have received.

We therefore request an assurance from you that General Fries will make these specific statements.

We are glad, as we are sure that the representatives of the other women's organizations will be, that we can report your favorable reply to our conventions and that it will enable us to refute the slanders of any persons who hereafter claim to have the authority of the War Department in their unwarranted attacks on the Women's Joint Confessional Committee.

Source: Maud Wood Park to John W. Weeks, Secretary of War, April 2, 1924. LWV Papers on film, II. A.3. 0004–06. John W. Weeks to Maud Wood Park, April 16, 1924. LWV Papers on film, II. A.3. 0002. Maud Wood Park to John W. Weeks, April 22, 1924. LWV Papers on film, II. A.3. 0003.

After having missed the League convention in Des Moines, Carrie Chapman Catt was in Buffalo and in her customary good form, deriding the warmongers for their ignorance and chiding the peace-mongers for their timidity.

DOCUMENT 13: CARRIE CHAPMAN CATT ON THE NEED FOR WORLD LAW

A few days ago, there met a convention of a great, honorable, distinguished non-partisan organization of women, and it resolved in favor of a "safe and sane preparedness for war." I believe that is the first pronouncement of that character that any women's organization has made in any country of the world, since the Great War came to an end. I suppose that it is because of that subtle and persistent propaganda that has been going on for the last year and a half, which has veered all the way from declaring every woman who has spoken for the World Court or any step of peace no matter how small, up to the statement that the League of Women Voters and other organizations have been financed by the Soviet government. I suppose that this propaganda—it has called such women pacifists and Bolshevists, the two terms being exchangeable apparently—I suppose that society was justified in feeling that it ought to withdraw from such society and appear upon a plane of higher respectability.

It may be followed by the same expression of other women's organizations, I hope not. I hope every other one, in some form, will resolve for a safe and sane preparedness for peace. (Applause)

This issue brings us to the query as to what is a safe and sane preparedness for war, and that has been the question which has brought all the trouble into the world. When Germany found herself the central portion of Europe, surrounded by great nations that she believed were hostile, she began a "safe and sane preparedness for war." She accepted the philosophy which any militarist in the world will give you, that there is but one safe preparedness for war, and that is to build all the way along the lines of preparedness a machine which shall be greater than that of any other nation in the world. But in Europe, as always, that philosophy became infectious. The conscription of Germany was introduced into Italy and France and Russia and Austria, and they had for many a year a competition in safe and sane preparedness. It was inevitable that the time would come when a preparedness for defense would become a preparedness for offense, and now we are beginning to ask ourselves all the way around the world, what was that war all about? One man has introduced a resolution which did not travel far, to investigate its causes. I hope some day that may be adopted.

Mr. Girard said that it came about because the Germans were afraid. I have no doubt of it, and I can give my testimony that the women in Germany, whom I have known long, are firmly convinced that that war was a war of defense.

What I say is, the cause of that war was the safe and sane preparedness of the nations of Europe. (Applause) It was the breaking down of the whole damnable system of competition in armament and preparation. (Applause) . . .

I think I may assure . . . that the women of this country, in the majority, will support every proposed step that leads ever so little a way toward peace as they did support the Naval Conference, as they are supporting the World Court, they will support a Disarmament Conference, an Economic Conference, if they be called, or any other step. But I want to assure . . . that so far as in me lies, no woman in this country, or man either, is going to be fooled by any one of those things. (Applause) None of them are a cure of war. You can disarm, you can cut down all kinds of armaments and something new may come, and the nations may lead the world in aggression, in spite of it all.

There is but one cure of war, there never can be but one cure of war. You may evade it and avoid it all you will, but sooner or later you will see that there is but one road. All these other things are going by stagecoach across the prairies where there are no roads, compared with riding upon a steam train of cars along the iron rails leading to the goal where we would go, and that is when every nation in the world has made the solemnest pledge that any nation knows how to make, that it will not make war upon any other nation, and that if any difficulties arise, it will pledge itself to arbitrate that difference and abide by the consequences. (Applause)

Mr. Ingersoll once said that when courts were substituted for clubs, civilization began, and we may say that if we are to use a slogan of "Law, not War," it means to put into the courts, or commissions or whatever may be set up, the means of arbitration and making the settlement of our difficulties compulsory there. There is no other way. Then some kind of a contact all the way around the world, we must have every nation with every other nation. You may dodge that matter all you will, but sooner or later, the reason and the common sense of this nation will come to realize that fact. (Applause) There is no use in trying to reach it any other way. . . .

I, myself, want to stand here and testify that I believe from the bottom of my heart in the League of Nations. (Applause)   I believe the greatest blunder that this nation ever made was when it refused to ratify that covenant. (Applause) I believe it was a blunder which will leave its scar upon the politics of our nation for the next hundred years. (Applause) I believe that it came about not as some would have us believe, as a result of argument, it came about as a result of chance.

Do you realize that had we in our constitution the same jollity for the ratification of a treaty as we have for the declaration of war, if we had the same method with both houses of Congress ratifying a treaty by majority, that we would have been in the League of Nations, and that nobody in America would have been nauseated by the mention of the word. (Applause) . . .

Source: Excerpts from the Proceedings of the Fifth Convention. LWV Papers on film, II. A.6. 0420–37.

On the domestic front, national board member Belle Sherwin spoke of the state of affairs with regard to the direct primary, a favored cause.

DOCUMENT 14: BELLE SHERWIN ON THE DIRECT PRIMARY

The Direct Primary, that poor thing, but our own by adoption in three conventions, has been much discussed before League audiences in the past year. It will probably continue to be the subject of much discussion until we discover and advocate well founded modifications of the various Primary laws. It is a sorry fact that we have no such modification to propose for consideration this year. The politically wise, who recognize the League of Women Voters as sturdy guardians of the Direct Primary, have told us that we shall need all the help and strength we can muster next winter, when most of the states will have legislatures assembled with amendments to the Primary laws in their programs. In that connection, two incidents in the month of April are worth quoting as straws, showing the direction of the political wind. New York State has failed once more to get back her Primary law; once lost, the Direct Primary is exceedingly difficult to recover. From Maine, however, there is better news. Our chairman of Efficiency in Government has just written, "Neither of the two parties in convention have tinkered with the Primary law, although there was much pre-convention talk and many editorials against the law. There is no question but that the political bosses were afraid of the women, whose influence was never so clearly shown. The League of Women Voters, the Women's Christian Temperance Union and the Federated Clubs were united." The change in the law, which was proposed in Maine by at least one party, was the pre-Primary Convention, favored by powerful party men elsewhere. It was resisted as the entering wedge of a return to the old system of nominations.

The League of Women Voters cannot in all probability, do better than follow the example of Maine women for some time to come; cannot do better than prevent nominations from reverting to the convention system. We have thoroughly learned to accept this course of action because there are no facts on which to base constructive changes. There are only personal opinions of how well or ill a particular system of nomination has worked, the value of the opinion depending largely upon what the holder of the opinion favors as a result of the nomination.

There is a group of political scientists who tell us frankly that at last they are going to be scientific, and that in several years they will be prepared to answer our question—which is one of theirs—namely, what is the best method of nominating candidates to office.

Those men and women organized last September as a National Conference on the Science of Politics, with a round table on the Direct Primary. The object of the round table is to find out what is the best method of nomination in any particular instance, by testing the various existing methods with reference to the ends to be secured. For the present year they will work on nine tests as follows:

1. Type of candidate produced, as indicated by age, education, occupation, and previous political experience.
2. Cost of nomination to the state, to candidates, to party organizations, to private individuals and organizations.
3. Effect on the party system, including effect on such matters as party leadership and program, party organization, minority par-

ties, party methods, and party responsibility (with the understanding that the term requires clarification).
4. Effect on public interest, as indicated by the amount of participation, amount and character of discussion, kind of appeals made.
5. Extent to which corruption is fostered, as indicated by the evidence as to buying and selling of votes, collusion, undue influence.
6. Effect on continuity in office, that is, how frequently candidates
are re-nominated and re-elected, involving considerations of such
questions as the opportunity for building up "machines," for
compromise candidates.
7. Effect on majority control, as indicated by the extent to which
nominations are controlled by minorities.
8. Extent to which press dominance is furthered, as indicated by the
degree of correlation between successful candidacies and press
support.
9. Effect on campaign methods, involving the problems of press
domination, corruption, and public interest.

This group recommends also the organization of a round table to study party
responsibility. Their interests are much the same as those of the League, though
their way is longer than the League would choose. Yet there seems to be no
other way for the League than to await the results of those researches, while it
practices with vigor the tactics of the Maine women.

In the meantime, the League has immediate and important business as efficient citizens in getting voters to make use of the Primary, such as it is. If voters, precinct by precinct, everywhere had taken advantage of the opportunity to
vote in the Primary for the past 20 years, the League would be less occupied in
debating the value of the Primary today. Few political predictions are so safe as
that. A large vote in the Primaries would have answered positively some of the
questions, which unanswered, block progress in nominating methods.

Source: Excerpts from the Proceedings of the Fifth Convention. LWV Papers on film,
III. A.5. 0081–83.

*In September 1924 the president of the Alabama League wrote to
Belle Sherwin, who had been elected national president at the 1924
convention in Buffalo, and to Minnie Fisher Cunningham, explaining
the difficulties of meeting a seventy-five percent get-out-the-vote increase in her state. Similar impediments of voting could be found in all
the southern states.*

DOCUMENT 15: THE TANGLE IN ALABAMA'S ELECTION
PROCEDURES

I enclose copies of our plan for the Get-Out-The-Vote campaign, which I
understand must be on file by October 1st. While we are entering the competition for the cup we only do it because we want to be good sports and not because we have the faintest hope of getting the cup. The situation in Alabama is
rather peculiar. If we get out 25% increase of the 1920 vote we shall have to get

out about 3,000 more voters than there are at present qualified voters in the state.

During the summer I have been painfully collecting the statistics as to the qualified voters in 1920 and in 1924. This could only be done by applying to each individual county probate judge as there is no central depository in the State for these facts. No human being will ever know the accurate number of qualified voters in Alabama for 1920 for the reason that the poll lists were made up in April, the women were enfranchised in September and allowed to register without paying poll tax and also without being added to the official poll list. . . .

As you know it is a very difficult matter to qualify for the vote in Alabama, the registration books are only open three months during the even years and ten days during the uneven years and the poll tax books are open only four months every year. Hence after February 1st of any year it is a practical impossibility to increase materially the number of qualified voters in Alabama. In view of all these facts we have decided to set our goal at 75% of our qualified vote for this year, even though this will mean less votes than in 1920. As I explained before, the large vote in 1920 was due to the fact that women were allowed to register and vote without paying poll tax, and this was done because the tax books were open October 1st to the following February 1st. The election was in November and the women were "trusted" to vote in November and pay their tax before February 1st, which many of them failed to do.

I am sorry to bore you with all this detail but I want you to understand our local difficulties and why we have adopted as a goal a smaller vote than in 1920. We wanted to take something that was possible of accomplishment even though it cuts us out of the "National Cup Race."

I feel very much encouraged about our campaign since last Wednesday when we had a very successful luncheon at which more than 50 statewide organizations were represented. We organized a nonpartisan statewide Get-Out-The-Vote committee, which meets Monday. . . .

You will find our election statistics on the enclosed leaflet. Finally let me remind you that we are a one–party state, which is another difficulty in getting out a large vote in November.

Source: Amelia W. Fisk to Belle Sherwin and Minnie Fisher Cunningham, September 20, 1924. LWV Papers, Library of Congress.

An even more telling example of the impact of the League's voters service work was the report concerning a candidate in Wisconsin who could not restrain his indignation about the questions he was expected to answer on a League questionnaire.

DOCUMENT 16: A CANDIDATE FLAILS AT A LEAGUE QUESTIONNAIRE

Ever since the League organized to disseminate unpartisan political information, the circulation of questionnaires to primary and election candidates has been one of the most helpful and fruitful undertakings in the big job of political education. . . . A League in Wisconsin recently sent out a questionnaire to local candidates. One of the . . . men . . . called the League on the telephone. "I'm Mr. X," he said. "I've just received your questionnaire and I don't like it. Why you've asked me to answer questions I never heard of . . . why lady, I venture to say that there isn't a candidate running who could answer these questions. I've asked 3 officials at the City Hall and they couldn't answer them. You've asked my attitude on the ratification of the Child Labor Amendment. I never heard of such an amendment . . . you want to know whether I am in favor of reappropriation of funds to take advantage of federal aid for the Sheppard-Towner Maternity Act. Now, I don't know what the Sheppard-Towner Act is." An episode such as this has many aspects, but to members of the League it is a serious matter. It points the way for every League, for the 'Mr. X's in the political world are not confined to any one state or locality. To the intelligent and capable candidate the questionnaire is a veritable boon; to the less intelligent candidate, who has depended on the ignorance of voters on pull to put him in office, it comes as a tremendous shock and a rude awakening.

Source: *The Woman Citizen*, September 20, 1824, 3–4.

> In her farewell address to the 1924 Buffalo convention, Maud Wood Park documented the League's achievement over the first four years but also pointed to matters left undone and needs not yet adequately addressed. Among the latter was the need for more women in public office and the recruitment of young women to the cause of good government. In one of the more telling passages, she recognized that the millennium would not be a consequence of woman suffrage, but she remained hopeful that women would become more interested and that "the women's distinctive point of view" would "become increasingly important in public affairs."

DOCUMENT 17: MAUD WOOD PARK'S FAREWELL ADDRESS

The League of Women Voters from the beginning has stood for step by step progress. It has chosen to be a middle-of-the-road organization in which persons of widely differing political views might work out together a program of definite advance on which they could agree. It has been willing to go ahead slowly in order to go ahead steadily. It has not sought to lead a few women a long way quickly, but rather to lead many women a little way at a time. It has held to the belief that no problem of democracy is really solved until it is solved for the average citizen. . . .

In all the efforts of the League it has had the advantage of an extraordinary opportunity, the opportunity afforded by the enfranchisement at one time of approximately 20 million women. In the nature of the case, this opportunity will last only a few years and it can never come again. Only for a few years shall we have the possible advantage of an enormous number of new voters, untrammeled by carelessly made political affiliations, with no bad political tendencies to undo and therefore free to form good political habits from the start. Never again shall we have the impetus of the enfranchisement of a huge group of citizens, the great majority of whom are law abiding, with no political axes to grind and an honest desire that the community in which they live should be a good place for children to grow up in.

To be sure, many of these well-meaning new voters have not been accustomed to think in terms of government. Many of them were ignorant of public affairs and profoundly indifferent to their new opportunity. They needed awakening and a chance to learn. Large numbers of them need it still. That is why so much of the recent unfavorable criticism of what women have done with their votes is superficial. At the last presidential election the new women voters had been enfranchised less than three months, too late for the majority of them to have any part in the primaries. They did not know how to mark a ballot; they were largely unfamiliar with the questions at issue; they had not had practice in making the connection between their beliefs and desires in regard to public affairs and the actual processes of government. To expect women as a whole, in the brief period of four years, to become active in an entirely new field, to learn enough of politics to make their wishes effective, to qualify for and secure a large proportion of public offices, and to correct practically all the abuses of government is absurd to the point of childishness. I think well of women, their ability and their conscientiousness, but not so well as all that expectation implies. . . .

When I say that the great opportunity given by the Nineteenth Amendment will be ours for a few years only, I mean "few" in the relative, not the absolute sense. I do not mean three years or even six years, for I think it will take much longer than that to bring the knowledge of her opportunity to the average woman, much longer than that to measure the result of women's votes. Meanwhile, however, I look for increasing interest. Women do not have a larger part in this year's national party conventions than they had four years ago. I shall be disappointed if the women's distinctive point of view does not become increasingly important in public affairs. But I shall not be disappointed if during my lifetime the millennium fails to arrive as a consequence of woman suffrage. . . .

During the League's first year, much of this work was carried on in connection with the Department of Organization, which helped the states to arrange numberless demonstration classes to explain to the newly enfranchised women before the presidential election the proper way to mark a ballot and the other technicalities of registration and voting. Often these demonstrations were given in election booths set up in department stores, hotel lobbies, or public buildings; and there or elsewhere the League's policy was never to say who should be voted for, only how to vote in order to have the ballot legal.

After the election of 1920, a special effort was made to carry on citizenship schools for the study of the principles of government, local, state, and national, and since that time these schools have continued to be a striking and popular part of our work. Many of the schools are conducted with the cooperation of universities or colleges, others are arranged in a series so that a group of instructors can travel from one to another. . . .

Another important form of training for citizenship has been supplied by the standing committees dealing with subjects of special interest to women. . . .

During that preliminary year [1919], committees were appointed on child welfare, women in industry, legislation affecting the legal status of women, social hygiene, American citizenship (dealing largely with education), food supply and demand, and election laws and methods. These committees were continued after the League became an independent organization and have done valuable educational work in regard to their special subjects. . . .

The League's efforts to arouse and sustain intelligent interest in the obligations of citizenship are by no means confined to study courses, publications, and meetings. Every member of the League is advised to become an active member of the political party which best represents her views; to attend its caucuses, meetings, and conventions; and to vote in all primaries as well as in final elections. Particularly is she urged to take part in the political activities of her own election district and to do her best to see that only properly qualified men and women are nominated for party or public office.

There is another suggestion for future work that fires the imagination of a good many League members. This is the idea of a campaign to put more women into public office. To my mind, such an effort is justified only by one of two premises: that women are to be chosen who are better qualified for office than are their men opponents; or else that the qualifications being equal, more women in public office are desirable because women have distinctive opinions in regard to public affairs that men cannot express. Certainly League members will agree that a poorly qualified woman is never to be preferred, simply because she is a woman, to a well qualified man. On the other hand, most of us would be glad to see a much larger proportion of women in office for exactly the same reason that makes us stress the social welfare program in the League's work, namely, that women as a whole have a keener consciousness of the human side of public questions than have men because women have naturally more experience in dealing with our human resources.

The fact that we should like to see more women of the right sort in public office does not imply, however, that the League as an organization ought to start out electioneering for women. Obviously, if we did so, we should be in grave danger of running counter to our provision in the by-laws which forbids party action by the organization. In the majority of cases women candidates, if they are to be successful, must run on a party ticket. The League can help only indirectly by urging its members to act, each within the existing party best representing her views, in order to secure the nomination of properly qualified women. A bi-partisan or all-partisan committee of the League might serve to stimulate action of this kind, although it could not take any part in the campaign.

Unless the League is to make radical changes in its purpose and program, our own part in the high undertaking of applied democracy is reasonably clear. We are an organization of women to help women make the best of themselves as voters, both by intelligent participation in the responsibilities of voting citizens and by special attention to the human welfare side of government, in which women are particularly fit to be useful. First of all, we have to make more women alive to their great new privilege. Through our own membership and in cooperation with other organizations, we have already kindled the consciences of millions, but many more millions must be reached before that part of our task is done. Our citizenship schools must go into every street of crowded city districts; our publications must reach the busy, thoughtful women of every rural community. In order to do this our methods should be direct and practical, connected first with the needs of the immediate neighborhood. Hard working women have no time to waste over theories. They want to know how government touches them and the things they are familiar with. The work that we ask of them as good citizens must be made to fit into their other work. . . . We must see to it that the girls coming of age to vote are enlisted year by year in the interest of good government. Very few of them will come to us. We shall have to go to them and it will be useless to go with any dry-as-dust appeal. They must be made to feel the thrill in their possibilities as voting citizens. Youth likes adventure and there is no greater adventure than this of ours to make democracy real. For many girls in college, the foreign mission field has had a compelling call and for others, the social settlement. These are both noble causes, but causes to which the average young woman cannot give up her life. For her, the same religious fervor, the same sympathy with the down–trodden and neglected, should find an outlet in her activities as a citizen. She must understand that it is an illuminating experience to learn the politics of her own precinct, that outwitting the crafty and self-seeking in public office is an alluring adventure and that working with millions of her fellow citizens for a righteous cause is an undertaking that exalts and ennobles. All this these young women must be made to see and feel and then they must be set to work, for, though a thrill in a good cause is much to be desired, the only way to keep it going is to do something. So we must have plenty of work to offer them and self-direction and a chance to laugh at themselves and the rest of us. We must remember, too, that they will want to do things, at least in part, in their own way and that they will learn a great deal more through their own mistakes than they will from ours.

Once in a while I hear from an old suffragist that the glory has departed from our work now that the vote is won, or that working for one thing only, as some of us worked in the suffrage campaign, was vastly more interesting than working for many things as conscientious voters are obliged to do. It is not easy for me to understand such complaints.

When we worked for suffrage, I doubt that many of us believed that there was anything wonderful in being able to put some marks on a piece of paper and drop it into a box three or four times a year. We thought of the ballot as a tool with which great things were to be done. We had to have the tool and so we were willing to let other causes go in order to work for it. To my mind, however, there is no comparison between the interest of working for a tool, the means to an end, and the interest of working with that tool for the end itself. We are working for ends now and that is a glorious thing to be doing.

Source: Excerpts from the Proceedings of the Fifth Convention. LWV Papers on film, II. A.5. 0524–34.

Chapter 8

An Experiment in Political Education

Belle Sherwin succeeded Maud Wood Park as League president in 1924. Sherwin, born in Cleveland, Ohio, in 1868, was one of five children of the founder of the Sherwin-Williams Company, one of the nation's best-known paint manufacturing firms. After graduating from Wellesley College, with which she maintained a lifelong association as a trustee and benefactor, she taught briefly before beginning her career as a volunteer. She organized English classes for Italian immigrants in a Cleveland settlement house and then moved on to a position of leadership in the Visiting Nurses Association. Sherwin first joined the National College Equal Suffrage League in 1910 in response to Maud Wood Park's organizing visit to Cleveland. She did not, however, become active in the suffrage movement until 1916, a commitment prompted by the formation of a militant branch in Cleveland of the National Association Opposed to Woman Suffrage. In 1921 she was elected vice president of the National League of Women Voters. According to Louise Young's biography in *Notable American Women: The Modern Period,* "The ten years of Sherwin's presidency established the character of the League of Women Voters as a nonpartisan, goal-oriented organization, politically accountable for its policies and respected for the accuracy and objectivity of the educational materials prepared by its research staff." Also important to the LWVUS over the years was the service rendered by a series of Executive Secretaries (as they were then called) who managed the home office.

Source: Young, "Sherwin, Belle," *Notable American Women: The Modern Period.* Cambridge, MA, 647–48.

As Sherwin took hold of the League's reins, she had the advantage, as have most League presidents, of previous service on the national board. The memo below reflects the continuing presence and influence of Carrie Chapman Catt and Maud Wood Park concerning the League's interest in and commitment to the international dimension of the League's work.

DOCUMENT 1: BELLE SHERWIN'S CONFIDENTIAL MEMO TO THE EXECUTIVE COMMITTEE

I want to write you as promptly as possible with a report of my conference with Mrs. Catt on Saturday night and Sunday the 19th and 20th of July.

The World Court Committee

We spent the greater part of the time talking about our points of view in regard to making more adequate the work of the World Court Committee. We did not work out a perfect agreement, though I am sure we appreciated each other's point of view. It was finally agreed that I should write Mrs. Park asking her to say what she felt was the most desirable action to take.

I have therefore prepared the memorandum enclosed, which summarizes Mrs. Catt's proposals and arguments and our line of reasoning in support of the action taken by the Executive Committee Friday afternoon, July 11th. I am enclosing that memorandum which I hope you and Mrs. Catt alike will find a fair statement. I have written Mrs. Park enclosing the memorandum, Mrs. Cunningham having agreed with me that it was really only just to Mrs. Park to give her an opportunity to speak about what concerns her child, the Joint Congressional.

The Quinquennial

Mrs. Catt assures me that there is now no doubt that the International Council of Women will hold it's meeting in 1925 in Austria. When I expressed my satisfaction she raised her eyebrows and later told me that she had had correspondence, which made it seem not at all unlikely that Mrs. Haviland Lund at Copenhagen had instigated the change.

It appears that Mrs. Catt has had correspondence following her article "Poison Propaganda" in the *Woman Citizen* which has brought to her copies of letters sent by Mrs. Lund to both Mrs. Moore and at least one other woman in this country. The letters make amazingly interesting reading and include a suggestion to read certain books which are offered as correctives for the innocent point of view of organized women in this country. It is my understanding that Mrs. Catt will use this information in later articles in the *Citizen*.

Pan-American Association for the Advancement of Women

Mrs. Catt has not yet decided what action to take with respect to concluding her term of office with service, which is helpful to the Pan Americans and satisfactory to her. She has thought of a conference in New York this November, or a year later. This she thought might be held in conjunction with a Board meeting of the League. She also is considering not holding the conference at all but taking the summaries of the questionnaires she has sent out to the various countries and presenting them in person to each of the South American countries represented in the Pan American in the course of a trip which she would make next winter following the conference for the Cause and Cure of War in Washington.

In any event, she does not favor holding the Executive Pan American conference in connection with the League of Women Voters annual convention, chiefly, I understood, because she thought it would keep the Pan American ladies too long in America. If they should elect to hold the conference in New York she would suggest that it be strictly limited in time, to include a day in Washington. The number of delegates would probably not exceed thirty and probably be less. The League's name would be used in the invitation.

The Woman Citizen
Mrs. Catt tells me in confidence that the Leslie Commission has agreed to continue a subsidy to the *Citizen* for five years, provided that the present management in able to carry out its plans for increasing circulation, etc. This relieves us at once of the responsibility of planning for a bulletin, unless someone should wish to reconsider that possibility.

Conference for the Cause and Cure of the War
Mrs. Catt is full of plans for making this a very distinguished discussion. She thinks now that she would like to have two rooms in Washington, for work room and conference purposes, for about six weeks before the conference, probably from the first of December on. In that case the only possibility of finding so much space in this building is in the unleased rooms on the third floor, which are now offered far rent. Mrs. Cunningham agrees that it would be very desirable to secure them for the use of Mrs. Catt and her secretary, if possible.

I have given you these details at length because I think they will relieve your minds, and I will let you know what I hear from Mrs. Park at an early opportunity. Washington is some days very hot and some days very pleasant, and the office grows better and better.

Source: League of Women Voters Papers on film, III. A.5. 0011-12.

The League had been devastated by the failure of women (and men) to vote in significant numbers in the 1924 presidential election and disappointed that only one woman was elected to Congress—though several had run. (Mary Norton's victory was attributed in large part to the assistance provided her by the notorious Hague machine in New Jersey.) The get-out-the-vote exhortations and efforts of the League had apparently fallen on deaf ears. People began to doubt the much heralded promises of the suffrage campaign, and scholars scurried to find answers. So did League leaders. Their conclusion: the development of political women, both as voters and as candidates, would take time, perhaps as long as a generation. It was unrealistic to expect that great numbers of newly enfranchised women would rush to great numbers of newly enfranchised women would rush to the polls or run for office to express their political liberation. Years of prejudice against women leaving the domestic sphere for the political realm and years of put-downs when women tried to offer views on public issues made many women fearful of coming out to the polls. They also concluded that getting voters to the polls was not a periodic activity but a year-round continuing responsibility.

Other considerations impeded the progress of the political woman: the diversions of the Roaring Twenties; laws restricting job opportunities for women by denying married women the right to teach and by establishing veterans preference in public employment; the decline in college enrollment by women; and the replacement of notable women educational leaders by men who held very different views on the goals of education for women. In retrospect, it can be said that the sexual and behavioral freedoms enjoyed by women in the 1920s were not matched by comparable advances in either the economic or political arenas.

DOCUMENT 2: REPORT ON THE 1924 GET OUT THE VOTE CAMPAIGN

First of all, I would mention Mrs. Park, who, in the parlance of modern sport, "threw the ball into the field" at the Des Moines Convention; then our fine and intrepid leader of today, Miss Sherwin, who had the happy thought of the cup, turning the campaign into an inter-League friendly contest (I believe it was an inspiration); Mrs. Edwards, who contributed a report at Buffalo; Mrs. Cunningham, already charged with our great department of organization, accepting the chairmanship of this campaign, and setting us a wonderful example thereby of a double job. How well she did her work is history, strategic material produced at the psychological moment, first-hand aid given notably in her western tour, and all the time visualizing for us all, keeping our courage up, the goal that had been set before us. . . .

Thirty-five states accepted these terms, three of them enrolling in August, so eager were they, the first of all being Pennsylvania, followed by New Jersey and Wisconsin. Thirty-eight states were reported working in the *Woman Citizen.*

The underlying reason for it all, we know so well, was the dwindling electorate. In 1896, 80 per cent; in 1900, 73 per cent; in 1912, 62 per cent; and in 1920, after we had gotten the vote, 49 per cent. Certain states have a much better record than the record of the total, we must bear that in mind, and certain states have been handicapped by a drop in the population, as notably Delaware and Nevada.

Now, a few campaign characteristics, and this is where I ask you to reminisce in your own mind. Early in the field were we, it has been stated here that we were the first, and that later it became the very popular idea. Well do you remember our surprise when it was taken up by unexpected quarters? Our nonpartisanism was clearly defined. "Vote as you please, but vote!" We opened a door to a new service, stressing research work always, and always before everything else stressing cooperation. Wasn't that true? Not seeking credit but seeking the great end. The stimulation of party activity seemed to be a sort of by-product.

There were some general results which might stand out clearly, which no figures can show, such as reactions on the part of those of us who labored. Citizenship became a very distinct thing to us, like an adventure; it could never again be a drab affair, I am sure. Then our conviction, our growing conviction that the processes of election must be simplified and that that is a part of our job as citizens in America, to see that it is done. Then I believe we proved that one might be politically minded without self-interest. We proved that we could and did help all the parties, and we turned that time-honored taunt into a great asset, namely, that women in speeches, with slogans. We expressed our solemn conviction that majorities must rule in the United States.

Though there are two sides to the final results, an increased and a decreased percentage, 22 of our contestants are on the good side and only thirteen on the losing side, and we may honestly claim that wherever we labored, things were better because we tried to help. It was a stupendous undertaking, and let us frankly marvel at our courage to think we could do it at all.

There were two big divisions of work already referred to by Miss Sherwin, the registration and the voting itself, both in primaries and elections, today. The methods began, of course, with organization work, some of it particularly well done. Minnesota, Illinois, New York, notably by counties in Virginia, and by precincts in California.

Then there was the tackling of the regulations of registration. Did you ever know such forehanded rules as requiring registration at this particular moment, whenever it is, so long ahead of when it seems necessary! Why, in Alabama, the situation was tragic; not after February could they register, and in the preceding election, in 1920, the poll tax had been remitted to the new voters, so the poor women in 1924 did not know whether they had to pay their poll tax or not. But we tackled the situation as it was, we got longer hours wherever we could, we carried people to the clerk's office, and in California and Minnesota they even had members deputized as clerks.

Just this side of the campaign would give us enough results to fill a book, but the big fight came afterwards, and what was that? Making qualified voters want to vote! Stemming the tide of democracy's deserters! What were our tools? Again, words, but not alone words; we had a good many works too—house-to-house canvassing, planning meetings, and, perhaps best of all, the use of party machinery itself, the hearing of candidates, two opposing on the same platform became a great stimulus of this desire of the voter to vote. Illinois' famous "Fourteen Points," and then our own splendid League planks. The materials were simply endless, both national and state. The campaign surely exercised our brains. Nationally, we got the cup, we had the cartoon contest, we had the splendid speakers' bureau, we had outlines and suggestions in many pamphlets, especially fine was the preparation of the comparative party platforms with such of our planks as were accepted; posters, booklets, and then those famous "Seven Steps." It seems almost too bad to mention any, because we cannot mention all but you will pardon me. I am sure, such a variety that a full catalog would certainly exceed our time. . . .

We did not reach our goal of 75 per cent increase, but we did stem the backward tide or helped to, we did raise the percentage, or helped to, we did get over on to the majority side, as the president has reported, 50.91 per cent.

Source: Excerpts from proceedings of the Sixth Annual Convention of the National League of Women Voters (hereinafter referred to as the Sixth Convention), Richmond, VA, April 16–22. LWV Papers on film, II. A.6. 0519–21.

The League, struggling to cope with the difficult process of wooing a new constituency to political participation, began to erect an ambitious experiment in political education. Sherwin's thoughtful speech to the 1926 League Convention in St. Louis reflected her high hopes for a new and different kind of League-style education. Sherwin was intrigued with the relationship of education to the League's purpose and its procedures. She was convinced that women joined the League to learn and remained members to influence the curriculum (that is, the program). Under her stewardship, "study before action" and "consensus" became hallmarks of League work. This process, whereby members studied all sides of an issue and then reached conclusions that could be applied to the support of or opposition to legislation before the Congress, state legislatures, and local authorities could be agonizingly prolonged, but it provided a needed solidarity at a time when the nation had become increasingly conservative and frequently hostile to League viewpoints on issues of the day. In some respects, it proved easier for League members to immerse themselves in study than to take the next step of acting on their beliefs. Nevertheless, Belle Sherwin's administrative talents and her concept of experimental and experiential education in the form of what she called "a university without walls" have to be acknowledged as vital building blocks for the development of the League of Women Voters.

DOCUMENT 3: BELLE SHERWIN, "THE WAY OF THE LEAGUE"

The League of Women Voters welcomes you to share in the anniversary that we celebrate with rejoicing tonight. It is the anniversary of a great meeting of women held in this city almost exactly seven years ago. They met to commemorate the sacrifices and victories of seven times seven years devoted to winning the suffrage of women in this country. The end of the hard road was in sight. They proposed a memorial to brave departed leaders, a "living memorial" of patriotic service" to be called the League of Women Voters.

The new national body of voting women, without partisanship or political custom, was dedicated to definite tasks and a great expectation. It was "to rise its utmost influence to secure the final enfranchisement of women" here and "to aid in the struggle of women for their own in other lands." It was "to remove the remaining discriminations against women from the codes and constitutions of the several states that the feet of coming women may not stumble."

It was to "make democracy so safe for the nation that every citizen may feel secure." Complete enfranchisement followed in seventeen months. The legal disabilities of women are being gradually removed, state by state, and measure by measure. The evolution of democracy through the new influence is more gradual. There are signs that it is real. I wish to speak of the character of that influence and the promise it bears.

Given the right of all the people to share in government through universal suffrage the first essential of a democracy, is a standard of life for all its citizens, a definition of that security and good life for all which has been the immemorial expectation, of government by the people. A program of such standards was forecast by the convention in St. Louis seven years ago and adopted by the League at its own first convention in Chicago the following year. The program was not considered then nor is it considered now as supplying a complete picture of the conditions of life in an ideal democracy. Rather it is a series of proposals—for study and for enactment into laws—of measures prompted by the facts of life in this country at this time as tending toward the security of a greater number of citizens. It is concerned with homely matters which women instinctively understand and as elements of security, such as the protection of maternity and infancy, school attendance laws, the prevention of child labor, the limitation of the hours of working women in industrial occupations, the enforcement of laws relating to sex offenses without discrimination between the sexes, the prevention of unfair trade practices, the service of women on juries. It is concerned with election systems and governmental policies which women have learned they must understand in the interest of individual security-registration laws, the direct primary, executive budgets, the methods by which appointive offices are filled, taxation, and the vexed questions of Federal aid and states rights. In the last two years it has been identified with measures tending toward the security of citizens in all nations.

We in the League agreed in 1919 that democracy can only work out through education of the people. We thought of education then in terms of literacy and in great part rested our faith in the future of democracy upon the extension and development of the public school system even as our fathers did, In 1920 we thought of education in terms of the immediate need for political information on the part of women as new voters information about ballots, the requirements of public offices and the qualifications of candidates, issues in the campaign then imminent. Today we are thinking in terms of the continuing education of adults in a wider range of questions of government and politics. Some of its are bold to believe that the necessity for political education has led the League of Women Voters directly into a creative process of democracy. We are discovering in turn that democracy is itself a process. . . .

In the early days of small numbers in this country our new invention of public schools did in some measure result in the development of the individual in relation to the demands upon him and so laid foundation for a working democratic government. How far we are from realizing that ideal through our educational system in the complex of life in 1926 is a matter of too common observation. For the many, education today is both remote and limited to a brief period of life or is highly specialized for vocational purposes. Education for active citizenship has hardly been tried. It is demonstrated that reading and writing do not in themselves result in responsible voting. We know that the influence of increasingly practical courses in civics in the schools carries over to the voting age at most only a little interest, a little understanding, and a little information which requires to be brought up to date. We see that advanced courses in politics and government equip a few leaders yearly with varying degrees of encyclopedic knowledge. These leaders are welcomed by their home communities arid seldom escape being set to work in relation to a citizen organization. So information about government spreads and is put to use. But there is a better sign for democracy in formal education today than the training of leaders and the equipment of bureaus of research.

It may be found in modest attempts in the schools here and there to teach critical reading of the newspapers and other means of "avoiding mobminded-ness."

In the meantime in order to supplement a meager education or in order to meet new situations groups of adults have undertaken certain experiments in special education almost as a means of self-preservation. Such undertakings, of workers and women voters for instance, are worth observing as a method of educating the people in order that democratic government may succeed. They appear to possess a vital spark. Each group of experimenters is taking daily living—the job or some other human relationship or the vote as the raw material of self-education. Each experiment began with making up for deficiencies in information. Each has developed rapidly to dwell on issues, current practices, underlying principles, because something in the day or the situation called for more understanding.

The citizenship schools of the League, for instance, were planned to give in-formation about the structure of government and the history and organization of parties to voters who knew next to nothing of either. They were held in a great majority of the states in 1920 and 1921 and hailed with enthusiasm. When in-terest in them lagged and it was said, "women were not smitten with being edu-cated" neither the women nor the schools were properly indicted. It was the educational stuff of the schools that was at fault. As a cog in the machinery of democracy, citizenship schools are all inspired innovation in political fife. What the schools deal with determines their appeal and their power. They multiply today on demand to help women to form sounder judgments than they could otherwise reach on political questions which somehow press upon women for answers. Getting out the vote and just voting lead to the study of election laws which actually "matter" to the student. Jury service rouses a train of persistent individual inquiry. Espousal of a legislative measure develops a personal re-sponsibility to determine the validity of a political theory.

For this reason the experiment of the League offers a New Hope to democ-racy.

The schools deal with the intrinsic merits of questions but they do so with a refreshing difference from the academy. In every school someone asks some form of the question "What does this mean to me, a voter?" It is competence as a citizen that is sought, not the information of experts. It is an evidence of vital-ity that the political education of the League has developed spontaneously in a variety of forms. The schools of the first year almost uniformly followed a na-tional model. Fertilized by diverse experience in cities and states the seed of those first schools has yielded increasing crops of study groups, round tables, conferences, and institutes, each suited to the needs of local consumers. This gradually mounting number of schools and the number of women attending them cannot be called impressive in a country where great numbers are at once a boast and a problem. Only when it is realized that the facts back of the figures never existed before does the number of the League's undertakings in political education become significant. It is interesting that they appear most significant to men of largest affairs.

The distribution of these centers of political education throughout the coun-try is more impressive than numbers. Local organizations undertaking to inform citizens and support measures on a basis of fact are within the experience of many of us. A nation-wide coordinated undertaking of that kind is unique. We are happy in recalling the observation of an English journalist traveling in the United States in the past year to the effect that "in a land otherwise politically arid the League of Women Voters blossoms from coast to coast."

The flowering of citizenship schools in thirty-four states may attract attention but the fruits of political education as the League has tried it are not generally conspicuous. Our seven years are disappointing to those who wish to read as they run, who set a store by get-rich-quick methods, to those to who in spectacular advertising Spells Success. Here and there locally political education by the League is understood arid valued as a community asset.

During the past year for instance editors of city dailies, east and south, in the middle West and Northwest have volunteered comments on the League as a political factor to be reckoned with, because it "emphasizes education in politics," because its "candidates' meetings are eminently fair and enlightening" because a state "bulletin is an eye-opener which ought to come under more eyes," because a state League "sure in direction, skilled in method has brought out concrete instances of an uneconomical public administration." These editorial writers and others agree that the medium of political education, which characterizes the League, is "less buncombe, more facts," and that such use of the facts never happened before. Quite generally they hope it will happen again.

On the whole this is understanding of the potential value of political education. There are results that are matters of history, the first demonstration of a new working hypothesis. The conscientious, impersonal, and finely balanced use of facts by local Leagues has notably helped to clean out dusty corners in city administrations. Behind an editorial statement that a certain state League is "one of the strongest forces operating for political enlightenment" is "the acknowledgment of all unbiased observers," that that League was the citizen factor most responsible for putting through a measure for the re-organization of state departments. The way of the League there was an initial inquiry by a few, a distinguished institute devoted to the discussion of state administration, more than a score of one-day schools in county seats and city wards followed by a state-wide campaign in support of a simplification bill. Another state League more than four years ago initiated a request for a conference on the efficiency of state administration. Today that League reports the enactment by the state legislature of a reorganization measure for which the League has worked constructively through every stage of conference resolutions, commission studies, and an interpretive campaign.

Modern city charters in several instances definitely owe something to the educational work of local Leagues in offsetting purely political opposition. It is work quite distinct from that of charter specialists. Commissions lead the vanguard in formulating basic principles, leaders of the League frequently belong to those bodies, but the League as an organization of responsible voters comes into the movement in cities and states alike to interpret all the merits of the question what is at stake for the citizen, to answer the question—"Well, what does this technical thing mean to me, a voter?"

The results of political education in election campaigns and in support of a legislative program are not so easy to trace though there are instances in which it has been done. The largest returns upon political education are not yet capable of measurement at the polls. They are to be found rather in the gradual appreciable increase of the number of citizens concerned to become competent voters through understanding some aspect of government or some political situation which has come home to them. The test of the value of such education may, I think, be made quantitatively now. Yet a better test is the apparent quality of growth.

To increase steadily the number of citizens to whom government has come home as a personal trust has been a persistent problem of democracy.

Suffrage granted to all the women of this country at one time created a condition unknown in history. Women experienced suddenly a consciousness of a wholly new relationship in life. We do not know how many women because of that have already begun to develop power to understand themselves in relation to voting. We do hear continuously of those who in real numbers seek to do so. Upon that hinge of consciousness and personal experience and desire, the success if political education for democratic life and government must turn. The League of Women Voters is not led by its brief period of experimentation to believe that it has found so important a bit of machinery for universal use. The League does believe that it has found a way of helping to realize democracy, which actually works among a growing number of citizens.

The League is very young. It will be easy to say that it belongs to the "romantic age of politics" but if by romance, illusion is meant, the critics of the League will be in error. The realities of the campaign to get out the vote and to ratify the Child Labor Amendment put an end to the period of romance for the League in the sense of illusion. True romance the League does know, the romance of all creative work however small, wherever it may end.

We ask those who doubt that education as a basis for democracy call ever succeed to watch the development of political education by the League as they would observe a culture in a test tube. We ask those who are inclined to give the League's way the benefit of the doubt to support our progressive experiment as ail exploratory course deserves to be supported, substantially and with good will. The multitude of the indifferent we expect to shock some day by an explosion demonstrating what political education can do.

To the League of Women Voters, the demonstration of political education as a process of democracy in our midst is a challenge, a challenge to prove the experiment and to establish that which is proved. It means a new adventure for us all. It means plodding tasks in the course of which romance must certainly be obscure. It means new inventions and trial by error. It means persistence in little things. It means a very real share in one of the greatest of human endeavors. The League has been caught in the current of "a great force wise of old." If that force "has its whole way with us," there is for us and even more for those who come after us the chance o' the prize of learning the way of democracy. That way may make use of our modest beginning and "aeons hence gladden a golden year."

Source: Excerpts from the Proceedings of the Seventh Annual Convention of the National League of Women Voters (hereinafter referred to as the Seventh Convention), St. Louis, MO, April 14–21, 926. LWV Papers on film, II. A.7. 1010–12.

Following the 1929 Council meeting, an article by Gladys Harrison, one of the League's most influential executive secretaries, described the relationship of the League's educational process and its role as an advocate for particular public policies. It was a relationship that would often confuse the public and cause disagreement among League members, but with few modifications it remained one of the League's great strengths. Her report on the League's procedures is particularly illuminating.

DOCUMENT 4: GLADYS HARRISON, "PARTICIPATING IN GOVERNMENT"

What is the procedure by which a large organization can act simultaneously as an educational agency and as a supporter of a program of action? The two are apparently incompatible, yet in proper juxtaposition electric with energy generated and released.

The immediate relation of study to use and action is characteristic of adult education, even that which is not strictly vocational. The immigrant studies English and the Constitution in order to become a citizen. The bride-elect takes cooking lessons in order to feed her husband without fiasco. It is political education for and through participation in government which the League of Women Voters is attempting—vocational education by the laboratory and the "case" method. The method has proved itself stimulating to educational invention in a most neglected field.

"The League," said Miss Sherwin in her president's address at its recent General Council meeting, "is an experiment in political education to promote the participation of women in government."

It is to sharpen the challenge of the vote, to vivify the educational process of study and discussion, quite as much as to achieve the success of particular measures, that the League supports a legislative program. It follows that the League must constantly readdress itself to shifting needs and conditions. Such action is easy enough for a small group of like-minded people, which can leave its affair to a small governing body. The League, however, is large and the common denominator among its members, aside from sex, is no more than a general desire to use the vote intelligently. How can such an organization act on current controversial issues without disruption?

The answer is in a scrupulous regard for representative procedure within its own ranks. The recent Council meeting received the reports of two committees, which had been going over this procedure with a fine toothcomb. The recommendations for change were slight but all in the direction of increasing advance consideration of the program on the part of the local Leagues and individual members, and the understanding use of the program after adoption. Long ago, the practice was established of sending outs three months in advance of the convention at which of work with all proposed new matter indicated in red ink. This preliminary period is one of study, consultation and discussion-not of referendum. The deliberative freedom of the convention itself is carefully preserved. Two other points should be mentioned-items are customarily placed upon the study program for a year or more before going on the active lists and the number of items added in a year is small, the rate being about equal to that by which other items are written off through accomplishment.

The three additions this year illustrate with particular clearness the League's habit of dealing with "situations not subjects." The General Council, which takes the place of the convention in alternate years, is limited in action on program to proposals due to "altered conditions." To the program of the Efficiency in Government Department, therefore, was added the study of corrupt practices legislation. The Child Welfare program was modified so as to permit support of measures—state or federal—to continue programs of maternity and infancy hygiene in the states after the expiration of the Sheppard-Towner Act in 1929. In the Department of International Cooperation to Prevent War, arbitration has been for several years an item for study. There has now been substituted active "support of the settlement of international difficulties by arbitration or other peaceful means and support of treaties having the same end in view."

Thus the League has worked out for itself a procedure which spells vitality and health. It is, in briefs to seek first the facts, then a plan of action to meet the facts. The method is slow and often criticized by eager spirits who would press forward even though the rank and file trails helplessly and perhaps resentfully behind. Yet the League has found that the caution and care with which it makes commitments are in direct ratio to the constancy and valor with which they can thereafter be supported.

Source: Gladys Harrison, "Participating in Government." LWV Papers, Library of Congress.

Chapter 9

Unfinished Business

The mid–1920s represented a period of growth for the League in both organizational and programmatic terms. The League had refined its decision-making process and extended its reach in public policy issues. There were, however, two major disappointments: the Get Out the Vote campaign of 1924 did not produce the voter turnout the League had hoped for, and the Child Labor Amendment went down to defeat. During this period, the League also began to monitor the number of women elected to public office in local, state, and national elections, and its effectiveness in adult education became the object of scholarly research.

A press release introduced plans for the Sixth National Convention to be held in Richmond, Virginia, in April 1935 and heralded the event as an occasion for hundreds of women to gather and articulate their interest in world peace and a more efficient government also attentive to the welfare of needy citizens. It would be the first League convention to be held in a southern state and the first to be presided over by the new president.

DOCUMENT 1: PRESS RELEASE OF THE LEAGUE OF WOMEN VOTERS

Hundreds of women, whose interest centers in more efficient government, the establishment of an assured world peace program, and the various phases of public welfare in government, will gather in Richmond, VA, Thursday for a six-day annual convention of the National League of Women Voters. A brilliant array of national and international speakers will contribute to a program which covers twenty-two sessions and conferences, and includes twelve scheduled dinners and luncheons.

For the first time in the history of the League, since its organization in February 1920 in Chicago, the national convention is being held in a southern state. For the first time since her election to the presidency, Miss Belle Sherwin of Cleveland, will preside over convention sessions, and for the first time the convention is being welcomed to the home city of a director of the National League. Miss Adele Clark, of Richmond, is not only national director, but president of the Virginia League of Women Voters.

Members of the national board of directors are wending their way to Richmond today, in preparation for the opening of a three–day Board meeting that always precedes the convention. Presidents of state leagues will precede the delegate body to Richmond by one day, arriving Wednesday for a meeting of the executive council early Thursday morning. Special trains from New England, New York, and the Middle West, and automobile caravans from more adjacent states will bring delegates in time for the Department and Committee Conferences Thursday afternoon.

The program is rich with authoritative speakers. Mass meetings devoted to "The Background of the Program," international relations, and questions of the day schedule the presentation of a group of brilliant and instructive speakers, such as Brigadier General Herbert M. Lord, director of the U.S. Budget; Huston Thompson, chairman of the Federal Trade Commission; Glenn Frank, editor in chief of the Century Magazine; Professors James T. Shotwell and Arthur MacMahon of Columbia University, and John M. Gaus of the University of Minnesota.

One of the gala events scheduled is a finance luncheon Monday, April 20, with George Shephard Chappell, the widely known author and magazine writer, as the principal speaker. As "Walter E. Traprock" Mr. Chappell's entertaining wit is known far and wide. Elaborate arrangements, providing for a scenario and other unique features, are in the hands of Miss Katharine Ludington, of Lyme, Conn., national treasurer. She will be assisted by Mrs. Sumner T. McKnight of Minneapolis and Miss Gertrude Ely, of Bryn Mawr, PA. Special visitors from all parts of the country are expected for this luncheon.

Of the many interesting sessions, in which more than 100 speakers, including League members, will participate, the afternoon and evening sessions of April 21, a few stand out as particularly attractive. "Women in Public Affairs in the United States" from a mayor of a small town in North Carolina, to woman in legislative service, in a Governor's cabinet, a collector of internal revenue and those holding federal posts, will "tell of her job." It is expected to be one of the outstanding events of the session, and will be followed by a banquet, the closing gathering of the convention. Among the banquet speakers will be Mrs. Corbett Ashby, of London, president of the International Woman Suffrage Association, Miss Bertha Lutz, secretary of the National Museum at Rio de Janerio, Countess de Robillant of Italy, Mme. Branko Adjemovitch, wife of the secretary of the Serbian Legation, Miss Josefa Llanes, of the Philippines, and Mrs. Carrie Chapman Catt. Miss Julia Lathrop will preside.

Another day which gives evidence of being exceptionally interesting is Saturday, April 18, known as "New Voters' Day" and set aside to honor a large representation of new and prospective voters from college, Junior League, Girl

Scouts, business, industrial, farm and professional groups. The day will be crowned with addresses by Judge Florence E. Allen, Supreme Court Justice of Ohio, Mrs. Maud Wood Park, former president of the National League, and the representatives of the various groups.

Of the many impressive features, there will be the award of the silver loving cup to the League in the state showing the greatest percentage of voting increase in the last election. Mrs. Gifford Pinchot, of Pennsylvania, chairman of the committee of award, will present the cup.

Marked interest is being shown in the election of officers, terms now held by Miss Julia Lathrop, of Rockford, Ill., Mrs. Minnie Fisher Cunningham, of New Waverley, Texas, vice presidents, and Miss Ludington, treasurer, having expired. The nominating committee, of which Mrs. James G. Macpherson is chairman, will also suggest candidates for directors in each of the seven regions. The present incumbents are: Mrs. James E. Cheesman of Providence, RI, Miss Gertrude Ely, of Bryn Mawr, PA, Miss Adele Clark, of Richmond, VA, Mrs. William G. Hibbard, of Winnetka, ILL, Miss Marguerite M. Wells, of Minneapolis, MN, Mrs. Charles H. Dietrich, of Hastings, NE, and Mrs. W. A. Shockley, of Reno, NV.

Source: LWV Papers on film, II. A.6. 0725–26.

> Belle Sherwin began her presidential address to the League's sixth convention with a retrospective look at the League's Get Out the Vote campaign of 1924. While that effort had produced a minuscule increase in voter turnout, Sherwin remained optimistic that the League's work was making a difference.

>> The actual day by day work of the state and local Leagues was appraised by experienced campaigners as shrewdly practical, ingenious, and, above all, persistent to the finish. The now familiar forms of educational activity which went hand in hand with ward and precinct campaigning were almost embarrassingly praised as "aids to sound thinking and sound patriotism such as have never been developed in America before." It is conservative to say that the League gained in reputation in 1924, that it grew in the general esteem as a factor in the responsible citizenship of the country.

>> But the League's reputation had a negative dimension as well. Opposition to the League and to other women's groups had surfaced and was directed at their positions on behalf of social legislation and international cooperation. Sherwin noted: "The criticism resolves itself into three charges: Communistic programs; casual and baseless endorsement and adoption of legislative measures without understanding their relation to the purpose and limits of government; the support of Federal legislation to the exclusion of local responsibility and initiatives."

In response to the allegation that the League supported a growing federal government and shortchanged "local responsibility and initiatives," Sherwin had an impressive retort: In its first four years, the League worked for thirteen Federal measures, but in the same period, forty-five state Leagues had successfully worked on behalf of 420 laws. Statistics clearly refuted the notion of the League seeking a greater power for the national government over and above that of states and municipalities. As for communism, Sherwin asserted that the burden of proof rested with the critics: (1) to define communism and (2) to specify the ways in which the League program equated with that ideology. As for the Child Labor Amendment—symptomatic of the charges relating to an ill-informed support of certain public policies—President Sherwin acknowledged that the campaign would be long and uphill but insisted that the League's commitment would never be in doubt. Putting all this turmoil in perspective, Sherwin concluded her address with the remarks that follow.

DOCUMENT 2: BELLE SHERWIN'S PRESIDENTIAL ADDRESS TO THE LEAGUE'S SIXTH CONVENTION

If public opinion is ever to be leavened by facts it must be accomplished by the active working of the desire of many, many men and women. Citizenship, like religion, is an individual, personal experience, and one of its first fruits is a sense of active responsibility toward its own kingdom, whatever that may be. Just so far as the realization of citizenship in this personal sense has been deepened and widened among us by this year's work, in such degree has the year enriched us. If the purposes of the League of Women Voters, as they have been formed previously or as they are to be formed by you, here are to prevail in the future—far or near—they must be carried forward by the desire of a multitude of individuals finding expression in simple ways in the course of countless daily relationships, and, I would add, in the atmosphere of good temper which the whole facts carries with it. . . .

The almost exclusive discussion of one aspect of public welfare this year has introduced to our most thoughtful consideration now the larger question of the objective of a government that truly serves the people. We shall get only a glimpse of the significance of that question and the answers in this convention. The lessons of the year counsel us to look at it in the light of ascertainable facts, forgetting preconceptions and throwing overboard prejudices, if the League of Women Voters ever harbors such.

One other objective of our program is in the foreground of our thoughts—the Promotion of Peace. We are not able to report one item of that particular part of the program enacted this year, but I know you are to recount together here real gains made in the definition of terms essential to the promotion of the program and real gains made in the degree of support given to measures which must depend upon the expression of the will of many for their enactment ultimately.

Intangible returns, it may be said, in almost every case. It is for you to demonstrate whether they are as real as steam in the engine and the vigor of health in a body that has been exercised. What do we need today to meet the indifference we have met and to counter the alliance of money and "partial facts" which we have encountered? The citizen poet who best understood the forces and problems of democracy in this country once said to a pupil, "If reform is needed through you, begin to inure yourself today to pluck, reality, definiteness." Exactly these qualities seem to me to be the rewards of work won by the League of Women Voters in the past year. If pluck, reality and definiteness are ours, the morrow is assured. The convention will prove us. (Applause)

Source: Excerpts from the Proceedings of the Sixth Convention. LWV Papers on film, II. A.7. 1010–12.

The program of International Cooperation to Prevent War was humming with activity under the inspiring leadership of Ruth Morgan of New York. There were no results to point to in terms of legislation, but it wasn't for lack of trying.

DOCUMENT 3: REPORT ON INTERNATIONAL COOPERATION ACTIVITIES

You recall the man who, when asked why there was so little happiness in the world, replied: "Because there are so few people engaged in the manufacture." The same is true of peace. Before we can get that world order which is peace, in its outward aspect, we must build the machinery and the system, which is to displace the system and machinery of war, for war is the adjustment of international difficulties by violence.

What has your department done for this in 1924–25? The previous year we had educated ourselves about the World Court as the instrument of peaceful adjustment between nations. We had worked very hard to educate groups in our states and specifically to inform our representatives in the Senate as to our convictions in the matter. This year we have expanded our efforts in the direction of informing national public opinion on this subject.

The three outstanding efforts undertaken by the League of Women Voters were: First, aiding in the organization of the hearing before the Senate Committee on Foreign Relations on the bill providing for the entry of the United States into the World Court. Miss Marion Delany of California, Mrs. James W. Morrisson of Illinois, and your chairman from New York made a geographical representation from sea to sea on behalf of the measure. Incidentally it took your department six weeks of effort to get the hearing and to prepare for it.

Second, came the hearings before the conventions of the political parties. As one who took a strenuous part as a member of the League committee to present planks to the Republican Convention, we have been assured that the Court plank was partly driven in by our efforts and we were allowed to discuss its actual wording as acceptable or not to this group of women.

After the other party conventions came the summer work, involving intensive study as to the relation between international cooperation and those questions which were raised in every community where mobilization days and peace days seemed to come into conflict. This study was undertaken as part of the preparation necessary for any useful material to be published for our own educational purposes. . . .

It is only possible here to suggest one or two points: First, the Constitution plainly makes all citizens responsible for plans, money grants, and other needs relative to the adequate defense of the country. As Congress prepared and passed the much discussed National Defense Act, it can also amend or alter it. The Constitution is also emphatic on another point. Civilians are responsible for their own army and navy, but the latter have no peacetime responsibility for the opinions, education, or conduct of civilians. In other words, we as citizens are made responsible for the organization and control of our defense departments and this emphasis on civilian control was based on the experience of our forefathers in Europe with military and naval establishments, as they functioned there.

Why does military and naval preparedness enter into any modern discussion of foreign policies? For one reason, because it is the outstanding symptom of international non-cooperation. Every new demand for increased preparedness, every danger suggested and every suspicion aroused echoes and re–echoes in other countries. What one nation does compels the action of another country. What is done on other continents influences our military and naval plans. If the rest of the world fought with bows and arrows, should we need intensive preparation for chemical warfare? So long as one nation prepares to attack, we must prepare to defend. But we can restrict ourselves in alarms, in hates, and even in preparations, not only for our own sakes, but for the sake of the rest of the world. We can with absolute consistency prepare to defend ourselves in the remote contingency of our being attacked and at the same time go ahead to build a system of world order of which our nation shall be a part. In this field we have the leadership of great statesmen and responsible heads of governments the world over, and President Coolidge has offered us the most emphatic leadership for this double responsibility. We can back his disarmament plans and we should do so in the most whole-hearted fashion.

We now reach the third accomplishment for this year in the education of ourselves and public opinion. I like to recall the moment last year in Buffalo, when Mrs. Hooper won for us Mrs. Catt's leadership, which resulted in what I like to call Mrs. Catt's Conference. All of last summer Mrs. Catt matured her plans and she said that Miss Schain and myself with her should have no holidays. The director of your department, Miss Schain, was elected secretary of the Conference. Many of you went to the city of Washington, were it took place in January. Such a concerted effort by nine women's national organizations— such harmony such questioning! It was intended as a great movement in support of the World Court. As such it strengthened and indeed largely superseded the constant interviews with senators.

I do not hesitate to say that its effect on public opinion was incalculable and whatever effort and sacrifice was made by your department to achieve it, was repaid a thousand-fold by its results.

What your department does is only a feeble reflection of what the states really do. I can only illustrate by the extraordinary standing set by the state of Rhode Island, which held eighty-six large meetings on international affairs, twenty-five round tables and fifty other meetings where members of the League spoke on similar topics.

And now for one forward look! We must get the World Court with an estimate of 85 per cent of the country for it, and at least 75 per cent of the Senate favorable to it, with the President of the United States urging it and the opposition party demanding it. With the two great parties on record in the platforms for it, why not? Well, its enemies have not admitted defeat. They mean to fight all summer against it, up to the date, December 17, now set for the vote. We cannot afford to slumber or take anything for granted.

Source: Report of the Third Vice President (International Cooperation to Prevent War). LWV Papers on film, II. A.6. 0513–14.

The budget for 1925–1926 ($136,000)—even taking into account the lower costs of the period—seemed a meager sum with which to tackle such imposing issues as those defined by the League's program of work for the same year.

DOCUMENT 4: 1925–26 LEAGUE BUDGET

Topical Summary

General Administration	$ 8,167.38
Organization	48,132.39
Publicity	11,487.39
Publications, General	9,870.00
Public Welfare in Government	8,700.00
Legislation and Law Enforcement	8,747.37
Treasurer's Office	9,870.00
Efficiency in Government	8,612.37
International Cooperation to Prevent War	10,275.00
Secretary's Office	1,400.00
Board Members' Travel	2,500.00
Convention	6,500.00
Legal Services	500.00
Emergency	1,620.71
	$136,000.00

Percentages of Budget Chargeable to Major Divisions of the Work

General Administration, including Board Members' Travel, Secretary's Office, Executive Secretary's Salary	.08
Organization, including Regional Secretaries, Speakers' Bureau, Regional Directors	.37
Publicity	.08
Education, including Efficiency in Government, International Cooperation to Prevent War, Publications, Standing Committees	.28
Legislation	.06
Business Administration, Money Raising, Promotion	.07
National Convention	.05
Miscellaneous, Emergency	.01
	100.00

Source: LVW Papers on film, II. A.6. 0516.

DOCUMENT 5: 1925–26 LEAGUE PROGRAM OF WORK

To carry out the purposes for which the League was organized, the program consists of the following lines for study and action. Its first object is to increase the number of responsible voting citizens.

I   *Efficiency in Government (Standards, Legislation, and Law Enforcement.*

Nominations and Elections.
City Charters and State Constitutions.
Problems of Administration: public finance and public employment.
Law Making.

II   *Public Welfare in Government (Standards, Legislation, and Law Enforcement).*

Child Welfare.
Education.
Legal Status of Women.
Living Costs.
Social Hygiene.
Women in Industry.

III *International Cooperation to Prevent War (Education and Legislation).*

The National League of Women Voters is making a creative attack upon indifference and ignorance through training for citizenship and by supporting needed legislation.

The League believes in a program of education which prepares for action. It believes in a program which emphasizes practical methods in realizing ideals.

The League believes that qualified women in administrative offices, upon boards and commissions, and in legislative bodies, will contribute a necessary point of view to Government in the United States and to its international relations. The League, therefore, urges the principle of electing and appointing qualified women to positions in national, state, and local governments, and upon commissions and other bodies having international representation.

Source: LWV Papers on film, II. A.6. 0516, 0522–27.

A year later, at the St. Louis convention in 1926, national board member Marguerite Wells addressed the perennial issue of "how much government is enough" and the difficulties in reaching agreement due to differing priorities and new inventions.

DOCUMENT 6: MARGUERITE WELLS, "THE GREAT ADMINISTRATION"

You remember the oft-quoted observation of Mark Twain that everybody grumbles about the weather but nobody seems to do anything about it. Nowadays everybody is grumbling about too much government. From the press, from magazines, from the platform, out of the air, ring the phrases: "Too much government; too high taxes; too many laws; too much paternalism; too much centralization." Into the ears of thousands of people these phrases pour and out of their mouths come back: "Less government; lower taxes; fewer laws; no more paternalism; decentralization!" Into the ear and out of the mouth, by the shortest route!

For, with a few distinguished exceptions, nobody is discussing in a constructive way the problems these phrases involve. People will agree about reduction of taxes without agreeing on a single government service they all are willing to do without. I never heard anyone talk five minutes about fewer laws without proposing a new law. Men will oppose a federal appropriation of a few thousand dollars for the protection of babies or women because it is paternalistic, and then laud to the skies a federal appropriation of eighty million dollars for good roads, as an example of cooperation between state and nation based on the best traditions of American government. Farmers object to federal legislation against child labor as a federal encroachment and then go to Washington to insist upon the government's taking part in a plan to fix the price of grain. Businessmen oppose the scheme of the farmer as government interference with economic laws and turn about and vote for higher tariff.

What conditions have brought about expansion of government, whether they are desirable or inevitable, what must be done to cope with changing conditions, these are questions rarely asked and more rarely answered. Yet everybody knows that the larger and more complicated any affair becomes, the more need there is for rules and regulations. This is as true of children's playgrounds as it is of schools. It is true of the factory, it is true of the football crowd, it is true of the arrangements for a League of Women Voters convention. And the rules and regulations of a country are its laws and government.

Twenty-five years ago, if you had wished to drive from this hotel to the stores on Locust Street, you would have been outraged, and justly so, if the traffic regulations of St. Louis had limited the speed at which you might go, had forbidden you to stop at the curb here or to turn into a side street there, had permitted you to go only west on certain streets and only east on others. Today you could not arrive at all except for these traffic regulations. At least, only a few of the more ruthless and aggressive of you could arrive. As for the pedestrians, without the modern traffic regulations, they would be glued to the sidewalks or lose their lives in the fray. It is true that the traffic regulations have taken from you certain of your liberties, but as Mr. Farnam, the political economist, has recently pointed out, there are many sorts of liberty of which legal liberty is only one. By giving up certain legal liberties about how to drive you have secured for yourself liberty of arriving at your destination, while to the pedestrian, the modern traffic regulations ensures that equality of opportunity which is the very basis of our American theory of government. Pedestrians today would have no opportunity at all without modern traffic regulations. . . .

Another cause of expanded government is enlightened self-interest, or, as some prefer to call it, the wider social consciousness. In feudal days the baron was content to live in his castle, surrounded by every luxury his booty could purchase, while the town huddled at his gates, steeped in poverty, ignorance and dirt. When out of these conditions came pests and plagues, the baron and his family had to die with the rest. Today people know that there can be no personal safety unless the community enjoys a certain degree of safety too. Today people demand a higher standard of living than can be secured by individual enterprise, a standard that can be secured only by community effort.

In many states there are counties, poorer than the rest of the state. In such counties until recently the schools were poorer too. It was thought to be nobody's business but the parents of the community what sort of education the children had. Recently the people of the state have become unwilling that anywhere in the state children should be so poorly educated that when they moved from one community to another they carried ignorance with them, or that when they stayed at home they added to the ignorant vote for state laws and state officials. Accordingly there has been a demand for state aid of county schools, and this has meant more laws, more government.

You may call this enlightened self-interest or you may call it a broader social consciousness. Certainly there is closer communion today between the people of a state than in early days between the people of a township. This is fostered by inventions. Trains and rural free delivery, the automobile and the telephone, the radio, have brought the people of a state together and revealed the unity of their interests. So inventions as well as the tendency towards centralization play their part in the expansion. . . .

Centralization everywhere is an inevitable tendency. It nowhere shows itself so strongly as in business. Everybody knows that steel doesn't do business in any one city or in any one state but in every state of the country—and oil, and Fords. Even in the retail stores nowadays frequently do business not only in one town, but in many. There are few important industrial concerns that do not spread out into many communities, perhaps into many states. . . .

The trusts and the mergers of a quarter century ago are familiar phenomena, and the expansion of government to meet them under Roosevelt and Wilson. Within the last five years, however, there has come about an era of consolidation of business compared with which the Roosevelt trust is a pigmy. It is an era that businessmen refer to as a "commercial revolution," with all that term implies. The public is familiar with it in the case of bread and what it tried to do, and in the case of railroads and what they are about to do. The possible results and the possible effects of this commercial revolution challenge the imagination and outrun any calculation.

In the face of phenomena like these, commercial revolution, the transformation of conditions due to inventions, the new demand of people for government service, it is idle to ask if the expansion of government is desirable. It is inevitable. Our task is so to administer this new and expanded government that we may avoid its perils and minimize its evils. Our task is by attention to every unit of administration, local, state and national, to decrease waste and increase efficiency. Our task, above all, is to devise new forms of government to meet the new conditions and by an inventiveness in the field of political science to match the inventiveness in other fields that has brought about the need for expanded government.

Faced with a task like this, we cannot stand meekly by wringing our hands over too much government. We cannot sigh for the good old days. We cannot invoke those great men of our early history whose rules and regulations were adequate for a little band of three million agricultural people, scattered among the wilderness of the Eastern seaboard, living under conditions that had not changed as much for them in five thousand years as they have for us since that day. Or rather let us invoke those early heroes of ours, Washington, Jefferson, Madison, John Marshall, that we may profit by the example of their courage in the face of new conditions and their resourcefulness in adjusting to their new conditions old forms of government.

City charters and the manager plan, state departments and an executive budget, federal aid, taxation, civil service, do these seem to you dry and technical subjects, or are they a challenge to find for our great expanded government, a great administration? This is still a new country. We are still a young people. In our veins runs the blood of pioneers. Especially do the new voters possess some of the courage and enthusiasm that comes with new responsibilities and new opportunities. Let us then stand up to our great task! Let us not be overwhelmed by its difficulties!

Let us even, in the words of the psalmist, "Rejoice as a strong man to run a race."

Source: Excerpts from the Proceedings of the Seventh Convention. LWV Papers on film, II. A.7. 1040–43.

Maud Wood Park delivered an informative speech to the same convention about the early days of the League—the kind of memories that do not often find their way into recorded history.

DOCUMENT 7: MAUD WOOD PARK ON THE LEAGUE'S EARLY DAYS

Actually the beginning of the League was in 1919. The Suffrage Amendment was not then through the Congress but the great leader of women in this country, Mrs. Carrie Chapman Catt, realized that we were soon to be enfranchised. In 1919, therefore, the states which were already fully enfranchised or which had Presidential or Primary suffrage formed the League of Women Voters, of which Mrs. Charles Brooks of Kansas was national chairman, as a branch of the National American Woman Suffrage Association.

Thus at the time of the enfranchisement of some twenty odd millions of women, there was an organization ready to help them get the necessary information for their early votes and an organization to bring forward the special ideas of women in regard to legislation. In that preliminary year, before the 1920 Convention, there were organized in the League of Women Voters a number of committees covering virtually all the subjects in our present division of Public Welfare in Government.

There was also a Committee on Election Laws which later became our Department of Efficiency in Government. The only present department that was not represented in that preliminary year was our Department of International Cooperation to Prevent War. That was not established until the Cleveland Convention in 1921. . . .

The rest of the committees were started in the preliminary year, because Mrs. Catt felt that there were, at that time, certain subjects in which women had particular experience, and, therefore, particular interest and that one of their great services as voters was going to be the insistence that the women's experiences in those particular subjects should be reckoned with in legislation. That purpose was one of the chief objects of the League, just as it is today, and the other objective was the general political education of women.

The great difference that I see today, is therefore not in the idea, which was that vital wonderful forethought of Mrs. Catt's—the difference is in the method of application of that idea. Let me illustrate by what happened to us in that Convention.

The actual By-laws were not worked on by any member of the first Board. They were drafted on the way to Chicago by a group of women who happened to be on the train going out, and that group of women were so enthusiastic about the possibilities of the future that they believed we could run the League of

Women Voters exactly as a business corporation is run by a Board of Directors who meet occasionally to vote on decisions, leaving all the active work in the hands of a manager. For that reason our first set of By-laws provided for a General Manager of the League of Women Voters, who was to do all the real work of the National League.

Now, a large part of our trouble that first year came from our efforts to get such a National Manager. I wish you knew how many agonized conferences the Board held in its attempts to find some woman who could live up to the qualifications that we vaguely understood were necessary. Then suddenly, about the middle of the year, we realized that if we found the woman we hadn't the money to pay her, and, so, though our By-laws directed us to appoint a manager, I had to go to the Convention next year and explain why we had violated that By-law, because in the first place we could not find a woman with the necessary qualifications, and in the next place, we could not pay her.

Our other great agony was over money. The fact that the National American Woman Suffrage Association was not continuing and nobody was really certain whether the League of Women Voters was going on as an independent organization, led to a situation in which nobody had any real responsibility for raising the money. And if Mrs. Marie Edwards of Indiana, our wonderful first Treasurer, later Vice-President of the League, had not realized suddenly that she was going to be treasurer without funds to work with and persuaded Miss Mary Garrett Hay to raise pledges in the Convention for forty thousand dollars, including a large one from the Leslie Commission, I do not know what would have happened to us.

I, who happened to be the first national chairman of the League, was not elected for that purpose. I was elected as a director-at-large, but when the Board organized we had to divide up offices as well as we could. The other directors-at-large, Mrs. Gellhorn, Mrs. Edwards and Mrs. Jacobs, all had families and could not come to Washington to live. I could manage to be here part of the year and, therefore, I was made Chairman.

MRS. GELLHORN: "That was not the reason at all." (Laughter)

While the Board was meeting in a small room to choose the officers, the Convention was busily going ahead passing resolutions. I assure you that there were thirty-eight different measures involving legislation endorsed at that first Convention of the League of Women Voters. . . . Now if any of you think we are severe about our limitations on general resolutions at conventions, you bear in mind that some of us had that early experience.

We were extremely anxious to have the League a national organization, to keep it from being too Eastern by having a proper division of the work in various parts of the country. Therefore we decided to have four headquarters. We had our organization headquarters in St. Louis and our finance headquarters in Indiana, our Secretary's office in Alabama and our legislative headquarters in Washington. . . .

All the hope and all the enthusiasm that we had then, you have for exactly the same ideals, but your enthusiasm is chastened and made lucid by your experience and made efficient by the leadership of the very wonderful administrator who is now our President.

I think that today more than ever we see the need and the possibilities of this organization of ours. We realize that our task is no less interesting, no less stimulating than in those early days. But we have learned that it must be carried on with a degree of wisdom about methods that we had not at all anticipated at that time. And therefore I think the League is at the most hopeful point in its career.

We all know that Mrs. Catt's idea of the League was a great idea. We know that the League's service to the future of this nation is going to be a great service. We know now that we cannot go ahead "hit or miss," the way we went at a lot of our early work. We know that we have to give all the wisdom and the devotion that is in us. And the more of that wisdom and devotion we put into the work, the more we are ourselves committed to the future of the League.

Source: Excerpts from the Proceedings of the Seventh Convention proceedings. LWV Papers on film, II. A.9. 0554–67.

With the adoption of new bylaws by the 1926 convention, annual conventions became biennial, and General Council meetings (later shortened to Council) were held in interim years. These meetings were much smaller than conventions, and each state usually sent two representatives. At the first of these General Councils, Edna Gellhorn, one of the original board members, who was highly regarded for her wit, charm, and dynamic personality, delivered an important report—based on more searching reports requested from selected Leagues—as to why there had been such a low turnout in the 1924 presidential elections.

DOCUMENT 8: EDNA GELLHORN ON 1924 VOTER TURNOUT

Summarizing from studies made of different types of communities in five states by the League of Women Voters we may draw the following conclusions:

1. The percentage of women who use their vote is lower than that of men; in other words women are poorer voters than men.
2. The head of the family holds the best record as a voter. Next to the head of the family comes the son and daughter, and last the wife.
3. Persons belonging to the middle age group have the largest voting percentage; those of the youngest group the lowest voting percentage.
4. The better the education, the higher the voting percentage of the group.
5. In surveys which covered several elections it was proven that a much higher percentage of persons vote at one or more elections than is shown in a survey of a single election. A very small percent of the total eligible voters never use their vote. . . .

Moreover from these studies and additional data it has been demonstrated that there is evidence in plenty to justify concern over the non-participation of the American people in their government, but upon careful analysis of figures used in get-out-the-vote campaigns it would seem that conditions are not quite as appalling as we had feared. The following facts have direct bearing on the total number of votes cast and prove that more persons voted than we have counted.

1. The vote for president which is taken as the basis for the number of votes cast is not always the highest cast at an election; frequently the vote for the candidates for governor, some other state officer, U.S. Senator, etc., is much larger

than the vote cast for president. For example in 1924 in 10 states there were 400,854 votes in excess of the vote for president.

2. The number of defective ballots has not been calculated in the total number of votes cast. In New Jersey in 1920 there were 10,979 rejected ballots; in 1924 in the same state 6,006.

3. In some states, one party states, more votes are cast in the primary than in the general election.

On the other hand the calculation of the number of "eligible voters" has not been exact. Criminals, idiots, and insane have never been deducted from the census figure for native born and naturalized citizens. Nor have voters disqualified by special provisions such as residence requirements, poll tax requirement, literacy test, registration requirements, lack of absentee voting laws, etc., been subtracted from the number of eligible voters.

With the number of "eligibles" reduced and the number of actual voters increased as indicated above, the percentage of those voting should be considerably higher than the one quoted for the past two general elections.

The failure of women to exercise their newly won rights of the franchise is the chief concern of the League of Women Voters and the reason for its existence. The League believes that the change will come not by intensive campaigns shortly before election days but by an all the year round persistent effort through political education to stimulate the participation of women in government.

The National League has definite recommendations to make to the state and local organizations to strengthen this experiment in the education of a whole generation of women that has grown up without the tradition and experience of a responsibility to share in the glorious drama of being a citizen of these United States. . . .

Following Gelhorn was Mrs. F. W. Wittish who had chaired the Minnesota survey and who provided a witty postscript.

DOCUMENT 9: REASONS FOR NON-VOTING

Concerning the reasons for non-voting, of course, by far the largest number fall into the difficulty of indifference, and then, of course, there was a small group of women who admitted that they did not care to go to the polls because they had never been there and felt somewhat timid about it. A great many of the women particularly said that they would vote, if a group of them could go together, so they are planning groups of voters, preceding the next election, to go in a group.

One woman complained that the booths were too small, which was literally a fact, I am told. (Laughter) Some people had not time, or were too tired, they were too busy, and several women said they had not formed the habit and did not care to do so, that woman's place was in the home. One woman said her husband had not been at home to remind her of the fact. The professional ball player who went hunting was rather interesting. A butcher said his wife voted and he thought that was sufficient for the family. Another man said he did not vote because he did not care for the type of people who were elected. (Laughter)

Source: Press Department, National League of Women Voters, April 30, 1927. LWV Papers on film, II. A.9. 0544. Excerpts from the Proceedings of the General Council of the National League of Women Voters (hereinafter referred to as the 1927 Council), Washington, DC, April 26–30. LWV Papers on film, II. A.9. 0021–0033.

Another request from the National League produced a report—again from selected Leagues—on the numbers of women holding public office in 1927.

DOCUMENT 10: REPORT ON WOMEN ELECTED OFFICIALS

MRS. OTJEN:

It is impossible, you will realize, to make a report on women in office in detail, because there is lack of statistical material, and states have not made these summaries, generally speaking, and so, the remarks that I have to make are based, almost entirely, upon the material that was sent to the National office from the few states where these surveys were made, and these were made at the suggestion of the National League of Women Voters, in Minnesota, Connecticut, Ohio, Alabama, Washington, Kansas and Wisconsin. These returns, however, are not altogether complete, and since no general form was followed in making these surveys, the material collected is not uniform. Minnesota perhaps deserves the credit for having made the most complete and detailed report. . . .

Basing my remarks then upon the surveys mentioned, I find that the 1926 returns from Connecticut show that there were 97 women holding Municipal, County and State offices. . . . Minnesota had a total of 125 for the year 1926, as compared with a total of 209 for 1927, showing an increase of 66%. It is interesting to note that the greatest increase was in the number of women holding municipal and local offices.

In Wisconsin, there were 61 women holding county and state positions in 1925, as compared with 70 women holding similar positions in 1926. The Wisconsin survey gives no figures for women in municipal office. Ohio shows a total of 91 women holding county and state positions in 1927 and Kansas' report for 1927 gives a total of 228 women in county and state positions.

As to the various county positions held by women in Wisconsin, in 1925 Wisconsin had one woman district attorney, none in 1926. The 1927 reports show for the office of county clerk, in Ohio, a total of 13, in Wisconsin 11, and Kansas 8. County treasurer: in Ohio 11, Wisconsin 10, Minnesota 3, and Kansas 24. For recorder and register of deeds: Ohio 25, Wisconsin 10, Minnesota 7, and Kansas 63. County superintendent of schools: Wisconsin 29, Kansas 72, Probate judge, Ohio 4, Minnesota 2, Kansas 11. For sheriff: Ohio 1, Wisconsin 3 and Kansas 3.

It is apparent that the office of county superintendent of schools is as much a woman's job as a man's. Progress is in the right direction when women fill positions that they are best qualified to hold. It is possible that women will predominate in the smaller political units, such as the town and county, because it is these offices which require the ability to classify the interest most likely to be found among women. It is the women who give the business-like attention to detail, as a rule, and furnish the kind of service which these offices require. It is not surprising, therefore, to find an ever-increasing number of women holding these positions.

It is, perhaps, more unusual to find a woman holding the office of sheriff. There are three county sheriffs in Wisconsin this year. This is accounted for by the statutory provision prohibiting a sheriff from succeeding himself in office.

These women recently elected to the position of sheriff are merely succeeding their husbands and thus, by appointing their husband as deputy sheriffs they keep the office in the family, and the deputy sheriff does the work.

Not so many statistics are available for women holding city, village or town offices. Minnesota shows a total of fifty-eight in such positions in 1926 as against one hundred and thirty-four in 1927. In Connecticut, the increase is even greater, eighty in 1926 and three hundred and thirty-nine in 1927.

Just a word or two about women in state offices: In Ohio, Judge Florence Allen is the first woman to sit on the bench in the State Supreme Court, and, of course, you know a great number of the states have women in their state legislature as members of the Lower House, primarily, and some also in the Upper House. The women elected to the 1927 state legislatures total one hundred and twenty-three.

The totals for all the states having women in the legislature are Upper House 13, Lower House 110. This number is slightly less than that recorded in 1925 and 1926, when approximately one hundred and thirty women were members of state legislatures. Fourteen states have no women representatives. The largest representation appears in Connecticut, a state which, up to the very last, opposed Woman's Suffrage. Fifteen women sit in its 1927 legislature. Wyoming, the first state to recognize equal suffrage rights, elected but one woman. The East, generally, has the most women legislators. Iowa, up to 1926, declined to recognize the right of women to sit in its legislature; on November 2, 1926, Iowa voters ratified a state constitutional amendment removing the obstacle to women serving in its legislative service, by striking out the word "male" in its provisions for qualifications of members.

As to women in national and federal positions, you are all, no doubt, familiar with the number of women who have been elected to Congress: six women have been elected to Congress since 1922; only one other woman, Miss Jeanette Rankin, of Montana, has been elected to Congress. She was elected in 1916 and served one term. . . .

Source: Excerpts from the Proceedings of the 1927 Council. LWV Papers on film, II. A.9. 0576–85. With regard to Jeanette Rankin, it should be noted that she was elected again in 1940 and again served only one term, a brevity of service influenced by her unpopular votes against U.S. participation in World Wars I and II.

At about this same time the passage of child labor reform, which was one of the League's earliest priorities, was consuming a lot of the organization's energies. Although Congress had enacted the original reform legislation, the Supreme Court declared the law unconstitutional. Congress then passed a proposed constitutional amendment, and, in preparation for the ratification debates certain to occur in state legislatures, the Women's Joint Congressional Committee established a subcommittee called Organizations Associated for Ratification of the Child Labor Amendment; it was chaired by Florence Kelley of the National Consumers' League. What initially had seemed a sure victory ended with a severe setback with opposition coming from a strong coalition of business, agricultural, and southern textile interests. The *amendment went down to defeat initially in states of the South and then in New England (areas populated by textile plants) and, for one reason or another, had hard sledding in other states. Although the amendment failed ratification in 1925, the League persisted in championing the cause until the essence of the reform finally saw the light of day with passage of the New Deal's Fair Labor Standards Act in 1938. A colorful account of the amendment's defeat in the Massachusetts legislature, given some years after the fact by Dorothy Brown, a participant in the failed effort to secure ratification, described the process and the outcome.*

DOCUMENT 11: THE CHILD LABOR AMENDMENT CAMPAIGN IN MASSACHUSETTS

The Massachusetts experience was the more fantastic because Massachusetts had so long been a leader in the movement for a constitutional amendment. In those days Massachusetts thought of herself as a leader in social legislation and believed that because of her labor laws she suffered in competition with the unenlightened 47 other states. So her Senators and Congressmen introduced amendments galore—to equalize conditions—one, by the late John Jacob Rogers would have given Congress power to legislate on the whole field of wages and hours for children or adults. Conservative newspapers like the *Boston Herald* urged the passage of a child labor amendment. In the winter of 1924 the Massachusetts Great and General Court (our legislature) petitioned *unanimously* that Congress pass the amendment. It is safe to say that no one in Massachusetts expected anything but a cordial welcome for the amendment and its prompt ratification.

The amendment was passed by Congress on June 3, 1924. Our legislature, which until very recently met annually, was in session, but was nervous and irritable and having a row with the Governor and it wanted to go home! The Massachusetts League of course wanted our state to be the first to ratify. A League delegation waited on Mr. Loring Young, then speaker of the House, and he told us that he too wanted immediate ratification as "a feather in the cap of Massachusetts," which he could make the most of when he went out to campaign for Calvin Coolidge for President!

But a difference arose in the legislature as to whether it could properly act on an amendment which had in fact passed both houses of Congress, but had not yet been certified to the states for action by the Secretary of State; and a further difference came up as to whether an amendment to the Federal Constitution should be acted on without the formality of regular committee hearings. Then some miscreant remembered that Massachusetts—always awfully annoyed about Prohibition—had recently passed the so-called "Public Opinion Act" which provided for the submission of various things to advisory referenda. What with the procedural questions involved, the quarrel between governor and legislature, and the passionate desire to go home and not be kept in session any longer for anything at all, the House suddenly adopted a resolve directing that the amendment be submitted to the people, under the Public Opinion Act, for an advisory vote—and then adjourned.

We were annoyed and disappointed but not dismayed. The amendment was still correct, socially and politically, and Massachusetts Party Platforms urged its ratification. Mr. Curley, then Mayor of Boston, made an eloquent speech for its adoption at a Boston League Benefit Pop Concert late in June.

But as July followed June the clouds began to gather. Sinister rumblings were heard—the amendment, long the cherished child of the politically orthodox of both parties, was becoming a radical step-child—born and nurtured in Bolshevist Russia.   A statewide committee was organized to oppose the amendment, but not under that name. No indeed—it was the Massachusetts Committee to Protect our Homes and Children! Prosperous reactionaries gathered at the Parker House and were told over the tea cups that not Henry Cabot Lodge and George Wharton Pepper were the sponsors of the Amendment but Lenin and Mme. Kolontai! Instead of an enabling act, permitting Congress to legislate, the Amendment was declared to be a law prohibiting all labor for persons under 18—even doing the farm chores or helping mother wash the dishes! Advertisements appeared in farm journals—an especially appealing one showed a large hulking boy of 17 sitting on a fence watching his frail old mother chop the wood—with the caption "Sorry, Ma, the government won't let me help you!" Literature of this kind was poured into the state. Radio time—then a new way of campaigning, but already expensive—was freely used. The literature "to protect our homes and children" was traced to its sources—the office of the National Association of Manufacturers and that of the Southern Textile Bulletin. Local money was easily raised because of the Bolshevist bogey and distrust of federal interference—the latter caused by Massachusetts' irritation over the Prohibition Amendment.

Meanwhile we too had not been idle! We organized an ad hoc committee— the Massachusetts Committee for Ratification of the Child Labor Amendment, with representatives of practically every state organization on it. We got up a Child Labor Caravan of cars—manned largely by labor women and League people, who spoke and gave out fliers at mill gates all over the state. We had a speakers' bureau of men and women busy day and night. We got favorable statements from the best legal and constitutional authorities, educators, ministers, statesmen. We raised some money, but the powers of darkness were more prosperous than the angels of light! The flood of propaganda engulfed the state. We knew we had not time or money to spread the truth in the farming districts so our hope was in the mill towns and cities. Suddenly, Cardinal O'Connell and his diocesan paper "The Pilot" came out against the amendment as Bolshevist radicalism and interference with family rights. Curley flipped and decided that the amendment was a vile Russian plot. The working people in the cities, largely Catholic, were as bewildered by this tale as the farmers already were. We knew our cause was lost. One League husband, as deep in the fight as his wife, said, "Anyway you'll get more votes per dollar than they do," and that was true. The opposition committee reported expenses 11 times as great as ours— and the vote was three to one against us.   The combination of reactionary Yankee Republicans and reactionary Irish Democrats influenced by one of the most shocking campaigns of falsehood and deceit ever seen in American political life, was too much for us and the Amendment.

But the referendum was only advisory, so we went grimly ahead when the 1925 Legislature convened and arranged a spectacular hearing—the star of which was that great lawyer and liberal Senator Thom Walsh of Montana— whom we shall always remember with gratitude because, though one of the leading Catholic laymen in the United States, he was willing to beard our local lions in their den and he did it magnificently. But it was only a gallant gesture.

their den and he did it magnificently. But it was only a gallant gesture. The members of the Legislature knew better—after all they had petitioned for this amendment only a year before!—but their districts had spoken and they no longer had minds of their own! The vote was overwhelmingly against ratification.

From that day on the Child Labor Amendment was the annual League nightmare. We had put our hands to the plow and we could not turn back— but each year we slaved over hearings, arranged interviews, made speeches— knowing it was hopeless. As the years went on a generation grew up in the Legislature who did not know from their own experience the respectable antecedent of the Amendment and really began to believe the things they said about it!

There were a few very bitter episodes—among them the vicious and slanderous attacks made year after year on our beloved Mrs. Kelley—largely by fanatical females clutching "The Red Network." There were interesting ones— such as the year when we decided that the Cardinal really did not know anything about the subject and that we would go and tell him, which we did—a charming call which paved the way for a formal interview between his Eminence and several labor leaders which in turn brought about a temporary truce and a letter about the Amendment, saying he was not opposed to it. The next year, however, his representative at the hearing denounced the Amendment as "The reddest thing that ever came out of Red Russia," so we were back where we had been before! Then there was the year (1934, I think) when people denied that President Roosevelt was for the Amendment so we tried a direct inquiry and got back a personal letter beginning "Of course I am for the Child Labor Amendment" which we kept secret till the day of the hearing—when we had photostatic copies ready for the press!

Finally there was the happy year when an annoyed and stubborn committee chairman shut down on a hearing before the proponents had had their say; the legislative agent of the A. F. of L. protested, was ordered to sit down, walked out of the hearing in protest. . . the CIO representative called on everyone else to do likewise and the League of Women Voters, the P. T. A., the Consumers' League, and miscellaneous other enraged citizens found themselves out on the sidewalk in front of the State House, marching around and around after the Labor representatives, solemnly picketing the Committee on Constitutional Law! It was a beautiful example of the solidarity of Labor when enough annoyed at someone else; the CIO marched side by side with the A. F. of L.—and we followed after! A League husband passing the State House at a distance saw the parade and asked his companion what those morons were doing up there in the cold—but he found out when he saw the evening paper and saw a picture of his wife along with most of her League friends, picketing away for free speech!

Altogether we learned a great deal in those years. We learned that one way that the enemies of good legislation use to defeat it is to think up a bad bill that sounds noble and work for it instead! Some of you will remember the effort to treat the products of child labor like prison–made goods—the Wheeler-Johnson bill and the Vandenberg Amendment—using the words "for hire"—in 1938. We learned that reactionaries on one subject are vary apt to be reactionaries on others; it is interesting to observe that the National Committee for Rejection of the Twentieth Amendment in 1924 had as a board member Colonel R. E. Wood of Chicago! The Amendment campaign was the isolationist fight of that day— the business-as-usual battle!

But it was not only for the sake of the children who gained protection that we welcomed the passage of the Child Labor provisions of the Social Security Act!

Fighting the good fight is all very well but also enough is enough!

Source: Excerpts from the Proceedings of the Fifteenth Annual Convention of the National League of Women Voters, Chicago, IL, April 28–May 1, 1942. LWV Papers on film, II. A.19. 0651–57.

At the Eighth National Convention in Chicago Belle Sherwin reflected on one of her deepest concerns—how the League and League members could most effectively involve themselves, along with men and women outside the League, in the necessary practice of self governance.

DOCUMENT 12: BELLE SHERWIN, "TAKING PART IN GOVERNMENT"

I would not even hint that the educational experiment of the League is complete. Far from it. The technique of all adult education is only beginning to take shape. Even in our limited field, it is difficult to keep pace with the possibilities open to us—witness discussion groups and the radio. We know that education by and for participation in government must be continuous. We have learned that it is a necessary process of popular government.

Nor do I wish to imply impatience because the suffrage of women has not produced more immediate and striking results, seen either in numbers of votes cast or in a marked change in political habit, notoriously of tough fiber. We in the League believe that change in both instances is practicable, but that it should come slowly, durably, through systematic and continuous effort in the gradual course of political development. Women can now point with pride—traditional in political groups—to the increase in legislation for the protection of children and the establishment of their own legal status.

I do not think this presidential campaign year finds women surprisingly or disturbingly lacking in meeting political obligations. I do think this year does and should put conspicuously to the test the work of the League intended to help women meet those obligations—but it is not a final test. Rather, it is a trying situation to be met with resolution now and anticipated with growing confidence in years to come.

Obviously a campaign year presses the League to make the widest possible use of whatever methods it has found practical in extending political interest and consequently political action among women. . . .

Five years ago the League first addressed its energies specifically towards increasing the number of eligible voters taking part in primary and final elections, undertaking then what has since become popularly known—though not popular!—as getting-out-the-vote, espoused in campaigns by many organizations, either long-established or newly organized for the purpose. . . .

Those who are in dead earnest about getting-out-the-vote must find out what changes in registration and other election laws seem most likely to make voting simpler, and, accepting those proposals as a continuing program for gradual enactment, put the power of organized demand behind them.

I think the League is in earnest in this respect.   In the election of 1924, many of its members observed that the number of votes cast was limited by certain difficulties in registration. In 1925 registration laws were made a subject for study in the League's program of work. A valuable little pamphlet was prepared as a text. This year the proposed program recommends that permanent registration be adopted by the convention for legislative support. Again, it was familiarity with the direct primary through study and support since 1921 which led the convention in 1924 to include a "shorter ballot" in the section of the program of work recommended for legislation. A short ballot is essential to the success of the direct primary because it presents only a few offices to be filled by election. For the same reason a short ballot would go further toward making voting simpler, and in a sense more interesting also, than any single change in election machinery which has been proposed to date. . . .

I think there is something more fundamental—that until men and women are conscious of their citizenship as an active principle in their lives, external helps toward participation in government will always fall short of our expectations. Work for a short ballot, determined and vigorous, ought not to be left undone, but the slow weaving of individual interest into the processes of government must be done until individual interest begins to function of itself and finds its own expression in obedience to law or in casting a ballot or insisting on the efficient administration of law. . . .

Personal interest in government may begin anywhere as long as somewhere in the "round of littles which large life compound"—in corporation taxes or the baby's food, in the electric light bill or in calendar reform. What makes the connection depends upon what one does, where one lives, with whom one talks. Wherever the beginning is made, personal interest leads—or may be led—to inquiries and discoveries. One finds one belongs to a group with a similar interest in government and a common fund of information which it is natural to appropriate. Other groups with opposing interests appear, possessing a disconcerting store of counter-information. Friends and neighbors belong to both groups. It becomes necessary to have more knowledge about the starting-point of interest, and to have confidence in one's knowledge.

At this stage of experience it is good fortune to realize that taking part in popular government has actually begun—in seeking to think for oneself what government ought to do in any single instance—in regard to corporation taxes or teaching infant hygiene. The next step is to find sources of recorded information which can be trusted and to test what is gathered by whatever experience and current fact are available, certainly by those of the disturbing opposition. Finally, what bears these tests must be circulated as widely as may be. It ought to be the discovery of each interested citizen that knowledge about the subject of interest is sterile, worth little or nothing, if it is not widely shared. . . .

Some such experience is the first phase of relating the individual to government. It is as important as birth and the period of infancy always are to the individual, to the family, and to society.

The second stage of the groping citizen's experience is that of individual action. At first it means voting, service on a jury if called, visiting that part of government which is visible in relation to the newly discovered interest. It rouses curiosity about what a vote accomplishes, and it causes discouragement because the accomplishment seems insignificant or futile. Merely voting is seen to be a small part of that political activity which is either apparently or mysteriously going on all about one, and an election is obviously only a final step in it. Association with that preceding and enveloping activity is evidently as necessary as belonging to the group which shared one's original interest in what government does. Therefore one joins a political party.

It is difficult to agree with any party in all respects, but it is apparent that parties help to organize the political action of the people, so that it becomes definite in some respect. Thus the third stage of taking part in government begins and a new host of confusing questions arises. The original interest in government, the ties of political association, loyalty to the government as the source of public well-being, all need to be very strong indeed in order to enable one to drive through a maze of personal problems, to reach some conclusions as guides to conduct.

I believe that honest and patient thinking leads to an agreement with Mr. Elihu Root—that "the American who feels the responsibility of citizenship can do his duty better by entering the organization of one of the political parties. . . . The better educated, the more intelligent and active the citizen is, the greater reason is there to seek the increase of effectiveness which comes from association, combination, and organization." Staying outside a party organization because there are abuses in parties, or because conflict of loyalties arises, may mean keeping oneself unspotted from the world, but it is not the counsel of courage. Staying outside because one can get nowhere inside seems to me the counsel of impatience. I should like to think with Mr. Root that "there is never a time when a man of character and ability entering into the active work of a party cannot gain the influence and power to which ability entitles him, or cannot contribute materially to a change of control—provided he is willing to take the pains and give the time and effort necessary. . . . Of course, a new recruit cannot do it."

It is time now to see more women of education, intelligence, ability, and character attempting to prove that. And the new recruit must begin by taking part in each least process of party activity open to her in caucus or precinct. I wish to repeat that the League of Women Voters by no means prevents the activity of women in the parties, though that is sometimes said to be the case. On the contrary, the League urges today, as it began to do in 1920, that its members seek action through the political parties of their choice. And that urgent counsel does not contradict the conviction that a common meeting-ground is needed by women, for the discussion—free from party bias or organization precedent—of "measures for which women see the need most clearly." In such a year as this the policy and counsel of the League may seem difficult to follow. Therefore I repeat what I have had occasion to say frequently this spring, that the extent to which officers who are publicly identified with the League should participate in partisan activities calls for careful consideration in each individual instance. As a general principle, the National Board advises "that League officers be as active in their respective political parties as it is possible to be without prejudicing or hampering their influence in the League. A League officer ought not to give the public any reasonable cause to doubt the unpartisan character of the League, composed of members of all parties." . . .

There is need for the resolute action of groups as well as of individuals in the public interest, irrespective of party affiliations. There are questions well known to members of the League which transcend all party lines. Action by groups may be required in support of a legislative measure or in the interest of honest and efficient administration of a measure which has been secured. It may be required in getting out a vote in a local issue intentionally obscured or when partisan groups hesitate and the general public is tired. We wait now to hear what a gallant League has accomplished in the special election held in a great city today in a manful effort to hold a modern charter against the assault of a political faction. . . .

Where public officials are personally known, interest in government quickens. The families and friends of the more than two and one half million government employees are interested in government and are counted at the polls. Therein may lie a way to beget more interest. It was in August 1920, that I asked a thoughtful young businessman not particularly interested in government nor the suffrage movement what he considered the likeliest way to create or discover political interest in women. "Try to get women in office," he replied instantly. This year there will be opportunity in several sections of the country to prove whether that was good advice.

Encouraging women to seek public office is an obligation today as it was not in 1920. We did not then and do not now wish to see women in office because they are women. We want qualified women in office as we want qualified men, and eight years of political experience have qualified many women to be effective in legislatures and to hold administrative positions with the sophistication that is required. We want more women in office, as we want more men, to give disinterested service. It is important now that such women should take part in government to the full extent of their capacity. As candidates they will undoubtedly interest voters, as elected officials they will help give new values to votes. They will introduce as they have already new vital spots of social experience as objects for which votes can be cast.

Because the League of Women Voters is at all times scrupulously careful to make its unpartisan position plain, it is often perplexing to know how to encourage women to seek office. But the nomination and endorsement of individual members of parties is not the only way to take; to study and to proclaim the opportunities for public service by women as office holders, to create understanding of women who seek and hold office, and when possible to set the fashion oneself may prove better ways. The emphasis should be on the need for finding a way.

"It is not exceptional ability," said a sagacious young fellow-worker to me the other day, "it is character and courage that count in public office—character and courage to stand for the public interest." And that is true for men and women at every stage of taking part in government from the time the initial interest lifts its head and the will to take part asserts itself. Possibly most women require a higher degree of courage to overcome their handicap as newcomers in a strange field.

Character in the sense I have quoted it implies several qualities. I think the chief of them is self-control, for men and women do not continue to take constructive part in government without it, and "popular government" which requires the participation of men and women "is organized self-control." Through the length of human history other qualities have been built into self-control and helped to advance it. Such qualities are the competence gained by workers following trades and arts, the trustworthiness proved by excellent performance, and the spirit that rises with danger. These are the qualities which have been the source of work and institutions which have endured. They are the qualities we must rely upon today. . . .

It will be necessary to perceive that the results of your work will come in the course of time, not now nor even soon, and you must be willing that this should be so. It will be necessary to give impulse to the qualities in human nature which have won lasting results. Do not doubt their ultimate success. Do not constrain yourself and others to act only from a sense of duty. Cultivate interests in government.

Try again and again to see the public interest in compelling form. Its beauty still remains to be told.

The founder of the League has challenged us to be bold—and we need to be. The first president of the League taught us by most persuasive example to be persistent. That we should never cease to be. Now out of the four years in which I have been learning more surely what the League has to do and how it can be done, I wish to say, be confident! You have reason to be—and "in confidence shall be your strength."

Source: Excerpts from the Proceedings of the Eighth Annual Convention of the National League of Women Voters, Chicago, IL, April 23–28, 1928. LWV Papers on film, II. A.9. 0633–37.

In 1930 the League celebrated its tenth anniversary in Louisville, Kentucky. Suffrage pioneers were invited, and these "ancestors of the League of Women Voters" were honored with appropriate recognition, festivity, and funds raised in their names on behalf of the League. Even in the era of the Great Depression and even with the League not immune from those hard times, the National League received contributions that came close to its goal of $250,000. Belle Sherwin's address captured the essence of the League at that point in time—the importance of the program and the contributions of the organization as an innovative experiment in political education.

DOCUMENT 13: BELLE SHERWIN, "TEN YEARS OF GROWTH"

For the sake of realizing together the continuous current of growth in the League and the new point of departure to which it has brought us, let us supplement the history . . . by a review of the development of the League within itself. Even so short a history as ten years divides naturally in periods. I find four. The first is the year of the inception of the League, 1919–1920; a dramatic year of work for the ratification of the Nineteenth Amendment; a year of preparation gathering material for a program. Then followed that four years which Mrs. Park recorded imperishably at the Buffalo Convention in 1924. The bearings of the League had been taken and the direction of its course set. But the course was not charted. A craft equipped to sail the sea of unpartisan political action had not been fashioned. Yet in any craft obtainable the League was under way in 1924.

The three years following were spent growing in understanding of the League and the tasks it imposed. We were able to define both somewhat to our satisfaction at the first meeting of the General Council in Washington in 1927. Since then, it is plain that the League has been occupied mastering its technique. Thus we may say the League possesses today a controlling idea as of 1920, and an equipment to realize this idea—in general policy as of 1924, in conception of its character and place in the life of the country as of 1927, and in serviceable structure and procedure so far as it has come in 1930. Looking forward now, the need is obvious, the wish inevitable for more power, for more and fuller sails. . . .

From even so brief a summary of its origin and evolution and present character it is obvious that the program of the League cannot be described as radical. It explores new ideas. It has gradually incorporated some of them which bore certain tests. Each item has been subjected to the question: Does the experience in life of the majority of members represented in the convention justify giving place and time to studying it, or does the majority, after realizing the relationship of the item to the whole round of life, think it important to support it by work? A second test has more recently been applied. Can the necessary information for study be supplied at this time and the necessary work paid for by the provisions of the present budget? The program is obviously a pragmatic program.

It is a liberal program. If you will take pains to check through each section, you will find that its items for support are consistently conceived in the desire to promote the public interest, recognized often as a neglected interest. This is obviously so in the case of the Departments of International Cooperation to Prevent War and of Public Welfare in Government. It is basically true of the program of Efficiency in Government, which began with a defense of the direct primary and declares that efficient government is "representative, responsible, and responsive; stronger than any economic group; capable of rendering with the least waste and at equitable cost, services adapted to the needs of life of all the people." Upon examination it is clearly true that the program to give women equal status with men under the law is in the public interest. For only in the day in which there is real equality will women move freely in all the walks of life and contribute to its work—with the confidence born of unconsciousness—whatever of talent, capacity, and wisdom they possess. Thus it is seen that the program of the League is not advanced in thought, though new currents of thinking run through it. It is also to be seen that it is not primarily or consciously a program of thought. Its distinction is that it is a program of work, originating in the experience of the majority. In active support of its items the League will be found in the van. In so far at least the League proves itself a living memorial of the women of the elder day we celebrate this year.

The program of the League is part and parcel of its ten years' growth. In fact, as the League makes its program, the program is making the League—finding out its members, forming in them habits of independent thinking, guiding individuals into habits of controlled action, providing channels for swelling currents of conviction. It leads the League on this or that item into cooperation with other women—and men—in order to mass opinion behind this or that particular effort to bring order or greater well-being into the common affairs of the nation or of nations. In brief, today the program "is the thing," the inner core of the continuous growth of the League.

Ten years of growth have made the League a novel educational body. The members who enter it to learn remain to shape their curriculum—the program. It is their experience which prompts the choice of its active courses to be worked for rather than "taken" in the current year. It is upon their demand that the League publications have acquired their number, form, and quality. The methods of organized study which have multiplied are those the members find practicable, suited to give them what they need to possess in order to take part in government without upsetting the other claims of an abundant human life.

I hope I shall be understood as saying something deeply true, not in the lease fanciful, in declaring that the League has become a living organism of education. I believe it offers a type of adult education more deserving of study and development than many more formal educational experiments receive.

"There is no orderly, systematic, inclusive attempt at adult political education based on scientific knowledge of the principles of government," reads the report of a most distinguished Committee on Policy of the American Political Science Association. "There ought to be such an attempt. . . . The committee is . . . of the opinion that adult political education is one of the most important means of improving the quality of government in our democracy. The education of the electorate on public questions is too exclusively left to partisan effort in which not truth but distortions of the truth are the staple commodity. A very honest and well conducted attempt at political education is being made by the League of Women Voters. This movement is, however, much limited by lack of funds, and there is no League of Male Voters."

We, you and I, who have ourselves become a part of the organism of the League, and who have at times seen its problem whole, can but agree with that distinguished committee and accept its valuation. To just about that point of honest educational attempt and good conduct on a limited scale have we come in ten years. We are aware, however, as even acute observers cannot be, that we possess something more than a good educational pattern often effectively used. We are conscious of a tingling current of life within the League, which is our capital. Our question at the end of ten years is how that capital is to be invested that it may work on a larger scale.

I know you will not bury our talent in the earth to preserve it. I think you will agree with me that the way of the League cannot be trusted to grow as the kingdom, likened unto "the leaven which a woman hid in three measures of meal till all was leavened." The idea of which the League was born is vital, but its time is not yet so fully come that it can be hidden in any measure of meal we know and left to do its yeasty work of itself.

To keep what we have gained in ten years strains our resources. We run to stay where we are. And that is a good thing to do and must be done if no more forceful way be found of going further. It is a necessary thing to do—in order to hold that frontier of political education in democratic habit which we have gained. The League is alone on that line. It is challenged to hold its gain until the day comes when the progressive way of democracy is more generally seen as the way of political education, natural and desirable, continuous and cumulative in interest.

In the meantime the League may be creative and come to its own aid with power. We put our trust in work and work often begets insight. Work done with imagination may reveal new sources of power—so that honest attempts shall not be hampered. For creative work of that sort I look to you—members of the League throughout the country—with hope. The League does not take work as mere drudgery. It adventures in work. Therefore, with expectation of a wider future, I charge you to meet the next ten years. Let not one of us dare stay the current of growth we have recorded in gratitude together. Hidden but real, it is a fresh current in democratic life, it gives new impulse toward the realization of democratic government. Let no one delay it! Search the way to quicken it.

Source: Excerpts from the Proceedings of the Tenth Anniversary Convention of the National League of Women Voters, Louisville, KY, April 28–May 3, 1930. LWV Papers on film, II. A.1. 0069–82.

Chapter 10

The Tennessee Valley Authority

The League's support of policies designed to preserve and protect the environment grew out of an initial concern with the cost of living. In the aftermath of World War I, a shortage of domestic fertilizer resulted in higher food prices. Muscle Shoals, a plant on the Tennessee River in Alabama, had been built during World War I to produce nitrates for explosives. Because the chemical industry chose not to invest in the conversion of that plant to produce fertilizer, proposals for a governmental investment began circulating in the Congress. Doing something about the Tennessee River had been before Congress since the turn of the century, but primarily for the purpose of harnessing the river to provide hydroelectric power. Coupling the concept of power with fertilizer, George W. Norris, a progressive U.S. senator from Nebraska, began developing a proposal for comprehensive river basin and regional development, although he did not introduce the measure in the Senate until May 1928.

Some years before, in 1921, a League delegate from Huntsville, Alabama, had offered the following resolution at the League's national convention.

DOCUMENT 1: RESOLUTION OF THE COLBERT COUNTY (AL) LEAGUE OF WOMEN VOTERS
"BE IT RESOLVED, by the Colbert County League of Women Voters, that

"WHEREAS, the United States Government, in order to create an independent domestic supply of nitrates for war purposes, has constructed at Muscle Shoals, Alabama, a nitrate plant whose raw material is the nitrogen of the air, at a total cost in excess of sixty-one million dollars, which plant is capable of producing one hundred and ten thousand tons of ammonium nitrate per annum for explosives in time of war, and two hundred and fifty thousand tons of ammonium sulfate for agricultural purposes In time of peace; and

"WHEREAS, this plant can be economically operated only by the installation of at least eighty thousand hydroelectric horse power, and

"WHEREAS, the United States Government has partly constructed within a mile of U.S. Nitrate Plant Number Two, at the foot of Muscle Shoals in the Tennessee River, a hydroelectric dam on which the Government has already spent more than fourteen million dollars, which dam if completed will not only furnish power to meet the Industrial needs of an area in excess of seventy thousand square miles, comprising parts of seven states of the union, and

"WHEREAS, the nitrate plant can be devoted to agricultural purposes without in any way affecting its value or utility as a munitions plant, and both the additions necessary to the manufacture of fertilizers and the work of completing the dam, can be accomplished for less than the cost of one battleship; and

"WHEREAS, the operation of the plant for agricultural purposes will not only insure to American agriculture two hundred and fifty thousand tons of ammonium sulphate per annum, but will render it certain that there will be available at all times a sufficient force of trained executives and operatives to make the plant immediately available for the manufacture of explosives in the event of war, and

"WHEREAS, the life of a battleship is of relatively short duration and it has no peacetime value, while the life of the plant in question would extend through several generations, and the life of the great concrete dam would extend through the centuries; and

"WHEREAS, if the plant and dam are scrapped, the seventy five million dollars heretofore spent on their construction will be wasted; therefore, be it

"RESOLVED, in the interest of American agriculture, in the interest of the conservation of coal through the use of water power, and in the interest of preparedness on the part of our Government to meet any war condition which may arise in the future, we hereby urge upon the Congress of the United States that some definite and practical plan be speedily enacted looking to the completion of the Muscle Shoals Dam and the operation of U. S. Nitrate Plant Number Two."

I believe that contains the argument.

Source: Excerpts from the Proceedings of the Second Convention. LWV Papers on film, II. A.2. 0152–54.

As the nation advanced into the 1920s, a conservative mood became increasingly dominant, and differing opinions with regard to private or public ownership of utilities and manufacturing companies provided the framework for the debate over the future of Muscle Shoals. That same debate infused the League as well, but the majority of delegates, after extensive discussion on the convention floor, refused to go

*along with Lucy Miller's effort to transfer the issue from "For Legisla-
tion" to "For Study."*

DOCUMENT 2: LEAGUE OPINIONS ON MUSCLE SHOALS

MRS. MILLER (Pennsylvania): I would like to ask the Chair some points of
Information in regard to Muscle Shoals, which is on our Legislative Program.
What is the total amount of money invested by the Government in Muscle?

MRS. COSTIGAN: When the Wilson Dam is completed on July 1st of this
year, the Government will have expanded about $150,000,000 at that time.

MRS. MILLER: What are the estimated expenditures for its completion to
get this economical power and fertilizer, also?

MRS. COSTIGAN: This is the estimated completion coat of the Dam. If the
Government takes charge of it there will be extra expense for establishing
transmission lines.

MRS. MILLER: We do not know what the estimate is. There has been no
estimate.

Is the Committee in favor of the Underwood Act or the Norris Act in regard
to Muscle Shoals?

MRS. COSTIGAN: The Committee did not take action on any particular
bill.

MRS. BALDWIN: Mrs. Miller, as you know, a Commission has been appointed by the President to go into the study of the Muscle Shoals situation.
That Committee is for recommendation purposes only, and must bring its recommendations to the attention of Congress, when it convenes in December. As I
understand it, before the present Chairman was appointed, the League Committee on Living Costs had gone on record as being in favor of the Norris Bill. As I
further understand it, the Norris Bill does not include as much in favor of the
distribution of electrical power as we should like to 800. In view of the last
year's hectic session of Congress, on the Muscle Shoals question, we have not
taken any stand on any definite bill, because we are waiting for the recommendation of that Commission which is now sitting, and a now stand will have to be
taken next winter when Congress reconvenes.

MRS. MILLER: May I ask one other question? It does not quite answer my
question. There are certain fundamental differences underlying the Underwood
Bill and the Norris Bill, and if I am not incorrect, those fundamental differences
are: The Underwood Bill presupposes Government ownership, but not Government operation and the Norris Bill presupposes both. It seems to me, again, we
are being very loose if we say we are for something of this kind when we do not
take a definite stand or a very definite economic principle whether the Government will own and operate, or whether it is going to own.

MRS. BALDWIN: The Committee on Living Costs stands for Government
ownership and Government operation with a Muscle Shoals corporation, consisting of an electrical engineer and a chemist.

MRS. MILLER: Then, we are not waiting for the report of the Commission.
That is what I wanted to understand that we might be asked for our Legislative
Committee to go out and ask our Congress to go out and ask for operation, and
Pennsylvania would be opposed, at this understanding of the question, to Gov-
ernment operation, because We do not think it is economical.

CHAIRMAN SHERWIN: The Chair has given you three minutes. Mrs.
Baldwin (the Chair thinks) did not quite understand your question. The Chair
thought your question was what was the theory.

Board of Directors, National League of Women Voters
Chicago Convention, February 1920

Top row (L to R): Miss Katherine Ludington, Hartford, Conn. director 1st region; Mrs. Richard Edwards, Peru, Ind., treasurer; Miss Della Dortch, Nashville, Tenn., director 3rd region; Mrs. George Gellhorn, St. Louis, Mo., vice chairman and director 6th region; Mrs. James Paige, Minneapolis, Minn., director 5th region; Mrs. C. B. Simmons, Portland, Ore., director 7th region; Mrs. Solon Jacobs, Birmingham, Ala., secretary.

Bottom row (L to R): Mrs. Maud Wood Park, Boston, chairman; Mrs. Grace Wilbur Trout, Chicago, chairman hostess committee; Mrs. Carrie Chapman Catt, New York, honorary chairman.

Carrie Chapman Catt, *Founder and Honorary President 1920–1947*

Maud Wood Park, *President 1920–1924*

Belle Sherwin, *President 1924–1934*

Marguerite M. Wells, *President 1934–1944*

Anna Lord Strauss, *President 1944–1950*

Percy Maxim Lee, *President 1950–1958*

Ruth S. Phillips, *President 1958–1964*

Julia Stuart, *President 1964–1968*

Lucy Wilson Benson, *President 1968–1974*

Ruth C. Clusen, *President 1974–1978*

Ruth J. Hinerfeld, *President 1978–1982*

Dorothy S. Ridings, *President 1982–1986*

Nancy M. Neuman, *President 1986–1990*

Susan S. Lederman, *President 1990–1992*

Becky Cain, *President 1992–1998*

Carolyn Jefferson-Jenkins, *President 1998–*

VOTE

BALLOT
BOX

Bonhajo

League of Women Voters

MRS. BALDWIN: There was mentioned—on the Commission, which is to recommend to Congress what shall be done with Muscle Shoals—an electrical engineer. The Committee feels if there is Government ownership and Government operation, that there should be on that Board, which conducts the operation of Muscle Shoals, both an electrical engineer and a chemist.

MRS. MILLER: It has not been clearly answered me whether or not the Committee favors Government operation.

MRS. BALDWIN: We do.

MS. MILLER: Therefore, I move that this section in regard to Muscle Shoals be transferred from "For Legislation" to "For Study."

... The motion was seconded by Mrs. Ellicott, of Maryland. ...

CHAIRMAN SHERWIN: It has been moved and seconded that the section on Muscle Shoals in the report of the Committee on Living Costs be transferred from "For Legislation" to "For Study."

MRS. MORRISSON: It seems to me that our whole action on this thing must await the findings of that Commission. I can not understand or believe that the League of Women Voters is so committed to the theory of Government operation that we believe In it, irrespective of the findings that that Commission may make, and it seems to me what we are interested in after all is in seeing that the rights of the public, as a whole, are safeguarded in this thing; but it does come down to a question of facts of what sort of terms can be made with a private corporation for the operation of the thing and of what the estimated expense of completion and operation would mean if we got Government operation.

I grant you that there is a theory. There are some people who are opposed to Government operation at all costs, and some people think we ought to have Government operation, but I think we are not committed to one theory or the other. What we want to do in safeguard the interests of the community and we do depend upon our knowledge of the facts.

Now, opposition to the Underwood Bill was based on the fact that it gave us pretty bad terms. It is entirely a question of what kind of terms we could make on it, and I think it is unfortunate if the League were beforehand committed to a policy of Government operation before the Committee brought in its findings and showed on what terms that kind of operation could be had. (Applause)

MRS. BALDWIN: As I understand it, this Convention assembled, in this Program, is not committed to Government operation. I am simply stating how the Committee on Living Costs feels about this plan, and how we have brought it out of our conference in answering Mrs. Miller's question.

MRS. COSTIGAN: Madam Chairman, all the Committee's report says is that we believe in the thing which, after all the investigations are made, seems to be for the best interest of the people.

The discussion on Muscle Shoals, for a great many years, has brought out these dividing opinions of Government, whether it is in the best interest of the people to have it operated by the Government, or whether it is in the best interest of the people to have it operated by private interests.

Now, Muscle Shoals go clear back to 1903, when a bill was passed through Congress giving Muscle Shoals to a private corporation, and the bill at that time was vetoed by Theodore Roosevelt, who said when the Government built a dam and a lock it established such an immense power that it ought not to be given into the hands of private interests. That was in 1903.

When this question was discussed In 1918, 1918 and 1921, hearings before Committees, the Secretary of War, at that time, Newton Baker, called attention to the fact that at Muscle Shoals we have the greatest gift In power of any country, and he called attention to the fact, that at that time it was like giving away to give that into the hands of private interests, like giving away all the coal in a certain large district for one hundred years, or even giving it away for fifty years; and at this time when everybody knows that developments in the line of electrical power are going ahead by leaps and bounds, and the people who get control of this power at Muscle Shoals, even for as short a space of time as fifty years, may have a control that will be greater than that of any other organization in the country.

I do not want to go very much into this, but just to call attention to the fact that there are these two opposing points of view, and to this fact on the floor of Congress, after all the evidence was brought in, after attention was called to the fact that where there is a big concern that has no competition, it is not in the interest of the people, because price is going up and up; whereas, if you have some other competing power that you do have a competition established that is able, in a measure, to bring prices to a level at which it is for the people's interests. I wish you would get the "Congressional Record" and go into all these propositions. So while the Committee did not go on record in favor of Government operation, it seemed to some of the Committee that it was in the best interests of the people that there should be Government operation. Of course, when the bills are finally brought before Congress, next year, we will have the question presented again as to what is for the best interest of the people; but it seems to some of us that the evidence was quite conclusive in this particular case, that in the interest of the people, the Government should keep its fingers on Muscle Shoals. They said they would not think of turning back the Panama Canal to private interests. We would not think of turning back the Parcel Post or the Federal Reserve Act, and the day I read that I saw this: "There will have to be an investigation of the Panama Canal, because the "blame" thing has turned in a dividend of $350,000. (Applause)

MRS. SMITH (Pennsylvania): I would like to ask the delegates in this room who feel that they have studied this thing enough to have an intelligent opinion to hold up their hands. (Ten hands raised) Then, I think we should put it on the program of study. We are not saying that we do not believe In Government operation. We want to study operation. We believe in Government ownership, but we do not know whether we believe in Government operation.

CHAIRMAN SHERWIN: The Chair has been asking Mrs. Baldwin to make a statement, which would clarify that feature of the discussion.

MRS. BALDWIN: The question, I think, was asked first regarding the Committee. I said that the consensus of opinion in the Committee was for Government ownership and operation; that the Committee had not voted out of the Committee to put into the program Government ownership or operation. I am simply stating the consensus of opinion of the Committee, when I say Government ownership and operation. When I read the program I am reading the Program as the Committee feels that it should go before this Convention.

CHAIRMAN SHERWIN: I wanted Mrs. Baldwin to bring out the fact, rather than the Chair, that the report of the Committee does not state anything about Government ownership or about Government operation, but Mrs. Miller, of Pennsylvania, asked Mrs. Baldwin what the Committee believed and the Committee has been talking about its belief. Mrs. Costigan has reported that its belief was not unanimous. . . .

MRS. MILLER (Pennsylvania): I rise to a point of information. Do I understand that in case the National felt it incumbent upon it to back some bill in the next Congress, because it is coming up, that this is on our Legislative Program?

Suppose that bill made government operation, you had a choice between Government operation and Government ownership, who is going to represent us as liaison officers between this League and Congress, and which would be their tendency to back, operation or the other thing?

CHAIRMAN SHERWIN: The Chair will answer Mrs. Miller's question by saying that if you vote for the adoption of the program, that is, not the amendment, you leave the power of discretion to the Board first, and to its Legislative Division in consultation with the Committee. You invest the power of discretion in those three agents, who are the liaison officers between the Council and Congress. If the Chair has not correctly stated that, she will call upon the delegate from Maine to restate it.

MISS CLARK (Virginia): Madam Chairman, I very much hope that this Item No. 4 will remain where it is in the Legislative part of our Program. I feel that it would be a backward stop to transfer it to the Study Program, and I see nothing contrary to the principles of the League in our endorsing what is stated here, because we are providing for a wide and economical distribution of electrical power, and providing for its production for the best interests of the people. I feel it is very clear we are not voting on details of this bill, but on the principle for which this League has stood for a number of years; and wishes to continue at this time.

MRS. BROOKINGS (Connecticut): Madam Chairman, may I point out that if the amendment were adopted, removing this Study Program, it would make impossible any protest by this body against a bill which would give away Muscle Shoals to a private corporation; that if the amendment is rejected, it does not commit this organization to Government ownership of the operation, but is a vote of confidence in the Board and Council of the League of Women Voters to exercise its judgment and discretion in the case of the many bills which will come up in the next Congress. (Applause)

MRS. MORRISSON (Illinois): Madam Chairman, in view of the fact that Muscle Shoals will, undoubtedly, be one of the main and first items in the work of the next Congress. I do not think we can "duck" this issue by putting it back to study. We must study it and be prepared to take action on it. The thing, as it stands, does not commit us to either Government ownership or operation, either for or against, and I am in favor of keeping it where it is. I think, however, it is a matter of importance to the Convention realizing that its Committee is in favor of Government own6ral to make, perhaps, some expression of opinion to the effect that while we do wish this thing to go through as it is stated, in other words, we wish above all things to safeguard the interests of the people, but we are not committed to any documentary theory, either for or against Government ownership.

I think we are agreed that a necessary Government operation is another story, and I do not think we ought to allow any theories for or against Government operation to influence us in our Judgment of the particular or specific bill that comes up. It is a question of the terms which can be made. I think we have confidence in our Board on that subject, but in view of the Chairman's statement of the attitude of the Committee, it seems to me it is desirous that we have this study, and make clear the fact that the Convention, as a whole, is not in favor necessarily of Government operation to the exclusion of any bill which may offer us good terms.

MRS. BALDWIN: May I speak to that Mrs. Morrisson, if you vote, today, to accept the statement as it is given in this program on Page 11? The Committee is bound to make an impartial report to the Board, if that question should come up during the winter. Even though the Committee has said that the majority of the Committee is in favor of Government ownership, of Government operation, it does not seem the right thing. The Committee is bound on what it has said on Page 11 of the Program to stand by the decision of the League of Women Voters. . . .

CHAIRMAN SHERWIN: The amendment is to transfer the item on Muscle Shoals from "For Legislation" to "For Study." You will understand that voting "yes" means moving that. All in favor of the motion, please say, "Aye"; opposed, "No." The Chair thinks the "No's" have it. The "No's" have it and the item on Muscle Shoals remains in "For Legislation."

Are there any further amendments to the original motion to adopt the report of the Chairman of the Committee?

Question called.

Source: Excerpt from the Proceedings of the Sixth Convention. LWV Papers on film, II. A.7. 0303–21.

A letter to Belle Sherwin from Adele Clark, past president of the Virginia League and second vice president on the national board, urged the League to take action in support of Muscle Shoals despite its status as "a hot political issue in parts of the South."

DOCUMENT 3:   ADELE CLARK TO BELLE SHERWIN, MARCH 20, 1926

I am in receipt of the "Statement and Recommendations of the Chairman and Sub-Committee of the Living Costs Committee, in regard to the Disposition of Muscle Shoals.". . .

I hasten to express my approval of authorizing the appearance of representatives of the committee at hearings in behalf of the principles engendered in the Morris Plan.

I feel very strongly that the League should do what it can to see that this great natural resource in which the government has invested so much money shall be developed for the public interest. The future of the South, to a large degree, depends on the proper use and development of Muscle Shoals. Of course it is a hot political issue in part of the South. I think I mentioned to you, after my trip to Alabama last year, some of the political background of the Muscle Shoals question.

I hope that I am not too late with my opinion.

Source: March 20, 1926. LWV Papers on film, II. A.5. 0008–09.

The debate over Muscle Shoals consumed many years in the League and in Congress. By 1926 the League had concluded that the conversion of the Muscle Shoals project should be completed. While members did not take a stand on the public versus private power issue, they proposed that Muscle Shoals could be used as a yardstick to measure the comparative costs and quality of service provided by public and private power. In succeeding years the League defined other

purposes they believed should be served by Muscle Shoals: to con-
serve the natural resources of the valley, to produce and deliver electric power to an area still dependent on lamplight, and to control ero-
sion and waste caused by perennial floods. In 1933 President Franklin
D. Roosevelt, who had given Muscle Shoals a more fitting name—the
Tennessee Valley Authority (TVA)—signed the legislation into law.

DOCUMENT 4: REMINISCENCES OF MUSCLE SHOALS

If it was "natural" for women to work on matters pertaining to children and
health and "logical" to insure through proper administration that these legislative
gains not be dissipated . . . it was considered decidedly improper and unnatural
to have such an unladylike concern as utility rates and public power. But this too
was a League interest and setting up Muscle Shoals as a demonstration for
power development and distribution can in some measure be attributed to the
League of Women Voters. Although the lion's share of the credit goes, and quite
rightly, to Senator Norris who so doggedly fought for Muscle Shoals throughout
the years, he himself credited the League with much of the basic educational
work necessary to get public understanding and support of the measure. The
League of Women Voters started support of Muscle Shoals in 1925 and perse-
vered until 1933 when it was passed and at no time did the organization advocate government ownership of all utilities—only of Muscle Shoals and as a
yardstick.

An eyewitness to the signing of the bill recalls, "On the occasion of the
signing of Muscle Shoals the whole group was in holiday mood and as President
Roosevelt took up his pen he said, 'Are we all here? Where is the Alabama
Light and Power Company?' Everyone laughed as that company had been bitterly opposed to TVA. The first pen went to the father of the bill, Senator Norris and others were presented to several of the men including to my amusement,
some who had fought the bill in its early stages but then when they saw it was
going through got on the band wagon and claimed to be uncle, grandfather or
close relative. And finally, when the signature was almost used up someone
said, 'Is there no pen for the League?' and the President said, 'Oh certainly,'
and he finished the signature with a flourish and gave the final pen to Miss
Sherwin."

Source: Excerpts from the Twenty-second Annual Convention of the National League
of Women Voters, Chicago, April 30–May 4, 1956. LWV Papers on film, II. B.7.
0571–75.

A year later, at the League's 1934 convention in Boston, David Lilienthal, then a member of the TVA's board of directors, thanked the
delegates for the League's vital role in the creation of the TVA.

DOCUMENT 5: DAVID LILIENTHAL ON THE LEAGUE AND THE TVA

It is a matter of particular gratitude to me to have the opportunity to speak to
this great League on the subject of electricity, for you have a two-fold interest in

this whole question. As a group of women united to take part in the political life of the city, state and nation, you have an immediate and direct interest in the community control of public utilities. As women of America, individually, you are the most important of all users of electricity—the users of electricity in the home.

This League for years has been distinguished by its alert and effective interest in public utilities and their regulation. Your organization has been singled out by more than one writer as being unique among associations of women because you demonstrated an independence of thought and action. Dr. Ernest Gruening, in his book, *The Public Pays,* makes special mention of this League as being one of the few women's organizations which remained free of utility influence during the great propaganda campaign of the 20s.

Not only has this League demonstrated an active interest in the field of public utilities generally, but you also have played an important part in the development with which I am now associated—I speak of Muscle Shoals and the Tennessee Valley program. There can be no question but that without the support of organizations of your prestige, Senator George Norris might have fallen short of victory in his decade-long fight to retain the great hydroelectric properties at Muscle Shoals for the use of all the people.

It is, therefore, particularly fitting that a year after the passage of the Tennessee Valley Authority Act, we should be making a report to you of the progress of that program which the League of Women Voters so ably championed.

Source: Press Release, National League of Women Voters, Hotel Statler, Boston. LWV Papers on film, II. A.14. 0869.

Louise Young provides a telling footnote to the Muscle Shoals debate. She called it "one of those dramatic coincidences that enliven history." The private utilities challenged the constitutionality of the legislation only to have their complaint dismissed with the decision that they "had no immunity from lawful competition." Florence Allen, the presiding judge, had been a suffragist and a League pioneer!

Although women's organizations—and the League was no exception—were primarily involved with the social issues of maternal and infant health, child labor, and education, Muscle Shoals involved the League in a major economic issue. That experience must have whetted the League's appetite; in succeeding years, the League tackled such issues as the cost of living, trade policy, and resource management. Economics became, for League members, not a dismal science but a lively issue. Young makes clear in her book, *In the Public Interest,* that the attitudes of League leaders had been shaped by the progressive movement, especially by Theodore Roosevelt, who articulated a critical view of the concentrated power of the American business community. He called not only for "antitrust" legislation but also for measures to advance social and economic justice. Consequently, it was not surprising that the League, however cautiously, came to the conclusion that it did—that the development of the TVA, by improving the economic well being of a poor and undeveloped region, would serve the national public interest. It might be noted parenthetically that the League's later interest in planning derived not from its work on Muscle Shoals but rather from the experience of local Leagues dealing with issues of local and regional governance.

With Franklin D. Roosevelt's election in 1932, the League could put behind the reluctance of three Republican presidents who, throughout the 1920s and the onset of the Great Depression, resisted changes to advance the general welfare. The second Roosevelt to occupy the White House brought a whole new attitude and approach to the role of government. The nation found itself on the threshold of the New Deal and the League also found itself with a new potential for achieving some of its programmatic goals.

Source: Young, *In the Public Interest,* 109–10.

Meanwhile, other activities continued to occupy the League's energies in the last two years of Belle Sherwin's administration; in 1932 the Detroit convention had adopted the following program and agreed to the following methods of work for the next two years.

DOCUMENT 6: 1932–1934 PROGRAM AND METHODS OF WORK

The National League of Women Voters is an unpartisan organization to promote the responsible participation of women in government. The League believes that a continuing political education is necessary to the success of a democratic form of government, in order that an increasing number of citizens shall base their opinions on facts and use their opportunity as voters to make those opinions effective.

Therefore the League offers the following program for study and support:

Efficiency in Government
      Nominations and Election
      Structure and Functions of Government
      Public Finance
Public Welfare in Government
      Child Welfare
      Education
      Living Costs
      Social Hygiene
      Women in Industry
Legal Status of Women
International Co-operation to Prevent War

The League believes that women contribute a needed point of view to government in the United States and to its international relations. Therefore the League of Women Voters urges the election and appointment of qualified women to positions in national, state, and local governments and upon commissions and other bodies having international representation.

Explanation of the Program

How the Program Is Formed

The vitality of the program of the National League of Women Voters depends upon the initiative and co-operation of the state and local Leagues. The program is framed tentatively by the national departments, each of which is composed of a national chairman and a member from each affiliated state League.

Not less than three months before the national convention the program as then proposed is sent to the state Leagues. Each state board is asked to submit the proposed program to its local Leagues and to report the suggestions and comments from the state to the national departments. At the pre-convention executive meeting of each department, a completed program is agreed upon, which is then presented to the national convention for final discussion and action.

The program as adopted consists of recommendations for study and for support to be undertaken as occasion warrants. In addition, League activities include work to be undertaken as occasion warrants. In addition, League activities include work to insure efficiency in administration and the enforcement of law. When an item is on the list of "Recommended for Study" the League aims to present all sides of the question. However, by placing an item on the list of "Recommended for Support" the League takes a definite stand on that item and thereafter is not obligated to present points of view contrary to the position it has taken. It is understood that items on the legislative program are to be supported by continued study.

Federal Legislation

The policy of the National League on federal measures is determined by the consensus of opinion of state Leagues expressed in national convention. It is understood that state Leagues shall not take action which is contrary to the policy adopted by all the states acting in common.

The General Council gives the National Board authority to decide which measures, adopted in principle by the convention, shall be made subjects for active federal legislative work. When such measures have been chosen, the officer of the National League in charge of federal legislation may call upon the state Leagues to contribute support as necessary.

State Legislation

The state Leagues of Women Voters choose from the recommendations for state legislation adopted by the national convention whatever subjects for legislation are most needed in their respective states, and decide upon the time for introducing those measures. The office of the National League may be called upon by state Leagues wishing advice and help in securing the passage of measures. National department chairmen may be called upon at any time for counsel and for publications explaining their programs. In particular they will give information about methods which have proved successful in working up interest and support for legislation, efficient administration, and the enforcement of laws. Conferences with these officers may be arranged to meet urgent situations in the states.

State Leagues may find it advisable to work for laws which have not been recommended by the convention. However, measures in opposition to any portion of the program adopted by vote of the national convention should not be included in state programs.

Methods of Work

The indispensable basis for carrying out the program is organization and finance, including: organization according to political units; a budget that insures efficient service and businesslike methods; a unified plan of money-raising for the League—local, state, and national.

Informing and Discussing
Through public meetings on special subject.
Through candidates' meeting.
Through ballot-marking classes.
Through study groups and round tables.
Through voters' schools.
Through institutes of government and politics.

Observing
Through fact-finding groups.
Through visiting legislative bodies, administrative boards, court of law, and public institutions.
Through comparing observed facts with standards and with procedure in other places.

Conferring
With public officials on special problems.
With experts on technical questions.
With individual citizens, or with special agencies, on community undertakings.

Training
Speakers to present fact.
Leaders of group discussion.

Publishing
Digests of laws, particularly of election laws.
Pamphlets on the points of the program.
Bulletins reporting information and programs.

Encouraging Participation
By all qualified voters, in every step of the processes by which public officials are nominated and elected, including caucuses, primaries, conventions, elections.

Source: LWV Papers on film. II. A.14. 0756-58.

At the 1933 General Council meeting, Sherwin spoke to the more solemn matters of the League's role in Depression-wracked America.

DOCUMENT 7: BELLE SHERWIN, "POINTING THE WAY IN 1933"

Our sense of the need for wise and swift governmental action is far deeper than a year ago. The future seems more predictable only as requiring longer and more concerted effort on the part of all citizens and officials. In our separated and often lonely posts of League responsibility we have though of this Council as our opportunity to see the course of things more clearly—in our national life and in the League. . . .

But, before you can speak, I must try to answer our common question. If what I say proves to be just wooden dolls, you must knock them down. As a matter of fact, my answer is yours. I have found it in your bulletins and letters and reports telling what the League has done since last April. I read, for instance, of a superb two-day Institute on Economic Control initiated by a big city League; of a really thorough study of county government which paved the way for a League in a small city to make a detailed budgetary study with recommendations to certain officials; of a League dinner of commanding influence in an aristocratic old town that formerly did not know the League or recognize the just claims of unemployment insurance for prompt consideration. I read that an amazing record of legislative success by one state League could not have been made without two years of preliminary study by all the local Leagues in the state I find that in at least two states all the local Leagues have been engaged in the study of some sort of reorganization of local government. I am told that the study of school revenues under the leadership of the League in an important city has so far formed public opinion that the people elected the candidates for the School Board who came out for the things for which the League stood. . . .

It is natural that the local Leagues should be the active agents of our common purpose at this time. It was in our communities, large and small, that the hard facts of the depression were first felt. It is still there that they must insistently press for relief. Actions, which may bring relief, depend on understanding of the facts and on the cumulative force of opinion generated in our communities. This is true whether the means of relief is state legislation providing for unemployment insurance and changes in the state system of taxation, or is found in administrative reforms for economy and the reduction of deficits in city halls and schools. It is equally true that the President cannot put through great remedial measures without the support of the men and women living in our communities who comprehend the purpose and something of the methods proposed. Even international questions that do not originate in communities must be comprehended there before they can be settled. Nowhere, after you begin to think about it, is the contrast between our vaunted scientific progress and what may be called our institutional lag so apparent as in our local governments.

All these things account for the direction of League activity in the past year and indicate clearly to me the part the League will take in what at best will be a long, slow period of reconstruction. We must enter upon it without delay. At worst, we may be too late. . . .

There is a beautiful sequence of method shown in some of the reports you will analyze this afternoon. More than one is a story of what may happen anywhere—of study in the League over a long period leading to opinion confidently held, then to the expression of that opinion at significant times and places, to the recognition by fellow townsmen that that opinion was authoritative, and finally to giving it official weight. It is a demonstration of how naturally knowledge becomes power presupposing the patience to pursue it, the sense to use it, because unused it withers away, the faith that its truth will prevail. By this route, truly, the participation of women in government is promoted; by it, public opinion is leavened; by it, the judgments of communities are made sound; by it, leadership is gained.

All League work begins in some kind of study. I have been told it too often ends there and I have also heard that the injunction to study sometimes becomes odious. In the latter case, I would say call it something else—getting information, digging out the facts, knowing and thinking before speaking, searching for truth. By any name it will be as potent, but its essence cannot be unnecessary. If study does not precede action and even accompany it, action is abortive. If study becomes an end, it is a dead end.

In either case, our failing is that we conceive action as collective and public and wish it might be dramatic. We are not well satisfied that our part in the great slow movement for world peace should be "writing and writing to our Senators," even though we know we are doing that in company with a host of other letter-writers. Particularly, we underestimate the part—the action of the individual in forming public opinion. We do not urge that as a responsibility of every member. We have not set it up in our thought and listed it in our methods of work, as a conscious individual art, to be practiced like painting or modeling and used with deliberate skill.

At this time, when every resource in the country is needed for recovery or reconstruction, whichever it may prove to be, I ask you to consider how the potential value of League study may be realized and its investment cashed in the action of individual members in forming public opinion. That will not call for publicity on any stage. It will require of the individual a plan, perhaps a conscious limit of effort and a goal. It can be undertaken on a small scale, be repeated, and improved upon. It does not necessarily imply argufying and controversy or the imposition of the personal opinion of the artist. It should mean bringing out the facts and "letting" them prevail. Moreover, as is the case with all arts, it is the best of good fun when practice begins to tell. And the gain to the League will be in almost inverse ratio to the effort—yours and mine—as well as to the individual members undertaking a new part. For, of course, it is not what we hear or read and in that sense learn that makes our strength, but what we think about what we near and read, what we do with what we learn. . . .

On the basis of matured understanding the League has already taken a vital part in the problems of the hour. On the Platform for the Times, 1932–1934, it has supported federal grants for relief, state provisions for unemployment compensation, the forward-looking stabilizing measure for a system of public employment exchanges, the Disarmament conference, and the World Economic Conference. In spite of rapid enactments in the Congress, we have still to test the strength of the League in support of them all in the states. Since last April, the League has hastened the ratification of the "Lame Duck" Amendment; it has notably pushed the ratification of the Child Labor Amendment in nine state legislatures, successfully in four. There, also, in the state legislatures, the state Leagues have supported and helped secure hours of work legislation, workmen's compensation, and minimum-wage legislation for women and children; have pressed for the passage of laws providing more adequately and equitably for school revenues; and have defended state welfare divisions. In safeguarding what we have called the essential services of city, state, and federal government, the League has already a record of effective action, and its task in this respect is only begun. The challenge of that record and of those beginnings is not what more to add but how to work to win what has been undertaken to hew to the lines the League has drawn and make its promise good. The promise is in the power generating now in the local Leagues throughout the states, a fuller reservoir than any figures show. Let us see to it, you and I, that the power is applied to useful ends in 1933.

Source: Excerpts from the Proceedings of the General Council Meeting of the National League of Women Voters, Washington, DC, April 25–27, 1933. LWV Papers on film, II. A.14. 0572–81.

At the same Council meeting Katharine Ludington of Connecticut, an impressively talented suffrage leader and National League board member, whose fourteen-year board service would conclude in the next year, gave a tersely worded and explicit statement on behalf of the League's Committee on Program Realignment.

DOCUMENT 8: PURPOSE OF THE LEAGUE'S PROGRAM OF WORK

At this time when we are considering Improvements in the form and set-up of the Program of Work, it is important that we should remind ourselves of the purpose it is intended to serve in the life of the League.

Any survey of the history of the program shown that our tendency has been to conceive of it, not as a syllabus of the whole field of government nor a "credo" which states our political philosophy, but as a program of *work; the series of commitments, self assumed, which define and direct and limit our activities.* The program sets the tasks of study and of support, to which we have put our hands. It limits these tasks, not so much in the interest of caution as in the interest of effectiveness.

If this conception is accepted, certain things necessarily follow from it. If it is a program of work, it must be highly selective; we cannot work at everything in the field of government. If it is selective, it cannot at the same time be perfectly balanced, rounded out and comprehensive, even within the fields of our chosen departments.

If it is selective, we must have tests or touchstones by which to make our selection. Let us consider what these touchstones have been. They are all implied in the title of the program, in the words "Voters," "Women" and "Work."

We are a League of *Voters* and we are concerned only with those matters that affect us as citizens or that are affected by our votes. We deal with matters of government.

We are *Women* Voters and our emphasis has been on the whole on those things for which women feel an especial concern and which might be neglected unless women took an interest in them.

Finally, our program is a program of *work* and each item must be tested by its workability. Since we take on our study and support items as jobs, they must be within the capacity of the League to comprehend and carry out—capacity in workers, time, study material, brains, and money. This has sometimes meant that we must steel our hearts against adding some subject of intrinsic and immediate importance if we could not see our way to making an effective job of it.

The program therefore should be re-examined and realigned first from the point of view of League organization before we can consider it from the point of view of the experts in the subject matter.

It is this way of conceiving of our program that has made the League the unique organization that it is. We long ago abandoned the old organization habit of passing resolutions and "taking a stand." We take on work to be accomplished and we toot ourselves by performance.

Marguerite Wells in Detroit said it for us with finality when she said, "The League to not so much concerned with pinning a flag to a masthead as with bringing a ship into port."

Source: LWV Papers on film. II. A.14. 0633.

Belle Sherwin had introduced several organizational initiatives during her three terms in office. She developed a publication policy that required national board approval of all materials prepared by the research staff. She stretched out the program-making process to insure adequate time for deliberation and discussion by state and local Leagues and thereby added consensus to the League lexicon. The outcome of that study, representing the opinion of a majority of members, constituted the League's primary strength in its role as an advocate for public policies, whether it be on behalf of the Child Labor Amendment, the direct primary, or for a federal department of education. Although the League also had to deal with uncertain financial support and unstable memberships, it kept going and was growing in importance. She kept a committee on the realignment of the program of work until 1934. A 1933 report suggests that the problem of containing the scope of the program, or at least keeping it manageable, seemed almost endemic, given the breadth of public policy issues and the eagerness of League members to address so many of those issues.

DOCUMENT 9: 1933 REPORT OF THE COMMITTEE ON REALIGNMENT

To understand the reasons for realignment it is helpful to review recent history. A committee of the National Board has been considering realignment for a number of years with Mrs. Roscoe Anderson, former vice-president, as its chairman since 1928. The committee reported to the Board in December 1931, that consideration of the possible realignment of the program had led to the conclusion that it was necessary to have the committee chairmen as members of the Board of Directors. The almost prohibitive expense of adding eight members led to the decision that a reorganization of the Board was advisable. This was accomplished at the Detroit Convention in 1932.

The Realignment Committee then set about to show how the program as adopted at that Convention could be rearranged under fewer committees. Their report presented to the General Council of 1933 recommended six departments instead of eight and a special committee. The Realignment Committee was then discharged and the Board designated the six departments recommended, to be set up at the 1934 Convention. The national department chairmen next undertook the realignment of the items. The results of their consideration are now submitted to the department members in the state Leagues and their responsibility in forming the program now begins.

The six departments designated by the National Board are to be:
Government and Its Operation
Government and Child Welfare

Government and Education
Government and Economic Welfare
Government and the Status of Women
Government and International Cooperation

National League of Women Voters   726 Jackson Place   Washington, DC
September 12, 1933

Source: "History of Realignment." LWV Papers on film. II. A.14. 0650.

*At the close of the 1933 General Council meeting, the League is-
sued a press release summarizing the legislative measures then receiving League support. The next to last paragraph hints of things to
come with the presidency of Marguerite Wells in 1934.*

DOCUMENT 10: PRESS RELEASE ON THE LEAGUE PROGRAM

Support of international agreements which will control the manufacture and
shipment of arms to aggressor nations in conflict, and revision of war debts
were voted yesterday as new legislative measures on the program of the National League of Women Voters.

A proposal to restrict support of an arms embargo to shipments only was defeated by the General Council, in final session at the Hotel Washington. Miss
Ruth Morgan, New York City, chairman of International Cooperation, and Mrs.
Elsie A. Zinsmeister, Louisville, declared that without control of the manufacture of arms, as well as the shipments, any international agreement would be
"weakened."

The Council also added support of "Adequate appropriations for the Office
of Education, Department of Interior," to its program.

Eight measures, three of which relate to unemployment relief, Muscle
Shoals, and reorganization of the federal-state employment service, and are now
pending in the special session, were selected for immediate emphasis in the
1933–1934 legislative program. The other five measures call for adequate appropriations for the Children's and Women's Bureaus, the Bureau of Home Economics, Trade Commission, and Office of Education.

The Council, on recommendation of its legislative chairman, Miss Marguerite M. Wells, Minneapolis, Wells, voted to continue its advocacy of the merit
system in the civil service, in all branches of the government, as of pressing
importance in the maintenance of efficiency standards.

Following adjournment, delegates went to the Capitol to call on their respective Senators and representatives, and to tell them of the League's federal
legislative program.

Source: LWV Papers on film. II. A.14. 0604.

Chapter 11

The Deserving Public

After Belle Sherwin's decade of League leadership, she was succeeded by Marguerite Wells who served for another ten years. No other League presidents have served for so long. Despite the budgetary constraints of the Great Depression, the League of Women Voters continued to make its mark. Its visibility was enhanced by the remarkable energy poured into the campaign to replace the existing "find the job for the man" spoils systems with a civil service system assuring selection of men and women based on merit.

The year 1934 marked the end of a decade of leadership by Belle Sherwin and the beginning of a decade of leadership by Marguerite Wells. The two women shared many common characteristics. They were both from the Midwest, Sherwin from Ohio and Wells from Wisconsin, North Dakota, and, in her adult life, Minnesota. Sherwin and Wells were the oldest daughters in the family and had close relationships with their successful fathers. Sherwin graduated from Wellesley, Wells from Smith, and both spent time in service to their alma maters as college trustees. The correlation between League leaders and graduates of women's colleges was noted in a 1934 preconvention press release.

DOCUMENT 1: LEAGUE MEMBERS SERVING AS WOMEN COLLEGE TRUSTEES

Being trustees of a woman's college is a distinction which appears to go in hand with the activities of leaders in the National League of Women Voters. Several of these outstanding women will be in Boston this coming week for the League convention at the Hotel Statler.

Miss Belle Sherwin, League president, has been a trustee of Wellesley College for many years, and is chairman of the grounds committee. Miss Marguerite M. Wells, Minneapolis, chairman of legislation, was trustee of Smith College for ten years, and was the proponent of the plan to have trustees serve ten years, instead of for life.

Four other leaders, Mrs. Henry Goddard Leach and Mrs. F. Louis Slade, New York City; Mrs. William G. Hibbard, Winnetka, Illinois; Mrs. Herbert Knox Smith, Farmington, Connecticut, are members of the board of directors of Bryn Mawr College. All but Mrs. Leach have been members of the national board of the League, and Mrs. Leach was president of New York State for several years.

Mrs. George Gellhorn, St. Louis, a former national League vice-president, is a former director of Bryn Mawr College, and is also life president of her class at the college.

Miss Mary Bulkley, Hartford, Connecticut, director of the New England region, is a trustee of Connecticut College for Women, and Mrs. David Chandler Prince, president of the Pennsylvania League, is a trustee of Skidmore College. She is also a director of Smith College Alumnae Association.

Source: LWV Papers on film, II. A.14. 0977.

Neither Sherwin nor Wells ever married. They had participated in the suffrage movement. The precipitating reason for Wells's affiliation is not clear, although she shared from an early age, her father's interest in politics. In 1917, after volunteering her services in the office of the Minnesota Woman Suffrage Association, she gave her full attention to woman suffrage and soon found herself serving as the right hand to the organization's president, Clara Ueland. In 1920, after Clara Ueland resigned her eight-month-long Minnesota League presidency, Wells succeeded her and in 1922 began her simultaneous service on the national League board.

Belle Sherwin presided over her last convention in 1934 wielding a gavel once owned by Susan B. Anthony; the authoritative—but perhaps not entirely accurate—inscription read, "Order is the first law of heaven." Boston was the convention city, and some of the distinguished guests included Carrie Chapman Catt, Maud Wood Park, Alice Stone Blackwell, and Ada Comstock, president of Radcliffe College. Blackwell reminded the delegates that the first national rights convention had been held in Boston in October 1850. The speakers repre-

sented a who's who of political scholars and practitioners, but the star
of the show appeared to be the young David Lilienthal, then a director
of the Tennessee Valley Authority. A joke was told about a woman introduced to a congressman as a League member, and he replied, "Yes,
the League of Women Voters—Maternity and Infancy, Lame Duck, and
Muscle Shoals." In her presidential farewell address, Belle Sherwin
spoke of the issues surrounding the efforts of the Roosevelt administration to formulate new economic arrangements as the nation struggled to emerge from the Great Depression.

DOCUMENT 2: BELLE SHERWIN'S FINAL ADDRESS AS LWV PRESIDENT

The Hard Road

Questions as to the direction the government and economic life will take in
this country quicken about us daily. The answers vary almost with their number,
and certainly with the bias of the person speaking. One constant quality they
have, however. Prediction or caution, optimism or alarm clearly depends on the
particular vantage point of the speaker, on his impressions or knowledge or understanding of where we are. In other words, knowing whither we go is of less
immediate importance than whence for all of us who are wayfarers today. And
in our ears, like the constant din of a great city, is a whir of ideas and purposes,
of activities and new administrations, exciting, disturbing, short-circuiting our
thinking.

A few weeks ago, one editor, asking "where are we going" answered by
isolating as evidence the two dominating efforts of the Federal Government, the
A.A.A. [Agriculture Adjustment Act] and the N.R.A. [National Recovery Act]
and declaring that "our concern now must be with consolidation through good
administration and intelligent explanation of what we have gained" in those
major attempts at private cooperation under public supervision. "The best barri-
cades against reaction," he continued, "are intelligent and thorough administration and widespread understanding," and, on the other hand, he said in conclusion that he held progress so much to be desired lie would not have it come fast.

More recently, a student of government, writing in a popular weekly, advanced as his opinion that "the battle behind the facade of the N.R.A. is a conflict between economic and political philosophies" which promise continuing
debates rather than gradual progress through working out difficult administrative details with patience and judgment.

A leading industrialist, in a position to have any amount of data, has just said
publicly "it is impossible to draw any definite conclusion either as to the possibilities for a better economic and industrial order or as to the form which it
might ultimately take." In his opinion, "whatever evolution may bring about,"
bitter strife is almost certain. And the same day the press quoted a cabinet officer as saying, "we must look forward to more and more reliance on voluntary
cooperation and view proposals for regimentation with skepticism."

That "we may blaze another new trail in history" is the conclusion of still
another student in the field of government and economics, provided, he says,
"the American characteristics continue which have given the New Deal a spirit

of tolerance, respect for individual and group rights and the effort at voluntary action."

It would be easy to multiply quotations of conflicting views from sources that command consideration. But to do so would almost certainly introduce specific issues and probably lead to some indication of partisanship which I wish to avoid now. What I wish, rather, is to point out the fact that old issues, as for instance between business and labor, have been more sharply drawn in the past year, and newer issues, as between owners and managers, or producers and consumers, have been uncovered by the effort at private cooperation in the field of industry under the guidance of a persuasive government.

Those issues are now becoming personal and almost universal. Translated from the realm of easy-going attitudes or prepossessions, from convictions or general resistance to change, into terms of individual adjustments in matters of detail—adjustments of ideas and habits and wills—they involve practically all of us, either as owners of property and stocks, or as managers of business or producers of goods, or as workers and consumers. In one week or month, the conflict between the new requirements of cooperation and the force of old custom has been more evident, as between farmers and distributors, in another as between distributors and consumers, or, again, as between management and labor. But gradually, throughout the year, it has grown increasingly apparent to observers that we are all involved in one or more ways as competitive factors, in a common economic life.

Today we are reaching the point at which it must be determined whether we will exact from ourselves—as economic factors—the renunciations as well as the commitments which the way of cooperation calls for, or whether we will act on the old lines of indifference or resistance, giving occasion thus to regimentation by government and irresponsibly and shortsightedly permitting the strife of self-interests to break out with waste and destruction in their course.

. . .

The famous gold fish bowl of the N.R.A. has made visible many features of these far-reaching changes otherwise obscure to most of us. At times, the hearings have been veritable revelations of democracy becoming articulate. Only an all-perceiving eye and mind could gather up all that was offered there as data. Only an all-patient being could assimilate it, and only one all–wise could, in limited time, reach just conclusions. [For] what became clear is that the public interest lies in the fine balance of a multitude of interests, each making claims which must in fairness be taken into account, no one of which but must suffer some abridgment or compromise. Only gradually, by adjustment and readjustment, can the public interest in industry be secured.

This is a conception of the public interest which goes beyond what is perhaps its most common acceptance—the greatest good of the greatest number gained through legislation—and challenges voluntary cooperation to the utmost. It transcends the idea that the public interest means only the negation of dominance by special interests, for it would recognize all interests and require all to be pruned. It runs counter to the belief—fairly widespread—that the consumers' interest is identical with the public interest and admits that the producers' welfare and the welfare of workers are also essential. . . .

Out of the clamor and confusion of interests in the harmonizing of which the way of public interest is to be found, there has emerged one phrase which may well serve as a standard for new conditions of industrial cooperation by all the group interests concerned—the phrase, "the necessary social costs of production." . . .

For or a few moments now I wish to go on to note with you what the program of the League of Women Voters has to say about socially necessary costs and the public interest. I do not mean to rehearse tiresomely the items of the program but to summarize what the program, taken as a whole, declares.

In the first place, the League is on record there as having accepted responsibility for the support of many socially necessary costs to be paid by taxes exactly where and as the majority of us have become aware of the necessity within the fields of social and economic welfare. This is most notable, as would be expected, in Education and Child Welfare and in the promotion and safeguarding of the interests of women in industrial and public life. It is more occasionally yet importantly the fact in the larger fields of labor and economics to which we are newly addressing our attention in this Convention.

As you must realize, items of the program in the field of industry have not been generally concerned with wages or purchasing power, or with the problems of production and distribution. In the last few years socially necessary costs in the field of employment have been increasingly supported by the League as the times emphasized successively the need for employment exchanges, unemployment compensation and unemployment relief. The principle of collective bargaining has been incorporated in the League program since its first formulation in 1920.

Consumers' interests have been featured in our program as separate from other group interests; in the study of the regulation of public utilities and rates, in the development of commodity standards chiefly for the benefit of housewives and house managers, and finally in the support of government agencies tending to lower living costs, to promote fair trade practices and to prevent those that are unfair. . . .

The meaning of the public interest in the League program is plainly stated as the public welfare in which particular social and economic factors have been selected for support. Those features are, as it were, important way–stations along a great public highway on which the League desires to see this country go forward as rapidly as it can do so successfully. The program is also perfectly definite as to the form and method of government the League desires to see continued—a representative, responsible and responsive government, perfecting the potentialities of those three Rs on the middle road of democracy.

That is the bias of the League of Women Voters, then, when it comes to answering the question: Where are we going today? Its judgment cannot, of course, be unanimous as to where the country is, in the course of the concerted effort to recover economic well–being with more security than heretofore. The impressions of the members of the League must be as various as their local experience, and as their exposure to opinion throughout the states. Knowledge of what has been gained by attempted cooperation must at best be fragmentary, whether gain is viewed as improved business, reemployment and purchasing power, or as just and hopeful compromises of conflicting purposes, or as understanding of the next difficulties to be met and overcome. It is not possible at this time to estimate the relative strength of the elements in conflict as efforts are pressed to carry out the terms of cooperation under the new acts.

In any case, it would be out of character for the League of Women Voters to prophesy. The League can but do as others do—see where we are in part only and suffer understanding of the situation of the country to be colored by pre-disposition. But the check of the League program against what the new administrations have in hand, what the government has undertaken, does give us ground for hope of continuance. The League has faith in its reasoned purposes.

It has faith, too, in the case by case, step by step, sort of education on public questions that it has worked out for itself. And such education is challenged more compellingly now than in previous League experience. From every source, on all sides, observation and explanation must follow each new undertaking of government.

The League is only one of many agencies that must meet the need for new types of education, each in its own way. The path of continued advance on the lines of voluntary cooperation is marked out for hard-working pedestrians, administrators, cooperators, and educators. The way of each is hard. The forward march of public understanding must be slow. But its course must be ensured; to help obliterate sharp lines of separation on the one hand and, on the other, to make social purposes plainer and the end of economic theories clearer to most of us, who are, we are told, lazy, who think only wishfully and harbor only hazy ideas and muddled prejudices.

Source: Excerpts from the Proceedings of the Eleventh Annual Convention of the National League of Women Voters (hereinafter referred to as the Eleventh Convention), Boston, MA, April 23–28, 1931. LWV Papers on film, II. A.14. 0863–68.

At convention's end, Belle Sherwin elaborated on her valedictory address, "The Hard Road," with these words: "I cannot say, 'thank you.' I have had a better time than almost any person who has been entrusted with public or semi-public responsibilities. . . and what I want to end with. . . I have saved until now. I commend you to the hard road, because I like the hard road for the people I love. The hard road is the rewarding road, far more than the easier way and if you do not know it now, you can find it all day in the League of Women Voters."

Source: Louise M. Young, "Sherwin, Belle" and Jeannette Bailey Cheek, "Wells, Marguerite Milton," in Barbara Sicherman and Carol Hurd Green, Eds., *Notable American Women: The Modern Period.* Cambridge, MA: The Belknap Press of Harvard University Press, 1980, 646–48, 723–25. Excerpts from the Proceedings of the Eleventh Convention. LWV Papers on film, II. A.15. 0585.

Throughout the 1930s the League remained true to its original conviction that the best means of advancing the rights of women was not the sweeping Equal Rights Amendment supported by the Women's Party but, as indicated by the following report, by specific legislative measures removing barriers to the equal treatment of women under the law.

DOCUMENT 3: REPORT ON THE STATUS OF WOMEN

The chief emphasis of the Department through the last two years has been on preventing discriminations against married women in public employment. Again and again, both in the states and at Washington the League has insisted that fitness for public service should be measured by merit and not by sex alone or marital status.

There has been need also for repeating the League's firm belief in equal pay for equal work. This has focused on the NRA and AAA codes. Early in the code making process the League filed a general protest with General Johnson and the deputy administrators against wage differentials on the basis of sex. As hearings on the code proceeded, such differentials were protested by the League in over one hundred codes. When opportunity was given by the Administration for individuals and organizations to specify their criticism of the codes the League again appeared insisting on equal pay for equal work regardless of sex.

Chief among the items for study and group discussion in addition to the above have been the property rights of married women and the nationality of children. Fourteen states have been actively concerned about jury service for women. Marriage laws, including a waiting period between application for a marriage license and its issuance, have been important questions in eight states with Iowa after a valiant fight losing their law and Oregon securing the passage of theirs.

An occasion arises we continue to voice our opposition to the so-called "Equal Rights Amendment" and to other forms of blanket action such as the Montevideo Nationality Treaty.

Source: Julia, M. H. Carson, "Summary Report on the Legal Status of Women for the Biennium April 1932–April 1934." Press Department, National League of Women Voters. LWV Papers on film, II. A.14. 0989.

An exciting moment for all national League meetings has been the message received from the president of the United States—or his appearance (e.g., Lyndon B. Johnson at the Pittsburgh convention in 1964) or the invitations extended by the first family to the smaller Council delegations to come to the White House for teas or receptions.

DOCUMENT 4: MESSAGE FROM FRANKLIN D. ROOSEVELT TO THE 1934 LEAGUE CONVENTION

I wish to extend my cordial greetings to the Eleventh National Convention of the National League of Women Voters. The splendid work of your organization in promoting the ideals of intelligent citizenship and study of national affairs has helped in no small degree not only to further the successful participation of women in public life, but also to extend knowledge of national, state, and local problems throughout the community. This type of educational work is of vital importance in our national life, and is more needed today than ever before when the solution of new and baffling problems challenges the cooperation of all our people. It gives me great satisfaction to send to your members assembled in Boston my appreciation for their contributions to enlightened citizenship and my sincere good wishes for the success not only of their present deliberations but of their continued efforts in behalf of the public welfare.

May I take this occasion to say how much I appreciate the fine work of your president, Miss Belle Sherwin, in the interests of humanity, and to compliment you in having had her understanding and intelligent leadership for so many years.

Source: Message from President Roosevelt to the National League of Women Voters Convention. Press Department, National League of Women Voters, April 25, 1934. LWV Papers on film, II. A.16. 0987.

The League program adopted by the delegates reflected their unrestrained enthusiasm to have a say on all the important issues of the day.

DOCUMENT 5: 1934–1936 PROGRAM OF THE LEAGUE OF WOMEN VOTERS

The National League of Women Voters is organized to promote the responsible participation of women in government. The League believes that a continuing political education is essential to the success of a democracy, that citizens may have opinions based on facts and may, as voters, make these opinions effective.

The League of Women Voters supports and approves political measures and policies. It does not as an organization ally itself with nor support any political party.

This Program of Work was adopted by the National League of Women Voters in Biennial Convention, April 1934, after it had been submitted for advance consideration by the membership. The post-convention Council, composed of the president and one other representative from each state league and the National Board, has selected from this program certain federal measures for legislative emphasis. In the interim between meetings of the Council, the National Board decides what measures, adopted in principle by the convention, shall be selected for active support.

State Leagues are expected to support Federal measures from the National League program when called upon to do so and local Leagues upon the request of their state Leagues. If state and local Leagues wish to take initiative upon any other federal legislation, it is understood that they will do so only upon measures not inconsistent with this program and after consultation with the National League office.

From this program state Leagues choose measures of state and local interest for their League programs of work. They may add other state measures which are not inconsistent with the National League program.

Government and Its Operation

The League of Women Voters understands efficient government to be a representative, responsible, and responsive government; stronger than any political or economic group; capable of rendering, with the least waste and at fair cost, services adapted to the needs of life of all the people.

The realization of efficient government depends upon making the laws, charters, and constitutions fit the needs of the people; upon the nomination, election, and appointment of responsible officials; upon the acceptance by citizens of participation in government as a public trust.

Recommended for Study

1. Structure of government.
   a. Administration and reorganization of national, state, and local governments.
   b. Law–making bodies.
   c. The judicial system.
2. Functions of government.
   a. Relative powers and responsibilities of the national, state, and local governments.
   b. Scope of governmental control under changing conditions.
3. Public finance.
4. Nomination and election procedure.
5. Organization and functions of political parties.

Recommended for Support

Structure and Administration of Government
1. Reorganization of state and local governments to promote efficiency and constructive economy.
2. The manager plan in municipal and county government.
3. A merit system in all branches of the civil service.
Public Finance
1. A budget system of the "executive" type with administrative control.
2. Reform of tax systems to provide adequate revenue for essential governmental services through an equitable distribution of the tax burden.
Nominations and Elections
1. Federal suffrage in the District of Columbia.
2. Improved election machinery.
   a. Permanent registration.
   b. A system of direct nominations of candidates for office.
   c. A short ballot of the "office" type.

Government and Education

The League of Women Voters believes in education supported by public funds scientifically apportioned and efficiently administered. Education supplied by properly trained personnel should be compulsory for all children and available to adults. The League urges wider use of the school plant for the good of the community. The purpose of the Department of Government and Education is to emphasize the responsibility which rests upon the voters to secure and maintain high standards in education through sound systems of administration and finance.

Recommended for Study

1. School finance—national, state, county, and district.
   a. Budgets.
   b. Ways of equalizing the burden of school support.

    c.   Ways of meeting problems created by raising the school age.
    d.   The relation of the new systems of administration to school finance.
    e.   Federal aid to education in the states.
2. Boards of education and state departments of education.
3. Teacher retirement funds—state and local.
4. School systems in cities.
5. The public library.
6. The federal government's emergency projects in education and their possible future.

Recommended for Support

Federal
1. Adequate appropriation for the Office of Education, Department of the Interior.
State
2. Sufficient funds for public education of high standard based on adequate sources of school revenue.
3. Equalization of educational opportunity through:
    a.   County and state school funds scientifically apportioned.
    b.   Larger units for school taxation and administration.
4. Compulsory education for children between 6 and 16, nine months yearly, and part-time attendance for young workers through the seventeenth year.
5. Adequate state requirements for training and experience of teachers and school administrators in rural and city schools.
6. Free textbooks.
7. Public education for adults, including illiterates and foreign born.

Government and Child Welfare

The League of Women Voters is concerned with discovering to what extent the child is protected and cared for by government and with attempting through public opinion and legislative action to secure adequate child protection. The immediate emphasis is on maternal and child hygiene, on opportunity for education and training, on the abolition of child labor, on the care of the handicapped, and on the support of public agencies whose work is directed toward child welfare.

Recommended for Study

1. Measures for child protection.
    a.   Recreation.
    b.   Sex education.
    c.   Constructive work of visiting teachers, attendance officers, and policewomen.
    d.   Laws covering age of consent and child marriage.
2. Provision for handicapped children.
    a.   The physically handicapped.
    b.   The mentally handicapped.
    c.   The socially handicapped.
         Dependent and neglected children.

Children born out of wedlock.
Children in industry.
Children handicapped by poor living conditions.
Delinquent children.

Recommended for Support

Federal
1. Adequate appropriation for the Children's Bureau, United States Department of Labor.

Federal, State, and Local
1. Adequate provision for maternity, infancy, and child hygiene.

State
1. Ratification of the child labor amendment.
2. Child labor and school attendance laws that conform to best modern standards.
3. Adequate mothers' aid.
4. Coordinated state and local public welfare organization.
5. Coordinated state and local public health organization.

Government and Economic Welfare

The League of Women Voters is concerned with the effort to promote economic welfare through governmental action. It studies the problems of citizens as producers and as consumers and looks for their solution in the public interest.

The League emphasizes the problems of women gainfully employed because of the importance of their health arid security to society. As a new group and a minority group in our economic life, their problems call for special consideration.

The League adheres to the fundamental principle of collective bargaining as a means of giving workers a share in the control of the conditions of their employment.

Recommended for Study

1. Government and economic planning.
   a. Factors affecting the balance between production and consumption and governmental efforts to adjust them.
   b. Tariff adjustments and trade agreements.
2. Government and the woman in industry—her health, safety, and economic security.
3. Government and public utilities.
   a. Utilization of electrical resources from the standpoint of the public welfare.
   b. Regulation of public utilities and holding companies.
4. Housing as a part of a public works program.

Recommended for Support

Federal
1. Appropriations for:
   a. Women's Bureau, United States Department of Labor.

    b.   Bureau of Home Economics, United States Department of Agriculture.
    c.   Federal Trade Commission.
2. Activities of the federal government which tend to protect the interests of the consumer.
3. Efficient administration of the Muscle Shoals project under the Tennessee Valley Act as a demonstration of power production and control.

Federal-State
1. Effective operation of the federal-state employment service.
2. A system of federal, state, and local unemployment relief.
3. Unemployment compensation.
4. Collection of labor statistics and their publication by sex.
5. Cooperative extension work in home economics.

State
1. Labor administration.
    a.   Well organized, administered, and financed labor departments, including agencies for women in industry.
    b.   Enforcement of labor laws.
2. Labor legislation.
    a.   Shorter hours and a shorter week for women in industry.
    b.   Prohibition of night work for women in industry.
    c.   Effective regulation of private employment agencies.
    d.   A minimum fair wage for women and minors.
    e.   Old age pensions.
3. State and local laws affecting living costs in the interest of the consumer.

Government and International Cooperation

The League of Women Voters seeks the prevention of war by international cooperation. It believes that much international friction could be avoided by dealing with controversial issues in international conferences and commissions. Furthermore, the League believes that, if disputes develop, they could be satisfactorily settled by such pacific methods as arbitration, conciliation, and judicial settlement.

In order to make the citizen's interest in international cooperation effective, the League of Women Voters considers as a primary function the creation of an informed public opinion upon international affairs.

Recommended for Study

1. The foreign policy of the United States and its conduct.
2. Domestic policies affecting international relations.
    a.   Immigration.
    b.   Tariff.
    c.   The new nationalism.
3. Cost of war.
4. World cooperation.
5. International economic relations.

Recommended for Support

1. Adherence of the United States to the Permanent Court of International Justice.
2. Membership of the United States in the League of Nations.
3. Codification of international law.
4. Implementation of the Pact of Paris.
5. The use of arbitration, conciliation, judicial settlement, and other peaceful means, in international disputes.
6. Consultative pacts.
7. Official participation of the United States in international economic and humanitarian conferences and commissions.
8. International reduction of armament.
9. Government control of manufacture and shipment of arms.
10. Revision of war debts.
11. Treaties, agreements, and national measures in the interest of peace.

Government and the Legal Status of Women

The object of this department is to remove the discriminations which preclude women from sharing an equal opportunity and a true equality with men before the law. It will be important to examine closely every measure proposed to see whether it affects a federal or a state law and whether, in view of the actual biological, social, and occupational differences between men and women, it tends to secure for women an equal opportunity and a true equality. In the accomplishment of this object, "blanket" methods of legislation are disapproved.

Recommended for Study

1. The content and administration of laws affecting women in the exercise of private rights:
   a. Age of majority.
   b. Acting capacity.
   c. Contract rights.
   d. Property rights.
   e. Liability and immunity in criminal procedure.
2. The content and administration of laws affecting the rights of husband and wife and the interests of the family:
   a. Marriage laws.
   b. Domicile.
   c. Rights in regard to the children of the marriage.
   d. Causes of divorce.
   e. Rights and obligations in the event of termination of the marriage.
3. The content of laws and the administration of justice relating to women offenders, particularly sex offenders.

Recommended for Support

Federal
1. The removal of discriminations against women in immigration and naturalization laws.

2. The removal of discriminations against women in the laws and administrative practice affecting the nationality of children.
3. Amendment of federal statutes where needed to permit the removal of discriminations against women in the territories and possessions of the United States.

Federal, State, and Local

1. Specific measures necessary to give women effective equality with men, such as:
    a. In the exercise of public rights:
        (1) Office holding.
        (2) Admission to public employment including promotion and the salary scale.
        (3) Participation in party management.
        (4) Liability for jury service.
    b. In the exercise of private rights:
        (1) Equal guardianship of children.
2. Removal of discriminations against women in administrative practice.
3. The right of each spouse to testify in an action where the other is a party.
4. The permanent establishment of women's bureaus in city police departments and the appointment of properly trained and qualified policewomen in all communities.
5. Adequate provision for women held pending trial and for women serving sentences.
6. Vice-repressive laws which would protect the community and not discriminate against women.

Source: LWV Papers on film. II. A.14. 4516–20.

With the change in leadership came other changes. At the very time that the League was burdened with thirty-eight program items, its membership was at an all-time low of forty-one thousand, a consequence of an aging population and the Depression. Marguerite Wells argued that the program was top-heavy and no member could possibly be fluent in all these diverse issues. Remember, said the new president, that the League's central purpose was citizen responsibility. Fewer program items could suffice "to restore the habit of direct citizen participation in government." This excerpt from a publication written by Wells in 1938 explains her reasoning:

DOCUMENT 6: MARGUERITE WELLS ON THE LEAGUE'S LONG PROGRAM

Almost the first contribution to the newly enfranchised women made by the League of Women Voters was the setting up of a new concept in women's minds about what being effective in government really meant. It set about breaking itself of an inveterate habit exemplified in jumping up at the end of a persuasive speech to "take a stand" on the cause presented. Expressing an opinion, taking a stand, passing resolutions—the League recognized that these were the very least of the stuff of which effective participation in government consists. Instead it insisted upon the necessity of considering a subject a long time before deciding what to do about it, and upon the necessity of preparing many people to help before the thing decided upon could be done. It set up innumerable self-denying rules and regulations for the establishment of these new habits, and there is no doubt that the fund of information in its possession today is due to the habit such regulations inculcated.

To consider well before undertaking action and to prepare well before beginning to act—this may be called a religion with the League of Women Voters. It is true that the important thing about a religion is that it shall remain alive and effective, and that the dangerous stage in all religions comes when ritual, designed to give effect to, tends to become a substitute for religion. The League will need to take care as the years pass that in preparing for action, ritual does not take the place of religion. Putting more on a program of work than prospects for carrying it out warrant will be no less a mere "expression of opinion" for being without the "whereases" and "therefores" of the usual resolution. Nor has the League earned its reputation of knowing what it is talking about by virtue of developing a few experts. Indeed, sometimes knowledge pursued too avidly by the few slows up participation by the many. The long program is an obstacle to success.

Source: Marguerite M. Wells, *A Portrait of the League of Women Voters.* Washington, DC: Overseas Education Fund of the League of Women Voters, 1962 (originally published in 1938), 10–11.

Marguerite Wells proposed to focus the League program load with the selection of two issues for special attention: civil service reform and tax reform. The League's involvement with both issues was not new, but there was a practical as well as a nostalgic reason for the selection of civil service reform. As long ago as the League's third convention in 1922, Helen Gardener, a highly revered suffrage leader who had been appointed by President Woodrow Wilson to be a member of the U.S. Civil Service Commission, had made a persuasive speech to the delegates, refuting the prevailing practice of "to the victor belongs the spoils."

The League convention delegates in Boston in 1934 responded affirmatively to Marguerite Wells's reminder that the two basic questions affecting the operation of governments were who provided governmental services and how to pay for them by adopting a "Two-Year Campaign Resolution" designed to replace the spoils system with a merit system for the selection of public personnel. (The tax item, also adopted, proved to be far more complex and for less spectacular in its results.) The civil service campaign lasted far more than two years, and it catapulted the League into a leadership position among government reform groups. Speeches, petitions, slogans—League members bombarded their communities with information to bring merit to employment in local, state, and national governments. The facts were *simple. Only about one-half of federal employees were in the civil service system; only nine states and only a small percentage of cities, counties, and other local units of government had civil service laws. By way of preparation, Marguerite Wells presided over an all-department conference of the convention to have delegates discuss the program as a whole. She spoke eloquently about the purpose of the League program as "in the public interest," of its makeup as "middle-of-the-road"—and amusingly of the League's preoccupation with detail.*

DOCUMENT 7: INTRODUCTION TO THE ALL-DEPARTMENT CONFERENCE

No one, who knows the program as well as we in this room, can fail to note that it gives evidence of striking agreement about its purposes within the League of Women Voters. Obviously it is a program in the public interest; not in a variety of special interests; not in local or class or economic interests. Special interests have always been well represented politically in this country. Not only selfishly by their own adherents but special interests, themselves weak in political power, have been represented politically by altruistic organizations in their behalf, such as labor, for instance, by the Consumers' League. What has been lacking from the time of the passing away of the generation of founding fathers to our own day has been an interest in government for the sake of the whole, the country itself. This need the League of Women Voters seems to me to have been organized to meet. The League may indeed be said to constitute a pressure group for the most neglected special interests in these United States today, the very *special* interest of the public, the American people, the nation as a whole. . . .

The program of the League of Women Voters has always been a middle of the road program. It makes no pretenses of being either right or left wing. Members of the League are both—I shall not say radical and conservative, terms too generally used to mean anything—but let us say, both patient and impatient. We must be grateful for those of impatient temperament who prevent patience in the League reaching the point where it ceases to be a virtue. We must be grateful for the patient and prudent among us who keep the League on the road and steadily going when the urge to go faster threatens upsets. The program, product of all of us both cautious and impatient, no doubt includes many a subject to astonish the cautious as its omissions sometimes must grieve the impatient. It is a program of next steps, but as everything the League has undertaken, however proximate and harmless and appropriate it may appear at the beginning, has involved a battle royal, aroused relentless opposition, and been a fight to the finish, what more can the most impatient ask?

When we speak of the program of the League of Women Voters, it is natural for us in this room today to think of the National program of work, so called, but the actual League program from which the League should be judged and classified as an organization is rather the sum total of all the working programs adopted by state and local Leagues everywhere. This program in our hands today, containing items voted by previous conventions, is really only a list of standards. It is a sort of reservoir from which the state Leagues draw. This year we know better than we have ever known before just how the state Leagues have used that reservoir. An analysis has been made to show what state Leagues undertook to do during the last biennium, that is to say, during two years of legislative sessions. We find on the program of state Leagues five hundred fifty-nine subjects of political work. Of that number, only thirty-six are not found in the printed National program. It is evident that state Leagues do consult the nationally adopted program for standards. Of the thirty-six measures that do not appear in the national program, fourteen were concerned with tax reform. Study them and you will see how it came about that obstacles met in the pursuit of other legislative ends lead straight to the conviction that reforms of antiquated tax systems were imperative. At the convention two years ago there was a demand for more specific national leadership to help Leagues meet the emergencies of the times. Accordingly a platform was produced, listing the subjects upon which the League was prepared to act, which were already in this program, the importance of which were emphasized by the emergency. One-half of these subjects do not appear on the state programs of the past biennium. . . .

One thing is certain. The test of the League of Women Voters is not in the adoption of a program here, but in its operation everywhere. To learn of the League's condition of health, we must go to the states. If you cannot go often enough or stay long enough to observe everything, let me tell you where to find a pulse from which you can diagnose. Sit in on that meeting, board or other, when the proposed state program of work for the coming year is first considered. If discussion begins with consideration of the program of the current year, what has been accomplished and what left undone, what must be continued, and what may be discontinued, if new items are considered not merely on the merits of the subject but on their timeliness, and especially on the preparedness of the League to undertake them, that League is healthy. If, on the contrary, discussion begins with suggestions from department chairmen in rotation, who select from the national program much as they would choose a meal on a menu, and if there is a disposition to insist that no department be slighted, that League is, if not unhealthy, at least immature.

It is in the state Leagues that League healthfulness is to be judged, not at national conventions. To use loosely Lincoln's most famous words, it is not what we say here, but what they do there that the public will longest have occasion to remember.

Not what we say here—and yet may not the time have come when we should set about searching a way to say more than we do! Conventions give us the sounding board, and the spotlight is on them. The press sits day after day among us. The wires are waiting our stories. We have only to speak to be heard. And lo, we are so busy adding drop by drop to our "reservoir," drops that may or may not soon be drawn off! More than once I have been aware of lost opportunities as an entire convention has forgotten itself in excitement over a close vote to make some item "2 a" under study to "3 b" under study, while ladies and gentlemen of the press, with closed notebooks and pencils tossed aside, yawned and fidgeted. Whatever we think we are doing at such times, this much is certain, we are not "telling the world." Certainly not in words the world understands. We are such wise and foresighted virgins at conventions, busy trimming our lamps for some far off use, we quite neglect the auspicious opportunity to put our light on a stand for the world to see.

You notice on your program for the last session of the convention "DIRECTION AND DRIVE OF THE LEAGUE OF WOMEN VOTERS." It seems to me that in these words I catch the very accents of our president, [Belle Sherwin] who is always a little ahead of us in her thinking, and always possesses the patience to wait while we catch up. In its beginning the League of Women

Voters turned thumbs down upon passing resolutions. To express ourselves in heated language upon matters about which we were not prepared to act effectively was never the League way. But it is possible that the time has come when the League may resolve in public because it knows itself to be prepared to carry out its resolutions.

Let us now discuss whether there is in our minds this year matter for resolutions. Let us discuss whether there is some matter upon which we wish to mobilize all the League and all League members everywhere in a campaign for the next two years. Let us discover what is the direction we wish to take, and what drive we can promise ourselves to make. If we agree on a direction, let us consider whether already today the time has come when we can trust ourselves to make a pledge before the public because we know we are prepared to redeem it.

As a result of the discussion by the Conference a committee was ordered to make recommendations for concerted action to the convention. . . .

Source: Excerpts from the Eleventh Convention. LWV Papers on film, II. A.14. 0837–39.

The 1934 convention chose not to limit the program but to single out for emphasis civil service and tax reform as two essentials of good government and as prerequisites for the achievement of other programmatic objectives.

DOCUMENT 8: THE TWO-YEAR CAMPAIGN RESOLUTION

The League of Women Voters, in Convention assembled, has again expressed through its program, its steadfast belief in the maintaining by government of essential public services and in the protection and regulation of those services in the public interest.

The League has become increasingly concerned with the threatened collapse and, in some cases, the actual breakdown of those institutions and agencies which make for the permanent social values of our American life. We realize that those things for which we so deeply care are seriously menaced by two causes which, unless promptly and effectively dealt with, will make the possibility of future achievement in these directions entirely unrealistic and valueless.

Unless the American people can be aroused to a determination to reorganize in their entirety our antiquated tax system, and thus to distribute equitably the cost of government, there will not be the necessary money for our schools, our welfare services, our public health programs, for any orderly and well-directed social life. And unless the citizens of this country awaken to the appalling waste in every unit of government and the menace to every needed public service caused by the "spoils system," our form of government is doomed.

The League frankly recognizes these two facts:

1. No governmental reform, however well conceived, can be effective without the permanent service of qualified trained personnel.
2. Essential government activities cannot be carried on without increased revenue, which necessitates a complete readjustment of the tax system.

This assembled Convention, therefore, accepting with deep seriousness the responsibility assumed in urging added demands upon government, does hereby pledge, in the name of the League of Women Voters, united and continued effort for the next two years to action designed to bring to government service, standards of professional quality, and to effect reorganization of local, state, and national tax systems.

Source: Excerpts from the Proceedings of the Eleventh Convention. LWV Papers on film, II. A.14. 0840.

The new president, following the adoption of the resolution, expressed her pleasure with its substance.

DOCUMENT 9: MARGUERITE WELLS ON THE TWO-YEAR CAMPAIGN RESOLUTION

I am glad you have made this pledge, I am glad you realize that when you continue to ask for more services from government, you must also do something about helping to reform those antiquated tax systems and to set about immediately and urgently to do something about establishing a permanent, trained personnel for the administration of them, without which, asking for the services and getting them would be unsafe, really.

I am glad, especially, that what has happened in the Leagues, in the last two years, what they have learned and what they have done has encouraged you and justified you in assuming this campaign. I can promise you, I think, and I am encouraged by Miss Sherwin to say that perhaps the National Headquarters can give you a little special service, more than ordinary, in the direction and leadership in such a campaign.

I warn you that, two years from now, we shall have to decide by the results of this campaign, whether or not the time has really come when we can trust ourselves to make resolutions before the public, because we know that we can keep them.

Now, just one word about what is going to befall us when, in a moment, Miss Sherwin brings down the gavel on this convention. Every member of the Board and every member of the Staff and every delegate to the convention will leave this room with a little heavier burden of responsibility on her shoulders than she had when she entered it. I want you to realize that responsibility, but I do not want you to be afraid. I am not afraid. To be afraid now would be to be unworthy of the League of Women Voters that Belle Sherwin has built for us. (Applause)

Source: Excerpts from the Proceedings of the Eleventh Convention. LWV Papers on film, II. A.15. 0578–80.

Seven years later an article in The Members Magazine *conveyed the depth and intensity of feeling that accompanied the long campaign on behalf of the merit system.*

DOCUMENT 10: KATHERINE GREENOUGH ON THE ISSUE OF PATRONAGE

"This Human Wriggle and Struggle"

Say the words, *merit system*, to any hundred women almost any place in the United States and you can pick out the members of the League of Women Voters instantly. They respond to the words as to a battle cry. Indeed, why shouldn't they? For the past five years, the struggle to substitute merit for patronage in filling government jobs has been kept at a campaign pitch.

Why this constancy to one idea in a growing and changing organization, not to mention a growing and changing world? Doubtless the practical aspect of the problem has had a compelling force. It is good common sense to have the services of government performed by employees qualified to do the jobs. It is such good sense that the complexities of the solution, which demand not only a positive program of recruitment and practical, honest, testing methods, but also up-to-date handling of employees, once they have jobs, do not seem to deter League members.

But there is a reason for making the change from patronage to merit that goes deeper than the practical reasons, compelling as they are. It is so fundamental that it underlies our whole philosophy of democracy. And members of tile League of Women Voters, who have been acquiring growing feeling of responsibility for our government during the past twenty years, who have learned to combine successfully careful study of problems with vigorous action to solve them, have become increasingly aware of this fundamental reason.

It requires only a casual political knowledge to realize that behind the facade of governmental structure, behind the Congress, the state legislatures, the city councils, behind mayors and governors and the President of the United States is the political party system. It is the force which makes the wheels go around. So it is no wonder that the fight to secure control goes on unceasingly.

Lincoln expressed it with characteristic vigor: "If ever this free people, if ever this government itself, shall become demoralized, it will come from this human wriggle and struggle for office: a way to live without work—from which complaint I am not free myself." This has always been true—this corrupting force of patronage of expecting government jobs, paid with taxpayers' money, as rewards for party work. It has put off many leaders of ability, who might otherwise serve gladly and gratuitously, but who will not subject themselves to being thrust into the "human wriggle and struggle for office."

But now when so much is at stake, it is too dangerous to be tolerated. Something other than selfishness is needed as the motive force of our government these days, when Herculean task must be accomplished swiftly and efficiently. There are vast reserves of selflessness and ability in this country. They have been tapped to some extent, and to this extent, have shown their power and effectiveness. But the way needs to be open for them to flow through the entire governmental structure with rejuvenating force. This can never come about in competition with political patronage. The parties must be rid of their dragging loads of patronage, and restored to their original vigorous function of being real organs of public opinion.

So, after all, it is small wonder that the League of Women Voters has been constant to the merit system. Belief in its practical value has been bolstered by proof of increased efficiency and lowered costs where it has been given a fair trial. Belief that the problems of our democracy can only be solved through political parties of principle, rather than through parties of patronage, has been deepened and sharpened by the present tragic crisis.

Source: Katherine Croan Greenough, "This Human Wiggle and Struggle," *The Members Magazine,* May 1941. LWV Papers on film, II. A.19. 0568.

In spite of its continuing problems managing program, the decline in membership and financial support during the Depression, and the myriad issues common to similar organizations, the League remained very much in demand by other groups and by its members to take on this or to do that. After one year in office, Marguerite Wells described the life of the League as she had experienced it.

DOCUMENT 11: MARGUERITE WELLS ON HER FIRST YEAR AS PRESIDENT

This is a year in which decisions may well be faced, for it is a significant anniversary. We are now fifteen years old. Fifteen is an age in which organizations should begin to beware of hardening arteries. At twenty it may be too late for changes. When an organization is five years old, it is in a position to decide whether or not it was justified in establishing itself. When it is ten years old it begins to feel the need of counting its achievements. When it is fifteen it may well ask itself are we going where we meant to go? Do we hold to our original purposes? Or have we changed them deliberately. Are the means we are using adapted to the ends we have chosen? It is those questions that I hope we are to ask ourselves from time to time during these Council meetings.

During the fifteen years that the League of Women Voters has been about this business of government there have been striking changes in national trends. What has been the League's relationship to the changing social, economic and political trends? Let me select a few instances for reply. There is a growing recognition that economic welfare and social welfare are inseparable and must be considered together, and that government must be concerned with both. There the League of Women Voters was in the vanguard. Such recognition was at the very root of the program we started with. There are the consequent new burdens that have been laid on government, the "new deal" that has been both fostered and feared these many years and came into great prominence with capital letters lately. Its best wishers express doubt and point out dangers in view of the people's tolerance of a civil service recruited through party patronage. The League of Women Voters early recognized this plight and is already well on its way to combat it. In respect to appointments to office there are no "deserving Democrats" nor are there any "deserving Republicans." There is only the deserving public and it deserves that its affairs be run by men and women chosen for ability and devotion.

During these fifteen years many new opportunities have been opened up for women. Today there are a considerable number of women in positions of conspicuous responsibility. That women shall make good in such places and other women back them up and all women prepare themselves for similar service, such is feminism new-style, 1935 variety. It is the League kind of feminism.

Feminism by crusade and proclamation has had its day. It was a necessary phase. But its day is passed.

All these fifteen years there have been peace societies. May they grow and multiply—there is need for them all. But all leave something untouched. Arousing and maintaining public sentiment against the ancient institution of war in a necessity of our time. But a government's foreign policy, like its domestic policy, calls as well for another kind of study and understanding. It is in giving such understanding and support that I see the League of Women Voters tending to take its place. The division of power between President, Congress and State Department, their adaptation to their purpose and their exercise in doing away with a war system by international cooperation as well as in keeping the United States out of war, are all fit subjects of League responsibility. The recent World Court debacle disclosed to all the world the worst faults and weaknesses of the American democracy. It is doubly dangerous that it should be precisely in foreign policy that our worst weaknesses are disclosed. I rejoice at the trend I seem to see in the League to look to the holes in foreign policy through which such dangers enter.

These have been years of confused thought and confused objectives. People have been bewildered and have scarcely known what direction to take nor whether the steps they took led where they wished to go. There has not been a day of the time that I myself have not been grateful to have been a member of an organization which had agreed upon its objectives, agreed upon first steps toward them and had set up methods by which these first stops one by one were possible to take. Today my wish for the League of Women Voters, if I may make one for the next year, is that every League everywhere and every League member should maintain faith in the League's objectives and respect for its methods, such faith and respect as will carry conviction to others wherever the League or its representative goes.

Source: Excerpts from the Proceedings of the General Council Meeting of the National League of Women Voters, Washington, DC, May 7–10, 1935. LWV Papers on film, II. A.15. 0778–89.

The League supported the legislation introduced in 1938 and 1940 by Representative Robert Ramspeck, chair of the House Civil Service Committee, which extended civil service status to thousands of federal employees. The organization also supported a provision of the 1935 Social Security Act (part of Franklin Roosevelt's New Deal), which required employees working at the state level with the program to be chosen on merit. At all levels, the League worked against Depression laws that discriminated against married women by providing preferences for veterans and others. The number of public employees under the protection of the merit system increased, and consequently the number of political appointees shrank. Civil service reform can be listed as one of the League's great hurrahs but neither the first nor the last. The effort by the League on behalf of the merit system was notable not just for its accomplishments but because the effort was such an apt example of what Marguerite Wells wanted the League to be—a means of demonstrating to League members that they could be effective citizens—not just by being informed about the issues, but by taking action to effect change in the public interest.

Source: Kathryn H. Stone, *A History of the League Program.* Washington, DC: League of Women Voters, 1949, 25-27.

Chapter 12

The Search for Peace

Louise Young has described the search for peace by the League of Women Voters as "the most exalted of its purposes." Clearly, it has been among its most persistent. From the time of the League of Nations to the era of the United Nations, the LWV has articulated and supported means of making the principle of international cooperation a practical reality. The League's initial support of the League of Nations in 1920 collapsed one year later in the bitter controversy and turmoil surrounding U.S. participation. It was one of the rare occasions when the League backed away from a position, and even the decision to form a permanent Committee on International Cooperation to Prevent War could not hide that fact. A publication described the League mind-set in 1930: "In the foreign policy area the League cherishes for its members the ambition that without being recklessly progressive or still more thoughtlessly reactionary, they can support a steady forward going foreign policy such as will eventually lead to genuine international cooperation."

The League inherited its approach to international issues, not from the Jane Addams pacifist strain (she was the first chair of the Women's Peace Party in 1915 and later, in 1919, elected first president of the Women's International League for Peace and Freedom), but rather from Carrie Chapman Catt's orientation. Catt, although opposed to war in principle, had supported U. S. participation in World War I. She saw the need for an effective instrument of collective action able to respond to any threat to the peace as well as the need to reduce the capacity of nations to wage war. Consequently in the early years the League, although retreating from support of the League of Nations in the light of adverse public opinion, concentrated its efforts on U. S. adherence to the World Court and support of a series of conferences designed to reduce the level of existing armaments.

DOCUMENT 1: CORRESPONDENCE ON THE DISARMAMENT CONFERENCE

My dear Mr. Christian:

The Executive Board of the National League of Women Voters meeting in Chicago on Friday and Saturday passed a resolution expressing its appreciation and pledging its support to President Harding in the work for the Reduction of Armaments.

The Board also endorsed the appointment of a woman on the American delegation to the Conference on the Reduction of Armaments if the size of the delegation warrants this. If it does not, the Board asks that women of the right qualifications be appointed on such Advisory Committees as are created.

This is in line with resolutions passed by our organization at the annual convention in Cleveland in April, and we would like an opportunity to present these resolutions to the President at such a time as he shall decide to receive our delegation. Mrs. Richard Edwards of Peru, Indiana, Mrs. Charles Sumner Bird of Boston, Mass., and Mrs. Sumner McKnight of Minneapolis, Minn. will represent the League of Women Voters on this delegation and we await the convenience of the President.

Thanking you for an early reply, so that our representatives may be advised when to come to Washington, I am,

> Sincerely yours,
> Maud Wood Park
> President

My dear Mr. President:

Please let me thank you once more, and very warmly, for your kind reception yesterday of the delegation from the National League of Women Voters.

We feel that your willingness to see us was particularly gracious when you were under the impression that our organization was responsible for a resolution doubting the real purpose of the Disarmament Conference, and we are grateful to you for giving us the opportunity to make it clear that our attitude, as shown in our resolution of July 22, has been one of sincere gratitude for your action in calling the Conference.

Believing that the questions to be discussed are of incalculable importance to this nation and to the world, I beg to assure you again of the earnest desire of the League of Women Voters to help in any possible way toward the successful outcome of the Conference.

> Respectfully yours,
> Maud Wood Park
> President

Source: Young, *In the Public Interest*, 122. Maud Wood Park to George B. Christian and to President Warren G. Harding, July 25, 1921 and August 18, 1921. LWV Papers on film, II. A.3. 0247–48.

DOCUMENT 2: MAUD WOOD PARK TO PRESIDENT WARREN G. HARDING

Please permit me to express for the National League of Women Voters as well as for myself great appreciation of the statement in your message to the Congress, favoring the entrance of the United States into the World Court. We are particularly grateful for your clear explanation that the "pending proposal presents the only practical plan on which many nations have agreed."

We are also very glad that you spoke in favor of the child labor amendment, a minimum wage for women, provision for Federal women prisoners, a department of education, the extension of the merit system in the civil service and law enforcement. These are all measures for which the National League of Women Voters is hard at work and our members rejoice at the help given by your statement to the Congress.

Source: December 10, 1923. LWV Papers on film, III. A.3. 0256.

In 1923 the League, under the leadership of Maud Wood Park, took up the cudgel on behalf of U.S. adherence to the World Court. (After her retirement from the League presidency in 1924, Park chaired the World Court subcommittee of the Women's Joint Congressional Committee.)

The League's high hopes for a successful outcome collapsed when an obdurate Calvin Coolidge refused to ask the Senate to reconsider, at the request of several foreign governments, a reservation (that he had authored as a senator) attached to the treaty prohibiting the Court from issuing advisory opinions.

At the League's fifth national convention in Buffalo, New York, Jessie Hooper, a Wisconsin delegate remembering Carrie Chapman Catt's impassioned plea for peace at the Cleveland convention three years earlier, approached Catt with a suggestion reflecting her earlier expression of interest in implementation. If the women's organizations having peace and disarmament among their goals would come together, their five million members would surely have an impact in rendering a favorable public opinion. Catt agreed and urged her to move forward with the idea. Initially contacting representatives of some of those organizations attending the convention as observers and assured of their enthusiastic support, Hooper asked Catt to take the leadership role in forming this new coalition for peace. Once assured of the collaboration of Josephine Schain, who had been one of the young rising stars of the suffrage movement, Catt set about this new task with her customary vigor and enthusiasm.

As Belle Sherwin made clear in a confidential memo to the LWV executive committee, there were some concerns about the relationship of this development to the Women's Joint Congressional Committee and its World Court subcommittee. Nevertheless, the organization of this new group continued on course. The issue of what to call themselves was among the first order of business. After long deliberations and research, they finally settled on the "Conference on the Cause and Cure of War," as the project name. The managing core became the "Committee on . . ." and in time the rather convoluted name came into popular parlance as "Cause and Cure."

DOCUMENT 3: LWV PRESS RELEASE ANNOUNCING THE FIRST CONFERENCE ON THE CAUSE AND CURE OF WAR

The National League of Women Voters will have a notable part in what should prove the most important gathering of American women in the history of the nation, the Women's Conference on the Cause and Cure of War, which will be held in Washington, DC from January 18 to 24.

This Conference will be held under the auspices of eight national women's organizations. Mrs. Carrie Chapman Catt, internationally known as a leader in world movements, will serve as chairman. More than 5,000,000 American women will be represented.

The Conference will be a constructive attempt by the women of America to face facts, and to substitute clear thinking for hazy idealism in the matter of war prevention. Its purpose is to arrive at a practical working program which may unify the independent efforts now being made in behalf of world peace by each of the organizations taking part in the Conference. These include the American Association of University Women, the Council of Women for Home Missions, the Federation of Woman's Boards of Foreign Missions in North America, the General Federation of Women's Clubs, the National Board of the Young Women's Christian Association, the National Council of Jewish Women, the National League of Women Voters, and the Women's Christian Temperance Union.

Speakers will be leading authorities on the issues of international peace. Among them are Dr. James T. Shotwell, who contributed a basis for the Geneva Protocol, Dr. Manley O. Hudson, of Harvard, Dr. Stephen P. Duggan, Director of the Institute of International Education, Professor Earle of Columbia, and John Foster Dulles of the Foreign Policy Association.

Miss Belle Sherwin, President of the National League of Women Voters, in her endorsement of the Women's Conference on the Cause and Cure of War says:

"I welcome the plans for the Women's Conference on the Cause and Cure of War because they afford an opportunity which it is difficult to contrive, and which many busy women covet—an opportunity apart from all daily preoccupations to collect and sift ideas upon a fundamental problem of life and governments.

"The divisions and topics of the program for the Conference are searching, the addresses promise to be illuminating, the discussions by women from all parts of the country are sure to be stimulating. But most important to my mind is the decision to set aside a week of the year like 'a quiet hollow scooped out of the windy hill' for the exclusive and thoughtful consideration of many aspects of one problem, and that problem world wide but dependent upon profound individual conviction for its solution."

Source: Lall, *The Foreign Policy of the League of Women Voters of the United States,* 5, 25–27.   Peck, *Carrie Chapman Catt,* 409–11.   Belle Sherwin to Dear Ladies of the Executive Committee, August 20, 1924. LWV Papers on film, III. A.5. 0017–19. Undated Press Release, probably issued in late 1924 or early 1925. LWV Papers on film, III. A.5. 0027–28.

For six days with three sessions each day, the 450 delegates attending the first Conference on the Cause and Cure of War in January 1925 listened to nearly forty speakers. Admonished by Catt not to discuss the horrors of war or to spend time in futile vilification of those who disagreed, the delegates instead identified two hundred fifty-seven causes of war and went on record in support of the World Court.

The League, both on its own and in concert with "Cause and Cure," waged a vigorous campaign for the United States to join the World Court, and year after year of setbacks did not deter the organization. The League learned that there was more to education than providing information; if education was to be meaningful, there must also be agitation, "a stirring of the subject," necessary for the passage of favorable legislation. The U.S. Senate administered the death blow on January 29, 1935, by a vote of fifty-eight to thirty-five, seven votes shy of the necessary two-thirds majority. Thus the matter was put to rest until it was resurrected with the post–World War II organization of the United Nations that included, as its judicial arm, the World Court.

The League became increasingly involved with a wide spectrum of foreign policy issues. The Japanese takeover of Manchuria in 1931 strengthened the League's conviction that the United States must be a part of an arrangement if the principle of collective security were to be implemented. Hence, at the League's convention in 1932, the organization finally went on record in support of "United States membership in the League of Nations." The League endorsed the Kellogg-Briand Pact to outlaw war, even as members were aware that, lacking an enforcement mechanism, it did not go beyond an expression of intent.   Disarmament was a hot item in the 1930s, and the League lined up behind every effort to limit arms. In 1932 a League representative delivered a trunk filled with signed petitions to the disarmament conference meeting in Geneva. The League backed the Senate's well-publicized investigation, under the leadership of Gerald P. Nye (R., ND), on the manufacture and sale of armaments and opposed the passage of the Ludlow Amendment, which would have added a constitutional change requiring a national referendum—except in the event of a direct attack—to declare war or engage in overseas warfare.

From 1922 until she died in 1934, Ruth Morgan, a dedicated internationalist from New York, guided the League through the trough of American isolationism. Morgan, a friend and neighbor of Franklin and Eleanor Roosevelt, possessed means, time, and energy that she devoted to the Department of International Cooperation. In the year before her death, Ruth Morgan gave a status report in which she described great activity prompted by the "installation of a new President of the United States with new views" and by "the rapid and important changes taking place in all parts of the world."

DOCUMENT 4: DEPARTMENT OF INTERNATIONAL COOPERATION TO PREVENT WAR, "REPORT OF CHAIRMAN"

The status of the department reflects a great activity because of the installation of a new President of the United States with new views; also the rapid and important changes taking place in all parts of the world. To cite one: The proposed amendments to the covenant of the League of Nations, partly as a result of the failure of the disarmament conferences, forces this department to publish something fresh on the League of Nations. The Montevideo Conference of the Pan American Union raises other questions, and the arms embargo excites the interest of most League members.

The National Committee on the Cause and Cure of War undertook to get a certain number of meetings and resolutions to the pre-disarmament meeting held in Geneva on October 15th by the Consultative Committee. To this appeal, the League of Women Voters responded much better than any other organization. It sent in 358 and 38 states and the District of Columbia responded. Both Miss Sherwin and the organization at Washington should feel deeply gratified by the promptness and the number of these responses.

In the discussion of program help, together with the subjects to be discussed, it would seem that the Pan American Conference, the arms embargo and the League of Nations together with economic subjects assume first importance. We suggest that a reference kit be made up of publications of other organizations together with our own, and that such a kit be a loan to a group studying department subjects.

In the publications policy, it would seem that two pamphlets at least should be issued by the League in the coming year to succeed the pamphlets on Consultative Pacts and manufacture and sale of munitions; one should be a pamphlet in the international economic field and the other on disarmament and the League of Nations.

Four newsletters have been issued since April and it is safe to say that no policy has been more popular than the policy of issuing up-to-date information. When the publications policy is discussed the inclusion of newsletters in the publications budget should be duly considered. On the whole, these newsletters very nearly pay for themselves [even] if they do not show a profit, and it would seem an extraordinarily valuable activity of the department.

Source: November 27, 1933. LWV Papers on film, II. A.14. 0161–64.

On the economic front the League in 1924 undertook a study on "the relation between tariff legislation and living costs." The League concluded that tariffs constituted a tax on products, thereby adding to the cost to consumers. Second, tariffs often kept out foreign goods and could be construed as isolationist in intent and practice. Tariff barriers escalated hostilities among nations, and those restrictions also depressed living standards. For all these reasons the League adopted without controversy in 1935 a program item, "Downward Revision of the Tariff through Reciprocal Trade Agreements." When the 1938 convention renewed that program item without any changes, it did so in the conviction that expanding world trade could be the nation's greatest contribution to peaceful change. At the 1940 convention, Louise Baldwin made the following comments with regard to the League's efforts on behalf of revision of the Neutrality Act and extension of Trade Agreements legislation.

DOCUMENT 5: LOUISE BALDWIN ON FOREIGN POLICY LEGISLATION

Since 1938, here are some of the things that we have been doing:

Fifty requests for action went from the National Office to the State Leagues from May 1938 to April 15th, 1940. In addition to general requests, individual services were given whenever we thought it was useful, including telegrams to key states, special information on attitudes of Representatives and Senators from different states, and information on the danger spots. Fifty-nine pieces of supplemental material accompanied these requests and they ran anywhere from one to twenty pages of mimeographed material. Thirty-seven press releases on legislative activities were issued. 232,972 copies of "You Can Help," the flier on neutrality revision, were distributed to the states. You know when they went, when they reached you, and the work that distribution involved. 36,521 copies of the "Key to Trade Program," the flier on the Reciprocal Trade Agreements program were distributed.

The League was represented before Congressional Committees either by statement filed or personal testimony on Neutrality, War Referendum, Trade Agreements, Logan-Walter—that is the exemption to the. . . Food and Drug Amendments—Civil Service Bill in both the House and Senate, the amendments to the Social Security Act, all kinds of appropriations, District Suffrage, and Discrimination Against Women in Immigration Laws.

Not only was the League point of view officially represented, but there were representatives of the League attending the hearings steadily during the course of the testimony. I think you will agree with me that it is not enough for us to go to the hearing the day we appear, make our statement, and then disappear. I think you will agree that we learn so much by sitting through the hearings, learning what kind of interests are represented, we know what kind of questions are being brought up, we learn sometimes that the men or members of the committee say one thing on the committee and another thing to you and perhaps a third thing to us, and so we find it of great value in sitting through the hearings.

The Trade Agreements was one of the hearings in which we sat for weeks, almost. For the first two and a half weeks of the Trade Agreements, only officials of the government spoke. It was intended that the officials take about four days, then representatives of six women's organizations were going on immediately afterwards. But the minority on the committee asked so many questions of the officials, and then the majority thought that in order to clear it up and bring out their points again, they must ask certain questions again of the officials, so that it was two and a half weeks before our turn came: and that awful suspense of going home every night and spending an hour or so asking and answering questions of yourself, thinking that tomorrow might be the day when you would be called, then the next morning trying to make the decision as to whether it was best or second best hat. Of course, if the style show had come before the hearing, there would have been no question, because there would have been the red and gray costumes.

Finally, the day came and, much to our amazement, because we have appeared before the Ways and Means Committee and we always felt in appearing before that committee that we were there by sufferance, but much to my amazement we were listened to with such deference, understanding, and respect, we could not believe our eyes or ears, and the witnesses who came later were patiently questioned by the chairman of the committee, who asked if they had heard the testimony of the women. And again in the Senate where we appeared, questions were asked of us and we had what seemed like a very pleasant reception. We do not think that every time.

Besides going to hearings, there are innumerable conferences with individual members of the Congress, with representatives of other organizations interested in the same measures, that we do all the time, with officials in the executive branch of the government, and a steady stream of correspondence went from the Program Chairman and the Program Secretaries to you.

This was particularly true on the Trade Agreements program, because there were so many questions coming up. Oregon would write in and say: "They say this and that about lumber; what do you say about it? Have we any answer?" Oklahoma would write in about oil. It was not that Oklahoma's faith and belief in the Trade Agreements was shaky, but because Oklahoma and Oregon and Missouri and all the other states wanted to have the very best answers to give to special Interests when those questions were asked. . . .

There were too few organizations with a specific program to have a Legislative Committee on the Revision of the Neutrality Act during the special session in 1939. That meant that there were not five national organizations who were supporting the revision of the Neutrality Act and, therefore, we could not have a legislative committee, but we did do together a great deal of work. There were four organizations, I think, and in the spring of 1939, Mrs. Wright appeared before the Senate Committee on Foreign Relations to present the views of those four organizations on the question of the revision of the Neutrality Bill.

Mrs. Wright's statement, if I remember, at that time was about twenty minutes, and she was on the stand for over two hours, the questions of Mrs. Wright were so numerous. The committee sitting, almost the complete number that day, recognized in Mrs. Wright someone who was representing the public interest and who knew what she was talking about.

So far, I have only indicated to you very roughly what was done and has been done in the last two years in the Washington headquarters. Now, I think we ought to talk about what you have been doing in the states.

Every state participated in the campaign for revision of the Neutrality Act during the fall of 1939. As already mentioned, you distributed flyers, you had special meetings, more editorial comment on League position than on any other subject except personnel. You got large numbers of League members to write thoughtful letters to Congressmen at a time when they were being flooded with cards, telegrams, letters, all expressing the hysterical plea, "Keep us out of war," "Don't repeal the arms embargo," and so forth. It was interesting in Washington to know that these letters, a tiny proportion of the mail that was being received, did receive the attention of many members in the Congress. They broke through the logjam created by the flood of communications; they did receive special attention, as attested by the many thoughtful replies that the writers received.

The halls during that special session, the galleries, the lobby, simply were alive with people, they just streamed in, and it was as much as your life was worth to get even a foothold inside the door of the gallery to listen to that debate. During that time, we saw those committee chairmen—we are not going to be modest today—we knew those votes were changed by reports from the League of Women Voters, because a number of men said their minds were changed or the League had. . . [made] up their minds. (Applause)

We saw, as we sat in the gallery the last two or three days of debate in the House. . . we saw the result of the League work, and I am going to tell about one state. We saw the result of New Jersey's work, because I think New Jersey had more members of the minority. . . I think there were more members of the New Jersey delegation in Congress, whose minds were changed after the debate started than perhaps any other, and before the vote was taken, New Jersey had already sent in a preliminary report of what they were doing in their state.

The minute the special session was announced, they sent a wire to each of their senators and then followed that up by a long letter, then sent a special delivery letter to all their Congressmen and telephoned some of them and wired some of them. They took Miss Wells' letter and had 250 copies made to send to especially prominent men and women throughout the state, sent it to the Foreign Policy Chairman, they sent it to the local Leagues, and answered all kinds of letters in their headquarters. They sent post cards to their members and said: "Be sure and write." They organized telephone squads to get people not only to write members of Congress but to talk to prominent men and women, and they had mass meetings. You can see that they got results.

So, in our role of "stone turners" in the National Headquarters, Miss Wells wrote to each member of Congress a form letter, explaining the position of the League. She did not do this until a day or two, I think the morning before the vote came, and she did that because she thought we would not leave one stone unturned. That was the very last thing we could do, it was just one more effort with little expectation that we would hear anything from them and, much to our amazement, a flood of replies to a form letter came to the office and they said things like this:

"It certainly is a pleasure to receive a plain, common sense letter from one who evidently gave our foreign policy a lot of thought and study." Another said: "I have always found the opinions of your group to be fair, and have found your group always anxious to obtain more information on any subject which they were discussing at any particular time. "I want you to know that I am grateful to you for your good letter of October 2nd.". . . "I appreciate the sound logic of this letter." Another wrote, if I remember: "You do not know what pleasure it was to get that letter, because you have no idea what insulting letters we sometimes get." (Laughter)

The key of that campaign, "Keep calm, think this through," was a contribution to the kind of sane action this country must continue to take as the war gains in intensity. That campaign proved that the educational efforts of years had taken hold, that the League had developed a group of citizens who could not be swayed by hysterical propaganda; who, in the midst of excitement, could think clearly and help others to do the same.

Trades Agreements was another job upon which all of us did a tremendous amount of work. We did such a variety of work, but I thought it was a good example to show what we had been doing in the last two years. I think in almost every state, there was a small group of League members who became almost experts on Trade Agreements, that is, they were the ones who tried to answer the questions such as, "What about the zinc mines? What about the lumber industry? What about shoes in Massachusetts and wool in Massachusetts?" And we got all kinds of reflections from that kind of a job. . . .

Then I think a third thing that we did in that work for Trade Agreements was the assistance that we had. We had made up our minds it was a decision that had come to us, that we had arrived at as a result of sixteen years' work, and we were determined to see it through. We have all kinds of reports in the office of the things which you did, which have come under this heading, the letters which you wrote to editors asking for editorials, the conferences you had with them, the letters you wrote to newspapers correcting misinformation in the newspapers, the follow-through that you did afterwards with your Congressman.

One of the states wrote a letter to their Senator and the Senator sent back a wire and said: "I am for the Trade Agreements program," and that state president sat down and wrote to him and said: "We are glad you are for the Trade Agreements program, but how are you going to vote on Senate ratification?" That Senator was wavering, he was in that group of ten who went into debate with their minds not quite made up about Senate ratification, and I am pleased to report to you that he voted. . .[for] Senate ratification.

The states, I think, did a real job in educating Congressmen. (Laughter) I think that is evidenced over and over again in the letters that you receive back from them and certainly, over and over again, in our conversations with them during the debate, and you are carrying on that in cultivating them.

Wisconsin, for instance, knowing full well that its representatives in Congress were absolutely opposed to the Trade Agreements program, wrote to their representatives in Congress after the vote was taken, "Sorry that this has happened," and then commenting on the Trade Agreements program. I am sure Wisconsin is going right on in the hope that some day they may educate those men.

Indiana wrote so many letters to their Congressmen and Congressmen liked them so well that they all wrote back and said: "Thank you." And then because so many people from Indiana wrote to Congressmen and Congressmen were so impressed, they flooded the Indiana office with copies of the hearings before the Ways and Means Committee in the House and the Finance Committee in the Senate on Reciprocal Trade Agreements. There are four volumes about that thick in the House and I don't know how many in the Senate, so I hope Indiana's new headquarters is large enough to take care of those. At any rate, that was a reciprocal act on the part of the Congressmen.

Now, the reports:

I said that New Jersey reported progress to us before we came anywhere near the vote, and that was so helpful, because we knew just the men New Jersey thought were still doubtful. We knew those men who had given their promise to the New Jersey League that they would vote thus and so.

I am only going to cite one report that came in to us, but because it is such an exciting one, I think you would like to hear it. It is just about the best job we had on the federal measure in two years, and I wonder if it is because that state president is a member of the National Board and knows the value of reporting on federal measures to us who have to do your work in Washington.

This is what that state did, and it is not a very large state, either. The Board sat down and made plans for work on the Trade Agreements program, and there were twenty study groups in the state, working on that, studying the various angles, and helping to bring other people along with their line of thinking. There were three radio talks, four luncheon and dinner meetings, forty inter-views—those were not interviews with Congressmen, those were interviews with prominent men and women over the state—two articles in their "State Voter," and six requests from the state president to local Leagues for action. A pretty good job!

It seems to us, as we see it in Washington, that we have never had so much evidence of good state board planning for a job as we have had in the last two years, and particularly as we have had on the Trade Agreements program. During this two-year period, we have reaped the benefit of years of work. I think the success that we have had in the two years is due to work done since the beginning, in interesting women in government and in helping them to be effective in government.

We have been building an organization that can work as a whole. That is so evident again in your Trade Agreements program where we started sixteen years ago to study tariff, where some of the people in that very first meeting in Buffalo said they did not dare put tariff on the program because they were going back to sections of the country that believed in this and that kind of a tariff and they wondered what it would do to the League of Women Voters, as an organization, if anybody knew they were studying the tariff. From that beginning, we have come step-by-step until out of that we have evolved an opinion which is our opinion, based on study and fact, until we have come to the point where we are working for that opinion and we are working for it as one organization.

I think nobody puts that better than the article in the very first Membership Magazine, the article written by Avis Carlson, who is here and who wrote, "I Like the League," when she says: "Congress has just renewed the reciprocal trade agreements. On this project I really did spend some time, more than twenty hours. My twenty hours were nothing in themselves. They had no influence upon even a single vote—I know because both my senators voted nay. Yet as part of the thousands and thousands of other League-hours which did affect the final result, they gave me a right to the warm glow of triumph I had when the news of ratification came. These achievements all represent forward steps in government which I think are important. I did none of the front line trench work, but I have a feeling of having participated. And for someone who was once a rank individualist, that sense of success in a group activity is a grand feeling."

Of how many people is this true and how many people have had a part in government as a result of this activity of the League of Women Voters! (Applause)

Source: Excerpt from the Proceedings of the Fourteenth National Convention of the League of Women Voters, New York, NY. April 29–May 3, 1940. LWV Papers on film, II. A.19. 0006–20.

Despite these expressions of internationalism, it was difficult to resist the isolationist sentiment that permeated the nation in the late 1930s. The Ludlow Amendment, given a push by a Japanese attack on American ships on the Yangtze River near Nanking, nearly passed early in 1938. The League itself equivocated initially with regard to the Neutrality Act of 1935, but by 1939, with Europe in flames, League members could declare that they "had measured the dangers and decided that the victims of lawless aggressions should be aided by the United States."

Source: Van Voris, *Carrie Chapman Catt,* 198. Lall, *The Foreign Policy of the League of Women Voters of the United States,* 158–64, 173–74, 179–81. Stone, *A History of League Program,* 32–34.

Chapter 13

Two Endings and a Beginning

With the onset of war in Europe the League of Women Voters took a strong stand on behalf of aiding the Allies through its support of Lend-Lease legislation and its efforts to repeal of the Neutrality Act. The League also took steps to help build public opinion favoring U.S. participation in a post–war organization of nations to keep the peace.

All the sustained efforts of the League, other organizations, and many individuals to build an edifice to resolve conflict without resort to war began to look increasingly without hope as the war clouds gathered over the nations of Europe. Five months after these remarks by Marguerite Wells at the opening of the League's national convention in April 1938, an indecisive Britain and an uncertain France agreed at Munich to sanction the dismemberment of Czechoslovakia, revealing to the world the lack of political will by the European democracies to resist the rise of German militarism.

DOCUMENT 1: MARGUERITE WELLS ON THE THREAT OF WAR

Many times since the League of Women Voters was inaugurated, we have met in state conventions or in the National convention at a time of great perplexity and trouble and excitement, either domestic or foreign. In my experience, it has never happened once that we have not gone out, at the close of our convention, steadier and calmer than we came in. Today, we meet in the midst of a world of stark fear; wars, or the threats of war, are on every hand; people are being ruled by force and obeying through fear. Democracies are crumbling and the art of self-government is disappearing. Never did the most pessimistic man or woman alive expect to see a time like this return to this earth.

We have been thinking that, slowly but surely, a system was being built up to abolish war as a national policy. We have been believing that, one by one, every civilized country was founding a democracy, and that democracies were learning how to work. Now, Americans must realize that in all this world, theirs is the one best opportunity to prove that democracy can work. It cannot be proved by worship of the idea, it cannot be proved by pride in possession of the system of democratic government. It can only be proved by working it out, and in order to work it out, it must be understood.

Americans do not understand democracy well enough. Our forefathers worked at democracy, they created a democracy, they worked at it, and they bequeathed it to us. Thus, the Eighteenth Century bequeathed to the next century democracy, and, in proverbial fashion, the heirs to that bequest were spendthrifts and ceased to work at it. The Twentieth Century, in proverbial fashion, must return to shirtsleeve days and work their democracy.

Now, this is a familiar idea to the League of Women Voters. We have all long accepted the fact that democracy had to be worked for, and we are, therefore, to be congratulated. It is easier to work than to worry, and though ours may be only "the drop in the bucket," it is better, when the fire occurs, to be in the vessel line, though our vessel may be weak and leaking. So, members of the League, let us do the hard work of this convention with joy. (Applause)

Source: Excerpts from the Proceedings of the Thirteenth Annual Convention of the National League of Women Voters, St. Louis, MO, April 25–29, 1938. LWV Papers on film, II. A.17. 0633–35.

Two years later the convention in New York City marked two decades of the League of Women Voters. It proved to be the last time that the original League leaders would be together at a League convention. Carrie Chapman Catt, Maud Wood Park, Belle Sherwin, and Marguerite Wells were at the head table to hear one of their most distinguished members, Eleanor Roosevelt, give one of the banquet addresses. The League was in better health than it had been after the first decade, but the world was not. Barely one month after the convention's close, France fell to an onslaught by Nazi Germany. Marguerite Wells responded to that event with this communication on June 6, 1940, to state League presidents.

DOCUMENT 2: MARGUERITE WELLS ON THE DEFENSE OF DEMOCRACY

It is fitting that you who have assumed responsibility for the League of Women Voters in your state, and I, who have assumed the responsibility of helping you, should communicate frequently in these days of the League's great test. Since we last met scarcely a month ago the American people have united in plans for defense against an enemy outside the country and in other plans for defense against possible enemies within. It is peculiarly the responsibility of an organization such as the League of Women Voters to look not only in those directions but also beyond to the defense of democracy itself.

The pattern of things that are happening in Europe is perhaps becoming clearer as it develops. Many things have happened this past month whose meaning we could only guess at. The behavior of certain Norwegians when their country was invaded, the feeling of some Dutch against their Queen who fled when Holland fell, the conduct of the young King of Belgium, the disaster at Sedan, the lack of English equipment, and the changes of command in France—these cannot be unrelated incidents, but must have some common explanation. The easy word is "fifth columns," but fifth columns within the invaded countries could not have been "made in Germany." They must have been prepared for by people inside who have found it too hard to maintain that continuous devotion to and defense of free government without which government by the people cannot succeed. Fifth columns will not go far in a country where no longing eyes have been cast on the easier ways of dictatorship, no considerable number of citizens have shirked the responsibility of citizenship, no leaders have lost their faith that the democratic way is best and can prevail.

European democracies today stand at death's door not because democracy is a weak form of government, but because democratic people have not yet learned or not yet accepted the demands made upon them for the preservation of freedom. As we Americans watch their agony today, who is there among us who should not say, "There but by the grace of God go I?". . .

The time is ripe to bring home the truth of what a democratic government demands of its citizens. The time is ripe to justify to all League members the value of our own methods and of the discipline we have required of ourselves in order to help more people understand our democracy and practice it.

Source: Marguerite Wells, Leadership in a Democracy. Washington, DC: League of Women Voters, 1944, 13–14.

> With the escalation of the war in Europe, President Franklin D. Roosevelt proposed heroic measures, to aid any nation vital to U.S. interests. Foremost among these was H.R. 1776, the Lend Lease bill. On January 16, 1941, the national board announced its support and sent this "Request for Action" to the state League presidents.

DOCUMENT 3: REQUEST FOR ACTION

Your Board has decided that H.R. 1776, an Act to Promote the Defense of the United States, now under consideration by the House Committee on Foreign Affairs, should be supported by the League of Women Voters under its program item, "A foreign policy as a non-belligerent which permits discrimination against an aggressor." An analysis of the Act is enclosed.

You will see that the Act gives to the Executive very great and perhaps unprecedented powers, which may be modified by the Congress; that it sets aside much, if not all, of the various kinds of legislation designed to tie this country's hands in case of war; that it authorizes aid by a non-belligerent to one party at war and of a kind and extent heretofore unknown or even imagined.

It is an act of such far-reaching implications that it can not be operated without sacrifice, public and private, present and future, comparable to the sacrifices demanded by war itself. Yet it is not an act providing for war. On the contrary, it is a substitute for war.

Such a substitute the League of Women Voters has long sought. It comes now in a way we had never envisaged. It comes too late to prevent wars elsewhere, but not too late to halt their spread. It comes as an experiment to be made by one country alone: it is not multilateral, but unilateral. It is a bold experiment, but it is not war and the great powers it confers upon the President leave him free to carry out his repeated pledge not to take this country into war.

If successful, if it saves free nations from the attacks of violators of law and order and does this without participation in war, it will be the first and only demonstration on a grand scale of bringing pressure in war situations without recourse to war. It is an experiment that fits our traditions, our history, our genius, and our uniquely favorable geographical situation. It is an experiment no other country by itself could make. If we go to war in spite of it, it will have failed. If without going to war we help prevent a conquest of the world by aggressors, a practical demonstration will have been made of renunciation of war as an instrument of national policy. Once more as in 1789, when we made of the ideal of democracy a reality, our country will have set a light for the feet of men.

Will you ask every local League to call its board together to make clear all the risks and all the possibilities of this great experiment called an Act to Promote the Defense of the United States, but which may be made to mean an act to renounce war as an instrument of national policy? Will you ask them to carry the message to their members and to the public; will they tell their representatives in Congress what they think the Act means and can be made to mean and what they wish it to mean; will they tell the President of the United States?

Source: Request for Action. Washington, DC: League of Women Voters, January 16, 1941. LWV Papers, Library of Congress.

As the intensity of the war increased so did the great debate in the United States between isolation and intervention. The League perceived that the advance of Adolf Hitler's ambitions constituted a clear and present danger to democracies, including the United States. Led by the eloquent rhetoric of Marguerite Wells, the League made its initial moves with its campaign to "win the battle of production" and its support for repeal of the Neutrality Act of 1939 in the summer and fall months of 1941. Marguerite Wells pushed the League to examine the causes of public confusion over the direction of American foreign policy and to provide information in terms that could be easily understood by citizens. Under her leadership, the League expanded its outreach with rallies, broadcasts, slogans, and the like. Soon after the close of the 1941 Council meeting, she urged League members to "win the battle of production." A high water mark in this effort was the broadcast, over CBS in July 1941, of a speech given by Louise Leonard Wright, the highly respected and knowledgeable chair of the League's Department of Government and International Cooperation.

DOCUMENT 4: LOUISE LEONARD WRIGHT, "THE BATTLE OF PRODUCTION"

Some of you are fortunate enough to have special skills that can be used for the defense of your country; others have administrative experience of value. You know what you can do to win the battle of production. But there are other things that all members of the public can do.

We can immediately change our standards from business-as-usual to defense-first-of-all. This means that we must not expect to have the leisure or the luxuries that we have in more happy days. We are not to complain about shortages of supplies or less skillful services if we know that our personal deprivation is the nation's gain. Defense will be our yardstick for measuring all action.

We can pay our increased taxes not only cheerfully but gratefully, for the taxes offer proof that this country is determined to continue as a democracy.

We can make our decreased incomes go further if we buy more carefully and plan for paying the taxes by including them in the domestic budget.

We can release commodities for defense by not demanding them in consumer's goods and acquainting ourselves with satisfactory substitutes.

We can ease the transportation problem by buying the necessary coal now instead of in the September rush.

We can forestall inflation by buying defense bonds.

We can demand that no individual or special group profit at the expense of the success of the defense program.

We can help provide the necessary schools, housing and other facilities for the people in the new industrial and defense areas.

We can insist that our government be manned by competent personnel who are given an administrative set-up which speeds the defense program with maximum efficiency.

We can express confidence in our leadership and make our criticism constructive.

We can add our bit to the formation of an intelligent public opinion.

Of all these opportunities, public opinion is the most immediate. This is the job to which the League of Women Voters is directing its attention. If the American people want a thing badly enough they get it. No defeatism, no technical difficulties, no lack of energy will deter them. The vast majority of the American people want to stop Hitler. They have chosen to do it by becoming the workshop of the world, by harnessing their special genius to the production of immediate and ample war material for those nations who are fighting Hitler. This policy was determined by public opinion and it must be carried out by public opinion.

In a recent talk to the National League of Women Voters, Ralph Barton Perry, a distinguished philosopher, said, "The major force in a democracy is public opinion, which is no more than a sum of private opinion. There is no public mind, but only private minds and every private mind is made up privately."

The challenge before the American public is how to achieve unity among 130,000,000 private minds made up privately. Each of us has an individual formula for running the affairs of the world. We probably all wish that we could ignore the unhappy spot in which we find ourselves but few of us yield to that temptation. Those of us who recognize that the situation which we don't like is nevertheless the situation in which we have to live are willing to reach a decision even in the midst of doubt. An essential part of that decision is accepting the fact that this democracy must voluntarily achieve a single-minded purpose equal to that in a nation run by a dictator.

Unity of purpose and action will come if each of us assumes his or her responsibility for an individual share in the making of public opinion. Cracker barrel conversations have been moved to the cash and carry grocery, the streetcar, the beauty shop, and bus or commuter's train. Wherever we are, we talk. If our conversation includes a clear understanding of our national policy of aid to other nations, a recognition that this policy was deliberately devised to meet the brutal facts of international life, a willingness to subordinate our private or special group interest to the public interest, then our talk will not hinder the defense of our country but will help win the battle of production. . . .

Public opinion is the weapon, which each individual can forge to keep the war we don't want from coming here. We have made a plan, but are we carrying it through? We have been slow in recognizing the awful urgency of our task. This is partly because the situation in which the United States finds itself is wholly new and equally unwelcome. This shrinking world caught us unprepared for the impact of the policies of other nations upon us. . . .

The job to be done is unprecedented. For instance, a 14,000% increase in ordnance manufacture is under way. The United States Maritime Commission has already had its building program doubled. Production of many of the instruments of war started from scratch, plans weren't made, plants weren't built, and trained workers and technicians were not available at the places needed. Great progress has been made and greater progress will be made. But the program has been delayed in great part by the lack of public recognition of the necessary speed and the consequent attempt to maintain business and life as usual while building for defense on the side. Until each individual puts the force of his undivided support into this program it will fall short of the need. The challenge of Hitler is the challenge of machines, of assembly lines, of laboratories and technical ideas, the field where the United States has considered itself supreme. We know how to fight this battle-of-production. If we have the will, we will win.

Source: Louise Leonard Wright, Excerpts from "The Battle of Production," July 15, 1941. Washington, DC: League of Women Voters, July 17, 1941, mimeo. LWV Papers, Library of Congress.

All over the country Leagues swung into action on behalf of the battle of production. This sheet, reporting League activities, reflected the energy and creativity with which League members entered the fray.

DOCUMENT 5: BATTLE OF PRODUCTION "CAMPAIGN FLASHES"

"We are 'making friends and influencing people.' It's a grand sensation," reports one state League president.

How and Where:

In the Sky: A Mexico, Missouri League husband who flies his own plane will trail "Battle of Production" slogans across the sky.

At the Movies: Clatsop County, Oregon has a screen flash, with a sound track; the Illinois League has several slides in red, white, and blue, available to its local Leagues at cost; Grand Rapids and Saginaw, Michigan report slides still being used.

In the Newspapers: A full page Battle of Production "ad," with an arresting drawing of Uncle Sam in the Gleaners and Journal Sunday paper, sponsored by the Henderson, Kentucky League and financed by sixteen local business firms—not to mention the increasing number of editorials and countless news stories which tell of activity and more activity.

Via the Ether Waves: Seattle, Washington and Portland, Oregon will carry on the "battle" with a "Quiz of Two Cities" program, based on the campaign.

Louise Leonard Wright, national chairman of Government and Foreign Policy, will speak over the Columbia Broadcasting System on Tuesday, July 15, 6:15 to 6:30 Eastern Daylight Time. The Joplin, Missouri League gives us a cue: for state radio broadcasts they have organized drug store listening-in parties.

At the July Fourth Parades: A pony cart with Sparrows Point (Maryland) children and Battle of Production slogans in Dundalk; station wagon with Prince George's and Montgomery County (Maryland) League of Women Voters and Battle of Production banners in Takoma Park.

At Filling Stations: Minneapolis, Minnesota reports that Pure Oil and Standard Oil companies have taken 1,000 and 700 window stickers respectively saying "Help Win the Battle of Production" for distribution through filling stations throughout the northwest.

In Store Windows: Special displays and Battle of Production slogans painted on the windows featured in Mexico, Missouri.

With the Morning's Milk: Dodgers go out with milk bottles on Sunday morning, in Troy, New York "when pa is home to see it."

At Hotels: Enroute to League meeting at summer home—stopping at all resort hotels along the way to leave dodgers (Green Bay, Wisconsin); having dodgers placed in mail boxes at hotels while conventions were in session (Denver, Colorado).

At the Farm Bureau: A member of Kansas' newest League, Sedgewick County, gave a thirty minute summary of the Campaign to six hundred people, as part of the Farm Bureau program.

At a Labor Institute: The Mayor of Newark and Secretary of the American Federation of Labor in New Jersey used our "Battle of" Production" point by point in his speech before the Labor Institute at Rutgers University.

No wonder the Waterville, Maine League writes, " . . . It's such a grand project to be in, that we couldn't resist!"

Source: "Battle of Production Campaign Flashes," Washington, DC: National League of Women Voters, July 9, 1941. LWV Papers, Library of Congress.

The opportunity to repeal the Neutrality Act was welcomed by the League in a message from President Wells on October 22, 1941.

DOCUMENT 6: MARGUERITE WELLS ON REPEAL OF THE NEUTRALITY ACT

Outright repeal of the Neutrality Act is now before the Congress in the form of an amendment to the Administration's bill which asks repeal of Section 6, prohibiting the arming of merchant ships and which gives authorization to the President to proceed with arming merchant ships. The amendment to the Administration's bill is sponsored by Senators Bridges of New Hampshire, Gurney of South Dakota, and Austin of Vermont, all Republicans, and calls for outright repeal of the existing Neutrality Act.

Your National Board interprets this amendment as consonant with the League's program in doing away with a measure whose effect has always been to prevent discrimination between aggressor and victims of aggression. One section only of the Neutrality Act has ever been specifically approved by the League of Women Voters, the section providing for a National Munitions Control Board. This provision, proponents of the outright repeal amendment expect, will be exempt from the repeal or immediately reenacted.

The proposed amendment as it stands offers Leagues the opportunity they have so often given evidence of seeking, that of being effective in an effort to do away with that misguided piece of legislation called the Neutrality Act. For six years it has tied the hands of our government, Congress and Executive, prevented exercise of their constitutional duties during a period when flexibility and adaptability to circumstances have been most vital. Mercifully we shall never know to what extent this abnegation of ours has influenced for the worse the course of events. Vain regrets will not help but repudiation of the policy we now so much regret would certainly give a lift to our spirits and restore our self-confidence.

Source: Marguerite Wells, *Leadership in a Democracy*, 1944, 44–45.

Marguerite Wells put pen to paper to write a thoughtful analysis of one means of civic response to the current crisis confronting the American people.

DOCUMENT 7: "AMERICANS: REALISTS OR IDEALISTS?"

Americans have in the past been a practical people. Only practical people could have fashioned an enduring nation out of thirteen colonies of headstrong pioneers and set up democracy as a going concern at a time when anarchy appeared to be the alternative. Inventiveness, compromise, even opportunism were the ingredients out of which the plan for a United States of America was made.

Yet those realistic founders of our nation were never exclusively concerned with their own time or their own immediate salvation. In all the plans they made and sacrifices they endured they had future generations in mind. But perhaps a sense of responsibility for the future is so nearly instinctive that in this respect too it might be said that American tradition is one of practical realism.

Yet though this be true, what name shall be given to the constant concern of those early Americans that the democracy they founded should serve not only America but the world? Idealism? By whatever name, the wonder remains that those forerunners of ours should have been so often under its compulsion.

Looking back we see that the men who toiled in Philadelphia to establish our democracy always looked upon their handiwork not only as the salvation of Americans but as a beacon to mankind. They were constantly held to their task by the realization Washington expressed that the destiny of democracy as a form of government was staked on the American experiment. Almost a generation later Jefferson was warning that disaster to our democracy would persuade the world that man is incapable of self-government. Another fifty years and people heard Lincoln say that success of our Union would be the proof whether a nation conceived in liberty and dedicated to the proposition that men are created equal could long endure.

Thus throughout our history the theme runs: America's concern for freedom everywhere. It was that concern that took our own generation into the war to make the world safe for democracy. We fought that war not only to make the world safe for democracy. We fought it also to end wars because democracy cannot under modern conditions be safe while wars exist.

Twenty years have passed. Twenty years of failure to use the opportunity war had won, of failure to translate an ideal into practice. An entire generation has grown up who hate warfare as much as they love freedom. They have not helped abolish war but they *have* foresworn it: they have as it were taken vows against it, and to fight means to them a violation of those vows.

Now once more war comes to the world: once more and as never before freedom is at stake. What kind of Americans are facing this crisis today? Idealists or practical men? Distracted by what seemed to them irreconcilable loyalties Americans today have sought in vain to evade responsibility. Now finally they have begun to face up to their responsibility. They face it this time with a plan of their own devising, a plan made in the traditional American spirit, a plan for something vast and untried.

It is a plan for all-out production such as only Americans could hope to achieve. It is a plan for aid to one set of belligerents against another set of belligerents with all the risks such a course involves—a courageous plan. It is a plan for being effective in preserving freedom—a practical plan. If it succeeds it will offer the world a practical demonstration that by means other than war, compelling obligations may be met. It is in the tradition of our practical founding fathers, whose contribution to the world of their day consisted of a demonstration that individual liberty could be maintained without anarchy resulting. It is a plan that requires for success all the sacrifices, the devotion, the fervor of war itself. Only a people bred in idealism could hope to achieve success in such an undertaking.

Source: Special "Win the Battle of Production" Issue, *Member's Magazine*, August 1941. Washington, DC: National League of Women Voters, LWV Papers, Library of Congress.

On December 7, 1941, the Japanese attack on Pearl Harbor, "the date that will live in infamy," brought the United States into the war against the Axis powers. In her message to members, Marguerite Wells wrote in part: "Your first duty is to make clear to all the purpose for which America is united. This is no war merely of revenge against treacherous attack. It is part of the world struggle. America is at war to help rescue the cause of freedom everywhere, and free humanity from evil powers who seek its degradation."

Wells summoned the national board to Washington for approval of her proposal to hold a special council meeting in January in Indianapolis (the only Council meeting held outside Washington, DC) rather than waiting for the biennial convention scheduled for April. The outcome of that meeting in Indianapolis was reflected in a declaration released on January 2 and later, on January 14, with a plan for action.

DOCUMENT 8: THE LEAGUE DECLARATION OF ITS ROLE IN WORLD WAR II

The Emergency Council of the League of Women Voters meeting one month after the United States entered the second world war—the greatest in extent and the gravest in issue that ever faced a civilized world— recognizes that danger threatens, not only our physical territory, but in a more far-reaching and menacing way, threatens our national existence as a self-governing, free people. It recognizes that in the most literal sense of the word the future of government, resting on the consent of men, is at stake in this war. The mechanization of modern life has taxed the social ingenuity of men almost to a breaking point and sapped the fervor of their belief in self-government. The Council moreover appreciates that even to have the opportunity to develop a democratic future, the war itself has to be won.

In this knowledge the League looks to itself and asks not just what it may do better or differently, but asks whether it shall continue to exist. Has it a reason for being, sufficient to justify it in times when every non-essential commodity and activity is being sacrificed?

Approaching our situation in that mood, the League Council votes unanimous conviction that if an organization having the purpose of the League of Women Voters did not exist today, it should be created. That no grant of executive power in a war emergency, however great, lessens the importance of an alert, understanding, critical body of citizens, active continuously in relation to the functioning of government. Without this the people would become passive and democracy, at its very roots, die.

So in a real sense the League feels it should be reborn to do some of the tasks in some of the ways it has known before, in teaching both itself and others an understanding of government, but adjusted to the new requirements of winning the war, and winning the peace thereafter.

With that rebirth, the League of Women Voters commits itself to reaching a larger public than ever in its history, reaching them face to face with new methods including special enrollment and instruction of its members, with a new determination.

The League of Women Voters expresses the conviction that at the level of local government, whose importance is often underrated even in normal times and whose functions are eclipsed in public attention during wartime, lies a task of special importance.

The League of Women Voters will devise ways and means to see that a Congress is elected in November 1942, which is capable of dealing with the problems it will face, particularly that of post-war organization for peace. For upon this next Congress may well hang the fate of that kind of civilization for which we are now pledging our all.

Source: "A Declaration by the General Council of the League of Women Voters." Issued in Indianapolis, IN, January 8, 1942. LWV Papers on film, II. A.19. 0742.

Well before the end of World War II, the United States and its allies looked forward to the dawning of a new age in which a postwar organization of nations would keep the peace.   Throughout the war Marguerite Wells had been urging state Leagues to prepare citizens for the choice between international cooperation and isolation. Given its long history of support for measures to enhance cooperation among nations, it was not surprising that the League stepped forward to work on behalf of a bipartisan resolution introduced in 1943.   The resolution, known as B2H2, came from a group of Senate authors: Joseph H. Ball (R., MN), Harold H. Burton (R., OH), Carl A. Hatch (D., NM), and Lister Hill (D., AL).   Its purpose was to avoid a repeat of the Senate-presidential confrontation over the League of Nations and to put the Senate on record for the idea of postwar cooperation among the nations fighting the Axis powers. The League's forward motion was a bit hesitant. When the national board was polled by mail to determine if such a resolution was compatible with the League's longtime support of measures strengthening international cooperation, five members said "yes," six said they would support it in principle, and three were against any action at that time, indicating reservations that were generally prevalent in the nation.

DOCUMENT 9: MARGUERITE WELLS ON THE B2H2 RESOLUTION

You have undoubtedly been aware of the resolution introduced into the Senate by Senators Ball, Burton, Hatch, and Hill, advocating United States participation in an international organization. . . .

In the eyes of the world, the Senate action on any such resolution will be indication of how the Senate will behave on plans for postwar international cooperation. Although such a resolution does not commit the Senate to any future action, nor bind the President to any line of action, such an expression of opinion should be helpful and it gives the people a chance to express their desire for international cooperation. Senate passage would also give us a lever to use when specific measures such as trade agreements come up for action. We can relate such an expression of opinion to the issues at hand and show that the expression is valueless if contrary action is taken on specific issues. . . .

It is important that the objectives of the resolution be emphasized because controversy over the merits of various pending resolutions might defeat the chance of getting the Senate on record on any one of them.

Source: Wells, *Leadership in a Democracy*, 87.

As one of her last acts in office, Marguerite Wells drafted plans for a campaign to woo the American public away from its residual isolation and win its support on behalf of a foreign policy lodged in cooperation with other nations.

DOCUMENT 10: MARGUERITE WELLS ON A CAMPAIGN FOR MOBILIZING PUBLIC OPINION TO A NEW INTERNATIONAL COMMITMENT

I have followed eagerly reports of progress in preparation for a nationwide drive to recruit millions who have never been reached before, preparing them to make a choice between international cooperation and isolation when the time comes. In the near future I hope to make a report to every state League. Today I am sending you some answers to the questions most often heard. They are questions about how to proceed and what we hope to accomplish.

One question for which an answer is eagerly sought neither you nor we can answer: When will the time come when the American people will be faced with a choice? That is something that nobody knows and those whose guess is worth most, cannot say. Perhaps a few months from now we shall be ourselves better able to guess. Meantime there is more to gain than to lose in making haste. Every man and woman added to the number who has in his heart a strong feeling for international cooperation increases the prospect that the U.S. will choose well, whether three years from now or one year, or less.

I am sending under separate cover the sheet entitled "Answers to Questions about Mobilizing for the Foreign Policy Drive" in bulk, enough to each state League for distribution to its local League presidents.

Just before Labor Day the September CITIZENS ALL will go out. It will contain more help for understanding the League's foreign policy drive.

Over and over again we need to emphasize the simplicity of what we seek to do—open one more mind to an idea which Winston Churchill, with his genius for simplicity, once described as the desirability of nations becoming "somewhat mixed up together in some of their affairs for mutual and general advantage." The League's effort is based on the belief that when the time for choice comes, the man or woman in firm possession of that idea can be depended upon though others raise a multitude of vexed questions about details of an ultimate plan.

It has become clear that the allied nations are going to win the war and only the date of victory is unpredictable. Immediately a fearful doubt paralyzes allied plans for after the war: will the American people consent to U.S. cooperation or will they refuse as they did after the last world war? All the plans for cooperation will be in vain if a substantial part of the people are without a glimmer of feeling about our country's doing something to prevent another war. It is to increase the number of American citizens who have made a home in their thoughts for the simple idea of cooperation that the League of Women Voters has undertaken to present it person to person to millions who for various reasons have given it no thought. Leagues who are recruiting for the crusade find many questions to ask about how to proceed. We are sending you herewith some answers to a few questions most frequently asked.

1. How long will the campaign on foreign policy last?

    Answer: If within the next few months favorable war conditions bring into prominence the question of American's foreign policy critical for the whole world, it is unthinkable that the League of Women Voters would slacken its foreign policy campaign.

    If, as is more likely, the time of choice on foreign policy is postponed by a prolongation of the war, and other critical measures are at stake in Washington, the public should be reached by distribution of broadsides, etc. (through squads) on these other subjects.

    The drive should continue at white heat until we feel confident that the time for choice may not come soon. Even then beware of disbanding your squads. They are the League's most valuable equipment for "letting the people know" about all sorts of urgent matters. Recruitment should be completed by September 15.

2. If most members are engaged in the squads or in conducting them, who will attend to other League commitments both national and state or local?

    Answer: We often fail to realize how few members are usually engaged wholly or even partially in such other activities. Though in every League there will be a few League leaders who have not time to join a squad, you will probably find that many members are more, not less, useful in other work as a result of their work as distributors to the public, but the squad itself should not be used.

3. How many should each League recruit?

    Answer: In order to recruit a total of 50,000, each League must recruit a number of corresponding to its membership, plus 10% to make up for members who do not take part. Many women who are not members and some men will be interested to take part in the drive. If you do this thing well, you will no doubt find your membership increased automatically because of women who will be attracted by the new tempo of the League.

    The recent crisis has raised up many women who want to be helped to become good citizens, but are not satisfied with study for their own information.

4. How can 50,000 recruits reach enough people to make a difference?

    Answer: If each averages one-a-day, one and one-half millions would be reached each month. Three to five million people, not now interested, who become firmly convinced that this country needs a foreign policy of cooperation, would make this country safer than it has been for generations.

5. Can we plan on a new broadside every two weeks?

    Answer: You can plan for that or something else. If some point in a former broadside still needs to be emphasized, we will call your attention to it: If something new happens that the people need to understand, we will point that out to you. If we have something to tell you about successful methods in other Leagues, we will point them out to you.

6. How can recruits be taught how to open a conversation and what simple subjects should be introduced?

    Answer: Squad leaders of imagination and resourcefulness will show them how—at each fortnightly meeting of the squad at least three-fourths of the time should be used in discussing how to make the face to face contacts and in reporting on successful experiences. The rest of the time should be given to a discussion of the best subject to introduce, as indicated in the broadsides and other material. If interest is aroused in a face to face talk—the recipient of a broadside will be more likely to read it.

Ideas gleaned from those who have tried:

Begin conversation and wait for your cue

Follow the cue

Talk little—listen well

Use only the one fact or idea that seems most appropriate

Plant your seed and leave it to mature

Don't argue

7. If those who make the person to person approach are asked, "What is the League's position on foreign policy," what can they reply?

    Answer: Now and during the past 23 years the League of Women Voters has been for international cooperation. Not until later will the League formulate the specific plan it will support.

8. How can Leagues afford to buy so many broadsides?

    Answer: In every town and city there are people who would be happy to contribute to a special fund for such a purpose. It is an ideal project for a "five dollar contribution drive."

Source: Letter from Marguerite Wells to State Presidents and "Answers to Questions about Mobilizing for the Foreign Policy Drive," August 20, 1943. LWV Papers, Library of Congress.

On New Year's Day, January 1, 1944, Wells once again expressed her hope that League members would take individual as well as collective action in reaching citizens with information about the important foreign policy choices confronting them.

DOCUMENT 11: MARGUERITE WELLS TO SELECTED LOCAL LEAGUE PRESIDENTS

It is the first day of the year 1944, and as I write, the sun in Washington is just rising over the horizon. At whatever time by the clock that moment comes in every land, solemn thoughts are coming with it, and the world will be united for an instant in hopes for the future. The resolutions each one makes this year will be no ordinary New Year resolutions.

I am sharing mine with the presidents of certain local Leagues of Women Voters, chosen because of their special qualifications to make a thorough test of the new person to person way of helping to shape the future. Has the LWV found that way or must it seek another? That is the question to which you are asked to provide an answer. You know the essence of that new way—it is to reach more individuals, remembering it is individuals, their freedom and independence for whom the government of a democracy is instituted. It is not to preach to them, nor teach them, nor exhort them, but to help them do their part in making a success of that government. Those of you who accept leadership in such an undertaking have a hard task, but your reward, if you succeed, will be great. Your success will spread beyond the few with whom you work and far out of your sight and furnish evidence to those of less faith.

You will need help and it is that help I am now sending you. The subject upon which squad members are to give help will be the emergency subject of the hour; now it is foreign policy, tomorrow it may be choosing the best people for government office or it may be upon saving this country from the dangers of inflation.

If you can prove that the person to person approach can help about foreign policy, you will prove its usefulness on other great matters. The emergency about foreign policy continues. The danger is that it be not recognized. Recently I heard a confessed isolationist Senator say what amounted to this, "I voted for the Connally Resolution only because of the two-thirds provision for treaty ratification which, as in 1920, will give time for isolationist Senators to show the people how mistaken they have been in favoring plans for international cooperation." It is true that in 1920 great numbers who favored the League of Nations had merely followed the crowd. This time we must make sure that they lay hold upon some fundamental principles from which they can not be swayed by chicanery about details.

Already there are many people who cannot be fooled a second time and it is the League's task to make sure there are more.

Day before yesterday I saw a piece in the paper about a little book "Faith and Works," with the comment that the book infuses the individual with a sense of deep personal responsibility for political order. Then the commentator goes on thus, "Perhaps you will agree that it is fear of the complexities of international affairs that causes so many people to pass by on the other side. But . . . what the individual must commit himself to is a very simple principle . . ." That is what the LWV understands. It seeks to strengthen the individual's hold on simple principles.

My wish for you on this first day of the New Year is that by *your* faith and *your* works you may infuse thousands of individuals with a sense of deep personal responsibility for political order.

I do make that wish most earnestly and I am sure that you are as grateful as I am that we have work to do. Please share your successes and failures with me that I may know how to help you or pass on your help to others.

Source: Marguerite Wells to "Dear Local League President, January 1, 1944. LWV Papers, Library of Congress.

> Wells's quick action gave the League a head start in addressing not only the issues of the moment but in thinking about the world after the war. The program of the League of Women Voters for the years 1942–1944 reflected both the priority of the war and the organization's new programmatic division between an "Active List" that may take the form of study, legislative support, or forming of public opinion and a "Platform" representing prior League activities and reflecting its current attitudes about the appropriate role of government in society.

DOCUMENT 12: 1942–44 ACTIVE LIST

Plans for post-war international organization with special reference to economic problems.

Support of foreign policy adopted by the Congress which is to provide defense articles for the government of any country whose defense the President deems vital to the defense of the United States.

Financing the defense programs with special consideration of personal income taxes, commodity taxes, borrowing and reduction of non-defense expenditures.

Controlling inflation by legislative and administrative action, such as price control legislation, allocations and rationing, fiscal policies.

Full use of mediation and arbitration services of government for the settlement of industrial disputes.

Opposition to use of public funds for private education.

Special status for inclusion in platform

Government provision for medical care of the indigent.

Source: Active List, 1942–44, National League of Women Voters. LWV Papers on Film, II. A.19. 0608.

DOCUMENT 13: 1942–44 LEAGUE PLATFORM

The Platform is composed of those subjects to which the League has given sustained attention. Many of them are now part of the governmental pattern.

The National Board may select measures from the Platform if the League of Women Voters has previously worked for a similar measure or if an unexpected opportunity arises to do effective work on a bill which is in conformity with the Platform.

State League conventions select state subjects for state support which are in general conformity with, but not in opposition to, the statements on the platform.

Platform of the National League of Women

In a democratic government the authority comes from the people.

Unless the citizen gives time, energy and thought, there is no true democratic government. The citizen must vote, must watch administrative practices, must follow legislation, must help to form public opinion. The League of Women Voters, in the public interest helps the citizen to act.

The citizen must be free to reach decisions on which he bases his vote. The League of Women Voters works to safeguard the constitutional rights of the individual with special reference to freedom of speech, assembly and press.

In order to prepare the citizen to accept the responsibilities of democracy, the League of Women Voters works for a system, state and local, of compulsory public education for all children between the ages of six and sixteen and for educational opportunities and library service for adults. Academic freedom is essential to education in a democracy.

The League of Women works for extension of the popular vote to disenfranchise in the District of Columbia and abolition of the poll tax as a prerequisite for voting.

In our democratic government the authority of the people is delegated by them to elected representatives and officials and through them to appointed officers.

To make it easier for the voter to chose competent officials and representatives, the League of Women Voters works for permanent registration and for the short ballot which includes only policy-making officials.

The responsibilities of those to whom the people delegate their authority should be clearly defined and understood. Because referenda tend to decrease the sense of responsibility of elected representatives, the League of Women Voters opposes war referendum. The League of Women Voters works for organization of state legislatures which clarifies their relation to the voter and which expedites legislative procedures; executive responsibility for the preparation of and control of budgets; understanding of the fact that the official who represents the majority of all the voters and who is charged by the Constitution with the conduct of foreign policy is the President.

In democratic government efficiency is not easy to achieve.
The League of Women Voters attempts to increase efficiency by: employment of qualified personnel without discrimination on the basis of sex, marital status or place of residence; use of scientific procedures and the results of research in all fields of government; appropriation of funds adequate for the carrying out of adopted policies; development of a coordinated system, federal, state, and local, for taxation; development of a state and local system for public health and public welfare; formation of units of school taxation and administration large enough for economy and efficiency; adoption of the manager plan for local government.

Of the special responsibilities assumed by government, the League of Women Voters works for: provision for unemployment and old age insurance; slum clearance and publicly subsidized housing for low income groups; protection of the right to bargain collectively; protection of the buying public through standards of purity and quality, adequate information, and fair trade practices; minimum wages and maximum hours where sub-standard; public employment service; provision for relief and old age assistance; control of child labor; social security measures for children; protection of dependent, delinquent and neglected children.

Legal and administrative discrimination against women should be removed by specific state legislation.
The League of Women Voters opposes the Equal Rights Amendment.

The flow of trade is in the general interest and should not be obstructed by consideration of private interests, by interstate trade barriers or by excessive international trade restrictions.
The League of Women Voters works for a tariff policy as found in the trade agreements program.

Foreign policy should be conducted for the good of the nation as a whole and should recognize the fact that the nations of the world are interdependent.
The League of Women Voters has consistently advocated American participation in international agencies designed to settle disputes by peaceful means, to provide for peaceful change, and to solve common economic and social problems; limitation of armaments by international agreement; a foreign policy which permits discrimination against an aggressor and favors the victim of aggression; opposition to racial discriminations in immigration laws.

Source: "Platform of the National League of Women Voters," LWV Papers on film, II. A.19. 0598–60.

In the midst of war, other issues had to be attended to. One was renewal of the Reciprocal Trade Agreement Act. The League's contributions to that successful effort were described by Marguerite Wells in June 1943.

DOCUMENT 14: MARGUERITE WELLS ON THE RECIPROCAL TRADE AGREEMENTS ACT RENEWAL

The League of Women Voters deserves a great deal of credit for the comfortable margin by which amendments to the Trade Agreements Act were defeated. Up until the last moment in the House it was doubtful whether the amendments could be defeated. . . .

In the Senate, the bill started under a serious handicap by failure of the Finance Committee to defeat all the proposed amendments. The League of Women Voters did good work in interpreting the Committee (Danaher) amendment to the press and to members of the Senate.

The League was among the first to start telling the public to watch amendments, not merely the vote of final passage of the Act. The League stimulated newspaper correspondents to start writing about trade agreements from this angle; helped interest newspaper editors; pushed other organizations into action. The whole Stop Isolationism Now effort of the League contributed to public thinking on the issue. Our only regret is that had we been able to put even a small amount of extra effort into this first major test of foreign policy, we might have prevented passage of the one amendment. . . .

Source: Wells, *Leadership in a Democracy*, 72.

In all these activities Marguerite Wells tried to expand the outreach of individual members to the larger community. Concerned that members were set in their ways and simply content to educate themselves, Wells and her board identified structural problems (such as the departments' tight control of program) standing in the way of achieving the League's purpose to act in the public interest. Consequently, Wells and the national board proposed a sweeping revision of the bylaws that would establish a closer relation between members and the national organization. The dominance of the state Leagues within the organization would be downgraded if not eliminated, and the national League would become a unitary organization of local Leagues. Needless to say, such far-reaching proposals produced a rebellion in the ranks.

The Sixteenth National Convention in Chicago in 1944 found the regularly nominated slate of nominees contested by another slate organized by opponents of the proposed changes in the bylaws. Marguerite Wells had indicated her intention to retire from the presidency. Because Ruth Mitchell, the reform slate's nominee to succeed Wells, was also from Minnesota, charges of a "Minnesota dynasty" provided added ammunition for the opposition.

What may have been the most contentious convention in the League's history was nevertheless conducted with civility and mutual respect and ended in compromise. The convention elected Anna Lord Strauss of New York as president along with three other officers on the substitute slate. At the same time delegates adopted certain "reform" changes in the bylaws, thereby moving the League from a federation of state Leagues to an organization of individual members of local, state, and national Leagues.

The change was more than cosmetic. With the departure of Wells, the last of the suffrage leaders had retired from the scene. Strauss, though she could claim Lucretia Mott as her great-grandmother, represented the postsuffrage generation of League leaders.

A soft-spoken but highly efficient leader, this white-haired but vigorous and athletic Quaker went about rescuing the League from the postconvention trauma of having to recruit an almost entirely new board and staff. During her years in office, the League achieved unprecedented levels of membership and political clout.

Chapter 14

The Atomic Age

Even though the League had undergone significant structural changes, changes in the world were much more dramatic. Many knew in 1944 that the end of the war was in sight, but few knew that it would be a new kind of bomb that would hasten its end. The United States would emerge from World War II as an atomic and economic power the likes of which the world had never seen. But the perception of the nation's new world importance did not immediately register as the new crop of American veterans returned home. Reunited with their families, they went about the business of getting an education through the GI Bill of Rights, finding jobs, and building homes in new suburban communities.

The magnitude of volunteer and staff time required for implementing the League's program is clearly documented in the listing of legislative action and materials prepared in the two-year period from April 1944 to April 1946.

DOCUMENT 1: LEGISLATIVE ACTION AND MATERIALS ISSUED, 1944–46

1. *A war and postwar finance program based as far as possible on tax revenues, which takes into account control of inflation, fair distribution of the tax burden and minimizing postwar dislocations.*

Legislative action: None
Materials issued:
> Memo: Introduction to the Study of Business Taxation March 1944
> TRENDS articles (6)

2. *Curbing inflation through price control, rationing and curtailing purchasing power.*

Legislative action:
> Support of renewal of Price Control Act in 1944, 1945, and 1946
> Support of extension of Second War Powers Act (H.R. 4780)
> Support of the Patman bill for stabilization of housing prices (H.R. 4761)

Materials issued:
> Broadsides:
>> What Will Your Dollar Buy?—March 1945
> TRENDS articles (20)
> Stumbling Blocks or Briefs for Action
>> Is OPA Worth Keeping, April 1945
>> The Public Asks Some Questions About Food, May 1945
>> A Backdoor Way to End Price Control, June 1945
>> Questions and Answers on Price Control, April 1946
>> Discussion Outline on OPA and the U.S. Food Situation, May 1945

3. *Adoption of domestic policies which will facilitate the solution of international problems.*

Legislative action:
> Support of revision of Senate treaty rule (H.J. Res. 60, S.J. Res. 53)
> Support of extension of lend-lease (H.R. 2013)
> Support of reciprocal trade agreements (H.R. 3240)
> Support of British Loan (S. J. Res. 138)
> Opposition to Gassett bill to cut immigration by 50% (H.R. 3663)
> Support of bills granting immigration quotas to East Indians (H.R. 3517) and Filipinos (H.R. 776)
> Support of McMahon bill on atomic energy control (S. 1717)
> Opposition to May-Johnson bill on atomic energy control (H.R. 4566)

Materials issued:
> Memos:
>> Trade Agreements—Bridge to Peace, April 1945
>> Trade, Jobs, and Peace, February 1946
> Broadsides:
>> Trade Makes Jobs, March 1945
>> Is Lending Money to Britain Good Business for Us?, February 1946
> Stumbling Blocks:
>> What to Do With Atomic Energy, November 1945
>> The British Loan—Improving the Basis for Postwar Trade, December 1945
>> Progress Report on Atomic Energy, January 1946
> What's At Stake—The British Loan, April 1946

TRENDS articles (12)

4. *Participation by the United States in plans and machinery for world-wide relief and rehabilitation, for handling common economic, social and political problems, membership of the United States in a general international organization, eventually to include all peoples regardless of race, religion or political persuasion, for peaceful settlement of disputes with power to prevent or stop aggression.*

Legislative action:
Support of U.S. entry into the United Nations (United Nations Charter)
Support of Bretton Woods Agreements (H.R. 3314)
Support of appropriations for UNRRA (H.J. Res. 266, H.R. 4649)
Support of U.S. Membership in UNESCO (H.J. Res. 305)
Support of U.S. Membership in the Food and Agriculture Organization (H.J. Res. 145)
Support of legislation granting authority to U.S. Delegate in the UN (S. 1580)
Materials issued:
Memos:
Bretton Woods Monetary Proposals, January 1945
Peace Is What We Make It, February 1945
Fifty Nations Agree, July 1945
The United Nations: The Road Ahead, January 1946
Broadsides:
Foreign Policy—Essentials for Party Platforms, May 1944
Yours Is the Power, November 1944
What Happened At Dumbarton Oaks, December 1944
Power Politics or United Nations, February 1945
Victory is Not Peace, April 1945
Starving, May 1945
We the People are Forging the Peace, June 1945
Have You Caught Up With the Atom? January 1946
Stumbling Blocks or Brief's for Action
Russia and the San Francisco Conference, April 1945
The Public Asks Some Questions About Food, May 1945
Why Is Europe Hungry? May 1945
Is the Food Problem Still a Problem? August 1945
First Step In Peace Building—Food, September 1945
UNRRA's Future Hangs in the Balance, October 1945
From Blue Print to Growing Concern, March 1946
Other Materials:
Discussion Outline on Foreign Policy, August 1944
Suggestions for Seizing Our Second Chance, October 1944
Discussion Outline for Four Discussions, December 1944
How to Plan a Meeting on United Nations, December 1944
Discussion Outline For A Single Discussion, December 1944
Public Relations Is Our Job, December 1944
Bibliography on Dumbarton Oaks, December 1944
Suggested Outline For A Speech, December 1944
Opening Gun, December 1944
Dumbarton Oaks Chart, December 1944

Board Planning For UN Campaign, December 1944
Story of Dumbarton Oaks, January 1945
Outline For Discussion Meetings On Making UN Work, February 1945
Story of Bretton Woods, May 1945
Charter And the Press, May 1945
Discussion Outline On Food for Europe, May 1945
Windows Display On Food, September 1945
TRENDS articles (63)

5. *Policies for economic stability that take into account: demobilization of armed forces; reconversion of industry; fullest use of resources; a high level of employment; mutual responsibilities of labor and management.*

Legislative action:
Support of the Wagner-Ellender-Taft bill for a national housing policy (S. 1592)
Support of Patman bill for emergency housing measures (H.R. 4761)
Opposition to bill returning USES to state operation during reconversion period. (H.R. 4437)
Materials issued:
Memos:
Valley Authorities: Shall We Establish Regional Developments, October 1945
Full Employment and Democracy, April 1946
Our Housing Problem, April 1946
Stumbling Blocks:
A High Level of Employment, digest of the Murray Bill, bibliography, etc., October 1945
The Murray Full Employment Bill, December 1945
Factors In Labor Picture, January 1946
Tools for Leaders:
Housing Policies, December 1945
TRENDS articles (36)

6. *Strengthening governmental procedures to improve the legislative processes and the relationship between Congress and the Executive, including a constitutional amendment changing the procedure of the approval of treaties to a more democratic process.*

Legislative action:
Support of Manasco Bill to permit reorganization of the executive departments (H.R. 4129)
Support of proposals to amend two-thirds treaty rule (H.J. Res. 60, S.J. Res. 53)
Statement to Committee on the Organization of Congress on need for reorganization.
Materials issued:
Memos:
Reorganization of Congress, May 1944
The Two-thirds Senate Treaty Rule, October 1944
A National Government to Meet Today's Needs, January 1946

(Bibliography On Reorganization of Congress, August 1944)
TRENDS articles (9)

7. *Development of the social insurance program: extension of coverage; benefits for temporary and permanent disability; insurance for medical care; nationalization of unemployment compensation insurance.*

Legislative action:
Support of Child Labor Section in Minimum Wage Bill (S. 1349)
Materials issued:
The Future of Social Security, September 1945
TRENDS article (1)

8. *Federal aid to education administered through state departments of education.*

Legislative action: None
Material issued:
Memo:
The Case for Federal Aid to Education, February 1945
TRENDS article (1)

9. *Preservation of Civil Liberties and protection of minority groups against discrimination.*

Legislative action:
Support of equal pay bill (S. 1178)
Materials issued:
Memo:
Government and Our Minorities, August 1945
TRENDS articles (2)
Miscellaneous legislative action on basis of platform.
Support of Suffrage for the District of Columbia (S. J. Res. 9, H.J. Res. 62)
Opposition to "equal rights" amendment (H.J. Res. 49, S.J. Res. 61)

Source: "The Record: Summary of Action taken under Active List." April 1944–April 1946. LWV Papers on film, II. B.1 0145–48.

The exigencies of postwar reconstruction and recovery did not, however, distract the League from examining its own way of doing things. The League's perennial desire for a more manageable program found expression in this memo from Anna Lord Strauss to state League presidents.

DOCUMENT 2: ANNA LORD STRAUSS TO "DEAR STATE LEAGUE PRESIDENT"

As provided in the by-laws, the National Board has formulated the Proposed Active List for the consideration of the 1946 Convention and submits it to you at this time. It is now the responsibility of your State Board to consider it and to submit in writing any further recommendations it may wish to make. Your recommendations must be submitted twenty days before the opening of the National Convention, which will be held in Kansas City, April 30–May 3. The National Board will consider all such recommendations at its pre-Convention Board Meeting before submitting its proposals to the Convention for action.

A Shorter Active List

The first thing you will note about the enclosed proposal is its brevity. The National Board has found that many factors point toward the wisdom and the necessity for limiting the current agenda of the National League. The League has never aimed to set up and accomplish a complete program of political action. It has always aimed to select a few vital issues of fundamental importance, because such issues are best suited to the League purpose of promoting political responsibility of citizens.

One League member summarized succinctly what she wanted in the National Active List when she said, "If the League could just stop wars and prevent depressions!" Many have used more words to say virtually the same thing. Comments from state and local Leagues and League members are preponderantly in support of a shorter program.

Local Boards Bear a Heavy Load

It is the local League President and Board who know best why the National Active List needs to be shortened. On the local Board rests the responsibility of coordinating the programs and action of all three levels of League activity. It is the members of the local League who must do the work. They must answer National and state action calls on the major commitments, the current action items. They must be prepared to follow through on continuing responsibilities whenever they become live issues. They must plan and carry out local projects on which the prestige of the League in its own community so largely rests. They must carry on voters services and pre-election work according to the high standards that have become traditional with the League.

Not only must the local League Board take action in the name of the League [but] urge its members to act individually. It has come to see that this is only the beginning of the League job. The League conscience can no longer be clear unless the League is politically effective in its community. This means going to the citizens, exercising resourcefulness to gain their attention and interest, helping them to learn how to take political responsibility. It means more careful planning, better tools and more of them. It means setting higher finance goals and achieving them.

The Strength of the League

In considering the Proposed Active List we should bear in mind that a considerable proportion of our Leagues are in smaller cities and towns, and that they are relatively small Leagues. Seventy-two per cent of our Leagues have less than one hundred members. Almost half of our Leagues have less than fifty members. Only a few, five or six per cent, have offices and staff. This grass roots strength distinguishes our organization. We are the only national, non-partisan organization devoted to the improvement of government with live local organizations in towns and cities of many sizes. Public opinion in smaller communities has time after time been the decisive factor in the determination of important national policies.

We kill the goose that lays the golden egg when we heap upon state and local projects a long and complicated Active List on the National level. Add to this the continuing responsibilities, national, state, and local, and do not underestimate the time and energy that should continue to go into voters' services of various kinds. The League is the only organization in many, many cities which can be relied upon to do an accurate and dependable pre-election job year after year. The proportions of the League job are indeed formidable.

Each of the three items on the Proposed Active List embodies an important policy. The policy suggested for international cooperation is well developed and clear. The second item also embodies a policy well formulated by the League through its years of attention to the structure and functioning of representative government. The third policy proposed is in process of formation as a League policy. Some facets are familiar and well understood. Others of great importance need to be worked out if the League is to help to achieve economic stability, both for our nation and for the world.

The explanation of the Proposed Active List, which is enclosed, is intended to provide a basis for discussion, so that the Convention may express itself fully on many details of the three fundamental policies proposed as the Active List. Convention debate on the specific parts of the three policies will be guidance for future action. The final "Explanation of the Active List" will be written in the light of the whole Convention discussion.

It is the hope of the National Board that you will consider the Proposed Active List in the light of the whole League job and how the National League can best accomplish its part of that job.

The Platform is being revised and will be submitted to you before the time specified by the by-laws. Many items which have been dropped from the present Active List are being placed in the Platform.

Source: January 16, 1946. LWV Papers on film, II. B.1. 0011–12.

The League's push for the establishment of the United Nations had a dramatic effect on American public opinion. Following the August 1944 Dumbarton Oaks conference that drafted U.S. plans for the UN charter, a League pamphlet, "The Story of Dumbarton Oaks," sold more than one hundred thousand copies in just a matter of weeks. After more than a month of deliberations in the spring of 1945, representatives of fifty nations assembled at the San Francisco conference finally agreed to a charter for this new organization designed to maintain peace and security in the world. Anne H. Johnstone, a foreign policy expert, who had served both as a LWV staff member and board director, was one of several representatives of nongovernmental organizations who had the opportunity to express their views about the issues before the conference. To secure support for ratification by the U.S. Senate, "five thousand League members," as Louise Young reports, "were trained for a nationwide 'Take it to the People' campaign. . . . In the most successful community based contribution to public under-

standing of a major issue in which the League had ever engaged, over a million pieces of literature were distributed." In some respects it represented the high-water mark of the League's foreign policy achievements over the years. It is no exaggeration to suggest that the League's work in communities throughout the United State helped to generate a favorable climate of public opinion for acceptance of this new forum for international cooperation.

Nongovernmental organizations could appoint representatives to the United Nations, and the League found a UN observer in the person of Zelia Ruebhausen, who had, like Anne Johnstone, served both as a national staff and board member. This report from the League's energetic observer puts a human face on the goings-on in the new organization. Anna Lord Strauss noted, "Her first and amusing letter after she joined the observers indicated that the group seemed to think her appearance as important as the fact that Gromyko had come back to the Security Council. Everybody had been asking, 'Where is the League of Women Voters?' We had a flood of telegrams in Washington asking where we were."

DOCUMENT 3: REPORT FROM THE LEAGUE'S UN OBSERVER

I have had it on my mind to write you all week, but have been hopefully waiting for a typewriter. Since none is in sight I guess I'd better start my reportorial duties.

In the first place there was tremendous satisfaction both from the point of view of the other observers and the State Department that the League was finally represented. In their eyes our non-appearance was comparable to Gromyko's walk–out. I have faithfully attended every silly and non-silly meeting that was called so the League is now on par with everyone else.

Since the walk-out, and maybe before, I don't know about that, the Security Council meetings have been very carefully stage managed. When the notes from Iran and Russia came in, for example, Byrnes asked Mr. Ala what he thought of them. His reply was read and had been carefully prepared by his two American advisers, John Lord O'Brien and Jack Leland whom I understand is a former State Department employee, so the affairs of Iran are being carefully supervised by the U.S. By tacit consent of all the other nations the U.S. has taken the lead in this affair—all resolutions and comment on the situation being made by Byrnes. Stettinius just smiles and says nothing. From all I can see the Council did as much as it could in its present rather weak status, and as usual, James B. Reston has summed up the case in the most expert way possible. I am sure you have been reading his articles so I shall just add "amen" to everything he has written. My general impression is that with their limited power, the members of the Council are doing their damndest to make U.N. work. They seem especially sincere in proclaiming that collective action is the only solution to the world's problems, which I gather is different from the League where each nation tried to dominate for its own purposes and felt that it, as a country, was stronger than the group.

Because they have no rules of procedure as yet, the various countries try to jockey around with parliamentary rules and gain an advantage that way. As some of the delegates have never experienced parliamentary procedure, they are confused by it. The present chairman, Dr. Quo is weak because he never makes any procedural decisions. Instead of just announcing, for instance, that a certain motion has precedence, he appeals to the rest to ask them. That opens up the floor for a debate on the subject. The Committee of Experts, however, are presenting their report tomorrow on procedure, so that may help them to lay down a few definite regulations.

I attended one meeting of the observers with Stettinius and the State Department Division of Public Liaison. It didn't help me much because so many of the questions were along the line of "why aren't more women and more veterans represented?" These were quite easily squelched. The rest was taken up with how to get to Hunter, how to get tickets, how to present your ideas to the delegates, etc. The substance of what the Council was considering was not discussed. The observers themselves do not impress me. In conversations at the Security Council meeting they seem vitally concerned in whether the seats are going to be filled, and whether Cadogan is wearing the same necktie he wore yesterday. The trivia are of great importance to them. The other day a lone lady from Springfield sat next to me. I asked her what she represented. She said "the League." I said, "League of what?" She said, "League of Women Voters, of course." It was Mrs. Richard Anderson who had gotten a guest ticket for the day. She was thrilled to be there and thrilled to be sitting next to her National representative. I'd sort of forgotten how much prestige the "National" has. Anyway, I took her all around and helped her with an article she was writing for her local paper. . . .

I have been to one other meeting of women of all nations to discuss how international and foreign groups could be represented. The smartest thing they did was to name a small sub-committee to work with State Department officials on the problem.

There is another meeting of observers tonight, but as it is pouring rain, and the meeting is at 8:15 in New York City, and as I am cooking dinner in Rye I expect they shall miss the pleasure of my company. The quest for an apartment still goes on. We got a penthouse, packed up to move in today and then heard this morning that the management of the building has refused to let the Whipples sublet, although they have done it before. The truth of the matter is that Mrs. W. Wilkie wants the apartment so I guess we're licked. As going to and from to Hunter takes three hours I am anxious to move. Even so it is well worth it to be an observer and I am grateful to you for the opportunity. It is really an education. My very best to all.

Source: "Notes from Mrs. Ruebhausen during the United Nations Security Council at Hunter College, New York, April 1946. LWV Papers on film, II. B.1. 0149–50. Excerpts from Anna Lord Strauss's speech to the Seventeenth Annual Convention of the League of Women Voters of the United States (LWVUS) (hereinafter referred to as the Seventeenth Convention), Kansas City, MO, April 30–May 3, 1946. LWV Papers on film, II. B.1. 0276.

Another central League concern was to make the promise of "the atomic age" peaceful and not perilous. Confident that the United Nations represented the best instrument for international control and that domestic control should be in the hands of civilians and not the military, the League supported legislation to achieve those ends. Some flavor of that approach is contained in this excerpt from the presentation by national board members Kathryn Stone and Georgianna Mitchell at the Kansas City convention.

DOCUMENT 4: THE LEAGUE'S STAND ON ATOMIC ENERGY

MRS. STONE: The League of Women Voters has done a grand job in support of the McMahon bill. I think any neutral observer, not a member of the League, who has followed the fate of that bill thus far in Washington would testify to that. Many have told me so. . . .

The League of Women Voters strongly urges the immediate passage of the McMahon bill, S. 1717, a bill to provide for the domestic control of atomic energy through the establishment of an Atomic Energy Commission to be composed of five civilians. We believe that the citizens have demonstrated beyond a doubt that they wish to assure the fullest constructive uses of fissionable materials in the public welfare, and that the passage of the McMahon bill would provide for it.

The League calls attention to several minor provisions that it would like to see improved if possible. We believe that the internal divisions of an agency should not be specified by statute, as is done in the bill, since this would freeze the administrative pattern and would make it difficult for the Commission to adjust its organization to new problems as they arise. We believe that the General Manager should be appointed by the commission rather than by the President of the United States, since the Manager will be directly responsible to the Commission. We believe that would be desirable to insert provisions for a commercial type of audit similar to that of TVA and other federal corporations.

We wish to make clear, however, that in our opinion these objections are secondary in importance and do not materially detract from the over-all soundness of the bill. We consider it vital to the national welfare that the bill be passed by both Houses of Congress at the earliest possible date. (Applause)

I think we all feel the same way about this question of atomic energy—somewhat stunned and numb. It is going to take more time still to realize its implications. Some one said the other day that it is as if we had always lived in a darkened movie house with a flickering screen and two-dimensional figures and had suddenly been brought out into the full light of a three-dimensional world and the sunlight. It would take us some time to become accustomed to the brighter light and the changed conditions.

I think we have a big job ahead of us if we are going to follow through on this support. I should like to read a sentence from the "Purpose" as expressed in the McMahon bill:

"The significance of the atomic bomb for military purposes is evident. The effect of the use of atomic energy for civilian purposes upon the social, economic, and political structures of today cannot now be determined. It is a field in which unknown factors are involved. Therefore, any legislation will necessarily be subject to revision from time to time. It is reasonable to anticipate, however, that tapping this new source of energy will cause profound changes in our present way of life. Accordingly, it is hereby declared to be the policy of the people of the United States that, subject at all times to the paramount objective of assuring the common defense and security, the development and utilization of atomic energy shall as far as practicable be directed toward improving the public welfare, increasing the standard of living, strengthening free competition in private enterprise, and promoting world peace."

There, in broad terms, is our citizen job, to watch the development of these uses. I should like to call your attention more specifically to provisions of the bill which we will want to see carried out in provisions where we must be the watchdog, or where the citizens must be, and I do not know of any other group that will be a watchdog in the public interest so well as the League.

It is this provision: "When any use of fissionable material is developed to the point where it is of practical value, this Commission will report it to the President. In its report, it will estimate the social, political, economic, and international effects of such use and make a recommendation for legislation dealing with it. The President will then study it and make his recommendations to the Congress."

Remember that the Commission is empowered under the bill to issue licenses for these practical uses as they are worked out. It provides that no license for manufacture or use shall be granted until a report has been filed with Congress for ninety days. During that ninety–day period the commentators, the journalists, the League of Women Voters would be studying, would be discussing, would be thinking about the implications of whatever practical use was proposed. I think perhaps that is the best way of trying to get you to realize, all of us to realize, where we come in.

PRESIDENT STRAUSS: This subject is now open for discussion.

MRS. HENRY DeWOLF SMYTH (New Jersey): I should like very briefly to propose a vote of appreciation from this convention to the National Board for their ability to rise to the unusual demands brought upon them by the advent of atomic energy, by their extraordinary, clear presentation of its implications to the membership, both in the digests that reached us in the winter and the last brief of the Acheson Report, and for their willingness to realize that information about this to the public is one of our first charges. As a League member I am enormously impressed with their ability, and they deserve our great appreciation and commendation. (Applause)

Source: Excerpts from the Proceedings of the Seventeenth Convention. LWV Papers on film, II. B.1. 0604–08, 0368–74.

DOCUMENT 5: REPORT BY GEORGIANNA MITCHELL ON ATOMIC ENERGY WORK

MRS. MITCHELL: In the past few years the League of Women Voters has constantly called on our government to take leadership and champion policies of international cooperation. Those who have been around at meetings are conscious of how many times in speeches and literature we have said that the government must take the lead, the United States must lead.

With the report on International Control of Atomic Energy, our government is showing leadership. President Truman has said: "The release of atomic energy constitutes a new force too revolutionary to consider in the framework of old ideas."

The report outlines a new framework, an international framework to deal with this new revolutionary force. The government, I repeat, is leading now, and the question is whether the general public will understand the issue and follow quickly enough to avert the disaster which is impending unless a system of international control of atomic energy is developed by the United Nations.

The United States has taken a very clear stand in favor of such international control. I will just remind you of the sequence of events because it may shorten the debate later because it is a new topic to many.

1. Last November 1945, we had the Truman-Atlee-King Declaration advocating a United Nations Commission to work out international controls and safeguards.
2. The following December the foreign ministers of the United States and Britain went to Russia, and with the Russian foreign ministers and Stalin reached an agreement on a resolution to the United Nations for the creation of an atomic energy commission.
3. There was a follow-up on that. The first United Nations assembly created the Atomic Energy Committee. It was adopted by the assembly, and a commission has been established which is obligated to report to the Security Council, and when appropriate, to the General Assembly and to the Social and Economic Council, because the ramifications of atomic energy are not purely military.
4. The next move will be the meetings of the United Nations Commission. The State Department—for these United Nations negotiations, which are going to take place—has appointed a committee headed by Dean Acheson. Their job was to prepare what might become American recommendations of policy at the coming meetings. The Acheson committee, in turn, appointed a board of consultants, and it is this board of consultants—a very remarkable board—that has submitted the report that we term the Acheson Report. That report has been submitted to the American people for discussion.

The stand to be taken by our delegate on the United Nations Atomic Energy Committee will be to a great degree dependent on the reaction of the public to the report. What we think about it as individuals and what we do as a League is enormously important. We cannot over-accent that because the United States is now in the driver's seat on this question of atomic energy. We are the only ones at present who have the bombs and the ability to produce them. Other nations on this United Nations Atomic Energy Committee have asked us for our opinions, and certainly our delegate is not going there to make proposals which he does not believe, and which the executive department of the government of the United States does not believe the American people are going to back up. In other words, they cannot risk on this what happened with the Versailles Treaty. What they propose will be dependent upon what they believe the American people will support. That is why it is extremely important that all of us as individuals and as Leagues should say what we think about the control of atomic energy and how far we should go in international regulation.

I am going to refresh your mind on what the report advocates. This is going to be terribly brief. I hope all of you have read the digest that is in your kits, the brief that was done in the National office.

The report advocates setting up an international Atomic Development Authority. This Authority would have wide powers to insure complete control of all intrinsically dangerous operations connected with the production of atomic energy. Under the plan, the Atomic Development Authority would be the sole owner of the sources of raw material, the uranium and thorium mines, and primary production plants. The Authority alone would be able to extract the raw materials and produce fissionable materials, because they would control the sources and the primary production plants. There would be a large field of non-dangerous activities left in national hands, except for a minimum of licensing and inspection.

Step by step the report outlines plans for setting up the Atomic Development Authority and transfer of controls from national to international jurisdiction, beginning with ownership of raw material sources. This step by step transference is to insure protection for the United States and the other nations by retaining part of the controls in national hands until the Atomic Development Authority has gradually proved its ability to function.

Now, a word about the League's stand. The League of Women Voters stands for international control of atomic energy. In line with our platform stand for international agreements to limit armaments, the League of Women Voters took a stand in favor of United Nations control of atomic energy. The wording that came out read: "The Security Council should be responsible for supervising the production and use of atomic power. The Security Council should control weapons derived from atomic energy as part of an international program of arms control to which all nations would submit to such agreed upon controls as exchange of information, registration, inspection, or licensing."

I think before we open the discussion I shall do one further thing. I am not sure that all of you have had a chance to go to the numerous meetings that have been held throughout the country on control of atomic energy. Scientists themselves have played a large part in trying to tell people what they believe to be the situation. Out of this discussion and debate that has been going on now for some time, because you will remember that the first bomb fell in August, have come certain rather basic conclusions that seem to me be facts, rather than points open to debate. However, if you do not agree they are facts, you will have a chance to say so. I shall run through those.

1. Atomic weapons have a vastly greater power of destruction than that of any previously known explosive.
2. This greater destruction can be achieved with vastly reduced effort and at much lower cost. There are other statements, but I picked Arnold's: "Atomic bombing is six times more economical than conventional bombing." I think that is a conservative statement. "Ton for ton, atomic explosives will be anywhere from ten to one hundred times cheaper than the traditional explosives used in this war." That is a quotation from Oppenheimer.
3. Atomic weapons put a great premium on surprise attack.
4. With the development of the airplane and the atomic bomb, natural defenses such as oceans and mountains no longer afford protection.

There is no possibility of developing defenses adequate to give protection against an explosive of such magnitude.

5. We are already, in a sense, on an atomic arms race. The question is not "can a race be prevented?" but "will it continue or be stopped?" The United States is still spending roughly $500,000,000 yearly on production plants, producing materials that could easily be used for atomic bombs.

6. The United States will not be likely to maintain its monopoly for more than five to ten years. That is the general feeling.

With that as a sort of outline for discussion, we would like to hear what you think about this tremendously new and provocative thing that we have got to face as a nation.

MRS. J. W. MORRISSON (Connecticut): I think one of the most important jobs the League has to do is to see that the Acheson Report, the summary of it made by the National office, is as widely read and as widely understood as possible all over the country.

There must be international control of these atomic weapons. That is the only way out. We cannot have industrial powers bootlegging atomic bomb production. It will call for a job of supervision, an almost insuperably difficult one.

Source: Excerpts from the Proceedings of the Seventeenth Convention. LWV Papers on film. II. B.1. 0604-74.

The extent of the League's efforts with respect to educating the public on the relevant issues is captured in this report from a local League in Virginia.

DOCUMENT 6: REPORT BY ALBEMARLE COUNTY (VA) LEAGUE ON ACTIVITIES RELATING TO ATOMIC ENERGY

You have asked me to tell you some of our plans for Atomic Energy Week in Charlottesville and Albemarle County.

Our program starts on Sunday, May 11th, when local preachers have agreed to preach a sermon dealing in some way with atomic energy. They have all been given a copy of "12 Atomic Facts" for their information.

On Monday night, the 12th, we are to have the privilege of hearing Mr. Baukhage and Mr. Alfred Friendly speak at the Lane High School, capacity 923.

On Thursday, the 15th, Mr. Rorer of the Extension Division of the University of Virginia, is putting on an Institute similar to those which have been conducted throughout the State, with afternoon and evening discussions led by atomic scientists and members of the faculty of the Woodrow Wilson School of Foreign Affairs.

Beginning on May first, the city officials have agreed to stuff "12 Points on Atomic Energy" in with the gas and water bills which will go out within the following three weeks, approximately 5,500 of them. We plan to send a copy of the same flyer to every rural box holder of which we estimate there are about 2,500.

A young lawyer, the head of one of the civic clubs, is in charge of scheduling 16 mm movies among the monthly meetings of these clubs, to school assemblies, church groups and in the store, of which, more later. Each movie will be preceded or followed by a brief talk by a layman (in the schools, sometimes by a science student) and those speakers are in the charge of a retired naval officer, a member of the faculty. We expect to show "One World or None," "A Tale of Two Cities" and "Operation Crossroads."

There will be daily radio programs such as the play, "Pilot Lights of the Apocalypse" a message from Raymond Swing, brief talks in simple language prepared by a member of the staff of the Extension Division and, of course, spot announcements about the program of the day.

In a vacant store on Main Street we plan four times daily showings of the same 16 mm movies. It is here that we hope to really catch "the man in the street." The Salvation Army is lending its loud speaker for use outside the store before the movie showings to bring in anyone passing by. There will be exhibits, and each movie will be followed by a brief talk. We plan to open the store before the week actually begins so as to catch the farmers on two Saturdays.

The largest theater in town has agreed to run "The Beginning or the End" during the first part of the week.

We plan about 20 exhibits, a poster surrounded by literature with a program of events beside it. These are to go to the libraries, the City Hall, the biggest grain and feed store, the schools, and other places where people gather. We are asking the bookstores to feature books about atomic energy that week, and we have been given one other full window in addition to the one in our store.

Mr. Einstein has sent us a statement wishing us success in Atomic Energy Week and repeating his urgent plea for control.

The League of Women Voters of Albemarle has made a victrola record of questions and answers about atomic energy for distribution in these groups. "Mrs. Jones" asks the questions, the needle is lifted and the many Mrs. Jones discuss it and try to answer it. The needle is replaced, and a member of the faculty of the Woodrow Wilson School of Foreign Affairs then gives his answer.

There were about 25 local organization represented at the first meeting. We have drawn our committees from these groups. We have asked each one to contribute up to $25.00, but I fear we can not count on a 100% financial participation. The chairman of the budget committee, a member of a veteran's group, will follow up the letter by a personal visit. . . .

It is our purpose to show the citizens of Charlottesville and Albemarle County some of the background of international cooperation, the potentialities for good and evil in atomic energy, how it may be properly controlled, and what is the alternative to such control.

Source: Mary Stamps White to Kathryn H. Stone, April 21, 1947. LWV Papers on film. II. B.1. 0725–26.

Anna Lord Strauss initiated the campaign to build support for the United Nations by asking local Leagues to identify the principles that should guide such an effort. This initiative represented the first real test of the new direct relationship between the national organization and the local Leagues, and it proved to be a rousing success, with League members responding in unprecedented numbers. With the convening of the Dumbarton Oaks conference, Strauss proclaimed, "It is absolutely essential that the imagination and intelligence of millions of individual citizens be deeply stirred." She urged Leagues to reach

*the uninformed, the unorganized, the unconvinced, and the uncommit-
ted with information, and they did. Never before had a single League
community effort reached so many people. More than five thousand
League members were trained for a nationwide "Take it to the people"
campaign, and more than a million pieces of literature were distributed. As League members felt their power, the organization experienced a new surge of enthusiasm. Never mind that the initial high
hopes for the United Nations had been dashed by the realities of a rising clash between the ideologies of communism and democracy or,
perhaps more accurately, the contest for influence and control among
the world's major powers. The League was on the threshold of significant growth and influence within the public policy realm, as revealed in
this speech by Strauss to the League's national convention in Grand
Rapids, Michigan, in 1948.*

DOCUMENT 7: REPORT OF ANNA LORD STRAUSS AT NATIONAL CONVENTION

When we met in Kansas City we had hopes that 1946–48 would be a period
of turning to peaceful uses the discoveries and skills developed for war. We
believed that in this atomic age we would be using our scientific and techno-
logical abilities to improve economic, political and social patterns throughout
the world. We had hoped that the end of war would mark the beginning of
peace. We had hoped that the peace treaties would all have been written and that
the agreement of wartime allies would continue. We had hoped that the relief
and reconstruction stage of our foreign aid would be largely over. Most of all
we had hoped that the United Nations would be well launched, and would become the basis for the peaceful integration of the world community.

Instead we face a world in which the war is not concluded, a major task of
reconstruction is still ahead, our full hopes for the United Nations have not been
realized. The rift between East and West has widened steadily, bringing us face
to face with the gravest problem in our national history.

Today too many people are confused and discouraged. In their discouragement some are seeking an easy answer to our perplexities, a panacea, appealing
because of its simplicity. Others are returning to the pattern of the past, with a
cynicism that is the currency of the unmoral. They illustrate two groups, those
who run in too headlong a manner, and those who consider but do not run at all.
We will always have in our society those who race ahead regardless of what
may befall and the conservatives who hang back waiting to be shown the safe
smooth path. What is needed most of all today, however, is citizens willing to
build the road as they move toward their goal. That is a strenuous job that calls
for alert people with tempered judgment who learn from experience the effective moment when progress can be made and when compromise is necessary to
consolidate gains. Sometimes these citizens may be followed by eager and
willing fellow workers, but many times it will be a bewildering job to break a
trail through doubt and indecision. This very experience, trying as it may be,
will strengthen him and help him to reach his destination with a keener appreciation of the value of that for which he has worked.

One wonders whether our country that boasts of its educational opportunities has trained individuals to have the tough moral fiber that is needed in the complicated society we have wrought. Our job both within the League and in our individual lives is to help build a nation of character and self-discipline. Happily, League experience has equipped us to make an important contribution. The League develops habits of mind based upon self-reliance and pursuit of the facts as a basis for action. We have learned to ask the question in regard to every decision, "Is it in the public interest?" We have found that to question wisely is the best tool with which a citizen can equip himself. Moreover, questioning has beneficial results, for it clarifies the thinking of the questioner and the respondent.

The League has an enviable reputation for pricking the conscience of our public life. Its high standards of public morality are felt on four levels of government—local, state, national and international. Fortunately, I think we are justified in believing that the effectiveness of the League is at an all-time high.
. . .

The best argument that can be used against communism and dictatorship is the rightness of our political system; the freedom under law which representative democracies have developed, with the law determined by the majority of all of the citizens. Each weakness in our own system, whether it be in the law or in the administration thereof, is a vulnerable link. The weakness is not only a cause of dissatisfaction by our own people, but what is more important, it becomes a target for the protagonists of foreign ideologies, who build up their own cause by belittling ours. By the reiteration and over-emphasis they give to our inadequacies, they seek to deny the validity of our whole philosophy. It behooves us then to put great effort into perfecting our own political system, our educational pattern, our social thinking. The question of how much League concentration goes into international endeavors and how much into domestic is one of the questions we must decide during these five days that we are together, remembering always that within the League program we do not intend to encompass the whole of any member's political thinking or action. The League program is our tool for learning how to be politically effective. . . . Let us remember then in the decisions we make on behalf of the League of Women Voters and on behalf of ourselves as individuals that not alone the law must be right but the administration of it must be just. In our daily lives not alone our objectives must be sound but our means of obtaining them must be fair. We are not going to win for others a chance for free choices by restricting the thinking of those with whom we disagree. The United States is only as strong as its local communities and the people of those communities. The peculiar and traditional role of the League is to provide the dynamics needed to strengthen representative processes in those communities. We cannot overestimate the effectiveness of a good League at the grass roots where democracy must be nurtured or left to perish before the onslaught of other ideologies. Nor can we overestimate the importance of this local work in relation to the achievement of a peaceful, prosperous world.

The League as an organization has a vital role to play. We are gathered here today as representatives from our communities to formulate its program: to define our field of activity during the next two years. Our purpose is to stimulate many citizens to accept political responsibility. Let us not, in our desire to do our duty as citizens, so overload our organization that it is handicapped in fulfilling that purpose.

The demand of the hour is not only for a few inspired leaders. The need is for thousands, tens, and hundreds of thousands, of dynamic citizens of character and stamina, to see the right and to work for it. The need is for millions of citizens willing to forego temporary ease in order to perfect this country's form of government and to help this country play its part in world affairs. Ours is the land where each individual has the opportunity to help decide his country's destiny. To awaken citizens to use that opportunity is the work of the League of Women Voters.

Source: Excerpts from the Proceedings of the Eighteenth Annual Convention of the LWVUS, Grand Rapids, MI, April 25–30, 1948.   LWV Papers on film, II. B.1. 0824–28.

Meanwhile, League life consisted not just of momentous public issues but the daily business of organizational details as well. This brief report suggests that the potential for League expansion required and received assistance from the national office—board and staff.

DOCUMENT 8:   REPORT OF FIELD TRIPS

One hundred and thirty field trips were made this year compared with 76 last year and 86 of the year before. The total number of working days in the field was 698 as compared with 462 of last year and 227 of the year before.

All state Leagues were visited and extensive organization work was done in three states where provisional Leagues exist—Virginia, Idaho and Mississippi; and pre-organization visits were made to North Carolina, South Carolina, and South Dakota. Visits to state Leagues varied in number from one each in six states to nine visits to one state. Thirty-five visits were made to states where new organization is taking place.

Eight Board members, two non-Board members, and 11 staff members shared the fieldwork. Of the total days spent in the field, 197 days were spent by Board members, 20 by the two non-Board members and 481 days by staff members. Board members averaged 24.7 days of fieldwork. Two staff members, who have spent practically all of their time in the field account for 227 days of work. Nine staff members account for two hundred fifty-three and one-half. The average amount of fieldwork per staff member was forty-three and one-third days.

Visits for the purpose of discussing recognition under the new by-laws have been made to 31 states, 34 visits to discuss and advise on organization problems were made to 26 Leagues. Six Leagues received program visits; nine trips were made to organized states on finance; five were made on political effectiveness; six institutes were held. Organization and finance work accounted for all the visits to provisional Leagues.

Source: "A report of the 1949 Council meeting revealed continued League growth and continued concern over the workload." April 1, 1946–March 31, 1947. LWV Papers on film, II. B.1. 0742.

DOCUMENT 9: REPORT ON THE 1949 COUNCIL MEETING

Last week the League Council, composed of two delegates from each organized state and one from each unorganized state and the members of the national

Board, met in Washington to discuss League affairs, transact business and agree upon program emphasis for the coming year.

LEAGUE GROWTH CONTINUES   We were happy to learn that League growth is continuous, although the rate of increase is not so large as it had been in recent years. We now have 89,000 members in 720 local Leagues in 33 states, and the District of Columbia, and eight states where no state organization has yet been formed. For the first time, we had data on the number of members not renewing their membership. The figure totaled 7,000, and it was agreed that we should further analyze and meet this problem. A budget of $152,000 for national services was adopted, copy of which is enclosed.

THEME: THE NEED FOR CUTTING THE WORKLOAD   The theme of the Council developed unmistakably as the meetings progressed; it was the need for cutting the League workload to the point where members can perform it and "live too." It was particularly stressed by delegates at many points that the local League President has too much to do and that attention must be given to making the assignment more reasonable for a busy volunteer. The conviction was strong enough for the Council to resist the tempting and important opportunity of working on the Hoover Commission Recommendations. It was pointed out that individual citizen action in such an area could be encouraged.

FEWER PUBLICATIONS   Cutting the workload will mean fewer publications. No new program publications will be published until fall, when material in the field of collective security and a Memo bringing the federal budget facts up to date are scheduled for release.

KNOW YOUR UNITED NATIONS   We enjoyed the satisfaction of reviewing a big job well done on the "Know Your United Nations Year." This special effort was designed to help eliminate a dangerous lag in citizen understanding of the United Nations. Now that the year is over, the task of the U.N. chairmen is completed and our work returns to its regular channels. We recognize that the job of knowing the United Nations is a continuing one, as is the job of knowing our own government at home. Some Leagues have still to complete the special year's effort. Others are ready to carry the general educational job further where most needed.

FOREIGN POLICY ISSUES   The North Atlantic Pact was discussed at two sessions on two different days with special attention given to an evaluation of recent League thinking. The discussion was exceedingly helpful to the national Board in carrying out its responsibility for making the decision that the League is now ready to support the United States ratification of the Pact. League support for U.S. membership in the International Trade Organization will soon meet the crucial test as the ITO Charter comes before the Congress. Hard work will be necessary for the opposition is vocal and intense. Renewal of the Reciprocal Trade Agreements Act and appropriations for the Economic Cooperation Administration need our active support through this session of Congress.

FEDERAL BUDGET ITEM   Reports showed that an excellent start in the work on the federal budget item has been made, although there are some Leagues where the pressure of other commitments has postponed attention. In the coming year we will attempt to bring our knowledge of the federal budget up to date with changing conditions and examine the varying relationships between private and public economic activity in the United States. We will continue to build more widespread understanding throughout the League before supporting or opposing any measures in this field.

REGIONAL CONFERENCES ON VOTERS SERVICE Fourteen regional conferences on Voters Service are scheduled for next fall. The national Board is planning a new approach through popular material and techniques.

DELEGATES GO TO THE HILL While in Washington, council delegates took advantage of the occasion to talk with legislators on "The Hill," with a resulting increase in mutual understanding of the problems we face together.

NO VACATION YET FOR CONGRESS Though many of you are new having your annual meetings and some are finishing your year's work on local and state items, remember that Congress will be in session for many more weeks (perhaps into July) and that the federal issues on which we are working are yet to be voted upon. The decisive days are ahead and your action will be needed.

EVERY-MEMBER TRENDS Focus of great interest at the Council meetings problem was the national Board's recommendation for a new publication, an every-member TRENDS, to carry organizational news as well as the current interpretation of events of special interest. The new publication will replace ACTION. This proposal will be discussed and voted on at next year's Convention, and additional details will be presented to the membership in the next issue of ACTION.

AROUND THE WORLD My League training having finally taught me the value of public relations, I have decided to accept an invitation to go around the world with *Town Meeting of the Air* for a special series of seminars and broadcasts from many capitals. I shall hope to bring back a perspective about the international scene that will be helpful to all of us during the coming year.

Source: Anna Lord Strauss to "Dear President," May 6, 1949. LWV Papers on film, II. B.2. 0651–53.

> *The atomic age brought with it the fearful prospect of a hydrogen bomb in the making. A new coalition of diverse organizations sent this communication to President Harry S. Truman.*

DOCUMENT 10: PUBLIC DISCUSSION OF THE HYDROGEN BOMB

"The decision to make the Hydrogen Bomb has heightened the importance of issues which are basic to our democratic system. We are driven to defend ourselves by measures that could destroy the way of life we seek to preserve. These new threats to our freedom compel us to find ways of strengthening democratic participation in the formulation of public policy.

"Informed, extensive, and wise public discussion of issues of this magnitude is, in our judgment, essential.

"Confident that the President and the Secretary of State share this belief, we urge that a commission should be appointed to clarify and facilitate such discussion. This commission should consider all weapons of mass destruction in the context of over-all foreign policy. Its report should illuminate possible courses of action and the political, economic, and moral consequences of each, in order that the public may exercise an informed judgment.

"The commission should consist of persons chosen for breadth of experience, judgment and a belief that peace is possible. The members should be free to concentrate for a period of weeks—even months—on these problems. Their concentrated thinking when shared with the people, would stimulate and promote a sounder and more constructive public opinion. The nation would be better prepared to safeguard our freedoms and support our government in whatever steps become necessary in the critical years ahead."

League of Women Voters of the U.S.
United World Federalists
General Federation of Women's Clubs
International Association of Machinists
American Veterans Committee
Council for Social Action—Congregational Christian Churches
National Women's Trade Union League
Cooperative League of USA
Federation of American Scientists
National Farmers Union

Source: "Text of statement sent by the League of Women Voters and nine other organizations to President Truman March 10, on the subject of public discussion of the hydrogen bomb," March 16, 1950. LWV Papers on film, II. B.2. 0715.

In her farewell address as national League president, Anna Lord Strauss reiterated the League's continuing mission to broaden the base of informed citizenry and documented the League's impressive growth in the six years of her presidency. As she pointed to the League's accomplishments, she also identified shortcomings, particularly the League's failure to fully represent the diverse communities forming the mosaic of American society and the need to share more fully its skill at leadership training with other organizations.

DOCUMENT 11: FAREWELL ADDRESS OF ANNA LORD STRAUSS

No one need ever thank me for having acted in your behalf as the national President of the League of Women Voters. I have gained so infinitely much more from the job than I ever could have put into it, despite a lot of hard work, that the thanks are entirely in reverse. I thank you for having given me this opportunity of representing you—for your combined efforts have been recognized both in the United States and abroad to such a degree that we can all be very proud.

As I appear before you as president for the last time, I hope that you will forgive my taking a few minutes to look back to 1944 and use some comparative figures as well as recall to mind what is past history of which many of you probably have no recollection. For in this period there have been many new-comers to our ranks, younger women, deeply concerned about the future of our country, who despite the demands of young children and jobs have combined their spare time to be a real force in the community.

As of March 31, 1944, we had 49,242 members and this March, 93,090. This is a gain of 4,232 in the past year and a 90% increase in the last six years. We had 511 Leagues in 1944 and 739 in 1950, an increase of nineteen Leagues in the past year and a 45% increase in the last six years. In the year ending March 31, 1950, forty provisional Leagues have received local League status and 45 new provisional Leagues have been organized. . . .

In 1944 our national League budget was $74,731, as compared to $153,685 in March 1950, an increase of 105% in the last six years. Our total income from the sale of publications was $9,400 in 1944 and this year the total is $41,254 including Publications Service, a 338% increase.

In April 1944, our country still had more than a year of fighting before we were to win the war, but looking forward to victory the League was aware that the immediate problems of peace would present issues on which we must pre-pare ourselves. How to do this had caused some honest differences within the League which were debated on the floor of the Convention. Following the deci-sion that the delegates made, all but two of the former Board resigned and al-most all of the staff. Mrs. J. Hardin Smith of Missouri and Mrs. Harold Dyke of New York decided to continue on the Board, and I should like to register appre-ciation to them for their guidance in those rather forlorn first days. Bertha Pabst was the only established member of the staff who agreed with our position and for her fifteen years of devoted service to the League as Finance Secretary, we can be eternally grateful.

I shall not review those days when we adopted new by-laws. Every member who lived through it suffered severe headaches. But we can be glad that we have come through with an infinitely stronger League structure, a more closely inte-grated organization wherein the members have more authority than ever before, and with a pattern more suitable to serving the community as a whole. . . It is proper that you should be saying by now, "Yes, but where are we going next?" And I should rightfully leave that to you as the representatives of the local and state Leagues and to the new Board to be elected by you during this Convention. But I cannot refrain from saying a few things about the role that I foresee for the League.

Our purpose is to promote political responsibility through informed and ac-tive participation of citizens in government. But what does that mean in non by-law terms? Mrs. Dyke has expressed it well when she said, "Our job is to let the people know, make the people care, and help the people act."

We cannot look for a simpler life, for domestic and world problems are not going to be solved without much prayerful consideration and a true desire to understand other people's points of view as well as to analyze our own. The need begins with the development of individual moral and political character in our own country. The United Nations cannot be expected to have standards higher than those we as citizens live by and set for it, nor can any form of world government. There is need to make of our dreams a reality which will stand the strains and stress of those self-seekers who are not yet convinced that only through the good of the many can the individual ultimately benefit.

The League is a practical organization, a self-disciplined organization and we know that neither as an organization nor as individuals can we dig out all of the facts and prepare ourselves to help our communities think through all of the daily problems in order to reach constructive action. So our choice must be those subjects best suited to learning how to get at the facts, how to discuss them with a true cross-section of our community, how to arrive at decision in the public interest and then how to bring about our desired result. We learn by doing, but should that doing be scattered so thin that the net result is a state of confusion? In all honesty I believe that with our long programs of the past, we sometimes caused mental indigestion when we intended to be a clarifying force. . . . I believe that if we understand that the role of the League is not to think for us but to help us learn the essentials in tackling the problems of government, we will see our role as a training ground of leadership for our communities.

The League's role today is not the same as it was in the 1920's for the need has changed. In those early days there were comparatively few specialists in government. The League was generally forced to do its own research. Now there are many technical groups specializing in political matters whose services are available. They are eager to offer to the citizens the benefit of their work and of the Ph.D. students associated with them. There are many volumes on the shelves but all too few outlets into the community. The League having decided upon a problem which it is going to undertake, can benefit from the various technical studies which have been made and by presenting the information in a more popular manner combined with our go-see techniques can arouse widespread interest, discussion and action. Having awakened many citizens to the importance of the situation and having brought about needed change, we may have aroused sufficient concern in other individuals or groups so that our continued attention as an organization is not necessarily required. Individual citizen action should be the natural outcome of thorough and imaginative work on an important issue.

But how are we going to assure ourselves that the right decisions will be made in government on a wide variety of subjects? By electing better qualified persons. We must put more time and thought on our choice of men and women who will represent us in government. They must have integrity, character, they must have experience, judgment, willingness to learn and they must have a deep concern. We won't obtain this type of candidate unless public opinion stands squarely behind the truly public-spirited official. This does not mean only party support, though the political parties hold the prime responsibility for the nomination of candidates, it means a whole change in the climate of political thinking.

As we develop our Voters Service work, and encourage our members to be active in the party of their choice, the question comes to us, "Aren't these two ideas contradictory?" I don't think that they are, for I do not believe that anyone should remain indefinitely a member of a League board. We should learn within the League, take leadership in the League and at the same time join our party to become accustomed to its methods. Having served on the League board, some can progress into more active party work, taking leadership in their ranks and then eventually running for office or accepting appointment. Occasionally, there are seeming conflicts when a candidate is so outstanding that one would like to work hard to see him win, but certainly the standards which we have set should help many citizens be alert to the opportunity of supporting a well qualified candidate . . . .

There is a place in American life also for the specialized pressure group, one interested in a single concern or with a special slant. A special interest group may have come into being because of likeness of the training of their members. There are medical groups, legal, agricultural, manufacturing, labor and many,

many more. Then there are the people whose backgrounds may vary greatly but who have education, housing, international affairs, etc., as a prime interest. Each of these organizations can make an important contribution in different ways to the situations where their prime interest lies. It is important that the public and the government official evaluate the contribution that such groups make, taking due cognizance of how their decisions have been reached within their organization and with full knowledge of their special interests as contrasted with the public interest position of the League and other groups.

The social and political world must catch up to the scientific and industrial world. How is this to take place? The League has made a contribution and with its increased knowledge based on experience it can take a more important role as a public interest group. There are many people who want the League of Women Voters—they don't know that they want us, but they want what we have to give.

The League of Women Voters has complete confidence in the people. We are open to and welcome all people who believe in our form of government without any educational, social, economic, racial, or religious qualifications. Our method of conducting our League business has been developed to give the members the authority for making the important decisions. We take the little bit of free time that many people have to give who have other responsibilities both family and business. And by cooperative effort we make a distinctive contribution. There are times when the few of us with more freedom could not as individuals be a real force in the community; but our combined effort commands respect far beyond what may seem to be warranted by our comparatively small membership. You have heard, I am sure, as I have, people speak of the League's membership as five hundred thousand or even a million. Not realizing what a closely integrated organization we are with the program truly chosen by the membership, they cannot conceive of our being so influential with fewer members than they have estimated.

You have given me the privilege of knowing what your combined strength means and I feel deeply grateful to our Leagues when I hear the many compliments showered upon the League because of its effective work, because it *is a force with which to reckon.*

The need for citizen action is great and people are anxious to be of help. The genius of the League is to give the training—challenging in itself—to fit the citizen to serve. It is often difficult to find an interesting part-time job—volunteer or paid—but the League offers many such opportunities. . . .

Because I have taken some satisfaction in how far we have come, I don't want to leave anyone with the impression that we couldn't do a much better job. There are conflicting points of view within our own organization as to how this can best be done. There are those who think that the League should take a position on many subjects; others say that we should be educational only; others wish we would be more thorough; others want us to be more popular; others believe that unless we support candidates we are being ineffective. These are all important points to consider but I believe that the position we have arrived at, a compromise position is some instances, has given us the unique role that we hold today. And if it had not been for our care in sticking to our nonpartisan position, we would not still be in existence—thirty years after we were organized.

Is the League itself as good a cross-section of the communities in which we are organized as it should be? Do we really live up to the standards that we set ourselves of representatives from all of the different elements in the towns where we live? If we did, wouldn't it be even a more exciting group, with more varied points of view, each of us honestly attempting to find the common meeting ground agreement on the role of government? I doubt that we will ever be a mass appeal organization, but I think that we can look forward to the day when we may have infinitely wider influence because of our ability to train leaders—not a few leaders—but the great numbers that are needed in communities in all walks of life. The great cry is for leadership at all levels of activity. We hear repeatedly from non-Leaguers that when they want something done they turn to us for leadership. Why, if we have the ability to train leaders, don't we reach out and share with many, many others our methods and ideals?

In our zeal to tackle new situations, effect improvements where there is from our point of view, a crying need, let us not get too far out ahead. There is a place for the organization that plunges forward and for those with the militant approach, but that is not the way of the League of Women Voters. Our fundamental concept has been since the early days that only through education can one make gains that will last. Before we start on the legislative phase of a campaign we should ask ourselves how well informed are my neighbors—not only my next door neighbors—but the ones down the street and on the other blocks? I have been impressed with the number of legislators who refer to the increasing weight that is given to public opinion back home. Let us not forget that we alone are not public opinion; it takes lots of others agreeing with us to have weight. And of almost equal importance is the necessity for deep conviction which will fight to hold a gain, perhaps too easily won and therefore vulnerable to a high powered attack.

For the League to do a better and more influential educational job, it means more imaginative and widespread Voters Service work. What we do is good but in too many instances we reach so very few people. We are wasteful of talent. In a well-run business, the personnel policy is to use people at their top skills. And when they develop a good idea they obtain wide distribution for it. They wouldn't go to the effort of getting information on candidates for the benefit of a few thousand; they would carry through and in one way or another see that it was made available to tens and hundreds of thousands. . . .

The League of Women Voters is not an end in itself. It is a marvelous training ground. We awaken the apathetic, combine the few minutes here and there of many people and are the constructive expression of otherwise uneasy consciences. But don't let us kill ourselves off by overwork for we are needed and desperately needed for what is going to continue to be a long hard pull. Let's use our intelligence and experience to help many others to recognize that with freedom go responsibilities. Let us so improve the political climate that many more candidates with the potentialities to be statesmen will enter and remain in the arena to serve their fellowmen and their country. And in doing so let us remember that there is no more rewarding work than to develop that form of government which gives the utmost freedom of opportunity to all of the citizens.

I believe that one of our greatest difficulties at the present time is that we have so overloaded ourselves with work that we are exhausting our willing and eager leaders. There are two solutions that would help in this respect, I believe. One is to make full use of the material which the national League and the state Leagues make available for running the routine part of the job, so as to minimize the time which might otherwise have to go into thinking through the housekeeping problems of running the League. The other is to adopt a less heavy program load that is a more realistic set of programs, national, state and local. More time must be allocated, I believe, to what might be termed an expanded Voters Service work.

In my sixteen years of working with the League, I have had great satisfactions and interesting opportunities. It is only right that someone else should enjoy the privilege of representing this truly vital organization. I am convinced that the League has found the key to unlock boundless energy concerned with the perfecting of our form of representative democracy. The citizens of the United States have the discipline to rule themselves not only for their own advantage, but also as responsible members of a world society.

Source: Excerpts from the Nineteenth Annual Convention of the LWVUS, Atlantic City, NJ, April 24–28, 1950. LWV Papers on film, II. B.2. 0752–63.

Chapter 15

Years of Maturity, 1950–1970

With the dawning of the last half of the twentieth century, the League of Women Voters enjoyed a more visible and impressive persona marked by the largest membership growth in the organization's history. In the two decades from 1950 to 1970, the League increased its effectiveness as both educator and advocate, prompting Senator George Aiken (R., VT) to remark, "Only 135,000 of them? I thought there were millions." (In 1969, the League population peaked at 156,780.) During this time period, the organization was well served by four presidents: Percy Maxim Lee (CT, 1950–58); Ruth S. Phillips (IL, 1958–64); Julia Stuart (WA, 1964–68), and Lucy Wilson Benson (MA, 1968–74).

Percy Lee, the first of this quartet and an experienced national board member, succeeded Anna Lord Strauss and brought with her a forthright manner and a thoughtful eloquence that defined her leadership. A typical mix of humor and the idealism that has always bonded League members can be found in Lee's first address as president to the 1952 national convention.

DOCUMENT 1: PERCY LEE, STATE OF THE LEAGUE 1952

It is customary on these occasions for your president to give you, as best she can, an over-all assessment of the two years just completed—a bird's eye view of the whole League as seen from the President's desk.

It is a task to which I can turn with pleasure, since it seems to me that the two years just past have been among the best we have ever had. They have not been without problems—serious ones—but on the whole I think we have come far and fast. Much of this progress is the result of the careful groundwork laid by Miss Strauss in her years in office. A great deal of her work is coming now to fruition.

Perhaps before I go further I should say a personal word. These two years have been enormously rewarding to me, and I am grateful to you for the opportunities you have afforded me. I think it has been worthwhile to test whether it is possible for the League to have a President who does not live in Washington. Frankly, there have been scattered moments during these two years when I have myself wondered what the answer would be. Of course, the life of a nonresident President is not 100 percent a joyful one. Without infinite understanding and support on the part of my husband, and the cooperation of my household in Farmington, plus the patience and dedication of the resident Board and staff, the difficulties of living a divided life might have been insurmountable. Luckily, the cooperation has been unending, and I have managed to commute regularly from home to the office without any major crisis.

The only ones who have fallen by the wayside are a couple of dogs. The horse has had no exercise, the old setter is mournful beyond belief, and the new kittens have been legion. The humans, curiously enough, seem to be bearing up quite well. . . .

In Washington you now have working for you 35 people, doing everything from preparing material to mailing it, and from organizing new Leagues to sharing new ideas with older ones. You also have working for you a magnificent new machine—the multilith—bought last year, which has made it possible for us to publish material less expensively and more attractively than hitherto. . . .

As our membership grows, the use of publications skyrockets. We moved in 1950 to what we thought would be adequate quarters for years to come. In six months we were tearing down walls and doubling up offices to make more room for the publications department. As things stand now, there is hardly a spare chair for a visiting Leaguer to sit upon; and for months the Congressional Secretary only had a desk when someone else was away. Our Program people, who need peace and quiet on occasion, are hard put to find it. Those instruments of progress—electric typewriters and multilith machines—give us some of the aspects of a boiler factory.

Physical pressures are not the only ones. As our membership and prestige increase, the number of people who want the League to help with some project or other, the number of TV forums that would like us represented, the number of magazines who want articles on citizenship, and the number of conferences we are asked to attend or sponsor are constantly increasing. In the midst of these very worthwhile endeavors come invitations to shake the then Princess Elizabeth's hand, or more recently, Queen Juliana's. . . .

Prestige is an intangible thing, but we have a good deal of evidence that ours is increasing. We meet ourselves coming and going in print nowadays. Many of you have followed the outstanding "Political Pilgrim's Progress" series in the *Ladies' Home Journal* and have noticed how the League keeps coming into the picture. You may also have seen the article in the March issue of *McCall's* that starred the Ann Arbor League. Requests for help with similar articles come to us more and more frequently nowadays.

So, too, we are finding an increasing demand for public appearance on the part of the President and the Board—a demand that is more than the President, for one, can meet. Request for speakers, for TV appearances, for information, invitations to attend governmental conferences of one sort and another and important personages dropping in at the national office are all multiplying to the point that the public relations department is one of the real pressure points in our national headquarters.

The most gratifying experiences of all are, of course, visits from League members. We have even had the pleasure of meeting League husbands and the next generation—both girls and boys. . . .

I have referred to our growth over the past two years. Let me give you just a few figures. The number of local Leagues has risen from 740 in 1950 to 824 in 1952—an increase of 11 percent. The membership has gone from 93,000 in 1950 to 106,000 in 1952—an increase of 14 percent. Our total publications sales have jumped from $41,128 in 1950 to $52,269 in 1952—an increase of 28 percent.

I am sure you are as deeply stirred as I am at this evidence of League vitality.

I would like to mention that the phenomenal development in the West was made possible by the gift of $25,000 from the National American Woman Suffrage Association. Miss Sweeney has been at work out there since January 1951, and according to our present calculations that gift will keep her going until January 1953. After that, if we are to carry on, new resources must be found. On the basis of 14 months of operation, we figure that this organization work has cost about $833 per League. Since most of these Leagues are still provisional this does not by any means finish the job. It always takes a long time before any new League can be expected to carry itself, much less bear its share of the total financial outlay. But we believe this development to be of prime importance to the country and thus an essential long term investment.

For the development in the South, which is no less remarkable, we have drawn upon our own resources. I do not have a figure per League but we believe the cost is about the same for this work. For the first time we can honestly say that in the foreseeable future we will truly be a League of Women Voters of all the United States and we shall not ignore the Territories.

The finance picture is both good and bad.

It is good because we are coming to rely increasingly on non-member contributions, and are witnessing an increasing number of successful finance drives. There is greater understanding of the close relationship between public relations and finance. . . .

One of our continuing problems, as many of you who have grappled with it know, is that of the big city Leagues. The problems of the big city itself are reflected in any effort to promote political responsibility therein—size, complexity, the flight to the suburbs of money and talent, the presence of hard–to–reach groups and so on. We have long hoped to make some study of this question and this year such a study has gotten underway. It is called the Metropolitan Area Project, and is being financed by the Carrie Chapman Catt Memorial Fund. The first city selected for study is Philadelphia, and Mrs. Horner of our staff has been lent to CCCMF for this work. The project will encompass not only the League, but all voluntary organizations concerned with citizenship.

While we are on the subject of the CCCMF, I would like to give you some interesting facts. In 1947, when the CCCMF was established we knew that there would be great opportunity for carrying on Mrs. Catt's interests in education for citizenship and in developing international understanding. But we could not have foreseen how important a contribution the Fund would make in the latter field because the government's exchange of persons program was not then in operation. The statistics for this past year are impressive. The Washington office has handled the planning of trips and programs for 96 visitors from 12 countries. Without the cooperation of local Leagues this work would have been impossible. Seventy-one Leagues in twenty-seven states have participated in this program. In addition, the Washington and New York offices of the Fund are constantly called upon to work out local programs for international visitors. We know, too, that many Leagues get direct calls for help in this program so that the figures I have given do not cover the countless hours which have gone into this operation of international goodwill. The fund also made it possible for Mrs. Harold Dyke to be a member of a panel of women from American women's organizations who went to Germany for six weeks last year. . . .

If one of the earmarks of greatness is the loyalty engendered, then the League is indeed great. It has had through the years a remarkable group of women (indeed some men) who have stuck by through thick and thin, who have given so generously of themselves and their resources that some have given even after death. One of these was Anne Webster. When she died in Santa Fe in 1949 she left the League of Women Voters her entire estate. This generous act brought to us some rather curious involvements: a high bred dog whose marriage vows had been pledged but not consummated, chickens, goats, Indian dependents, and thirty buildings, all in Santa Fe. The amount of the federal tax has not even yet been divulged by the government and so the estate cannot be settled nor can it be determined exactly what funds will be forthcoming. But it looks like upwards of $50,000. When this does come to us, the national Board will put it to work for the benefit of the League as a whole. It is my own personal belief that our first obligation lies in strengthening our state Leagues so they, in turn, can extend greater services to the local Leagues. Whatever course the Board decides to pursue when we actually have the funds in hand, I can assure you this will not become idle money. . . .

Turning now to the larger matters involving the state of the world, I want to talk about our Program activity during the past two years. This has been an eventful period. Historical developments have taken place in our nation and in the world.

Six weeks after we went home from Atlantic City, the United Nations—for which the League had labored since its inception—faced its first overwhelming test. A clear case of aggression had taken place. I do not need to repeat the subsequent series of events, for they are familiar enough. Those events forced many of us to modify our basic assumptions. It became clear that the Communist nations would risk armed warfare to gain their ends—and that the military threat would have to be met with military might. . . .

The League was also prepared at this crucial moment to reaffirm its faith in the principle of collective security, and to support a program for the cooperative development of military and economic strength to meet the needs of the times. At the same time we continued our efforts in behalf of international trade and economic development.

Throughout our work in these two years there has been one very clear line of development: League members are aware of the necessity for military strength and security, but they are not beguiled into thinking that these things are ends in themselves, or that of themselves they solve any of the world's problems. Military power may temporarily preserve the life of the nation, but it cannot assure the survival of "liberty and the pursuit of happiness." This the League recognizes and in a quiet and resourceful way all over the country it has gone about its business of helping make our democracy work, of shoring up our national belief in the dignity and worth of the individual wherever its foundations are weakened, of asserting our conviction that humanity is worthy of the service of our government.

As I look back over this record I am proud of two things. One is that within the framework of democratic government, we were able to rise to the occasion and take action on the crucial issues of our day at the time when action counted. We have kept our eyes on first principles as well as on the far horizons. While pursuing a cause, we have maintained the essential integrity of the course. This I want to emphasize for I believe it of utmost importance.

It seems to me the League within itself must be a vital force demonstrating democracy at its best. The course we choose must be as highly principled as our objectives. This applies equally to our by-laws, our policies, our methods, our management, our selection of Program and our way of carrying out that Program. To support democracy, we must *be* democracy.

In a time of confusion, uncertainty, obstructionist pressures, fear the League has kept its head. We have neither forsaken the core of our governmental system—our local government, which sets the pattern of our nation—nor have we shirked the awful responsibility of making decisions on international policies that affect the course of history.

It would be a brave and maybe foolish person indeed who would attempt to give any final estimate of what has been accomplished since the Korean War began. But one can point with hope to several history-making developments: the UN action in meeting the North Korean aggression; the rapid development of cooperation in the North Atlantic Treaty Organization; the acceptance by France and Germany of the Schuman Plan; the acceptance by six European nations at Lisbon of the idea of a European Army. Surely no two–year period in history has witnessed any such basic advances. It is hard for me to give credence, therefore, to the prophets of doom. On the contrary, just stop and think that within the span of my lifetime (and though a grandmother and a president of the League of Women Voters I don't always feel so very aged) these things have been developed: movies, radio, television, automobiles, airplanes, atomic energy. The population of the United States has been increased by more than half. The total national production of the United States has tripled. The increase in the per capita share of the total product, which is a rough measure of the standard of living, has nearly doubled. The League of Nations was conceived and lost. The UN was established and is a living, growing reality. I cannot believe there is reason to despair. On the contrary, there is every reason to believe that no people has ever been presented with such an array of golden opportunity as the American people. In federal unity we found great strength. In international unity and cooperation we may yet build a total society which will benefit all mankind.

In the field of state and local program, your bulletins, your letters, the reports of Board and staff visitors, and the things we heard from you at Council last Spring all indicate a very lively development. "Know Your Town" and "Know Your County" studies are multiplying, and the published results are impressive. State government is receiving a great deal of attention, and an astonishing number of states are at work on some aspect of constitutional reform. Again, I must reiterate my profound conviction that it is in local and state governments where the heart of the matter lies. Here we establish direct citizen participation and influence. Here we set our standards—for morality or immorality, for freedom or tyranny, for social progress or social failure, for how much government. In our communities we create our nation. . . .

What the League calls Voters Service is our key to these things I have mentioned above. Through this work we build an understanding of our representative system and show citizens how to participate effectively. We link the candidate to the issue and try to make every voter cast an informed vote. Voters Service is enjoying a dramatic expansion and success. It represents our most powerful weapon against lethargy and apathy—the two great enemies of democracy.

And now I want to turn to a subject which I know has been of concern to many of you over the past two years, just as it has been to your Board of Directors. That is, the scattered attacks upon us from sources outside the League. Because I think it important for us to face this issue squarely, I would like to take a few minutes to analyze these attacks.

We have been accustomed over the years to being called "Republican" in some sections and "Democratic" in others. These charges tend to balance each other over the country as a whole and don't give us too much concern.

But lately—due partly, no doubt, to our increased effectiveness and partly to the temper of the times—we are charged in certain quarters with leading a parade to socialism, with being mouthpieces of the Administration, and even (as though this were insidious), with being "internationally-minded."

It is significant, it seems to me, that these attacks are not leveled alone at the League of Women Voters. They are directed at many of the major organizations of this country. These organizations are voluntary associations that have sought over the years to make this world a better place to live in. We in the League have every reason to be proud of our record. I believe we can justly claim that the vigor of organizations such as ours is one of the strongest foundations of our democratic society.

Why then the attacks? There are individuals and groups in the United States who do not agree with our views. So far, so good. If they were content to argue the issues on the merits and abide by the decision of the American people, we would have no quarrel with them. But when they resort to innuendo and inference to challenge our motives or pin "pink" labels on us—invariably so worded that one cannot bring libel—it is time for us to show some of the courage and determination of our predecessors in their long fight for suffrage.

The only way I know to combat this sort of thing is to have more and more people in our communities understand the League's purpose, program, and procedures; with understanding will come the kind of public attitude which will make unfair allegations rebound to the detriment of those who make them.

This solution is all well and good in the towns and cities where we have local Leagues. But what about where we have none, or are just beginning organization? There we have to rely on the reputation created throughout the country by each and every local League, each state League and your national Board—the organization as a whole. This Convention should know that there are delegates and observers sitting among us from new Leagues that—never having known the League of Women Voters in their communities—have nevertheless gone forward with organization in the face of obstacles which could quite understandably have discouraged many who had much more than faith to support them. These newest members have entered the League of Women Voters in its finest tradition and we extend an especially warm welcome to them.

I am sure I express the sentiment of the Convention when I say that ill-willed efforts to curtail our growth will not stop us, and that outside attempts to frighten us into abandoning our long-held positions will not succeed. Our objectives will continue to be set in democratic fashion by our membership. And I am convinced that that membership will make decisions—as it has in the past—designed to further the well–being of our country and to promote peace and human development throughout the world.

Source: Excerpts from the Proceedings of the Twentieth Annual Convention of the LWVUS, Cincinnati, OH, April 28–May 2, 1952. LWV Papers on film, II. B.3. 0326–34.

The League was concerned not only with weighty issues but with its own internal organization and way of doing things. Finances continued to be a problem. League members had to be encouraged and trained to ask for contributions from outside the League in annual finance drives. Some League members could afford to be generous, but the majority had discretionary time but not discretionary money. Nevertheless, the League—with characteristic frugality—squeaked by with a budget of $210,212 in 1952-53. By 1998, the League budget had increased to $2.6 million.

Reforms of various sorts were debated and rejected or adopted, influenced in no small part by the monumental 1956 survey of the League by the Survey Research Center of the University of Michigan. The magnitude of the program itself—always at issue—had been condensed in 1954 from a current agenda of broadly stated goals, a platform of thirty-eight specific legislative and policy commitments, and thirteen principles to a current agenda, eight continuing responsibilities, and eighteen principles. The dynamics of the League were in some respects the consequence of its willingness to change while always remaining within the perimeters associated with its good purpose.

Percy Lee's presidency coincided with the period when Senator Joseph H. McCarthy (R., WI) lent his name to an era of witch hunting. McCarthy, who saw the threat of Communist influence in many corners of American society, had initiated a slanderous attack on a range of scholars, public servants, film writers—anyone who did not hew to his anti-Communist demagoguery. In 1951, as a first step in refuting McCarthyism, the Carrie Chapman Catt Memorial Fund, under the presidency of Anna Lord Strauss, established a Freedom Agenda Committee and published a small pamphlet called Individual Liberty, USA. Three years later, convention delegates in Denver adopted as a new program item "the development of understanding of the relationship between individual liberty and the public interest." Subsequently, 797 Leagues in forty-eight states organized community dialogues to

give citizens an opportunity to exchange views on the meaning of indi-
vidual liberty, freedom of thought, and freedom of speech. Although
some of the heat of McCarthyism had subsided, other groups, includ-
ing the American Legion, found reason to criticize the Freedom Agenda
program and to charge the League with disloyalty. In 1955 Percy Lee
went right to the heart of the matter and in Indianapolis, the national
headquarters of the Legion, refuted their allegations and refused to
repudiate the Freedom Agenda program.

DOCUMENT 2: PERCY LEE ON THE LEAGUE'S FREEDOM AGENDA PROGRAM

I would like to comment on the importance of the work the League is doing in the field of Individual Liberties. It is because of its unwavering dedication to our democratic principles that the League recognized communism as a deadly threat to our national security. The question then was what could the League do to strengthen our national resistance and security. From its beginning the League has been involved in the free examination and exchange of ideas and with the fundamental role of freedom of opportunity in a constitutional democracy. We recognized that communism or totalitarianism destroyed these freedoms first of all. In 1954 at the League's National Convention we concluded that our best contribution would be to develop a widespread awareness in regard to our American heritage of individual liberty and its relationship to the national security.

This program is under way throughout the country and is meeting with considerable success. In over five hundred communities men and women are freely discussing these values and exploring ways and means to protect and strengthen them.

Now, of course, we realize from the start that freedom may be today a controversial subject in some quarters and variously interpreted. But it is good to know that the League has seen its role as a sort of catalytic agent to draw the community together, to spark its interest, to help organize discussion groups and then to leave them completely free to examine the subject as they choose. There has been no attempt whatever to exert influence or control.

The second and final thing I want to mention is our current difficulty with the Westchester County, New York, American Legion. The Westchester County, New York, Un-American activities committee of the Legion purported to investigate the Freedom Agenda Program. Subsequently they issued what is known as the White Report. This attempts to show that Freedom Agenda material is biased and that it leads the American people astray by failing to present the seriousness of the communist threat to the United Status. It recommends that the League of Women Voters repudiate the Freedom Agenda Program. This, of course, we will not do. We will indeed work all the harder to assure thoughtful and free discussion of our constitutional liberties and all other public questions of vital importance to the citizens of this country. The Westchester Legion attack only serves to reinforce our conviction that there is great and immediate need for the Freedom Agenda Program. Support of the principle of free discussion as guaranteed in the Bill of Rights was presented in my remarks to the Senate Judiciary Subcommittee on Constitutional Rights on September 17, 1955 and appears in full in your NATIONAL VOTER of that date.

Now, I believe fully in the rights of Americans to disagree and I do not pretend the League of Women Voters is infallible in its judgments. I *do* hold fast to the belief that in a free society people must not be intimidated or persecuted so that they cannot examine fearlessly all ideas and express fearlessly their own individual points of view. Incidentally, I would call your attention to the Legion's Committee report on UNESCO. This, known as the Murphy Report, is available and is an outstanding example of an objective and painstaking examination of the charges against UNESCO. It concludes that the charges are groundless and its evidence exposes the activities and methods of the extremist groups. I regret, of course, that the Legion Convention did not choose to honor the facts presented in this report which was made under the leadership of a distinguished past national commander.

Somehow I feel infinitely sad when, in view of the dreadful threat communism presents to my country, I see the name of a great and patriotic national organization used in an effort to set Americans against Americans; used in an effort to curtail the free exchange of ideas which has proved an unparalleled strength to us throughout our history. It saddens me immeasurably to find the name of the American Legion used in connection with an attempt to undermine confidence in honorable American institutions such as the Girl Scouts and the League of Women Voters. Surely, we all know that it is the *Communist* way to divide us, so we will destroy ourselves. It is astonishing and even frightening that the American Legion of all organizations should be caught by this tactic.

If ever there were a time for people of honor and belief in our American heritage to stand united, it is now. You cannot turn your back if you cherish the freedoms for which this nation stands. You must devote your energy and your support to those institutions which give it strength.

I am proud—inordinately proud of the League of Women Voters—and feel deeply privileged that I may be associated with it. Particularly in times of stress, it reveals a conscience, a sense of values and proportion, a power of discrimination and a dignity that inspires confidence and respect. I am proud of this and of the League's integrity, its never-faltering faith in this country, its fearlessness.

It has been said by a great historian that "fanaticism is not an enduring feature of a civilized society." It seems to me, we must strive unceasingly in the United States to assure that each succeeding generation gains sufficient maturity so that our society will be both civilized and enduring. I think perhaps Dr. V. Bush has put our goals into the clearest terms when he said:

> "We wish so to act that those who follow may be healthy men, unharassed, in decent and dignified relationships, free and individual; and to develop the powers of the mind to the utmost. If we build well, our children may indeed think more deeply and more surely."

"'To think more deeply and more surely"—this is what I wish *most* for the League of Women Voters and for the nation.

Source: Excerpt from remarks by Percy Lee to League of Women Voters of Indianapolis, October 17, 1995, LWVUS files.

Nor did the League forget the United Nations and its modest program of technical assistance to aid the economic growth of the world's poorer nations. This "inside story" of League efforts to restore cuts made by the House of Representatives in the U.S. contribution to that program provides insight into the positive impact of League action.

DOCUMENT 3: LEAGUE ACTION ON UN TECHNICAL ASSISTANCE

This is the story behind the Senate's restoration of the full amount, $15.5 million, for the U.S. contribution to the United Nations Technical Assistance Program, in the Mutual Security Appropriation for fiscal 1957. THIS CAN BE CHALKED UP AS A MAJOR VICTORY FOR THE LEAGUE AND THE OTHER ORGANIZATIONS WHO LET THEIR SENATORS KNOW OF THEIR INTEREST IN U.S. SUPPORT OF THIS PROGRAM.

What Happened on the Hill

The authorizing legislation for the Mutual Security Program, which contained the $15.5 million contribution to the U.N.T.A., was in conference between the House and Senate July 6 when the House Appropriations Committee reported the Mutual Security Appropriation bill (H.R. 12130). One of the "minor" reductions in the foreign aid money bill recommended by the Committee was a $5 million cut in the U.N.T.A. allowance.

House Appropriations Committee Subcommittees had been holding closed hearings, as is their custom, on the different parts of the program. When the report of the full Committee was made public, it was learned that the Foreign Aid Subcommittee had urged the full Committee to eliminate all funds for the U.N.T.A. program, partly on the grounds that our bilateral program is more effective and "wins us more friends" and that the two programs overlap. The full Committee decided to include $10 million for the UN program in the bill and defend this decision on the floor.

The Committee's action was big news in the League office and in headquarters of other groups interested in continued U.S. support of the UN Offices of friendly House members were consulted as to the best means of getting the funds restored. Because of "the temper of the House," these advisers said, it would be unwise to try to get the funds put back in the bill on the House floor. The Senate Appropriations Committee could be depended upon to make the restoration, we were told.

The House passed the Mutual Security Appropriation July 11, sustaining the U.N.T.A. fund cut.

Limited LWV Action

On July 9 Mrs. Lee had written the presidents of state Leagues with Senators on the Appropriations Committee, giving them background on the situation and asking them to get in touch with members of the Senate Committee. The Senate Committee had almost completed its hearings on the bill, but a League statement was prepared and sent to them July 12. The statement with a covering letter also went to all Committee members.

July 13 the Committee reported the bill. The House cut in U.N.T.A. funds had been sustained.

LWV Moves Into High Gear

The next day, Saturday, July 14, a Time for Action was sent by wire to all state League Presidents. Consultation with staff members of committees on the Hill had produced the information that the Senate, in a great hurry to adjourn, would probably move to consider the Mutual Security Appropriation Monday, July 23, and it was necessary to move quickly if a show of strength for restoring the funds was to be made.

Mrs. Lee also wired the President, the Vice President, UN Ambassador Lodge and Majority and Minority leaders of the Senate: "The League of Women Voters of the United States urges you to exert your personal leadership in helping to restore funds cut from U.S. contribution to the United Nations Technical Assistance Program. We believe it vitally important that U.S. in no way weaken its support of the United Nations."

Monday, July 23, Senator Mansfield (D., Mont.) introduced an amendment to H.R. 12130 which would restore the $15.5 million contribution. That day the Senate passed 150 bills and the announcement was made that H.R. 12130 would be called up on Tuesday.

In the meantime, Senate offices were being flooded by wires, letters and telephone calls about the U.N.T.A. fund. Leagues, other organizations and individuals all over the country were being heard from. This office had a call from the secretary of a Senator on Wednesday. She wanted to check some addresses with our file. "All I've been doing for the last two days is acknowledging messages about the United Nations Technical Assistance fund," she said. "It's all our office is talking about."

The Hill grapevine (and there is one) brought word that this was what was going on in a great many offices up there. Congress has seen a lot of lobbying this term, but this push for the U.N.T.A. was the grassroots speaking out. The Senate listened.

The Mansfield Amendment came up on the floor Friday, July 20. Senator Lehman (D., N.Y.) had joined Senator Mansfield as a co-sponsor, and both these and several other Senators supported the fund restoration in strong speeches. The opposition was led by Senator Knowland (R., Calif.) and Senator Bridges (R., N.H). Both urged reducing the U.S. contribution funds to one-third of the program budget. Senator Mansfield tried to get agreement to making our contribution one-third of all the funds involved in the program's operation, which meant including the amounts contributed by the countries receiving aid, in figuring the percentage. This was not acceptable to the opponents, and Senator Mansfield finally agreed to a modification of his amendment. As it was accepted, the U.S. contribution this year will be $15.5 million, but next year our contribution must be no more than one-third of the program budget. Senator Knowland, a member of the Appropriations Committee, agreed to take the modified amendment to the Conference between the Senate and House, and insist that it be retained in the final version of the bill. The modified amendment was accepted by voice vote. Final action on the bill was taken in the Senate July 24.

The Conference was announced for Wednesday, July 25.

And More LWV Action

Wednesday morning Mrs. Lee wired state League Presidents with Congressional representation on the Conference, asking them to get in touch with their Representatives and Senators to urge keeping the full $15.5 million in the bill. She also wrote letters to members of the Conference, and these were delivered by hand to their offices.

Late that evening, when the Conference was ended, Representative Gary (D., VA), who had been a member, wired her that the full amount had been granted.

Both the House, July 26, and the Senate, July 27, passed the version of the bill agreed to in conference. Funds for the U.S. contribution to the U.N.T.A. program were safe for this year.

This account of what happened in Washington and why state League Presidents received those wires on a hot Saturday afternoon has been prepared because the campaign to restore these funds seems such a good example of what an aroused public can achieve when it lets Congress know of its interest. It was not only League action as such that made such an impact; it was the good work done in communities all over the country by friends of the United Nations program in alerting other interested groups, individuals and the press.

Reports have come to this office from almost every state League and many local Leagues telling of the tremendous efforts made to follow through on the limited and the all-out Times for Action. This account of what happened in Washington is by way of being a thank you note from the national office for letting us know what induced the Senate to rise to the occasion so nobly. Here, we think the LEAGUES SHOULD TAKE A BOW!

Source: Report from the National Office, August 8, 1956. Document in author's possession.

One of the League's most innovative undertakings occurred in the mid-1950s when local Leagues were encouraged to conduct surveys of the impact of trade on their local communities. Over five hundred such surveys were made, constituting a great learning experience for more than thirty-five hundred League participants. Although the surveys ranged in content from elementary to complex, the results were in agreement: economic isolationism was on the wane, and the idea of a more liberal expanding trade policy was attracting wider public support. The studies also revealed that a surprisingly high number of respondents remained unaware of trade policy or its impact on their communities.

Source: *Facts and Attitudes on World Trade*. Washington, DC: League of Women Voters of the U.S., undated, 35 pages. Document in author's possession.

In 1958 Ruth Phillips became national president. A past Illinois president, Phillips was a businesswoman, engaged in a joint real estate enterprise with her husband. She was intelligent, personable, fashionably dressed, and persistent. League members—especially those who had the opportunity to work closely with her—understood that hers was "an iron fist in a velvet glove." During her six years as president, the League had a very strong programmatic commitment in foreign policy, particularly with regard to trade, aid, and the United Nations. At one point, from 1958 to 1960, the current agenda consisted of a single item—the review of U.S. foreign policy—representing a degree of *programmatic discipline never before (or since) achieved. The publication New Perspectives in Foreign Policy provided Leagues with a basis for analyzing all the League's foreign policy positions, an analysis that confirmed the validity of trade expansion, aid to developing nations, and continued support for the United Nations. In the decade following the League's trade surveys, the climate of opinion had definitely swung on the side of liberal trade, and President John F. Kennedy signed into law the landmark Trade Expansion Act of 1962.*

W. W. Rostow, counselor and chairman of the Policy Planning Council in the State Department, commented on the League's role in that legislative success: "The work of the League of Women Voters this year on the trade program is already legend in Washington." It was not surprising that the Department of State asked the League to describe its efforts in a national conference of nongovernmental organizations in May 1964.

DOCUMENT 4: AN EDUCATIONAL PROGRAM ON FOREIGN TRADE

The interest of the League of Women Voters in trade did not spring full-blown in the early sixties like Athena from the head of Zeus but evolved over a period of nearly thirty years. Two rather separate League concerns of the nineteen-thirties produced our first preoccupation with trade: one was a domestic issue—consumer interest, the other, an international issue—the economic causes of war. It is not hard to see how these two parents produced the progeny of liberal trade, and the League, like any parent, has agonized over the fits and starts of trade ever since.

There are two other historical factors which are especially meaningful in an understanding of the League's efforts in behalf of the Trade Expansion Act in 1962. Eight years before—in 1954—3,500 members of 530 local Leagues in forty-one states conducted 11,229 interviews in trade surveys to determine the impact of exports and imports in their own communities. Whereas all this research was not as precise as the contemporary computer may have turned out, nevertheless there was sufficient documentary evidence to substantiate the League's previous conviction that the liberalization of trade helped more than it hurt. And there were still many members in the League in the sixties who had worked on or who remembered the results of these surveys.

In more than a few cases, the surveys were really top–notch. For example, the University of Minnesota worked with the League in that state to design the survey, the League did the leg work, and the final document was published as a book by the Committee for Economic Development. The Connecticut League survey was cited as an "example of a good local study" in the recently published volume, *American Business and Public Policy*. Incidentally, one chapter in this book co-authored by researchers at M.I.T. contains a chapter entitled "The Ladies of the League" and states that "during 1954, the League must have been by several orders of magnitude the most active group to be found on either side of the trade controversy." More than three-fourths of the Congressional mail supporting the Reciprocal Trade Act originated in the League. But, says this same publication, "The letters which League members wrote to Congress may have been of minor importance compared with their general stimulation of public discussion of the issue."

The other relevant factor which must be cited to set the stage for the League's trade campaign was our very current concern with the elements of economic development in the rich nations and in the poor nations. So, at the very time that trade legislation was to be renewed or to be made new, the League was on the brink of evaluating trade as a means of strengthening economies at home and abroad.

The first component of League action is League knowledge. Like everyone else, we love to put words on paper so we put a collection of trade words into a publication called THE POLITICS OF TRADE. It turned out to be a surprising commercial success, but we were also reassured about its educational merits when 600 copies were purchased by the Graduate School of Business at Harvard University.

For those League members who like to dig—bless them—we issued a kit of trade materials which encouraged the pursuit of the facts about certain commodities which were then centers of trade controversy—textiles, . . . oil, shrimp, typewriters, lead and zinc. These case studies were especially useful to Leagues in communities where these products were produced or processed.

We also kept up a constant barrage of trade information in our national publication which goes to all 135,000 members. . . . For those members who were taking the lead in channeling information to members and to the community, we provided through the League's modest quarterly equivalent of *Foreign Affairs*, FOREIGN POLICY ROUNDUP, a measure of more profound information.

Finally, we rounded off this collection of publications with what we like to think was a fairly humorous little pamphlet called WORLD TRADE? WHAT HAS THAT TO DO WITH ME? This, League members could use themselves, of course, but it was designed primarily as something for members to give those citizens who may not have been especially concerned with trade one way or another—the fence sitters.

In short, we tried to reach a variety of audiences in a variety of ways with the printed word so that both in the League and outside the League, more citizens might be reached with both facts and opinion, the League opinion that trade is a good thing. We admitted our bias but we tried to be *objectively* biased, and I'm sure you all understand what I mean by this apparent contradiction in terms.

So much for the literature of League. Let's now turn to League action, but even this begins with and is sustained by the printed word.

In December of 1961, we sent a communication to all Leagues on the subject of League plans for "breaking the trade barrier." There we reported a bit on trade activity at the national League level: conversations with Howard Peterson, the President's Special Assistant on trade, and members of his staff; the unveiling of THE POLITICS OF TRADE at a luncheon for representatives of the press, radio, and television who gave us some very pertinent advice—and we reported that advice. With that as background, we went on for another seven pages with specific suggestions of how to do what when. We thought *we* had ideas—but they were nothing compared to what the Leagues did themselves. Let me tell you a few of these stories.

The Stamford, Connecticut League asked all members to abstain from their customary use or consumption of any item imported from any place abroad for a 24-hour period. This meant, of course, serving a meal without coffee, tea, pepper, or other spices; setting a table without linen, Danish or German or Japanese stainless steel ware, and so on. The novel scheme caught the interest of an area reporter and an article appeared in the *New York Times*, then a radio station asked Stamford's trade chairman for an interview.

The Mount Clemens, Michigan League held an International Trade Fair in cooperation with the Chamber of Commerce. The two-day event was at the town's civic center, with displays of products exported from Mount Clemens and of imported materials used in the manufacture of any goods made in the area.

With the help of the University of Iowa, the Iowa State League initiated a half-hour television show that was seen around the state. Owners of a gift shop and a bicycle shop were interviewed during the first 15 minutes as to how trade affected them, and during the last 15 minutes a panel discussed the question, " . . . . Is it possible that a trade policy can be too free?"

In addition to the unusual, the League did the obvious—meetings, meetings, meetings with speakers, speakers, speakers representing government, business, labor, agriculture, universities, and foreign governments and foreign businesses, too. League members peddled their publications, went on radio and TV, wrote letters to the editor, polled the public, and talked to their Congressmen and Senators. At our end of things, we informed Leagues of the progress of legislation, consulted with trade leaders in the executive branch and in the Congress, testified before Congressional committees, and worked in concert with our friends in other organizations.

Let me turn back for a moment to my previous mention of the League's evaluation of how trade can assist the process of world economic development. In the elaborate, difficult process we call consensus, we came forth with some refinements to our existing support for trade liberalization.

When the results of this recent League discussion and conclusion were revealed in March 1962, we issued a kind of position paper embracing past and present League thoughts on trade. In it, we said in part that we believed "a liberal trade policy will best serve the political, economic, and individual interests by paving the way for political harmony with other nations, stimulating economic growth at home and abroad, and expanding the opportunities for consumer choice among a wide variety of products." I won't enumerate here the six main points of our position except that I cannot resist saying in this building at the time the two trade conferences are being held in Geneva that our "Point 4" was, and I quote, "The principle of reciprocity in trade agreements should be maintained except when political and economic considerations call for special trade concessions to developing countries." But back to the subject—the fact that League members had so recently thought through their own personal convictions about trade had a very great impact on their collective commitment. It was this commitment which so distinguished the League's trade campaign.

We put much of what local Leagues said in our testimony before Congress. The fact that we quoted from Leagues in the districts or states of the Congressmen and Senators on the committees was hardly coincidental.

There is one thing more to be said. In a *Harper's* article (February 1962), Joseph Kraft said that it would take more than the League of Women Voters to gain support for the Trade Expansion Program. And he was right. It took Presidential and Congressional leadership, the support of prominent business and labor and agricultural associations, the general enthusiasm of the press, and the hard work of many of our colleagues in the non-governmental groups represented here today. All of these components were essential to the great change–

over in trade policy represented by the Trade Expansion Act of 1962. The climate of opinion was right but it was made right. New perspectives in U.S. foreign policy originate, for the most part, from political leadership, and these perspectives can become realities if we choose to make them so. We did with trade—a shining example of mobilizing public response at the right time to a very great opportunity.

As for the League itself, in the process we became politicians and economists. To be sure, we had an amateur status but I believe we can claim a professional status as citizens because we cared, we learned, and we acted.

DOCUMENTATION
1. Facts and Attitudes on World Trade
2. The Politics of Trade
3. Trade Kit
4. The National VOTER
5. Foreign Policy Roundup
6. World Trade? What Has That to Do With Me?
7. League Plans for Breaking the Trade Barrier
8. Statement of Position on Trade
9. Statement in Support of the Trade Expansion Act of 1962

Source: Rostow quoted in *It Makes a Difference There Is a League of Women Voters*. Washington, DC: LWVUS, September 1963, 11. "An Educational Program on Foreign Trade" (Presentation by Miss Barbara Stuhler at the U.S. Department of State's National Conference for Representatives of Non-Governmental Organizations, May 20, 1964). Document in author's possession.

The singular review of foreign policy from 1958 to 1960 was modified, however, by a number of continuing responsibilities requiring appropriate attention and action. Leaguers soon proved restless with such a restricted current agenda, and slowly but surely other issues began to be added to that category. Active in the area of the conservation of water resources, the League soon emerged as a leader on a continuum of issues relating to environmental protection. Similarly, civil liberties of the 1950s took a turn into civil rights of the 1960s, and equality of opportunity in education and employment emerged as a new League programmatic emphasis.

During the late 1950s and early 1960s, League members fretted about the process of consensus. Consensus, as Louise Young has suggested, proved to be one of the keys to the League's vitality. League decisions were not handed down. Rather, "they bubbled up from below." First, the issue to be studied was established in the program-making process. Staff and volunteers prepared materials and extensive bibliographies that were distributed as discussion guides and references for wide-ranging viewpoints. This coming-to-agreement after study and discussion could not be and was not measured quantita-

tively but emerged out of state and local League reports, out of visits by national board members, and out of council meetings and conventions. Still, there continued to be an uneasiness about how much one should know about the subject before coming to a conclusion. A fair number of League members worried that they did not know enough. Correspondence and other communications reflected that concern. League leaders, however, tried to persuade the doubters that they knew far more than the average citizen; and if they refused to act, those less well informed would be making decisions in their stead. A presidential address by Ruth Phillips in 1963 addressed this and other means whereby more League members could experience the "fun" of the League, the stimulation that came from "A Passionate Intensity" on behalf of the League's program and its growth as an organization.

DOCUMENT 5: RUTH PHILLIPS, "A PASSIONATE INTENSITY"

It is just a little over a year since many of us who are here in this room were meeting together at national convention in Minneapolis. At that time you will recall we were very much worried about the fate of the President's trade legislation. We were worried about the financial situation of the United Nations; we were concerned about the United States economy. And then, as sort of an afterthought, we were worried about our own financial situation. We spent an exciting evening hearing about five places where it really made a difference that there was a League of Women Voters and we were proud and pleased. . . .

Questions were raised and questions were answered in Minneapolis, but one question was not raised—at least not in so many words—but it underlay much of the discussion nonetheless and was perhaps related to the request that was made to the Board that we consider our whole Program structure in relation to League purpose. It has come forth again obliquely in the annual reports when over and over again we hear "there were not enough of us to do the job, the workload is too great for so few."

The question that we ask ourselves, not out loud, but we ask it just the same, is this: Why is it that those of us who enjoy the League of Women Voters so much, believe in it so deeply, and have found it the key to real participation in the mainstream of American political life—why is it that we cannot communicate this same feeling more widely—more widely even within the League itself? Why aren't there more of us?

The question has been in my mind all year—a year which showed that the Program we adopted at the national Convention in Minneapolis to be both timely and topical—a year in which we have all been glad that the League was in the forefront of those who believe that the United Nations is indispensable —glad that we are in a position to act in the very grave financial crisis which confronts it. This was the year when we have been proud, too, of the League's handiwork in building a climate of support opinion for the Trade Expansion Act, proud of the League's constancy on behalf of the economic aid for nations and peoples aspiring to a better life.

This was also the year when Leagues in over half the states were working hard for fairer apportionment at the polls and in their state legislatures. . . . courageous League leaders were battling the Liberty Amendment. This was the year that saw the successful culmination of 15 years of League work for a new constitution in the state of Michigan. I was in Michigan virtually on the eve of the election and was swept along with the excitement of the campaign and once more the question rose in my mind: Why is it that we can't communicate what this kind of experience can mean?

Is it because—as Yeats says in *The Second Coming*—"the best lack conviction while the worst are full of passionate intensity"?

I do not like to classify things or people as either "best" or "worst" but certainly we are finding "passionate intensity" in those who are against these days—*against* the United Nations—*against* economic aid—*against* the income tax.

Is it possible to have "passionate intensity" in favor of the UN—in favor of economic aid—in favor of fair apportionment—in favor of education? Do the "best" people lack intensity?

Sometimes as we look around us we see timidity abroad in our land even among those whose motives are the best. We are timid in the realm of ideas when the times call for boldness. . . .

Certainly we can't call the great majority of our people selfish, narrow and completely indifferent. How could one say that of a people who through their democratic government have given nearly a hundred billion dollars in aid to other nations since World War II, including former enemies? But because we sometimes give aid grudgingly and because sometimes we stress the selfish reasons for our assistance and because we sometimes seem to take a perverse pleasure in pointing out the cases where aid has been given unwisely—the effect on ourselves and the rest of the world is negative when it should be positive. If only we could undertake these positive actions with more enthusiasm—with more intensity.

In a world where the intensity—where the growth—seems to be on the side of those who are "against," it is encouraging to report that the League of Women Voters has increased its membership during the past year. We have grown by 3,000 members and are now 135,000 strong and have 1,164 local Leagues. We know that not all of these new members have joined us because of our stands on the United Nations, on trade, on economic aid, or even on apportionment, but we have learned of former members who had drifted away for one reason or another who have renewed their membership in the League as an affirmation on issues in which they deeply believe.

Even with this healthy advance we do not have as many members as we should have or that we need. Along with timidity we see a certain ambivalence abroad in the land. It is pointed up by something that happened early last winter. You may recall that in one month we had the pleasure of hearing Dr. George Gallup express his great and undying admiration for the League of Women Voters when he awarded me—as your representative—a citation from the National Municipal League and called the League "The greatest civic army of all time" and the next month read an article on women for *which his* polls provided the raw material. This was the article you may recall in *which women* from Maine to California declared loudly—or shyly—or sweetly—"All I really want is to take care of Charlie and the children" and went on to define "care" as filling their stomachs, ironing their shirts and if possible shutting out the rest of the world— including the world of school problems—tax problems—the problems of war and peace—the problems of economic development at home and abroad—the problems of polluted water and crowded streets—all of the problems you and I find a challenge.

But long before this article appeared in *The Saturday Evening Post* the national Board had planned to spend some time at our November Board meeting discussing membership in the League and what—if anything—we could do about it.

The first thing the Board did was to face the fact that the League had never really given as much creative energy to recruiting, orienting, and holding members as we have to the adoption of Program, study and action, voters service, public relations or even finance. Membership drives—while not exactly frowned upon—had never been encouraged. Even after the Michigan Survey indicated that there were women who would like to join the League if they were asked, a search for those women had never been effected with the same bloodhound zeal that we seek out an elusive fact on trade for example. . . .

Political victories are important but perhaps the most important reason for League growth—both in members and in participation within the League—is the evident need in this country and throughout the world for the truly committed individual.

Certainly whatever our favorite reasons for increasing membership in the League and for widening the circle of participating members within the League, the Board was agreed that there were undoubtedly barriers to both these things. Were the barriers that keep women from joining in the first place the same barriers that keep them from getting all they might from League membership?

Well, let's take a look as the Board did back in November.

First of all, we saw women entering the labor market—going back to school and preparing for new careers. We were told that one out of every two women in the forty to fifty-five age group is working.

We saw other organizations duplicating, in part, the work of the League. We saw adult education groups—courses on television—the Chamber of Commerce practical politics courses—many, many places to get some of the things that at one time were provided by the League almost alone.

We also found what has now become known as the Feminine Mystique. I think we have to face the fact, as the suffrage leaders did when women failed to flock, in to the newly formed League of Women Voters as they had hoped, that some women are simply not interested in government—just as some men aren't. But there are others, who, during their school and college years have developed interests in public affairs—have learned to use their minds—have found research, discussion, decision making exciting and stimulating. Then they get married and some mysterious intellectual affliction overtakes them. This is now becoming known as the Feminine Mystique. Perhaps some of you have read Betty Friedan's book of this title.

In the *Saturday Review* Lillian Smith said about this book—"The gist of Betty Friedan's thesis is that Nora is back in the Doll's House. It is now an air-conditioned split-level abode with her own car in the garage, but a Doll's House nonetheless."

The women who expressed themselves in the Hill-Gallup article in the *Saturday Evening Post* are the ones who are the personification of the Feminine Mystique. Mrs. Friedan blames Freud and Madison Avenue for putting Nora back into the Doll's House and then asks: Why do young women and their nice young men fall for it? Why don't they see that women can keep up their share of home responsibilities and still make their contribution in the outside world? Well, why indeed!

In discussing these barriers to League membership the Board decided that there isn't much that we can do about women going into the labor market—

many of our own members are doing just this. We can perhaps arrange for greater accommodation for working members—evening and weekend meetings perhaps—schedules adjusted to the working woman. As for the woman who is getting what she wants of political participation through working with other groups—what seems to be called for here is to encourage and accommodate.

And then we come to the victim of the Feminine Mystique. What do we do about her? Actually, it seems to me that the picture of life in suburbia is probably not as dire as Mrs. Friedan has depicted it or as rosy as the *Saturday Evening Post* contends.

I do not believe that every woman wants a career—at least not while her children are little. She wants the fun—as well as the responsibility—of watching them develop. This doesn't mean that she has to let her mind get rusty. In fact, for her husband's sake as well as her own, she will want to keep her mind very much alive. For her children's sake, as well as her own, she will want to know what goes on in the world beyond her own side yard. A mother really can't bring her children up to be good citizens unless she practices the rudiments of citizenship herself. And for her very own sake (or, as one mother of four put it, for her own sanity) she wants things to think about—even problems to grapple with—which are not her very own personal, demanding, ever-present problems.

I think the League has much to offer the young mother. Many young mothers think so too. One mother of three wrote that she really never had felt a part of the community—any community—until she had joined the League. But it sometimes bothers me that the individual young mother who really becomes enthusiastic about the League and becomes a League president at twenty-five or thirty puts almost too much into it. Which suggests, of course, that we should attract more of these young women so the full burden of leadership does not fall on a few.

Why don't we?

Perhaps we should look to the barriers to membership within the League itself—the barriers we may be able to do something about—we may catch the attention of the refugees from the Feminine Mystique and we might even catch the eye of Nora as she peeks out the picture window of her Doll's House. . . .

Recently I read a speech of a president who was retiring from office. It might well be entitled how to be happy though committed. She said in part: "If someone might ask me how I explain the exceptional success of the Leagues this year, I would say, first we have tried innumerable new ideas. Secondly, we were not afraid. We took our stands and worked hard for their accomplishment. Third, League members caught the excitement of our challenge and became personally involved. Fourth, we have tried to keep our members well informed so that they will know the reasons behind what we do. And last but not least, we have projected the image that being in the League is 'fun.' Which it is. . . . It has been a thrill and a privilege to serve as your president, and I will surely remember it as one of the happiest times of my life." Nonetheless, the over-worked leader—and her projected image—is a barrier to League growth. What else did we find within the League that might prove to be a stumbling block to membership? I report this next thought with some temerity and I'll even put it in the form of a question. Is it possible that we have become obsessed with decision making—and this is a barrier to some people?

I am aware that the Michigan Survey indicated that members who took part in decision making made for a stronger more effective League and I think our own experience bears this out. But I don't believe that the Michigan Survey meant that we had to take this dictum quite so literally. Sometimes it seems to me that we want everyone to participate every inch of the way—in suggesting the Program, in adopting the Program, in coming to consensus, in taking action.

In insisting on this participation are we likely to put a strain on the members and make nervous wrecks of the middlemen—the local Boards of the League of Women Voters—this same young president I mentioned earlier who takes her responsibility so seriously?

Some women join the League just to get League material or to feel that they are promoting a worthwhile cause. They may not have time nor want to participate in decision making and are willing to abide by the decisions of those who do participate. The safety factor is that of any democratically run institution—should a crisis or controversy arise, these non-active members can make their wishes known because the procedures are there.

If League leaders have shown that they are receptive to ideas, suggestions and even criticisms and if decisions are reported promptly and clearly the member may have all of the feeling of participation she wants or needs. On the other hand if we press too hard we may only inspire guilt in our leadership and membership alike and instead of increasing the degree of participation we may find we have frustration and discouragement.

Perhaps it is more important to see that as many members as possible participate in one decision on a subject about which they have thought deeply and on which they feel competent to make a decision that it is to vote a superficial "yes" or "no" on a variety of subjects on which they feel that both their knowledge and competence is limited.

And here I should like to quote a letter that Barbara Stuhler wrote a few months ago to a state chairman worried about member participation especially on consensus. Miss Stuhler said in part: "We are always searching for ways to strengthen the League by expanding membership participation in League stands. While we do this I think we should face up squarely to the fact that some members are going to be more interested in one component of the League Program than others but knowing how the League works should we be reluctant to let those knowledgeable and interested guide our decisions? Let me give you a specific example.

A little over a year ago I moved from Minneapolis where I had lived for ten years to St. Paul. I knew very little (and not much more now) about the local problems of my new city. But I turn to the League, and their judgments become my judgments. I don't feel any compunction about the fact that they make up my mind for me because I am confident in their methods and their conclusions. Congressmen and Senators have to work this way—have to turn to their colleagues whose views they respect on subjects they can't possibly master—why can't we?—why shouldn't we? I don't mean to imply that League members should become so highly specialized that they know nothing about issues outside their specialists but only that, in our highly complex society, we can't expect to know everything equally well."

I quite agree with Miss Stuhler and neither of us is suggesting that we return to the old department system of the League. What we do feel is that every member of the League should have the experience of going into at least one subject in such depth that the decision she comes to has significance to her and to the League.

And now let us take a look at another of our cherished concepts. "Program is a tool" we sometimes say, "It is a way we can learn to be participating citizens so it doesn't make much difference what governmental problem we choose for the demonstration." Have we adhered to this idea so tightly that what we choose to work on has no appeal to us emotionally? Has the objectivity of our study made us feel that we should also be unemotional about the results? Does the fact that we know that it sometimes takes years to realize a governmental objective—unpolluted water for example—make us too philosophical about accepting failure?

Some of us on the national Board have had the privilege of participating with some of you in three conferences on program structure in New York, San Francisco, and Chicago. As I did my homework for the Chicago conference and read the material on Program history which is in your Workbook, I was struck again with the sweep of League Program, with the relevance of League Program, and with the consistency of League Program over the past forty-three years. I am encouraged that the League has never shied away from broad and complex subjects. If we did so now, we would be at odds with a world whose distinguishing characteristic is complexity.

League Program is a great teacher. It teaches us that there are no simple solutions to the great issues of the day. It teaches us the many elements of political effectiveness. It makes us face up to the hard choices of decision-making. We learn from Program knowledge and know-how. The League has made politicians of League members, and I can think of no higher praise than that we have, in the first dictionary sense, become "experienced in the science of government."

Yes, Program is a teacher but is it something more? I think my answer to this question would be that it is. League Program is a commitment. I cannot conceive, for example, that the League would ever reject the necessity for international cooperation in trade, aid, and diplomacy. You do not lightly shut the door on a heritage of forty years of League support. I think we have an obligation to make better known to those who would join us the nature of this commitment. I think we should make more of our Principles, not solely as a basis for Program selection but also as a statement of what we believe. I think what I'm trying to say is that we should have more "passionate intensity" on our Program. . . .

We are back once more on the importance of the three steps in the League cycle—choosing the field in which we want our commitment to be—that is choosing the Program on which to work; making up our minds—making our commitment—and giving ourselves the authority to act and then taking action on behalf of that commitment.

If a member can have this experience on one problem on one level of government and see it through I venture to say that she will feel a part of the inner circle of the League—the place where all the excitement is. This feeling of being in the center of things is not always shared by the individual League member. All the fascinating tidbits of action or inaction, which comprise the political process, are not adequately communicated either. For when the member is excited about her involvement in a significant political experience—frustrating or satisfying—which was a central issue in her town, state, or nation that excitement is communicated to her friends and neighbors. Thus the inner circle grows.

How do we do this? I am not sure I know, but I suggest we try.

I suggest that we consider spending the next year in a campaign of expansion—continued expansion on the finance front—expansion of present member understanding and action in the League—and expansion of our membership.

The climate is ripe for growth. Men are interested in the League and this helps in recruitment of new members. There are some signs of retreat from the Feminine Mystique and we should be not only in a receptive mood but geared for reception.

Of course we have always welcomed new members in the League, but it has been on an every League do-it-yourself basis. There are great advantages in expanding together. There is a need for new materials for orientation—orientation geared to spark an interest in government first—League procedures second. Perhaps a simplified "Government in Action" course could be planned and combined with getting acquainted sessions with the people who run the local government.

If we should plan such a campaign of expansion we can, as always, look to our Leagues for inspiration and know-how.

There is a great reservoir of ideas for growth in the League. What we need to do is to get them from you and then pass them along to others of you. We want to know how you have combined courses in practical politics with specific Program items, ways in which you have made your new members become part of the League in a hurry, the kind of publicity you have used to project the League image clear and shining as a living invitation to the women who are "waiting to be asked." . . .

It is a little ironic that most of us have learned to communicate on everything but the League of Women Voters—what it means to us—what it means to our families—what it means to our communities—what it means to the country as a whole. We have learned political effectiveness. We know how to reach the "influentials," the "communicators," the "multipliers." We have learned in Voters Service that it is wasteful to spend hundreds of woman hours on a Voters Guide and then get it out to only 5,000 people—we have learned how to get that same guide into the hands of 500,000 people.

I suggest that we use these same talents to get members for the League of Women Voters and to attempt to instill in our present members who are outside of the inner circle some of the sense of commitment, some of the sense of excitement that motivates those of us who have found the inner circle of the League to be a "magic circle." For in the League the more the inner circle is widened the stronger the organization and, more important, as more and more citizens become knowledgeable, the more the very fabric of self-government is strengthened.

And all of us know that the fabric of self-government needs strengthening in this country. This country needs courageous, dedicated, committed, knowledgeable citizens. In all humility I think it needs the League of Women Voters.

Source: Excerpts from the Proceedings of the General Council Meeting of the LWVUS, Washington, DC, May 6–10, 1963. LWV files, Washington, DC, II. B.15. 0022-44.

The national convention in Pittsburgh in 1964 was also graced by a stirring speech by the highly respected economist Barbara Ward (Lady Robert Jackson) whose hour-long eloquence (with no notes) captivated an attentive audience of more than one thousand listeners. President Lyndon B. Johnson and Lady Bird Johnson dropped in—the first visit by an American president to a national League convention—and, after officially declaring "League of Women Voters Week," he used that platform to urge League support for his War on Poverty. League delegates were already on that wavelength having just adopted a new program item on equality of opportunity in education and employment.

The League had taken a giant step forward with the establishment in 1957 of the League of Women Voters Education Fund. Not only did the fund provide the League with a tax-exempt arm through which much of the League's voter and issue education work could be channeled; it also afforded the League the opportunity to do some cutting-edge exploration on issues where the League had no position. One such effort was undertaken from 1969 to 1971 with a series of regional conferences titled "Military Spending and National Security." Subsequently, beginning in 1982, the League itself took on an examination of military policy and defense spending.

Julia Stuart from Spokane, Washington, became the League's seventh president and the first from a western state, serving from 1964 to 1968. Her thoughtful manner, good humor, and quiet competence guided Leagues during the turbulent decade of the 1960s, a period when issues of civil rights, women's rights, and the war in Vietnam triggered protests, parades, and the disenchantment of young men and women who sought solace in merging the music of rock and roll, drugs, long hair, and a new kind of dress code.

Impatient with the League's emphasis on working within the system—although that remained a tried and true commitment—members joined forces in more overt demonstrations on the issues they supported (or opposed) by marching in the streets and forming coalitions with other groups. It proved to be a useful way of capturing public attention and motivating people to act. Much of the coalition building derived from the League of Women Voters Education Fund's Inner-City project, which brought together local Leagues and inner-city organizations to educate voters and to engage citizens as participants in the civic process.

Source: Nancy M. Neuman, *The League of Women Voters: In Perspective 1920–1995*. Washington, DC: LWVUS, 1994, 35–37.

At the 1965 Council meeting, Julia Stuart spoke to the League's prior experience in contending with crises.

DOCUMENT 6: JULIA STUART'S 1965 COUNCIL ADDRESS

"Why choose the League?"—why choose the painstaking, plodding, sometimes pedestrian method of working for desired changes that is represented by working actively in the League of Women Voters? Do our methods make sense in a fast-moving world? Are we so bogged down with procedures we can't move quickly enough? Are we so wedded to study and discussion and consensus before action that we never get off the ground?

Well our problem is, I believe, in relating to the crisis-ridden society and to this, I wish eventually, to address myself. But before I do, I want to share with you news of accomplishments that will make us all proud.

First and foremost, I want to tell you that your efforts to increase League membership have been successful. We have had a net gain of nearly ten thousand members. Membership has risen from 135,551 to 145,543 in the last twelve months. This is the biggest leap forward in membership since that 1952–53 boom and it has occurred all over the country.

Another reason to be proud is that we have kept pace with finance goals as we set for ourselves three years ago. And we have moved into quarters which are more nearly tailored to our needs and which we look forward to showing you tonight.

And we have had a larger sale and distribution of publications of *any* year in League history. One million three hundred and forty-nine thousand eight hundred and nine have been handled. And of these, 54,000 copies have been free publications to the Leagues and to the outside. These numbers represent more than just volume. Such figures as "over 60,000 copies" sold of *Prospects in Education and Employment* and over 50,000 copies of *Freshening East-West Trade Winds* indicate member involvement in Program as well. And as far as public recognition is concerned, we have no complaints.

In the last few weeks we have received a Freedom Foundation Award for the publication *Choosing the President*; and an award for Voters Service from the American Heritage Association; and just last Thursday I had the honor of accepting, on your behalf, the Meritorious Award of the Department of Defense for your efforts to provide members of the Armed Services with information helpful to them in casting their absentee ballots.

From all I have read and heard of our State Leagues—you too have been busy, productive, and generally appreciated. But in the midst of the ups and downs of our League life, we have been aware of, and sometimes involved in, various kinds of governmental crises. Indeed, we are getting so used to being confronted in crisis terms. A crisis is a result, however, of a long failure to deal with smaller problems, and each of the current crop has been with us for a long time. In a way, the fact that each is deemed a "crisis" is a triumph for the forces that are working to bring them to public attention. In other words, crisis sometimes can be a good thing, and an opportunity to move forward, the proof that something is happening that it may improve a situation which didn't bother people when it was not in the headlines.

So, the question for the League is: How do we relate to crisis? What is our role? Is there anything we can change to make our role more useful or important?

We stress the importance of individual action in the League and I am proud to state that our members *do* act as responsible individuals, but we want, in addition, the satisfaction of being identified with a group, *our* group, that speaks up on what we consider the *right* side. Can we always do this? Well, of course not.

As ever woman who joins the League quickly learns, we have patterns in the League, procedures, a way of doing things. And new members find an optimistic group all right, but they are quickly disabused of the notion that we can do everything, or that we can achieve everything we want to do as individuals through joining the League of Women Voters or any other organization. We do not encourage the fallacy that citizens need only ask, and they will be able to change the world, quickly, directly, and just as they please. This is a distortion of the town meeting concept of democracy. We are slow just as democracy is slow, but the League pattern includes taking action, vigorous action after certain other steps have been gone through, and we do not avoid crisis.

Indeed, we have learned that on every public question there comes a moment of crisis and opportunity to strike when the iron is hot. The trouble is that the moment of crisis does not always occur when the League has arrived at the proper moment in its study, discussion, and consensus, and is ready to take action. Sometimes the crisis comes before we are ready for it. And sometimes it comes on a subject we have been labeling "crisis" for years. But by the time the public has decided it *is* an emergency, we wonder what all the shouting is all about, and sometimes, quite often, we help precipitate a crisis. And once in a while, having done this, we then find that we cannot rise to confront the crisis head-on at the time that confrontation would do the most to give vent to our own frustrations. . . .

Obviously, if the leadership reflects membership choices and decisions, it, the leadership, cannot decide for itself what it thinks the members actually believe, and now having taken a look at the kind of an organization the League aspires to be, let us return to this matter of the League in relation to crisis and examine some of the crises the League has lived through and what we have done about them.

It just so happens that I joined the League in a time of crisis. It's why I joined the League. It was at the time of the Korean War, and those of you who go back that far will recall that the league took a strong stand and prompt action backing President Truman in his decision to send United States troops under the authority of the United Nations to stop the communist invasion of South Korea.

We did this by supporting the United States' position on the United for Peace Resolution in the United Nations General Assembly, and by conducting an all-out campaign for League opinion to be registered to the Congress in support of United States commitments to the UN and to NATO.

In the community in which I lived, this was a bitterly partisan issue and yet League members from both parties joined their voices with those of League members from all over the country in supporting this action in Korea. They had discussed and had debated and had come to conclusions and the action taken was in line with those conclusions. Now this is an example of the League response to a crisis on which it is well prepared.

Another kind of crisis which had the country in its grip about the same time, and this was the crisis over individual constitutional liberties. Federal loyalty-security programs had come into being in the late 1940s and early 1950s to cope with the danger of Communist infiltration of governmental and defense establishments. There was widespread criticism that the loyalty-security programs had grown so large that they had become unwieldy and that they were administered unevenly and that the rights of the individual were inadequately safeguarded. More importantly, there was a feeling of suspicion abroad in the land, and that little couplet "I sometimes fancy as I spy; I'm smarter than the FBI," epitomized the spirit of certain segments of the country.

Well, the League's answer to this crisis was the Freedom Agenda program. It was a series of discussions on the Bill of Rights, individual liberty in every League community in the land, and the climate *did* improve. Allen Weston, author and teacher and an authority in the field of individual liberty, attributes much of the change of attitude to the Freedom Agenda. "In community after community," he wrote, "I could see the difference after the program got started."

Sometimes crisis can be forestalled, and this happened in 1944. Remembering the defeat of the League of Nations because the public was ill-informed and disinterested after World War I, the League, was well-prepared for the results of the Conference at Dumbarton Oaks, which brought forth the tentative draft for the United Nations. With a tradition of twenty years of experience in combating isolationism and in working for international organizations of various kinds, and with a recent experience in going to the public on these issues, the League record between the end of the Dubarton Oaks Conference and the convening of the San Francisco Conference in March 1945 was nothing short of stupendous.

An excellent primer on the need for the United Nations organization sold over a one hundred thousand copies shortly after its release—with orders running at the rate of two thousand a day. In six months the League had trained five thousand leaders to carry the word about the UN to discussion groups set up in churches, businesses, settlement houses, foreign-born groups, and government workers. And some local League leaders gave as many as fifty to sixty short talks on this subject in a period of a few months. Letters of suggestions about what should be included in the United Nations poured into the State Department, over one thousand a day. So clearly the Dumbarton Oaks campaign was effective and clearly its effectiveness was due to the wholehearted commitment of the members to the goal of the organization.

What added to the effectiveness was that though the voice might be one with a Southern accent, or speaking with a Western drawl, or in the clipped speech of New England, the message was the same because the consensus behind that message had come from every part of the country.

And now back to the present. Many of you will remember the civil rights crisis in 1963, when it became clear that a real push was about to be made nationally on civil rights legislation. The National Board, encouraged by letters from many Leagues and individuals as well, did some soul-searching on what the League could do when the issue was not on the national Program and yet was such a basic issue of our time. Believing as they do that one of the responsibilities of leadership is pointing up different ways in which members and the organization itself can make a contribution in a given situation, the National Board asked Mrs. Phillips to issue a memorandum doing just that.

You may recall that the memorandum made suggestions and asked: Has the League made all the effort it could to reach all sections of the community with its Voters Service materials? Is it reaching those in the community who need clear-cut information on how and where to register to vote? Are there ways of getting information on the candidates and issues to minority groups? Will there be an opportunity for League members to be poll watchers to insure that there will be no infringement of the law at the polls?

And another suggestion was that local and state Leagues who felt strongly on this issue could adopt an Emergency Current Agenda in the field of political rights, making a community survey in the field of race relations, sharing this information with the community in a published report, was pointed out as a way in which to contribute.

And of course, individual action was stressed with the suggestion that local Boards might wish to provide leadership by adopting a more flexible policy with regard to what Board members might do as individuals in serving on citizen commissions, committees, and human rights councils. It was a good example of stimulation from the center in order to be a part of a coherent plan.

And our southern Leagues, many of them which for years have been plugging away on improving registration and voting procedures and feeling rather lonely about it, were encouraged to greater efforts by the knowledge that while they were part of a nation-wide effort, they were to make their *own* decisions about what *their* League would do, in the light of its own situation and its own needs.

Now, I cannot begin to spell out all of the activities the Leagues engaged in, ranging from conscious efforts to recruit Negro women as members to equally conscious efforts to master techniques of reaching those in the community who seldom participate in the civic process, including voting. And in the meantime, you know Mrs. Phillips who served on the President's Commission on Registration and Voting Participation, not only made a distinguished contribution to the work of that Commission but provided material, much of which formed a basis for the Commission's discussions, and this material was assembled and compiled by all of your Leagues and based on their work on election laws and on practices.

And of course, you know that Mrs. Phillips was one of a minority report, which mentioned the possibility of a national election law as really the most effective method of ending real discrimination against voters in minority groups.

So it is partly because of Mrs. Phillips' experience on the Commission and partly because the League feels it has much to learn in communicating with the consistent non-voter that your National Board asked the League of Women Voters Education Fund to undertake. . . pilot projects in voting and registration . . . The report. . . will be discussed during this council. . . .

And finally, the eye-opening effect of the Civil Rights memo caused many of us to take a new look at our own communities and the League's relation to them. I suppose we've all been aware that the struggle for civil rights was just the outward and visible sign of a deeper and far more far–reaching malaise. But beginning with the summer of 1963 and continuing through the fall and winter, League conscience stirred and League interest quickened.

When program-making time came along, we had suggestions from more than 900 local and state Leagues, and there were those who wanted a straight civil rights item; those who wanted a study of federal–state relations, and those who expressed concern about "human resources and educational opportunity." Then there were those who wanted to see congressional machinery improved, and it was clear that they were interested in this because they hoped that Congress would do something about "human resources, civil rights" or other issues which concerned them.

So during the program-making process, and on through the debate at Convention, we were fully aware of the need for a broader franchise. Our principles make clear what League members believe about civil rights as well as voting rights, so we could have adopted a broad or a narrow item in this field, but as all League members are well aware, we consciously limit our program so that we can be effective and we have to make choices.

It's always wonderful for me to watch what really happens at a national convention, because after we have been through our long drawn-out system of program-making, we do not find that we have a situation where a vocal group from one area of the country imposes on Leagues in other areas of the nation, either its views or its ideas on what constitutes the most useful. . . for League concentration. We really have a meeting of the minds.

Thus when we make a commitment in terms of League time and energy, we find that we almost inevitably adopt a program which is applicable and significant in all parts of the nation, and what we chose to work on, was the development of human resources, and I might add, that the two problems selected within this framework [included] "equality of opportunity in education" and "equality of opportunity in employment."

Source: Excerpts from the Proceedings of the General Council Meeting of the LWVUS, (hereinafter referred to as the 1965 Council) Washington, DC, May 4–7, 1965. LWV Papers on film, I. B.17. 0508–21.

Marjorie Pharis, national board chair of the current agenda item on human resources, interpreted the growing consensus emerging from League deliberations on policies relating to poverty and discrimination and on programs to provide equal opportunity in education and employment.

DOCUMENT 7: MARJORIE PHARIS ON LEAGUE CONSENSUS AND HUMAN RESOURCES

Annual reports are the League road map which shows us how far we have come, where we are at the moment, and where we may reasonably expect to arrive at a given time. From the nearly one thousand reports on Human Resources that came to the national office by early April, we have been able to discern the outline of a root that began with the adoption of the item a year ago. Our point of departure was a realization that wasted Human Resources create social, economic, and moral problems which affect the general welfare, and that government has a responsibility to share in the solution of these problems.

Our study has brought deepened and more sensitive awareness of the scope of the problem, the complexities that have caused it and some of the ways that may lead to its cure. We have raised our sights beyond the suburbs to depressed areas, both rural and urban, where inequality of opportunity is a "built-in" fact of life.

We have seen a close link between the denial of civil rights, and the denial of equality of opportunity for education and employment. We have developed a feeling of what it must be like to be born poor in an "Affluent Society," to sit before a teacher who says little that seems relevant, to be jobless and untrained when most people are employed. In short, we have some understanding now of what is meant by the "voiceless people," some conception of who they are, and why they may be voiceless.

Annual reports can never tell the whole story of a busy year of League work, and since this year's meetings are still going on, we don't have an entirely complete account of where we will be by summer, but the reports we have received are a rich source of ideas to mark the directions in which we are moving. We want to tell you the major points brought out in these reports, and we also want to discuss with you the National Board's thinking as to which of these ideas provide the most productive approach to the work of next year. A sizeable number of Leagues said they would like to study "education in general." To do so would go beyond the scope of the item as it was defined when adopted. . . .

Another group said they generally approved of the programs they have studied, that is they felt the programs were basically sound, and a step in the right direction. . . .

Non-discrimination was implied or explicitly spelled out in many of the comments.

It is this line of thinking about the role of government and people in solving problems of inequality that seems to us most fruitful for emphasis in the coming year. Some Leagues that have gone furthest in their studies expressed themselves rather fully, and indeed, they brought together what other Leagues said in part.

Here, for instance, is what Berkeley, California reported. This is a rather long quotation and I'll tell you when it's ended so that I don't have to keep telling you as I go along that it is still Berkeley speaking.

"In order fully to develop Human Resources, the problems of poverty must be attacked at federal, state, and local levels and by private agencies as well. Federal programs are necessary because more money is available at this level, because poverty is a national problem and because we have a mobile population. Local participation is essential to adapt federal programs to local situations. Communities, which can afford it, have a financial responsibility. Private agencies are often more flexible and imaginative, and their contributions are of great value.

"Programs which motivate the individual to help himself and his family give him the opportunity for a good basic education, and opportunities for vocational or professional training should be the goal of these coordinated governmental and private efforts.

"Our membership believes that the recent legislation on the federal level is an important step toward these goals. We refer specifically to Manpower Development and Training Act, the Vocational Education Act of 1963, the Economic Opportunity Act, and the Rural Redevelopment Act—which incidentally may now be replaced by the proposed Public Works and Economic Development Act of 1965.

"It is too early for evaluation of these programs. We are cautiously optimistic about their prospects and think it likely that they should be expanded in size at some future time. We are concerned that they be administered in such a way that the poor actually benefit, that the poor participate in planning, that no racial discrimination results, and that the programs not duplicate each other, that administrative costs be kept to a minimum.

"Because there can be no employment opportunities when no jobs exist, we endorse the federal programs designed to raise the economic levels of geographic areas, specifically the Area Redevelopment Agency and Appalachia programs." . . .

You will notice that the Leagues in the reports we are reproducing seem to approve the general concept of community programs authorized and financed in varying degrees by the Federal Government, and as I have already indicated, related threads run through a significant number of the reports. They also tend to enumerate the following criteria for such programs. . . .

One—All three levels of government, as well as private institutions, should be involved.

Two—People for whom community action programs are designed should participate in the planning.

Three—The programs should motivate the individual to help himself and his family.

Four—The programs should be non-discriminatory.

Five—Programs should be carefully tailored to the educational and employment needs of the group or groups they are supposed to reach.

Six—Programs may be closely related but should not duplicate each other.

Seven—Programs should be regularly evaluated to see if changes are needed.

Conclusions reached by some Leagues, by no means represent consensus on which we may act, nor do we want to imply that when consensus is reached, the League as a whole will necessarily agree with all the points we have just outlined, or that the criteria listed are all-inclusive, but these statements do indicate some areas where interest is high and where we might soon find League agreement.

Other questions on which we may wish to reach consensus are equally important. Most Leagues, we were interested to note, studied the major legislation covered by our item, but it seems that their liveliest interest centered on the Economic Opportunity Act as it began to be implemented this year. This may have been due, in part, to the total news coverage it is receiving, to the country-wide interest in community action programs, and to the emotional impact of the Act's emphasis on youth.

Here, however, are questions in other areas of our item which we think the Leagues may wish to consider also.

One—What approaches should be taken to the development of depressed areas?

Two—Should the Federal Government withhold grants, loans or contracts, supporting programs in education and employment that are discriminatory?

Three—Should the Federal Government provide advice and other forms of assistance to communities facing problems of integration in employment and education?

Specifically, this relates to the kind of help provided by the Office of Education, and the Community Relations Service established by the Civil Rights Act.

Four—Should the League come to agreement on whether it supports the idea of a "Federal Equal Employment Opportunity Commission?" What powers should commissions have? How should it relate to similar state agencies?

We suggest that League consensus on the criteria for government programs—this was the first group of questions—could be asked for by December 1st of this year. It should be an advantage for members to have reached agreement on standards for government programs before they propose what the League should do in the next biennium. Some Leagues might be ready to answer the other questions by that time too, but we think that the First of April 1966 is a more realistic deadline for the second group.

All these questions are open for discussion by this Council. We welcome your reactions and your advice now. (Applause)

Source: Excerpts from Proceedings of the 1965 Council. LWV Papers on film, II. B. 17. 1522-32.

Julia Stuart's presidential address at the Denver convention in 1966 provided a framework for the convention's discussion in an unconventional moment in American history. And once again, League members went on record against an overly long program.

DOCUMENT 8: JULIA STUART'S 1966 PRESIDENTIAL ADDRESS

And so I should like to begin with our response—your response—to the times in which we live. We are all aware that they are not exactly easy. In fact, the year 1966 has been said by someone to be the year we should feel comfortable about being irritable! (Laughter)

This is the year when probably more people are concerned about foreign policy than at any time since we were in a full-scale war and yet few feel entirely right about what we have. . . .The traditional lines drawn between isolationists and internationalists, or between the "good guys" and the "bad guys" [are not clear–cut].

And this is the year when our young are not apathetic and not necessarily alienated but distrustful—distrustful of the system in which we have implicit faith.

This is the year when, legislative triumphs behind them, some of those who worked for civil rights legislation, greater federal participation in education, and for funds to insure greater development of human resources, aren't sure what to do next. . . .

And this is the year when a cartoon in the *Saturday Review* showed two little girls in a school corridor. One is saying to the other, "It isn't that I don't like current events, it's just that there are so many of them." (Laughter)

And of course, this is the year when we are told once again that never before did the individual have to be so versatile, so knowledgeable, so reasonable, and so perceptive as today. We need at least a knowledge of world affairs, economics, communications, education, and politics! And if this is the year when we should feel comfortable about being irritable, League members should feel comfortable indeed. (Laughter) Because we are a bit irritable, and no wonder!

What a job you have been doing. We could write a book about what you have done in the field of Human Resources alone. You will recall that two years ago, we entered this field in response to a rapidly changing environment. We were behind on these issues and we have been kept exceptionally busy, sometimes to the point of harassment, in responding to a very dynamic situation.

And in response to the demand of the time, you have *not* confined yourselves to book learning on " Equality of Opportunity" in education and employment; there must be thousands of you—literally—serving on Community Action Committees, helping on Head Start programs, acting as two-way communications media between specific programs and the larger community.

In the process you have discovered—we all have discovered—that the complex of problems that we are tackling in this field are baffling, untidy, mixed up, unmanageable, contradictory, over-lapping, political, and never-ending. But you are making progress.

And of course, Human Resources is not the only thing you have been putting your mind to—you have done so much in Water that a book has been dedicated to you. You have been leaders in your community on the Celebration of ICY [International Children's Year], found time to defend the United Nations against its critics, obtain editorials on Home Rule for the District of Columbia, come to consensus on apportionment, and apparently joyfully, and of course, to keep up with all of the problems of government which engage you at the state and local level.

And some of you have had time and energy to spare and have organized huge meetings on the subject of United States relations with mainland China.

Such meetings were held in Massachusetts, Vermont, New Hampshire, in Seattle, Washington and Columbus, Ohio among others.

So you see we've been busy. But in your conscientious way you may even feel that you could have done more, or that you could have even done better, and that—along with the uncertain state of the world—adds to your irritation. And I don't blame you for feeling irritable—but you should also feel proud—mighty proud.

In reading your comments on the Annual Reports—and believe me we *do read* them—the National Board is struck with three things:

One is the desire for excellence in the League of Women Voters; second, is the diversity of the things you want the League to do and to be; and third, the almost universal conviction that the Program is too long. (Laughter) (Applause)

Source: Excerpt from Proceedings of the Twenty-seventh Annual Convention of the LWVUS, Denver, CO, May 2-6, 1966. LWV Papers on film, II. B.8. 0738-43.

The following report provided a capsule summary of the convention's deliberations.

DOCUMENT 9: REPORT ON THE 1966 DENVER CONVENTION

The twenty-seventh national Convention of the League of Women Voters of the United States met in the Denver Hilton Hotel in Denver, Colorado, from May 2 to May 6, 1966. Delegates came from all fifty states, the District of Columbia and Puerto Rico; they represented 815 local Leagues, forty-nine state Leagues, and twenty-two provisional Leagues. The delegate body consisted of 1,215 from local Leagues; 122 from state Leagues, and seventeen from the national Board making a total number of 1,360 voting delegates.

In addition there were 141 visitors from state and local Leagues, 71 special guests, 16 press and television representatives, 300 members of the local Convention committee, two members of state staffs, and 20 members of the national staff. The total attendance was 1,932.

Prior to the Convention, the Board modified the Program as proposed in January 1966. Further changes were suggested and adopted by the delegates. They selected a three–item Current Agenda limited in scope and outlook for work.

National Program 1966–68

The League of Women Voters, a nonpartisan organization, is dedicated to the principles established in the Constitution of the United States. The League works to promote political responsibility through informed and active participation of citizens in government.

Through its Program the League gives sustained attention to and takes concerted action on issues chosen by the members. Through its Voters Service the League provides nonpartisan factual information on the structure and function of government and of the political parties and on voting procedures, election issues, and candidates.

Current Agenda

Development of Human Resources: Support of policies and programs in the United States to provide for all persons equality of opportunity for education and employment. (As amended by the national Board and Convention.)

Foreign Policy: Evaluation of U.S. relations with the People's Republic of China. Support of U.S. policies to enhance the peace keeping and peace building capacities of the UN system and to promote world trade and development while maintaining a sound U.S. economy. (As amended by the Convention.)

Water Resources: Support of national policies and procedures which promote comprehensive long–range planning for conservation and development of water resources and improvement of water quality.

Continuing Responsibilities

Apportionment of State Legislatures: Support of apportionment of both houses of state legislatures substantially on population.

District of Columbia: Support of self-government and representation in Congress for citizens of the District of Columbia.

Loyalty-Security: Support of standardized procedures, "common sense" judgment, and greatest possible protection for the individual under the federal loyalty-security programs; and opposition to extension of such programs to non-sensitive positions.

Tax Rates: Opposition to constitutional limitation on tax rates.

Treaty Making: Opposition to constitutional changes which would limit the existing powers of the Executive and the Congress over foreign relations.

Two not-recommended Current Agenda items received the majority vote necessary for Convention consideration.

Development of Human Resources: Support of policies and programs within the United States to provide for all persons equality of opportunity for employment and education, and an evaluation of equality of opportunity in housing.

U.S. Congress: An evaluation of congressional structure, procedures, and practices and their effect on the legislative process.

Neither of these items received the three-fifths vote necessary for adoption. In voting down the addition of housing to the Development of Human Resources item, 525 voted in favor of the addition and 789 against, with 1,314 delegates voting. In voting down the U.S. Congress item, 525 voted for and 798 against with 1,323 delegates voting.

A move to reconsider the Development of Human Resources item to include equality opportunity in housing was carried but a move to adopt the item failed—596 voted yes, 602 no, with 1,198 delegates voting.

The not-recommended Continuing Responsibility, Loyalty-Security, as listed above, was voted down by the delegates but a move to reconsider carried and the item was adopted. . . .

Budget

A budget of $394,507 was adopted for the 1966–67 fiscal year. League support amounted to $357,927. This amount, combined with an increase in unsolicited gifts and a reduction in several expenditures, which will not curtail the essential operation of the League of Women Voters of the United States, left a $20,000 deficit which will be met by a withdrawal of that amount from the Reserve Fund.

Convention Highlights

Mrs. Stuart's speech "Response to Diversity" set the theme for the Convention. The diversified interests of the League were reflected back to the Convention through the speakers who appeared throughout the week and through special events such as the popular meetings on non-election Voters Service.

William J.D. Boyd told the delegates of the effect of redistricting on state legislatures and the effect of League action on the entire field of apportionment. In his address to the Convention, the Honorable Robert C. Weaver, Secretary of Housing and Urban Development, said that he was one of those who "believe it does make a difference that there is a League of Women Voters. It can make a significant difference in the effort to fulfill the promise of the democratic city."

The League heard from representatives of the two League-created Funds: The Overseas Education Fund of the League of Women Voters and the League of Women Voters Education Fund—both examples of League diversification and the ever-spreading influence of the League of Women Voters.

In his address to the Convention, "Financing the League of Women Voters Without Tax Deduction," League attorney Albert E. Arent suggested other avenues of expansion.

On the final morning of the Convention Congressman Henry S. Reuss (D., WI), C. Montgomery Johnson, Chairman of the State Republican Committee in the State of Washington, and Jim Fain, Editor-in-Chief of the Dayton News, viewed the political effectiveness of the League from the point of view of an elected official, a party worker, and a journalist and suggested ways in which the League could improve on its essentially sound techniques. The response of the delegates was enthusiastic.

But perhaps the greatest "response to diversity" within the Convention was in the adoption of the Program itself. The 1966–68 Program, while curtailed in response to member request for a smaller workload, includes both international and domestic issues, new and old interests, opportunity for study, for continuing education and for action, but not all on every item. The Program provides different kinds and different amounts of work. It is, indeed, a "response to diversity."

Source: "Convention Summary," May 9, 1966. LWV Papers on film, II. B.18. 0705–08.

A significant foreign policy initiative came in 1969 when, after three years of study, the League called for normalization of relations with China and the end of U.S. opposition to representation of the People's Republic of China at the United Nations. Given the hostility of the time—an outcome of the Korean War—and the timidity of most political leaders, the League's position was a bold step and would consume considerable time and effort until the goal was achieved in the aftermath of President Richard M. Nixon's historic trip to China in 1972.

Also on the foreign policy front, the Carrie Chapman Catt Memorial Fund (CCCMF) which had initiated the Freedom Agenda program, found itself giving more and more attention to the needs of Third World countries. The CCCMF began to expand its outreach, especially to women in Latin America and Africa. Although an independent entity, it was linked to the League by virtue of national LWV board members serving as trustees and electing members of the CCCMF board. By 1961, it had changed its name to the Overseas Education Fund (OEF) of the League of Women Voters, in part because the name of Carrie Chapman Catt had faded from public view primarily because it was a more accurate representation of its current mission. In 1970, by mutual agreement, the OEF became an independent organization. Due largely to a shortfall in government grants, OEF temporarily closed its doors in the late 1980s, only to open them again in 1992 as Women, Law, and Development, International. Serving now as trustees are some of the world's most prestigious women lawyers who are helping to transform women's rights into human rights.

In the late 1990s the League's Education Fund began to operate in the international arena through its Global Community Dialogue program in the independent states of the former Soviet Union, in the emerging democracies of Eastern Europe, and in Africa and Latin America. The League in the last half century has come full circle, reverting to its original commitment to the development of democratic institutions in nations where citizens have requested help.

Lucy Wilson Benson of Amherst, Massachusetts, who became president in 1968, prepared to celebrate the League's fiftieth anniversary. The League declared that anniversary in 1970 as "The Year of the Voter" and, with the help of a fiftieth anniversary campaign committee, raised the level of giving to the LWV. Although the campaign failed to reach its goal, major gifts—including one million dollars from Anna Lord Strauss's Ivy Fund, divided in equal thirds among the LWV, the Overseas Education Fund, and the Education Fund—provided those organizations with new resources with which to do their work. Benson, an

*outgoing and dynamic personality, conveyed her enthusiasm and en-
ergy in her 1970 convention presidential address.*

DOCUMENT 10: LUCY BENSON'S PRESIDENTIAL REPORT AT THE FIFTIETH ANNIVERSARY CONVENTION

A fiftieth anniversary or birthday is traditionally a time for introspection and stock–taking. Certainly, this convention has been no exception to that rule.

During the past week, we have taken a long hard look at ourselves, our organization and our objectives. We know where we have been and where we are now. We enter our fifty-first year—and the decade of the seventies—with confidence and with concern.

I know that we can be confident about the League and its capacity to grow as a constructive and viable political force. We can also be confident about the ability of its members to work for those things that will help fulfill League programs and themselves.

We also recognize that neither the League nor its members function in a vacuum. We are a part of society—responsive to the political and social forces of the times.

As we are sitting here conducting League business, the country is being rocked by a series of events which, at this moment have ripped holes in the fabric of our government, our political process and in the bodies of four young college students. Many of our universities have been closed down—many students attending those universities feel that they have been closed out. They seem determined to get back in. . . .

The League, as many organizations today, is at times concerned about its immediacy. We receive, from many sources, requests for League participation, help and support on great many important public issues. Often we can do nothing—the issue is not part of the League program. Our responses at times fall on incredulous and impatient ears.

We can and do explain—about the values of a limited program and the process of consensus; about the strengths of an informed, policy making—rather than rubber stamping—membership; about the importance of being able to concentrate rather than dissipate energies.

Our explanations make sense. The message gets across that when the League acts it acts from strength and conviction—that it will do exactly what it promises.

This, then, is a part of our confidence and a part of the confidence that others have in us. It is also a vital part of the confidence that League members have in themselves. League activities help us master the art of rational analysis—we learn how to look at issues and the disciplines and techniques essential to reaching goals. The process enriches the League. It enriches our members. It enriches the nation. . . .

Today the country is being forced to run a gauntlet of challenges. . . .The way in which an individual or a nation responds to challenge is a measure of its maturity, its wisdom, and its compassion. . . .

Lately, however, many of us who are being challenged, find that adequate responses are harder to come by. The old assurances don't seem as reassuring: our defenses become more defensive. We recognize, even if we don't always admit it, that both the charges and the counter-charges have elements of truth.

We are uneasy and for good reasons. Too much has happened: so much has changed.

All of us have deep, personal memories of the visual and visceral shocks of the bridge at Selma, the assassination of John Kennedy, Watts and Detroit, the streets of Chicago. But a wound eventually becomes a scar.

In 1970, we have become conditioned to shocks. In a few years, we have become used to police clubs, tear gas, mass protests and arrests, boarded windows and broken heads. We find ourselves watching procedures that yesterday we could not see ourselves accepting.

Today, if there is a scheduled protest or demonstration, it is standard operating procedure to call out specially trained police. The National Guard. The Army.

Today, we hear debates about the necessity of preventive detention: no–knock entries; increased wiretaps and electronic surveillance; prohibitive bail; raids on black militants, underground newspapers, extremist headquarters.

We read that the Civil Service Commission has allegedly amassed a file of one and a half million Americans who may have "subversive" intentions.

Dissent has become suspect and to challenge the system is subversive. We are admonished to be for something—not against.

Most of us remember Senator Joseph McCarthy and the effect he had on our government and our society. Then it was reds and subversives—in high or low places, it made no difference. Careers and lives were ruined—by smear, rumor, guilt by association, and through the timidity of many of our leaders and opinion makers. For all the hysteria, however, nobody went to jail—no heads were broken, no shots were fired.

It is different today. Now there are also the kids with freaked out hair or Afros, bizarre clothing, beards, beads; those who do not want to kill or be killed in Vietnam; the young people who have become strangers in their own land.

There are, of course, the truly violent, the new anarchists and nihilists. The bomb manufacturers and those who believe that change can only come from destruction—that destruction is an end in itself. Their wanton and desperate violence cannot be tolerated or condoned.

Nevertheless, the acts of a desperate few cannot be allowed to provide the pretext for controlling those whose dissent or protest takes other forms, or those who act out their frustrations and bitterness at rallies and in marches.

Some of our problems stem from our successes—the triumph of technology and America's unprecedented affluence. Some are due to the pressures of an ever-growing, ever-urbanizing population. Some are the result of our seeming inability to respond effectively to social and human problems. . . .

It is only a relatively few who, at this point in time, want to destroy or radically change the system. Although the pervading mood is one of impatience, the demands are not really for instant solutions or overnight change. In fact, the more simplistic answers seem to be coming from the forces of reaction rather than action. . . .

In the future there will be different issues and causes—the slogans and signs will change.

What seems much less likely to change are the basic causes of unrest. If today, we have grown accustomed to violent confrontations and their aftermath—what could we learn to accommodate tomorrow? It has been said that America can solve its problems "simply by putting its collective foot down and insisting: 'No more.' If that is to be our way out, a great many individuals could get trampled in the process.

At the beginning of 1970, the League put forth the concept of the Year of the Voter. In the context of what I've been discussing this morning, it may appear to be a somewhat forlorn and lonely standard. It is, however, a direct outgrowth of the League's historic concern with the individual and his place and role in our government. It symbolizes the open channels of communication, persuasion and change that the Bill of Rights intended.

As League members and as Americans it is our responsibility to keep that channel open—to foster and promote a climate that makes the vote not violence the basic instrument of change in this country.

If we can fulfill this responsibility, then we can be confident about coping with tomorrow's crises and changes. If we cannot, we may be looking ahead to a very different Year of the Voter—the presidential election year of 1984.

The League of Women Voters is an active and concerned organization fully engaged in meeting some of the nation's most pressing needs. The paths we follow are determined by our members—individuals who act in the world as well as the League. Each of you, in one way or another, has made a commitment to encourage participation in government. As League members you have learned about the system—that it can be changed, that individuals can make things happen, that old ways of doing things can give way to new ideas.

This is the kind of knowledge that is power. This is the kind of power to which the League of Women Voters is dedicated.

Today's concerns may shake our confidence—but we will not lose it nor will we allow it to be taken away.

Source: Excerpts from the Proceedings of the Twenty-ninth Annual (the Fiftieth Anniversary) Convention of the LWVUS, Washington, DC, May 4–8, 1970. LWV Papers on film, II. B.25. 0179–92.

Epilogue

Although the next three decades of the life of the League of Women Voters were not within the framework of Louise Young's history, it seems appropriate to name the presidents of this later period and to report the major events and changes that have occurred from 1970 to the present time. External forces—particularly the movement of women into the workforce—have dramatically changed the League and its *modus operandi.*

Since the League's fiftieth anniversary in 1970, seven women have served as national League president: Lucy Wilson Benson of Amherst, Massachusetts, completed her six-year term in 1974 and later served as Under Secretary of State for Security Assistance in the Carter Administration. Ruth S. Clusen of Green Bay, Wisconsin (1974–78), one of the pioneers in the arena of environmental protection, also served under President Jimmy Carter as Assistant Secretary of Energy in the Department of Energy and later received an appointment to the University of Wisconsin's Board of Regents. Ruth J. Hinerfeld of Larchmont, New York (1978–82) has been a stalwart supporter of international development and the United Nations, serving for many years on the national boards of the Overseas Development Council and the United Nations Association; she remains active in a variety of community affairs. Dorothy S. Ridings, then of Louisville, Kentucky (1982–86), was formerly a publisher with the Knight-Ridder newspaper organization, and subsequently was selected president of the Council of Foundations in 1996. She also served as chair of the advisory committee for the Education Fund's Vision 2000 capital campaign.

Nancy M. Neuman, of Lewisburg, Pennsylvania (1986–90), who earlier spearheaded the LWV campaign for the Equal Rights Amendment, has been a visiting professor at several universities and has written about the League in a pamphlet titled, "The League of Women Voters in Perspective 1920–1995." She has also edited *A Voice of Our Own: Leading American Women Celebrate the Right to Vote* published on the occasion of the seventy-fifth anniversary of the Nineteenth Amendment. A second book, also edited by Neuman and published in 1998 by the League, is called *True to Ourselves: A Celebration of Women Making a Difference.* Susan S. Lederman of New Providence, New Jersey (1990–92), who is the first foreign-born woman to be elected League president, serves as a professor at Kean University and as executive director of the Gateway Institute for Regional Development. Becky Cain of St. Albans, West Virginia, who will be remembered for her friendly manner and leadership with regard to easing voter registration and advocating campaign finance reform, completed her six-year term in June 1998. On that occasion, she was honored with the establishment of the Becky Cain Award for Visionary Leadership. Succeeding Cain as the League's fifteenth president is Carolyn Jefferson-Jenkins, Ph.D., of Colorado Springs, Colorado. She is a vice president of Junior Achievement and the first African American to serve as president of the League of Women Voters.

The first six presidents served a total of forty-eight years and the second set of seven for twenty-seven years. (Lucy Benson is included as one of the seven because four of her six years were after 1970.) The terms of recent League presidents have tended to cluster in the range of four to six years of service.

If, as stated in a League publication designed for the fiftieth year capital campaign, "the potential of the League is limited only by the capacity and endurance of its individual members" how can the League become more viable while recognizing that the capacity and endurance of members is more limited than ever before? In the past three decades, League membership has declined. The League has survived a significant downturn in membership and an accompanying reduction in financial resources from dues; yet, throughout this period League leaders have remained optimistic in the face of new challenges.

The fact that the League continues to lose members to work and education has meant that it had to figure out new ways of maintaining the organization without relying on hours of volunteer time. Could a League member remain in good standing if she did nothing more than pay her dues? Why not? How could members feel fulfilled if their activities were confined to work and home? How could the League survive without the volunteer? The League faced up to these issues in a series of self-studies in the 1970s and 1980s.

The conclusion of a 1972–74 study showed that the League was well aware of the problems, but it also expressed the inherent optimism of the organization: "We've got to get a move on." Subsequent studies, by a membership representation committee (1974) and an endangered species committee, referring to the volunteer (1976), produced more recommendations, but eventually the League wearied of inward gazing and bought into Ruth

Clusen's presentation to the 1978 convention: "It seems to me that we have engaged in too much self-flagellation during the last two years over the undeniable fact that women are going back to work and to school in ever-increasing numbers. The trend has become part of our rationale for decreasing membership and recruitment difficulties. I do not believe the volunteer is disappearing, but that the role of the volunteer is changing significantly.

Flexibility became a watchword and a practice, as the League found itself experimenting with a variety of innovations in order to accommodate to time restraints of volunteers. Local Leagues often have copresidents to share the responsibilities (and the time involved) of leadership.

Leagues—especially those in suburban communities—have merged to build a bigger membership and leadership base. Committees and boards often meet on weekends, over lunch hours, or in the evening. Where Leagues are large enough or have sufficient financial resources, staff members now do the work of writing, organizing, lobbying, and the like, and the board volunteers assume more the role of policy maker and less that of worker or doer. Through their education funds Leagues prepare proposals for foundations and corporations as well as governments and individuals to supply resources for a variety of projects enhancing civic literacy and activity. Web sites have sprouted up to inform the member and help the voter. So, even with all these self-assessments and concerns about the decline of the volunteer as we knew her, the League persisted in the business of education and advocacy in the public interest.

Perhaps one of the most significant steps taken by the League of Women voters during the period after 1970 was the 1972 convention decision to support the ERA. After years of opposition to this idea—from the time the ERA was first proposed by Alice Paul in 1923—the League had quietly dropped its objection in 1954, recognizing that the need for special protection for women workers had given way to the need for equal opportunities and equal pay—a need still unmet at the close of the twentieth century. In an acknowledgment that equality works both ways, men—who had not been barred from the League but seemed to be excluded by virtue of its name—were recruited and accepted as full-fledged members of the organization in 1974 (a Colorado League T-shirt said it best: "The League of Women Voters—not for women only").

As long ago as 1952 the League with NBC and *Life* magazine had sponsored the first televised primary debate of candidates for the presidency at the national convention in Cincinnati. By 1976 the League had assumed a leadership role in the sponsorship of televised presidential debates. It was a natural progression for an organization that had made candidates' debates an expected event prior to local and state elections. In 1988, because of rule changes giving control of the debate to the party candidates, the League, after failing to stop those changes, withdrew its sponsorship. The League, explained President Nancy Neuman, "has no intention of becoming an accessory to the hoodwinking of the American public."

The temper of the times changed with the onset of the 1980s. President Ruth Hinerfeld described the change and the challenge: "The 1980s will not be an easy time for many of our program goals. The broadly based support for civil rights that characterized the 1960s is ebbing in the face of fiscal austerity and new priorities. Now, at all levels of government, there is little heart for new initiatives – even though inequitable social and economic conditions still fester throughout the nation in schools, housing, employment."

The League supported the right of privacy in reproductive choices in 1983. It fought against the weakening of Title IX of the 1972 Educational Amendment Act, which banned sex discrimination in education; but a Supreme Court decision in 1984 had the effect of weakening all civil rights laws. For four years the League bent its efforts to secure the passage of the Civil Rights Restoration Act of 1988. The League took up issues relating to national security and, not surprisingly, given its long history of advocacy on behalf of international measures to secure the peace, endorsed programs of arms control and called for restraints in military spending.

Among the issues of the 1990s, the League found itself in a campaign to "Take Back the System" by reestablishing a sense of can-do participation by a citizenry that had become increasingly cynical and apathetic. It continued to labor in the vineyards of civil rights and expanded its work in the field of social policy. It took positions on health care reform in 1993 and on early intervention for children at risk and on violence prevention in 1994. The League continued to push for changes that would make it easier for citizens to register to vote. It became a key player in the passage of the National Voter Registration Act in 1993 ("Motor Voter"), which eased the process of registration by enabling citizens to apply at motor vehicle agencies as well as by mail and through public and private agencies serving the public. The League was represented by President Becky Cain, who joined President Clinton in the signing ceremony at the White House (and received one of his pens).

At this writing the League of Women Voters of the United States seems to have come full circle. Established in 1920 with a full plate of issues on an undifferentiated program, the program record has become more complex. In the years that followed, the League has formulated a platform (where old issues could be deposited and never die), decided on principles (a kind of credo for League action), and divided the active program between continuing responsibilities (where the League can track recent issues of concern) and a current agenda (which, as the name implies, can concentrate attention on study or action or both). More recently the principles have been refined, but the platform, continuing responsibilities, and current agenda have been merged into an integrated program with issues identified for emphasis. For the 1998–2000 biennium, the issue for emphasis is "Making Democracy Work," a kind of back to basics for League study and consensus. Four of the five major elements include programs to reconnect citizens through community dialogues; to increase diversity in membership, programs, and activities; to encourage more women and minorities to seek public office; and a

League perennial, to increase voter registration and voter turnout. The fifth is in the international arena: in the post–cold war world, the League has initiated programs to assist Russia and the emerging democracies of Eastern Europe and subsequently has extended those efforts to nations in Africa and Latin America as they struggle with the arts of democratic governance. On the domestic side of the equation, fending off attacks on Motor Voter and pushing for a realistic campaign finance reform measure high on the action agenda of the League. And the League is taking a new look at agricultural activity.

Source: Nancy M. Newman, *The League of Women Voters in Perspective, 1920–1995*, Washington, DC: LWVS, 1994.

The League Principles, as currently articulated, constitute not only a litany of prior commitments but also the goals to which the League has devoted its energies throughout the nearly eighty years of its existence.

DOCUMENT 1: PRINCIPLES OF THE LEAGUE OF WOMEN VOTERS

The League of Women Voters believes in representative government and in the individual liberties established in the Constitution of the United States.

The League of Women Voters believes that democratic government depends upon the informed and active participation of its citizens and requires that governmental bodies protect the citizen's right to know by giving adequate notice of proposed actions, holding open meetings and making public records accessible.

The League of Women Voters believes that efficient and economical government requires competent personnel, the clear assignment of responsibility, adequate financing, and coordination among the different agencies and levels of government.

The League of Women Voters believes that responsible government should be responsive to the will of the people; that government should maintain an equitable and flexible system of taxation, promote the conservation and development of natural resources in the public interest, share in the solution of economic and social problems that affect the general welfare, promote a sound economy and adopt domestic policies that facilitate the solution of international problems.

The League of Women Voters believes that cooperation with other nations is essential in the search for solutions to world problems and that development of international organization and international law is imperative in the promotion of world peace.

Where Do the Principles Come From?

The Principles are "concepts of government" to which the League subscribes. They are a direct descendant of the Platform, which served from 1942 to 1956 as the national repository for "principles supported and positions taken by the League as a whole in fields of government to which it has given sustained attention." During most of this period, the principles were grouped, along with specific legislative measures and policies supported by the League, under "Gettysburg Address–type" categories (Government of the People, etc.). By 1956, the Platform had disappeared from the League vocabulary, but the principles survived as "The Principles." Since then, the Principles have served two functions, according to the LWVUS Bylaws: 1) authorization for adoption of national, state and local program (Article XII), and 2) as a basis for taking action at the national, state and local levels (Article XII).

As for action to implement the Principles, the appropriate board authorizes action once it determines that member understanding and agreement do exist and that action is appropriate. As with other action, when there are ramifications beyond a League's own government jurisdiction, that League should consult other Leagues affected.

The national board suggests that any action on the Principles be taken in conjunction with current League positions to which they apply and on which member agreement and understanding are known to exist. The Principles are rather broad when standing alone, so it is necessary to exercise caution when considering using them as a basis for action. Furthermore, since 1974 most of the Principles have been an integral part of the national program, most notably in the criteria for evaluating government that appear at the end of the formal listing of program.

Source: *Impact on Issues: 1998–2000: A Leaders Guide to National Program.* Washington, DC: LWVS, 1998, 66.

In one sense, the League, on the eve of the twenty-first century, has remained, in the words of an old song, "bewitched, bothered, and bewildered"—bewitched that citizens shy away from opportunities to serve the public interest, bothered that many new voters and new citizens suffer the same malaise of apathy and lethargy, and bewildered by the increasing numbers of citizens failing to vote, failing to engage in the most fundamental act of citizenship. But the League has never been one to wallow in self-pity or be deterred by indifference to its efforts. It has continued to pursue its twin mission of education and advocacy in the public interest with courage and competence. Despite fewer members and new ways of going about its business, the League's reputation for civility, integrity, and effectiveness in the public arena has endured and is evident in its 1998–2000 program.

DOCUMENT 2: 1998–2000 NATIONAL PROGRAM

Government
Promote an open governmental system that is representative, accountable and responsive; that has a fair and adequate fiscal basis; that protects individual liberties established by, the Constitution; that assures opportunities for citizen par-

ticipation in government decision making; that provides sound agricultural policy; and that preserves public health and safety through gun control measures.

Agricultural Policy
Promote adequate supplies of food and fiber at reasonable prices to consumers and support economically viable farms, environmentally sound farm practices and increased reliance on the free market.

Citizen Rights
Citizen Right to Know/Citizen Participation. Protect the citizen's right to know and facilitate citizen participation in government decision making.
Individual Liberties. Oppose major threats to basic constitutional rights.
Public Policy on Reproductive Choices. Protect the constitutional right of privacy of the individual to make reproductive choices.

Congress and the Presidency
Congress. Support responsive legislative processes characterized by accountability, representativeness, decision-making capability and effective performance.
The Presidency. Promote a dynamic balance of power between the executive and legislative branches within the framework set by the Constitution.

DC Self-Government and Full Voting Representation
Secure for the citizens of the District of Columbia the rights of *self-government and* representation in both houses of Congress.

Election Process
Apportionment. Support apportionment of congressional districts and elected legislative bodies at all levels of government based substantially on population.
Campaign Finance. Improve methods of *financing* political campaigns in order to ensure the public's right to know, combat corruption and undue influence, enable candidates to compete more equitably for public office and promote citizen participation in the political process.
Election of the President. Promote the election of the President and Vice-President by direct popular vote and work to abolish the Electoral College; support uniform national voting qualifications and procedures for presidential elections.
Fiscal Policy. Support adequate and flexible funding of federal government programs through an equitable tax system that is progressive overall and that relies primarily on a broad based income tax; promote responsible deficit policies; support a federal role in providing mandatory, universal, old-age, survivors, disability and health insurance.

Gun Control. Protect the health and safety of citizens through limiting the accessibility and regulating the ownership of handguns and semi-automatic weapons.

Voting Rights. Protect the right of all citizens to vote; encourage all citizens to vote.

International Relations
Promote peace in an interdependent world by cooperating with other nations, strengthening international organizations, fostering long-term development, negotiating arms control measures and encouraging the successful resolution of conflicts through nonmilitary means.

Arms Control
Reduce the risk of war through support of arms control measures.

Military Policy and Defense Spending
Work to limit reliance on military force; examine defense spending in the context of total national needs.

Trade
Support systematic reduction of tariff and nontariff trade barriers and support broad long-range presidential authority to negotiate trade agreements.

United Nations
Support measures to strengthen the United Nations, in recognition of the need for cooperation among nations in an interdependent world.

U.S. Relations with Developing Countries
Promote U.S. policies that meet long-term social and economic needs of developing countries.

Natural Resources
Promote an environment beneficial to life through the protection and wise management of natural resources in the public interest by recognizing the interrelationships of air quality, energy, land use, waste management and water resources.

Resource Management
Promote resource conservation, stewardship and long range planning with the responsibility for managing natural resources shared by all levels of government.

Environmental Protection and Pollution Control
Preserve the physical, chemical and biological integrity of the ecosystem, with the maximum protection of the public health and environment.

Public Participation
Promote public understanding and participation in decision making as essential elements of responsible and responsive management of our natural resources.

Social Policy
Promote social and economic justice, secure equal rights for all, achieve universal health care coverage at reasonable cost, promote the well being of children, and combat discrimination, poverty and violence.

Child Care
Support programs, services and policies at all levels of government to expand the supply of affordable, quality child care for all who need it.

Early Intervention for Children at Risk
Support policies and programs that promote the well being, development and safety of all children.

Equality of Opportunity
Support equal access to education, employment and housing. Support ratification of the Equal Rights Amendment and efforts to bring laws into compliance with the goals of the ERA.

Health Care
Promote a health care system for the United States that provides access to a basic level of care for all U.S. residents and controls health care costs.

Meeting Basic Human Needs
Support programs and policies to prevent or reduce poverty and to promote self-sufficiency for individuals and families.

Urban Policy
Promote the economic health of cities and improve the quality of urban life.

Violence Prevention
Support violence prevention programs in all communities.

Whatever the issue, the League believes that government policy, programs and performance must meet these criteria: competent personnel with clear responsibilities, coordination among agencies and levels of government, adequate financing, effective enforcement, and well-defined channels for citizen input and review.

1998–2000 ISSUE FOR EMPHASIS
Making Democracy Work

Source: *Impact on Issues 1998–2000*, 1–2.

I would like to introduce the final document in this League history on a personal note. As a very young staff member of the League of Women Voters of Minnesota, I attended my first national League convention in Atlantic City, New Jersey, in 1950. One of the speakers was Louise Young who spoke about the recent transfer of League files to the Library of Congress. This was long before I had any particular interest in history (except recent political history), and I had no idea then that I might spend some years of my later life toiling in the relatively unplowed fields of women's history. I do remember one thing, however, about Louise Young's presentation. She had my undivided atten-

tion; I was absolutely riveted by what she had to say about the achievements of the League of Women Voters. I learned from her that I should take great pride in this organization, and I have—from that day to this.

DOCUMENT 3: LOUISE M. YOUNG, "OPERATION IMMORTAL"

NOTE: On Wednesday, March 1, 1950 Miss Anna Lord Strauss, president of the League of Women Voters formally signed over to Dr. Luther Evans, Librarian of Congress, the non-current files of the League of Women Voters. Dr. Young served as the League' special representative in arranging for the transfer and is currently engaged in helping the Library to process the manuscripts for use by students of social and political history. The papers weighed more than two tons, and comprise the largest single collection of non-governmental papers in the Manuscripts Division.

In telling the Convention the story of the preservation of the League's history, Dr. Young said in part. . . .

"The records of the Departments of Child Welfare and Legal Status of Women so far surpass all others in bulk as to be a very impressive memorial to your primary concerns and your most important accomplishments—and also to the deep original sources of your power. In these areas no legislatures could permanently gainsay you and you clearly got what you wanted. . . .

. . . . As for Child Welfare—here you were the supreme innovators. The idea of grants-in-aid from the Federal Government to the States for maternal and child welfare services was apparently Julia Lathrop's—embodied in her famous Annual Report of the Children's Bureau for 1917, but it wasn't until the Sheppard-Towner Act clothed this idea in legislative reality that the principle withstood the Constitutional test and the way was opened for the whole flood of social legislation based on the fiscal principle of grants-in-aid which pulled us through the Depression of the Thirties. And while Sheppard-Towner only survived until the late twenties, the substance of the bill was embodied in the Social Security Act of 1935.

"This is a very great achievement—a social invention of the first order—and how you persuaded a reluctant Congress to pass the Sheppard-Towner Bill is here for all to see. Again, you had help, but your record clearly reveals what you did, and what the others did—and how collectively you established the theory of social responsibility at the Federal level.

"You may be surprised to know that social hygiene has one of the bulkiest records, and here students of cultural change will find the policewoman rising up in all her majesty, knocking down one of the last props of male superiority; also informed discussion of the need for sex education in schools, for public attention to the care and prevention of social diseases. Curious inquirers will find you avidly demanding sterilization of the unfit in some quarters, but at the same time consistently sidestepping the question of birth control in spite of much agitated pleading from the race improvement lobby. These are social facts of great importance because your reasons for doing or not doing are always copiously recorded, and the analyst can look deeply into the cultural context. . . .

The political scientists, the historians, the sociologists and the social psychologists will go to your records to observe the democratic process at work at the grass roots. They illuminate the whole pattern of our complex and intricate society.

First of all, the historian will value you because you arose, young and beautiful like the Phoenix, from the self-immolation of the suffrage movement. Only a few of you realize how deep your roots go in the movement for the emancipation of women, and how you still draw your leadership and your strength from the top root of the suffrage movement. This fact puts you in the main stream of one of the broadcast currents of American historians, etc.

The constitutional historian will use your records for the light they throw on the amending process. This may well prove to be one of the most valuable parts of your record for future historians, etc.

The institutional historian will turn to you for data on the history of the radio, of adult education, of sweeping curricular changes in public and higher education. Like the social psychologist, he will be interested in what you can tell him about public opinion formation—how the public will is shaped, clarified and finally expressed.

The economic historian will find your records valuable because of three things you did. The first was quite simple: you taught women a few things about taxes as the price they paid for government. Since women are primarily consumers, they learned to look at taxes not in terms of how low they were but how much they got for their money. A volume could be written about the development of your early rudimentary interest in taxes to your present highly sophisticated fiscal approach to general problems of welfare and education. You also developed in your membership a sense of personal responsibility for the management of their own affairs. It took two decades to teach local Leagues to make budgets, but what you accomplished was to light up the economic gloom in which most women all too happily dwell. . . .

. . . A third thing you did in the economic field was perhaps most ingenious of all and has had the most far-reaching consequences. In the middle twenties you dug a deep trench and call it the Committee on Living Costs. Into this you diverted the normal interest and curiosity of consuming citizens regarding the destination of their consumers' dollars. Under this Committee's banner you did many things but two at least were world shaking—you studied the tariff, and you peered into the thick controversial fog surrounding some nitrate plants down at Muscle Shoals.

Where your studies of the tariff took you everyone knows. The path leads straight to the ITO [International Trade Organization]. You were prepared to embrace internationalism in the economic area long before you were in the political area, and are still ahead of your husbands. As for Muscle Shoals and the principle of public development of power resources, the historian give much of the credit for this victory to the late Senator Norris—while he, in turn, gallantly gives it to you, his most faithful supporters—and the story of this is in your record.

Historians of our international relations will find in your papers a vast mass of primary data on the transformation of cultural attitudes toward international responsibilities, which everyone knows took place between 1920 and 1940. You have, quite generally, the reputation for having been in the vanguard in this movement, and your papers reveal that your attitudes were composed of many strands - - not merely an academic interest in the World Court and the League of Nations. . . .

. . . Even as much as the historians, the political scientists will go to your records for evidence of how procedural changes have been wrought in our governmental machinery. You've been obsessed with the desire to tinker with the machinery, to elaborate and improve it; and you descended like a scourge on the professional politicians. Your attitude toward the parties and the professional politicians deserves careful study because you represent a microcosm of our democratic society; and I'm sure it will get it. If the boss is on his way out, he probably blames part of it on you. If local government has been revitalized in the last decade or so, you are partly responsible. Your innovations in this field have been remarkable. You invented the citizenship institute, the jury school, the candidates' questionnaire, the know-your-town and know-your-country surveys, and these things have left a permanent mark on our lives. . . .

In these records, however, it is women who are making history (men wander in and out from time to time but are kept firmly in their place) and the story of the impact of women on our social life in the last half-century is here for the telling.

Not just any women but *you.* It will be you the historians of the future find on the shelves when they search out answers to how our democratic processes really work—the minutes you have written, the meetings you have planned, the legislation you have supported or opposed, the projects, surveys, institutes, study groups you have carried on. Here is how the public will is being translated into public policy, the historian will say, and be inordinately grateful that his little segment of the public has so admirably recorded it for him. And since it is you, and not another, he has found on the shelves, it will be you and your accomplishments which will be clothed in the shining garments of immortality.

Source: Louise Young, *Operation Immortal.* Washington, DC: LWVS, 1950, 3 pages.

Bibliography

Most of the references in the text are obviously from the papers of the LWV in the Library of Congress. The other references cited in the text are listed here together with sources previously read that proved particularly useful as background information. A separate section includes publications of the LWV.

Blackstone, William. *Commentaries on the Law of England*. New York: William Ed. Dean, 1853.

Buechler, Steven M. *Women's Movements in the United States. Woman Suffrage, Equal Rights, and Beyond*. New Brunswick, NJ: Rutgers University Press, 1990.

Chafe, William Henry. *The American Woman: Her Changing Social, Economic, and Political Roles, 1920–1970*. New York: Oxford University Press, 1972.

Chambers, Clark A. *Seedtime of Reform: American Social Service and Social Action, 1918–1933*. Minneapolis: University of Minnesota Press, 1963.

Cott, Nancy F. *The Grounding of Modern Feminism*. New Haven, CT: Yale University Press, 1987.

Evans, Sara M. *Born for Liberty: A History of Women in America*. New York: The Free Press, 1989.

Flexner, Eleanor. *Century of Struggle: The Women's Rights Movement in the United States*. Cambridge, MA: Belknap Press of Harvard University Press, 1959.

Fowler, Robert Booth. *Carrie Catt, Feminist Politician*. Boston: Northeastern University Press, 1986.

Griffith, Elisabeth. *In Her Own Right, The Life of Elizabeth Cady Stanton.* New York: Oxford University Press, 1984.

Horowitz, Helen Lefkowitz. *The Power and Passion of M. Carey Thomas.* New York: Alfred A. Knopf, 1994.

Lall, Betty Goetz. *"The Foreign Policy of the League of Women Voters of the United States Methods of Influencing Government, Effects on Public Opinion, and Evaluation of Results."* Ph.D. dissertation, University of Minnesota, Minneapolis, 1964.

Lash, Joseph P. *Eleanor and Franklin.* New York: W.W. Norton and Co., 1971.

Lemons, J. Stanley. *The Woman Citizen: Social Feminism in the 1920s.* Urbana: University of Illinois Press, 1973.

O'Neill, William L. *Feminism in America: A History,* 2nd rev. ed. New Brunswick, NJ: Transaction Publishers, 1989.

Park, Maud Wood. *Front Door Lobby.* Edited by Edna L. Stantial. Boston: Beacon Press, 1960.

Peck, Mary Gray. *Carrie Chapman Catt: A Biography.* New York: H. W. Wilson Co., 1944.

Rosenberg, Rosalind. *Divided Lives. American Women in the Twentieth Century.* New York: Hiss and Wang, 1992.

Scharf, Lois, and Joan M. Jensen. *Decades of Discontent. The Women's Movement, 1920-1940.* Westport, CT: Greenwood Press, 1983.

Scott, Anne Firor, and Andrew Mackay. *One Half the People: The Fight for Woman Suffrage.* Philadelphia: Lippincott, 1982.

Sicherman, Barbara, and Carol Hurd Green, Eds. *Notable American Women: The Modem Period.* Cambridge, MA: Belknap Press of Harvard University Press, 1980.

Stanton, Elizabeth Cady, et al. *History of Woman Suffrage,* 6 Vols. New York: National American Woman Suffrage Association, 1881-1922.

Stevens, Doris. *Jailed for Freedom: American Women Win the Vote.* Troutdale, OR: NewSage Press, 1995.

Stuhler, Barbara. *Gentle Warriors: Clara Ueland and the Minnesota Struggle for Woman Suffrage.* St. Paul: Minnesota Historical Society Press, 1995.

Tilly, Louise A. and Patricia Gurin, Eds. *Women, Politics and Change.* New York: Russell Sage Foundation, 1990.

Van Voris, Jaqueline. *Carrie Chapman Catt: A Public Life.* New York: The Feminist Press, 1987.

Wheeler, Marjorie Sprull, Ed. *One Woman, One Vote: Reconstructing the Woman Suffrage Movement.* Troutdale, OR: New Sage Press, 1995.

Young, Louise M. *In the Public Interest: The League of Women Voters, 1920-1970.* Westport CT: Greenwood Press, 1989.

Publications of the League of Women Voters

Miller, Helen Hill. *Carrie Chapman Catt: The Power of an Idea.* Washington, DC: Carrie Chapman Catt Memorial Fund, 1958.

Neuman, Nancy M. *The League of Women Voters in Perspective, 1920–1995.* Washington, DC: League of Women Voters of the United States, 1994.

Perry, Elisabeth Israels. *Women in Action: Rebels and Reformers, 1920–1980.* Washington, DC: League of Women Voters Education Fund, 1995.

Stone, Kathryn. *A History of the League Program.* Washington, DC: League of Women Voters, 1949.

Wells, Marguerite. *A Portrait of the League of Women Voters.* Washington, DC: Overseas Education Fund of the League of Women Voters, 1938, reissued in 1962.

Other useful references included the League publication that began as *The Woman Citizen* (acquired from the Suffrage Association) and is now called *The National Voter,* and program record (Kathryn Stone's cited above was the first), is now issued biennially as *Impact on Issues*—both invaluable sources of information on the progression of League program and policies.

Index

About the Author

BARBARA STUHLER, prior to her retirement, was Professor and Executive Associate Dean, Continuing Education and Extension (now College of Continuing Education) at the University of Minnesota. From the 1950s through the 1970s she served on the state and national boards of the League of Women Voters and served as the League's representative on the U.S. National Commission for UNESCO. In recent years she has devoted her energies to writing women's history and to increasing the representation of women in politics.

ISBN 0-313-25316-1

HARDCOVER BAR CODE